VISUAL QUICKPRO GUIDE

PINNACLE LIQUID EDITION 6

FOR WINDOWS

Paul Ekert

Peachpit Press

Visual QuickPro Guide
Pinnacle Liquid Edition 6
Paul Ekert

Peachpit Press
1249 Eighth Street
Berkeley, CA 94710
510/524-2178
800/283-9444
510/524-2221 (fax)

Find us on the World Wide Web at www.peachpit.com.
To report errors, please send a note to errata@peachpit.com.
Peachpit Press is a division of Pearson Education

Editor: Karyn Johnson
Production Editor: Gloria Marquez
Copyeditor: Rebecca Rider
Proofreader: Liz Welch
Compositor: Owen Wolfson
Indexer: Julie Bess
Cover Design: The Visual Group

ISBN 0-321-26916-0

9 8 7 6 5 4 3 2 1

Printed and bound in the United States of America

To my wife Lotti

Acknowledgments

I'd like to thank everyone who helped create this book. This includes (but does not exclusively cover) the following wonderful people.

Everyone at Peachpit Press, whose expertise and professionalism allowed this book to become as good as it is. Special thanks to Marjorie Baer for bringing together the great team I worked with: editor Karyn Johnson; production editor Gloria Marquez; copy editor Rebecca Rider; proofreader Liz Welch; compositor Owen Wolfson; indexer Julie Bess; and technical editor Jeff Sauer.

Everyone working with the Liquid Edition development team including: James; Ali; Matthias; Markus; Jens (the DVD man); Anne; Claudia; Ziggy; HaPe; Kurt; Klaus; Manfred; Alex; Dan; Mike; and a special thanks to Marcel Stiller for being on call for those 1000 and 1 technical questions I had for him. Also, I'd like to personally thank the external Toledo Webboard testers for helping to squash those bugs and for doing such a good job of finding them.

A special thanks also to Semir Nouri of JVC Europe for providing me with an HDV camera.

I'd also like to thank my family and friends for letting me share their images that appear throughout this book; and I'd like to thank everyone who contributed to my general well-being and happiness during the production of this book.

And last but not least I'd like to thank my wife for having the presence of mind to encourage me back to writing.

TABLE OF CONTENTS

INTRODUCTION

I first started to use Liquid Edition when I was working in the QA development center for Pinnacle Systems. Because I was an old-school Adobe Premiere user, this "single-track" solution wasn't a working environment I felt comfortable with initially. However, I soon came to appreciate the power of unlimited video layers and saw immediate advantages to using off-the-Timeline DVD authoring and the real-time preview of filters and transitions—especially because I could access all these features without expensive or difficult-to-install hardware.

Finally I had discovered a way to edit and create DVDs, complete with special effects and titles, from within the one application, Liquid Edition. These features are the reason I now rarely use any other program to create my videos.

Although Liquid Edition offers affordable power and an incredible potential for creativity, you should still realize that no matter what type of video you are producing, you must make sure it is clearly and cleanly presented. Otherwise, your carefully nurtured production looks amateurish, the interest of the audience wanes, and you find you've wasted your time.

The secret to avoiding this painful scenario is simple: You must understand how to get the best from the software you are using—in this case, Pinnacle Liquid Edition 6. Once you know this, you are free to be as creative as you want.

Using This Book

This Visual QuickPro Guide, like others in the series, is a task-based reference book that uses each chapter to focus on a specific area of the application. For this guide, I use plain English to explain each function and I accompany each with a series of illustrations that explicitly show how each of the steps should work. Where necessary I use sidebars to illustrate particular topics in more depth.

This task-based approach—as opposed to a project-based one—allows you to use your own media or download the sample files from the publisher's Web site (see accompanying sidebar) while learning the techniques in this book. You can then choose to follow each chapter in order, or simply dip in and out of the areas you find most difficult to understand.

Going Pro

The "Pro" in the title of this book refers to the capability of the software rather than the aspirations of the reader. Liquid Edition is designed with a high creative ceiling. Users can produce simple, short videos for the Web or they can make a surround sound DVD movie. The only real limitation of Liquid Edition is the user's imagination.

The Pro in the title is also not a reference to the Liquid Edition Pro package. Remember, all versions of Liquid Edition share a common base program; those versions sold with extra hardware simply have advanced output facilities that any Liquid Edition owner with the relevant hardware can access.

This Book's Companion Web Page

To support this book Peachpit Press has a special area just for Liquid Edition users. Go to www.peachpit.com/liquid6vqp and you'll not only find details on where to download a fully working demo of Liquid Edition 6, but you can also download some of the sample clips used as examples throughout this book. I'll also use this area to update you—the reader—of any software updates and any changes these updates might make to the software.

Demo Version

If you want to try Liquid Edition 6 out before you buy it, you can download a demo version or call a special CD order line. For details, visit the Peachpit Web site at www.peachpit.com/liquid6vqp. The demo version has a time limitation and certain usage restrictions, but you can complete most of the task-based exercises in this book using the demo version.

Resetting the Interface

Liquid Edition 6 displays a demo sequence on the Timeline after the initial installation. This demo sequence can be used in the Appendix to test your computer; however, a new sequence must be started in order for your interface to match the screenshots in this book.

Figure i.1 The MovieBox 5.1 Pro version allows you to monitor the output when you're developing a surround sound project.

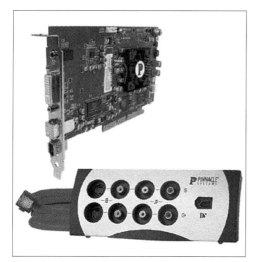

Figure i.2 The ATI Radeon 8500 adapted and rebadged by Pinnacle as the Pro card.

Figure i.3 The MovieBox. A USB DV/analog converter with a case designed by Porsche no less!

Liquid Variations

Liquid Edition 6 is sold as:

◆ Liquid Edition DV

◆ Liquid Edition Pro

The important thing to remember here is that the software remains the same in each version; the only difference is the hardware included in the packet. Here is the breakdown:

◆ Liquid Edition DV supplied with a standard FireWire card

◆ Liquid Edition Pro supplied with a USB DV/Analog converter with input and output sockets for Analog Composite, Component and S-Video, and also 5.1 surround sound. The analog output from this device allows you to monitor real-time previews on an external monitor such as a portable TV set (**Figure i.1**).

✔ Tips

■ If you never need to output your projects directly to VHS or if you never need to capture from VHS, then you probably only need Liquid Edition DV. However, remember that the Pro version offers one very important advantage: It can display Realtime filters and transitions on a TV set without having to be rendered first.

■ The Edition Pro card—a special Pinnacle 64 MB AGP card with analog out, supplied with Liquid Edition 5.x (**Figure i.2**) —and the MovieBox Deluxe—a USB DV/analog converter supplied with Pinnacle Studio (**Figure i.3**)—will both give you access to the analog features of Liquid Edition 6.

To which version does this book apply?

Software programs change their version numbers in gradual increments over their lifetime (from 1.0 to 6.0, for example). Often, the version numbers change in even smaller increments (from 6.0 to 6.1, to 6.2, and on up to 6.58, or something similar); these smaller increments often represent service packs (once know as bug fixes) and/or patches that allow users to access recently released hardware, such as advanced DVD burners with dual-layer capability.

Historically, these version increments don't significantly change the operation of the program. Therefore, this book applies to any version of Liquid Edition 6.*x*, where *x* is the number you have installed on your computer.

Liquid Variations

Adobe Premiere Translations

Adobe Premiere Pro is another popular NLE program, and many of the terms this program uses are now standard with most NLE users. However, not all of them are used in Liquid Edition, and sometimes the meaning of an identical function may be lost in translation.

To avoid confusion, I provide sidebars throughout this book that translate Liquid Edition features into something Premiere users recognize. For example, transferring media from DV tape to the computer is called *digitizing* in Liquid Edition and *capturing* in Adobe Premiere.

What's New in Version 6?

Version 6 isn't simply an upgrade; it's the concept of Liquid Edition matured. If you have worked with previous versions, you'll instantly notice that the interface has been redesigned with new users *and* professionals in mind and that it has a selection of exciting new features. Here are just a few:

◆ **High Definition Video (HDV).**

HDV is a high-definition version of the popular DV format that uses MPEG-2 compression to fit HD content onto the same DV tape stock. HDV uses a much higher resolution than DV to create clear, concise screen images. The difference in clarity is stunning.

Liquid Edition 6 includes native support for HDV resolutions, which means you can capture directly from an HDV camera without having to convert to AVI.

Although an HD film contains much more detail than Mini DV or Hi-8, it doesn't take up an exponential amount of space on your hard drive. This is because HD is MPEG-based, not AVI-based. This means the compression method is much more efficient, thus allowing for a smaller file size despite the greater resolution.

◆ **MPEG editing.** Native MPEG editing is now available. This means Timelines can contain MPEG formats such as HDV, VCD, SVCD, elemental streams, and even VOB files.

◆ **Multi-format Timeline.** You can mix AVI clips on the Timeline with MPEG film clips and vice versa without having to render the "alien" media. This is because Liquid Edition 6 has a new render system called SmartRender, which is able to use clips from a variety of different sources.

◆ **Improved Audio Editor.** Before the arrival of version 6, the audio side of Liquid Edition was a weak point. In version 6, the Audio Editor has been rewritten to include VST plug-in support, 5.1 surround sound, Timeline Panning control, and a variety of improvements to the audio interface itself.

Obviously the most exciting addition is the ability to create a 5.1 surround sound DVD using the included Dolby AC3 encoder.

◆ **A redesigned interface.** The Liquid Edition interface now sports a much needed dab of color and the choice between two different menu systems: the new Drop-Down interface designed for users new to Liquid Edition; and the Classic Start-Button system, which is based on an older interface style and may be more comfortable for old-hand Liquid Edition users.

◆ **Intuitive FX editors.** In this version, the look and feel of FX editors has also been altered to include a parameter curve editing system and an easier-to-use interface.

◆ **Greater scope for creativity.** The ability to add and subtract effects has also been enhanced. It now includes Global Track FX (with which you can add an FX to the whole track).

◆ **More wizards.** Previous versions of Liquid Edition featured just one wizard—the DVD Export wizard. Now import and export tasks are fully supported by wizards that attempt to ease you through the various ways in which you can bring in material to edit and then successfully export it again.

◆ **Multicamera editing.** If you've ever used more than one camera to film the same event, you know the problems that can occur when you try to match up two (or more) films into the one edited video. There are a hundred workarounds to do this, but now version 6 allows you to capture these clips as virtual cameras, which can then be edited into one clip via a numbered Picture in Picture display.

◆ **Backup and export projects.** Version 6 allows you to export a project with all its associated media (clips, sound, titles, and so on) to an external point, such as a DVD or an archived folder on your hard drive or network. This function allows you to back up your projects and also send them in an easily contained form to any editor in the world.

◆ **Matte and subtrack support.** In version 6, you can simplify the process of using Matte Track by adding a secondary Matte Track to the Timeline instead of using a filter. The effect is real-time, and you can collapse the Matte track and subtracks allowing you to save on screen space.

◆ **Audio Timewarp.** You can now apply a linear Timewarp filter to an audio clip, although its use is restricted to a value range between −50 and +200 percent.

Plus more...

Obviously this list is just scratching the surface of what's new in version 6.0. On the technical side, there have been huge advances in the rendering department and in the overall operation and workflow of the application.

Below is a short list of some of the other features that are new to version 6. The majority of NLE editors will probably find these interesting.

◆ Pinnacle Studio 9 project import and plug-in support

◆ Ability to export to WM9 with custom presets

◆ Surround sound mixer

◆ Four-point editing

◆ Dual-layer DVD support

◆ Ability to update Waveform after it returns from XSend to WaveLab

Again this is not a definitive list, but it does give you some idea of the advances version 6 has made.

The Minimum System Specification

- ◆ Windows XP SP1 or Windows 2000 with SP3 (Mac systems aren't supported by Liquid Edition 6)

- ◆ 1.8 GHz CPU

- ◆ 512 MB of memory

- ◆ A large second hard drive, either SCSII or EIDE/SATA (EIDE/SATA drives must have a minimum spin speed of 7,200 rpm (revs per minute).

- ◆ A graphics card with at least 64 MB of on-board memory

- ◆ A sound card that is DirectX 9 compatible

- ◆ An IEEE1394 PCI card (also known as a FireWire card)

- ◆ A CD-ROM (to install the program)

✔ Tip

- ■ Windows XP is seen as the OS of choice for Liquid Edition 6. Windows 2000 users should bear this in mind.

A Second Hard Drive

A second dedicated video hard drive is essential if you want a reliable NLE computer system. This rule applies to any video editing software, not just Liquid Edition. Video editing on one hard drive (i.e., the one that Windows XP lives on) is not just a viable option because slow disc performance is one of the major bottlenecks in a PC. The secondary drive should be one that is as big as you can afford and has a spin speed of 7,200 rpm. Drives that spin at 5,400 rpm don't offer the performance you need for video editing.

The second drive should also "always" be formatted using NTFS. The alternative—FAT32—can only store 4 GB (approximately 18 minutes) of video, whereas NTFS can store up to 12 TB (more than you'll ever need). Serious editors will only use NTFS.

For details on hard drive use, see the Appendix, where you'll find a range of tips for improving the performance of your computer.

The Recommended System Specification

This type of program demands a performance level that exceeds most programs available today. Where high performance is required, there is only one simple rule to follow: Bigger is always better. If you are serious about video editing, you need something like the following:

◆ 3.0 GHz or dual-processor system using 2x2.2 GHz CPU.

◆ 1,024 MB of fast, reliable RAM.

◆ A fast graphics card with at least 128 MB on board and DirectX 9.x support.

◆ A DVD burner. This is essential if you want to author DVDs or create an archived backup of your project.

◆ A sound card with ASIO 2.0 compatibility. To edit in 5.1 surround sound, you need a sound card that supports this and a speaker system that allows you to accurately monitor the results.

◆ A certified USB 2.0 interface. This is required if you're going to use MovieBox and MovieBox Pro. For a list of which USB interfaces are certified, visit the support page for Liquid Edition (www.Pinnaclesys.com).

HDV System Requirements

If you intend to do the bulk of your editing in the HDV format, you need even more power than the specifications I recommend.

Your CPU should be at least a 3.2 GHz with hyperthreading enabled, and your graphics card should be a PCI Express card with 256 MB on board and pixel shader support. The more RAM you have on your motherboard, the better.

Liquid Edition with a Laptop

You can also use Liquid Edition on a laptop but only if the laptop is powerful enough and is equipped with a graphics chip that has enough muscle to power the effects. To use Liquid Edition on a laptop, you'll also need an external FireWire hard drive on which to store your media clips.

Additional Equipment for the Power User

A Power user is a kind of superuser of NLE software. Typically, they start out as hobbyists and then progress until they are making money from their hobby by filming events such as weddings or training videos. Some even go on to make this a full-time career. If you are a budding Power user, you'll need a little more equipment:

- A second VGA monitor so you can have a dual-screen layout.

- MovieBox Pro if you want to output 5.1 surround sound.

- A DV deck to transfer your tapes to the computer. Yes, you can use your camera. I do. But there is a price to pay if you do so—double the work means half the shelf life for your camera.

- A quality VHS deck to output your projects onto tape and to capture from analog.

- An EIDE/SATA expansion card. You'll use this to add more drives to your system, either as separate units or linked together in a RAID, forming one big drive from up to four others.

- A removable drive bay. The alternative to a large hard drive or a RAID is simply to swap out hard drives for every project you work on.

GETTING STARTED

Before you launch into this book, it is essential that you familiarize yourself with some of the terms, phrases, and main features found in Liquid Edition. They are simple enough to learn, but obscure enough to seem impenetrable to the absolute beginner or to users migrating from other software programs.

This chapter looks at the interface and, for the benefit of total beginners, some of the basic concepts of nonlinear editing, which is often referred to as NLE. But don't panic, I deal with all of these features in far more depth in the relevant chapters, so you won't have to learn too much too soon. The latter part of this chapter does deal with customizing the interface and saving these customizations as templates, so you can learn some of the basic concepts of customizing your interface to suit your own particular workflow.

General Installation Tips

Setting up and using video editing software can be problematic, and the more you can do to ease this situation, the better. Installation is a good time to start; try to do as many as the following as humanly possible.

- Make sure Windows XP has the latest patches installed. Use the Windows Update short-cut to check this.

- Ask yourself how clean this Windows setup is. For instance, do you have a dozen different trial programs that might cause complications? If so, uninstall them before you install Liquid Edition.

- Turn off all background tasks before you start the Installation wizard; this includes any Messenger programs and any virus-checking programs or software firewalls. Obviously, if you do disable the virus checker and/or firewall, you should also physically disconnect your machine from the Internet. Don't forget to reenable firewalls and virus checkers before you reconnect to the Internet. Rebooting the computer may automatically do this for you.

- Disable the screensaver and all Windows' power-saving features.

- Defragment the hard drive. Once all background tasks have been disabled, you should take advantage of this situation and defragment the drive onto which Windows XP is installed. If you are looking for optimal performance, you should also defragment your system hard drive *after* you've installed the software.

- Check the system properties of your computer for problems. These will show up as yellow exclamation marks. Make sure you solve these before you install the software.

- Make sure you are using the most up-to-date drivers for the various components of your PC. That includes—and I cannot emphasize this enough—the chipset drivers for your main board. You can update these via the manufacturer's Web site. You should always update because a large percentage of performance problems experienced with NLE programs can be directly attributed to using an out-of-date chipset driver.

- Use the Windows XP restore function to create a Restore point before you install the soft-ware so that you can roll this installation back if you need to. You might also consider buying a disk image software program to make an image of your hard drive.

- Once you've completed the installation, don't forget to check the Pinnacle Web site (www.Pinnaclesys.com) for any updates or patches that you may need to install.

Figure 1.1 The autorun.exe shortcut. Click this to start the Installation wizard.

Select Destination Directory

Please select the directory where the Pinnacle Liquid files are to be installed.

C:\Program Files\Liquid 6   Browse

< Back   Next >   Cancel

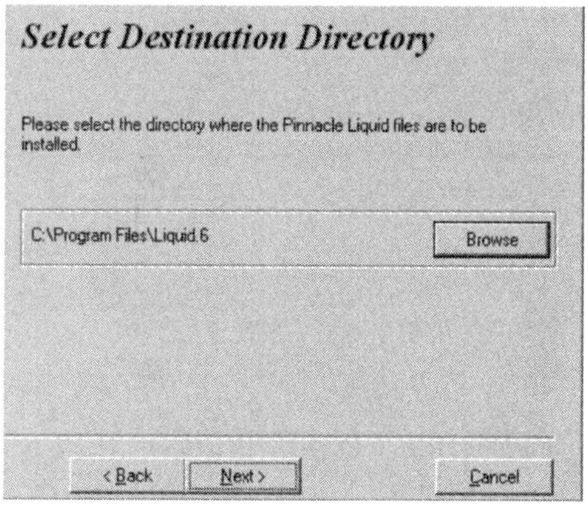

Figure 1.2 First choose where to install Liquid Edition...

Premiere Users, Read This

If you are migrating from Adobe Premiere, you may find the terminology in Liquid Edition particularly strange, because many common functions have a different name. When this occurs, I will include a sidebar (similar to this one) in which I will translate that function from one system to the other.

For example, what Premiere users would call capturing, Liquid Edition users would call digitizing. Essentially the process is the same; only the name is different.

Installing Liquid Edition 6

If your computer did not come preinstalled with Liquid Edition, you will need to install the software from CD. This is a simple operation, largely automated by wizards, but you should be ready to answer such questions as these: To which hard drive do you want to capture video clips? On which hard drive will you want to store render files?

✔ Tips

- If you create a folder called Capture on your intended capture drive and another folder called Render on another drive before you install, you will greatly simplify this situation.

- Please read the "General Installation Tips" sidebar before attempting to install Liquid Edition 6.

To install Liquid Edition 6:

1. Insert the Liquid Edition CD into your computer. This should automatically bring up the Installation wizard. If it doesn't, browse to your computer's CD drive and double-click the autorun.exe file (**Figure 1.1**) found in the root directory of the CD. Some versions of Liquid Edition 6 may display a file called Setup.exe.

2. Select the install language and click OK. This brings up a license agreement page.

3. Click Yes to agree to the license agreement and click Next at the welcome screen.

4. At the prompt, select the drive to which you want to install the software. Unless you have a specific reason for doing so, it is always best to install the software to the same drive that holds Windows XP (**Figure 1.2**).

continues on next page

5. The next screen asks you to choose which video standard and system language you want to use. This should default to the standard being used by Windows. Again, leave this set to the defaults and click Next (**Figure 1.3**).

You can also choose to install the drivers for Jog/Shuttle controller or Moviebox from this screen if you have this hardware.

6. Choose a drive on which you will store your render files (**Figure 1.4**). The optimal location will be a separate partition or hard drive that does not hold your operating system.

Choosing the optimal location is important because render files are created when:

▲ Real-time FXs are being displayed.

▲ Non-real-time effects are being rendered.

▲ A DVD is rendering prior to the burn process.

7. Click Next and you will be asked to select your video drive (**Figure 1.5**).

This is where your video clips will be stored when either digitized (captured) or imported. Approximately 16 minutes of digital video consumes 4 gigabytes (GB) of hard drive space, so clearly you'll need to select a very large hard drive to get the best out of this program.

8. Click Next again and Liquid Edition will begin to install.

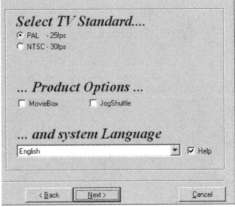

Figure 1.3 ...then which TV standard and language to use...

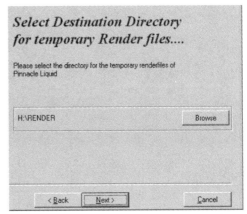

Figure 1.4 ...then the target location for your render files...

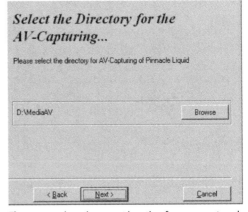

Figure 1.5 ...then the target location for your captured media...

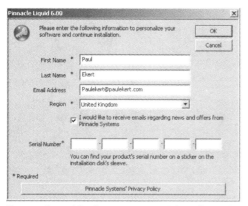

Figure 1.6 ...and finally, enter your serial number and personal details, and wait for the installation to finish.

9. Enter the serial number from your CD case. Make sure you enter letters in upper-case and then click Next. You'll also need to put some personal details in the required fields (**Figure 1.6**).

It may take anywhere from 5 to 10 minutes to completely install the various components that make up Liquid Edition. The Hollywood FX component is particularly slow to install, and in the beginning, it may appear as though nothing is actually happening. However, if you leave it for a while, the install process will eventually carry on.

At the end of this process (depending on which setup you have) you may be asked to install Title Deko. This process is largely automatic; just stick to the defaults and let the Installation wizard do the rest. Once all the components are installed, you may also have to reboot the computer.

✔ Tips

■ Although both Render and Video locations have to be selected during installation, you can change them later using the Control Panel. See Chapter 4, "Managing Your Media."

■ Further advice on setting up your computer and which hard drives to use for what can be found in the Appendix.

DV MovieBox Install Prompt

Users of the DV MovieBox—supplied with Pinnacle Studio 8 and 9—will be asked to insert the original Studio CD during the install process. This is only a verification check and does not install any files from that CD.

Opening and Closing Liquid Edition

Version 6 introduces a new type of interface—the Drop-Down Menu interface—while retaining the old, so-called Classic Start-Button interface. These two menu systems require two different methods to open and close them.

To start Liquid Edition with the Drop-Down Menu interface:

Do one of the following:

◆ Double-click on the desktop shortcut (**Figure 1.7**).

◆ Go to the Windows Start menu and select All Programs > Pinnacle Liquid 6.00 > Liquid 6—not Liquid 6 (classic).

To start Liquid Edition with the Classic interface:

◆ Go to the Windows Start menu (since the desktop icon created during installation opens the Drop-Down Menu interface) and select All Programs > Pinnacle Liquid 6.00 > Liquid 6 (classic) (**Figure 1.7**, right).

✔ Tips

■ Depending on how many plug-ins you have installed and the speed of your processor, loading Liquid Edition can take as much as a minute, possibly longer.

■ The first time you launch Liquid Edition 6 you will be asked to activate the program (**Figure 1.8**). To do this, click on the top button and follow the on-screen instructions. An Internet connection is required to complete this part of the installation.

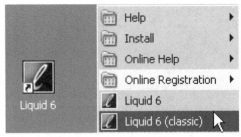

Figure 1.7 This icon on the left should appear on your desktop by default. Double-click it to launch Liquid Edition with the Drop-Down interface or, if you prefer, use this shortcut to launch the Classic interface.

Figure 1.8 The activation screen appears when you launch Liquid Edition for the first time.

To exit Liquid Edition in the Drop-Down interface:

Do one of the following:

◆ Click the window's X in the top right corner of the screen.

◆ Press Alt+4 on the keyboard.

◆ Go to the File menu and select Exit Pinnacle Liquid 6.

To exit Liquid Edition in the Classic interface:

◆ Click the Liquid Edition Start button and select Exit.

In both cases, a small Exiting Application window will appear while Liquid Edition clears unwanted temporary files from your hard drive. This process may take more than a minute and should not be interrupted. Once this window has disappeared, you may turn off your computer.

Start a New Sequence

Liquid Edition 6 opens with a demo sequence on the Timeline. So that the screenshots in this book match your computer display, you will need to start a new sequence by clicking on the New Sequence button [ ] at the top-right corner of the Liquid Edition interface. See Chapter 5 for more details.

Why Are There Two Interfaces?

In version 6, the decision was made to provide an interface that fell a little more into line with the Microsoft Windows ethos. Regardless of what you might feel about Microsoft, the Drop-Down menu approach is pretty much a worldwide standard, understood by millions (possibly billions) of users. Version 6 attempts to capitalize on this by giving new users an immediately recognizable interface to work with; something the original Classic interface did not always do.

But, there is also a hard-core user group whose members have been editing with Liquid Edition since the dawn of time. These people like their solid, somewhat confusing, and often impenetrable interface. For them, the Classic option is the only option. To avoid alienating the hard-core group, but with an eye toward wooing the new user, Pinnacle has produced the best of both worlds; they are allowing users to decide which interface they really want to use.

This book uses the new Drop-Down interface, partly because it is easier for beginners to understand, but mainly because it is the default interface displayed once the desktop short-cut is double-clicked.

For users of the Classic interface, you'll find a number of sidebars throughout this book that explain how to access the same option in the task-based descriptions.

OPENING AND CLOSING LIQUID EDITION

Touring the Interface

When you first launch Liquid Edition, it displays the main interface showing the Timeline, and the two windows on the left and right called the Source and Master/Timeline Viewer. Both are controlled by the buttons directly under the inlays or by using the mouse and keyboard shortcuts (**Figure 1.9**).

The Timeline is the root of all the various interfaces Liquid Edition has to offer, and at some stage during your edit process, your Project will be completed here. This makes the Timeline arguably the most important interface of them all.

Therefore I will touch on the Timeline in pretty much every chapter of this book, but specifically when I discuss editing techniques in Chapter 6, "Fine-Tuning Your Edit."

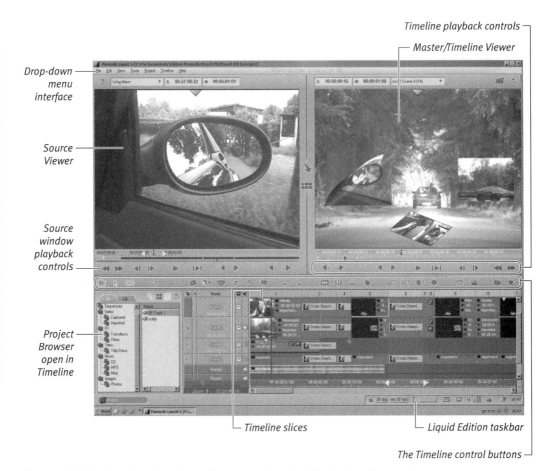

Timeline playback controls

Master/Timeline Viewer

Drop-down menu interface

Source Viewer

Source window playback controls

Project Browser open in Timeline

Timeline slices

Liquid Edition taskbar

The Timeline control buttons

Figure 1.9 The Timeline view; shown here with a complex layout of clips, both audio and video.

TOURING THE INTERFACE

Working with buttons and keyboard shortcuts

You interact with Liquid Edition by using a variety of buttons and keyboard shortcuts. To use a button, simply click it with the mouse. This action will open an interface, create an event, or perform an action, depending on which button you press (**Figure 1.10**).

continues on next page

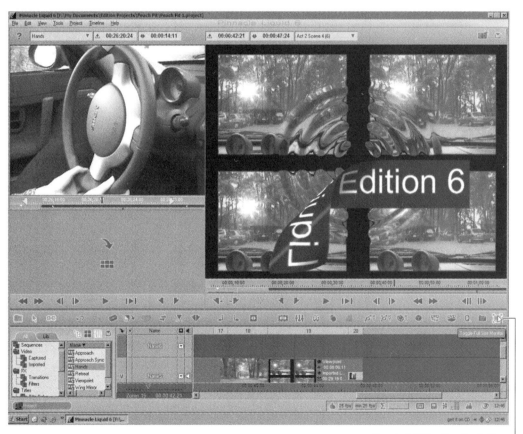

Toggle Full Size Monitor button

Figure 1.10 The Toggle Full Size Monitor button has been clicked to increase the size of the Master/Timeline Viewer.

If you are unsure of what a particular button does, just hover the mouse over it and a small tool tip will pop up and give you a brief description of what that button does (**Figure 1.11**). In some cases, the text is very brief, but it will at least give you a clue as to the button's ultimate purpose. From there, the answer is but a reference manual away.

The other way to access a feature is to use a keyboard shortcut. This is often a simple matter of pressing a single key, but other times, you may need to hold down a combination of keys and mouse buttons. Clicking the Keyboard button 🖮 (down in the taskbar area—the bottom-right corner of the interface) will bring up a template that shows which keys are assigned to which functions. Again, you'll be able to access a tool tip to figure out what all those icons actually mean (**Figure 1.12**).

✔ Tip

■ Once the keyboard template has opened, clicking anywhere in the interface will toggle the keyboard shortcut window to show the shortcuts for whatever area has just been clicked.

Figure 1.11 The Toggle Full Size Monitor displaying a helpful tool tip.

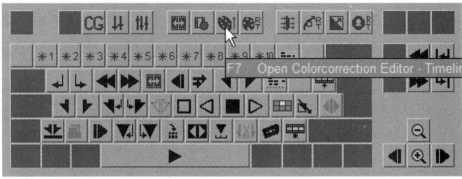

Figure 1.12 The keyboard template for the Timeline/Master shortcuts.

Technobabble— What Is an Inlay?

The term *inlay* refers to an area of a Windows-based interface that is capable of displaying a video or still image.

When you first open Liquid Edition, it displays a black area in the Source and Master/Timeline Viewers. This area is where the image of a media clip (video or photograph) will appear, and it is called an inlay.

You will also see inlays in the Logging tool, the FX editors, the Trim tool, and the Clip Viewer.

Some of the more common inlay problems and possible solutions can be found in the Appendix.

Summing Up— Other Interfaces in Liquid Edition

Although the most important, the Timeline is just one of the many interface screens that Liquid Edition uses. The other interfaces of primary importance include the following:

◆ **The Storyboard view.** This view provides a simple way for you to choose the running order of your clips. This interface is an essential part of any moviemaker's planning. It's one of the more underused interfaces of Liquid Edition, but Chapter 5, "The First Assembly—Storyboarding," details how to get the best from it (**Figure 1.13**).

OTHER INTERFACES IN LIQUID EDITION

The Trash icon — Button to select Picon View — Button to select Text View

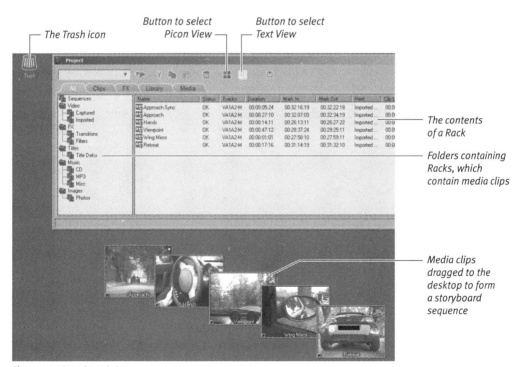

The contents of a Rack

Folders containing Racks, which contain media clips

Media clips dragged to the desktop to form a storyboard sequence

Figure 1.13 Storyboard view.

◆ **The Logging tool.** If you want to transfer
(digitize/capture) material from a DV/HDV
device or analog player, this is where you
will do it. The Logging tool is daunting at
first glance, but it simple to use in practice.
Chapter 2, "Logging and Digitizing,"
explores the possibilities (**Figure 1.14**).

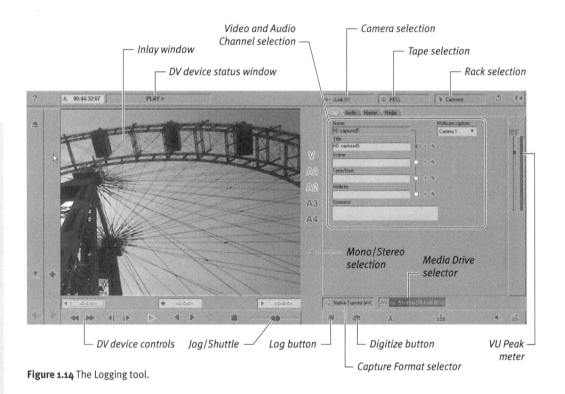

Video and Audio
Channel selection ──

Camera selection ──

Inlay window ──

Tape selection ──

DV device status window ──

Rack selection ──

Mono/Stereo
selection

Media Drive
selector

DV device controls   Jog/Shuttle ──   Log button ──   Digitize button   VU Peak
meter

Capture Format selector

Figure 1.14 The Logging tool.

◆ **The Effects Editors.** Liquid Edition
has several Effects Editors for a variety
of different operations. Although each
FX editor has a different function, each
operates on a similar principle of adjusting sliders to alter the properties of the
effect and adding key frames to create
effects over time. These features are
dealt with in Chapters 8, "Working with
Transitions" and 9, "Working with
Filters" (**Figure 1.15**).

FX editor parameter controls   Parameter Curve editor   One-Click tools

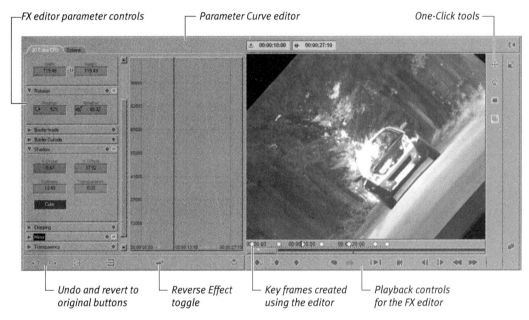

Undo and revert to   Reverse Effect   Key frames created   Playback controls
original buttons   toggle   using the editor   for the FX editor

Figure 1.15 The Effects Editors.

◆ **The Audio Editor. Figure 1.16** shows
the Audio Editor with the new 5.1 interface that is a new feature of version 6. To
access this, you must have a sound card
with ASIO 2.0 compatibility and a 5.1
speaker system. Further details are in
Chapter 7, "Working with Audio."

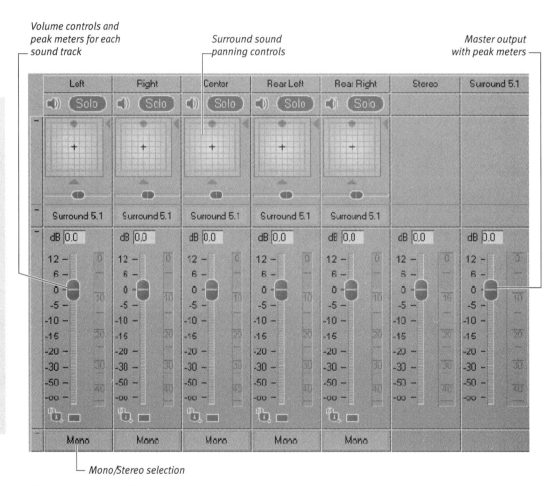

*Volume controls and
peak meters for each
sound track*

*Surround sound
panning controls*

*Master output
with peak meters*

Mono/Stereo selection

Figure 1.16 The Audio Editor.

OTHER INTERFACES IN LIQUID EDITION

◆ **The DVD Editor.** One of the most exciting features of Liquid Edition is its ability to create DVDs from the Timeline without first having to export the whole movie to a third-party application. **Figure 1.17** shows the Preview window open, which allows you to check that your menu and its buttons are working as expected before you commit yourself to burning the Project to a DVD. Chapter 12, "DVD Authoring," has more details on this cool feature.

Various DVD editing tools

Tabs to access the
DVD editing functions

DVD preview
controls

DVD preview
window

An animated
DVD button

Additional subtracks added automatically
by the creation of a DVD menu

Four DVD tracks have been added to create three
animated buttons and an animated background.

Figure 1.17 The DVD Editor.

◆ **The Trim window.** You use this interface to trim media clips. Actually, it's much more complex than that, and it's also one of the interfaces that causes the most problems for new users. Chapter 6 has more details on understanding the complexities of the Trim window (**Figure 1.18**).

◆ **The Control Panel.** This interface controls the various preferences and settings used to optimize and customize Liquid Edition. Chapter 4 has more details on this (**Figure 1.19**).

The Running Man—Used to exit the editor

Timecode and Duration information

The outgoing clip

The incoming clip

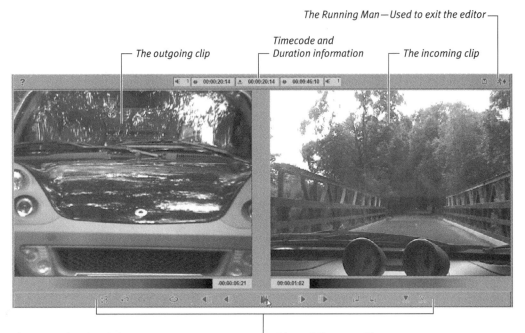

Figure 1.18 The Trim window.

Trim and Play control buttons

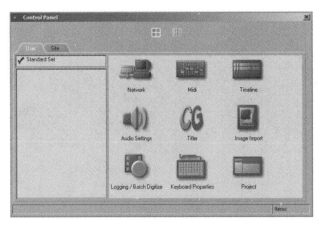

Figure 1.19 The Control Panel

A Media Clip

This is a generic term that refers to anything you bring into Liquid Edition, either by capturing it or by importing it. This is normally a video clip, but it can also be an audio file, a title, a photographic image, or an animation.

◆ **The Clip Viewer.** This is a small, compact interface that is uncluttered and fast to work with. It also has a number of features that allow you more editing opportunities than are afforded by the Source window. It's, sadly, a vastly underrated part of Liquid Edition's tools. See Chapter 5 for details on how to open and use the Clip Viewer (**Figure 1.20**).

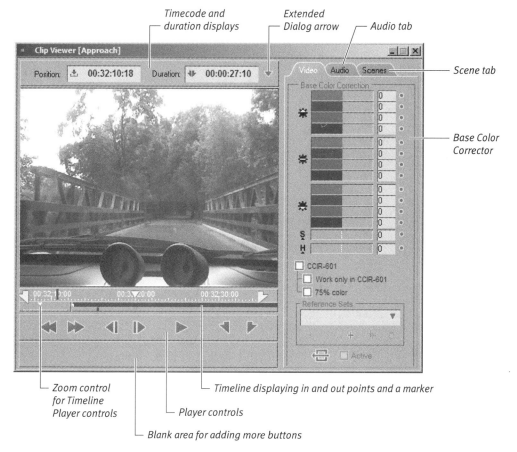

Timecode and duration displays

Extended Dialog arrow

Audio tab

Scene tab

Base Color Corrector

Zoom control for Timeline Player controls

Player controls

Blank area for adding more buttons

Timeline displaying in and out points and a marker

Figure 1.20 The Clip Viewer. The right-hand side of the interface is displayed by clicking the Extended Dialog arrow.

OTHER INTERFACES IN LIQUID EDITION

◆ **The Project Browser.** All the media clips you work with are stored in the Project Browser. You open this area of the interface by clicking once on the Project Browser button. Once it is open, you can access and manipulate your clips (**Figure 1.21**).

The Project Browser has a second tab called Lib, which is used to access the FX library. Liquid Edition has a comprehensive range of effects you can use in your video projects. You'll find a full explanation of how to use these in Chapters 8 and 9 (**Figure 1.22**).

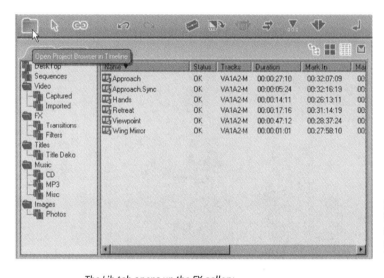

Figure 1.21 The Project Browser is the heart of Liquid Edition, shown here in List View. Anything that is placed on the Timeline will be stored here.

The Lib tab opens up the FX gallery.

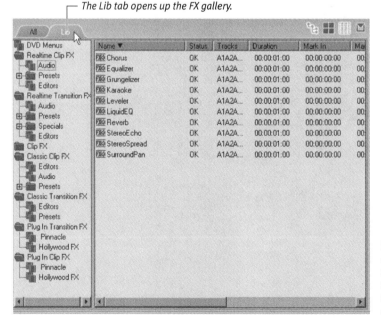

Figure 1.22 It is also the home of Liquid Edition's Effects Suite, where you can access an impressive range of filters and transitions. Here the new Audio filters are displayed.

Instant Save

One thing Premiere users will fail to locate is a Save button. This is because Liquid Edition automatically saves your work thirty times a second, which means even if a crash should occur, you are unlikely ever to lose any of your work.

Undoing information from previous sessions

The save function also retains all the undo information from previous sessions, allowing you to undo several days' worth of alterations if you needed to. This undo information is retained even if you close the program and switch off the computer.

If you have ever watched several hours of editing go south courtesy of a program crash only moments before you thought, "When was the last time I saved this?" you will really appreciate this particular chore being done automatically.

If you are worried about overwriting something important, Liquid Edition also allows you to save various copies of Projects which you can refer back to.

✔ Tip

- If a crash should occur, Liquid Edition will always restart the Timeline with a new *empty* sequence. Don't panic; your sequence is safe; it's just hidden from view. Go to the Sequence drop-down menu in the upper-right corner of the interface and you will find your sequence there; usually it is the next one down on the list.

How Nonlinear Editing Actually Works

The important thing to remember about nonlinear editing is that it's a safe, nondestructive form of editing that does not alter the actual clip stored on your hard drive. You can:

- Alter the length of that clip.

- Add a filter to it.

- Change its color tones.

- Speed it up or slow it down.

...anything you like—it doesn't matter because the original clip will always remain intact. This is creativity without the worry.

How does Liquid Edition do this?

By using the original clip only as a reference point, the software can display a proxy version created from temporary files stored in memory or on the hard drive. If you decide the media clip should lose 10 seconds from the start and 30 seconds from the finish, Liquid Edition won't actually delete 40 seconds of media; it will just adjust the way in which it looks at and displays that media clip. Similarly, if you decided to adjust the red tonal color of a media clip, then the software would simply create proxy files to display a red media clip but leave the original clip—yep, you guessed it—unchanged.

In a nutshell, this means you can happily experiment with your media clips, adding super-looking effects to video, adjusting sound levels, and so on, until you end up producing the most experimental video any art house would be pleased to controversially screen. What's more, you can do all of this secure in the knowledge that your original clips will remain in their original form, ready to be used again in another Project—perhaps one a tad less experimental.

The exceptions to this rule are the commands Consolidate and Condense (covered in Chapter 14, "Advanced Techniques"). These are special functions that will produce copies of the media clips that are different from the original. However, these commands will not delete the original media clip unless you specifically ask for this to be done.

INSTANT SAVE

Creating Projects

Each time you start working on a new production you should also start a new Liquid Edition Project. Think of a Project as being similar to an office ring binder—it allows you to place all the relevant documents in one place. This has several advantages, not the least of which is that you can export an entire Project to an archive or transfer it to another editing station without too much fuss. This simple operation alone can become overly complex if you have not given a unique Project name to each of the productions you are working on.

With this in mind, try to get into the habit of creating a new Project for each production you are working on The process of creating a Project only involves a few mouse clicks and is a sound investment for your future NLE sanity.

✔ Tips

■ Creating a new Project is also a good idea if you want to retain the default Liquid Edition settings. Every time you alter an element of the interface, Autosave will save it. Effectively, this means the default settings will be lost forever unless you make a backup copy or always work with a new Project name. The only other way of restoring the default setting is to reinstall the software, something you should be keen to avoid.

■ Liquid Edition saves your work every 1/30 of a second, which means once a Project has been created, it will continue to be updated every moment the application is open. This is yet one more reason to create a new Project for every production you are working on.

To create a new Project:

1. Select File > New > Project (**Figure 1.23**).

2. Browse to a directory in which you would like to store your Projects, give the Project an original name, and click OK (**Figure 1.24**).

   For details on the last option, Template, refer to the template section later in this chapter.

✔ Tip

■ By default, Liquid Edition saves its Project files to the Pinnacle root folder, the place where Liquid Edition is installed. If you need to reinstall the software or install a service pack, then this Project data may be deleted. Therefore, it is best to use a folder on another hard drive to store your own project files.

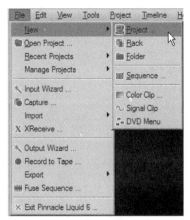

Figure 1.23 Creating a new Project via the drop-down menu.

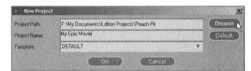

Figure 1.24 Picking a unique Project name and a Save location outside the Pinnacle directory.

Classic Interface

Users of the Classic interface can access all of the Project menus by clicking the Start button and selecting Project > Open/Create Project (**Figure 1.25**). This brings up a slightly different file browser. To create a new Project, you need to click the New button (**Figure 1.26**).

All other actions are identical to those described in this chapter.

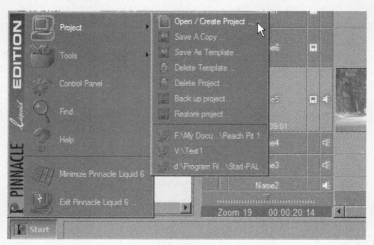

Figure 1.25 Creating or opening a new Project using the Classic interface.

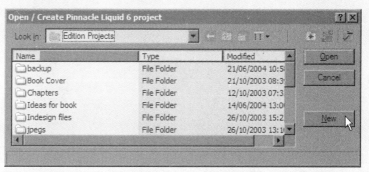

Figure 1.26 The slightly different file browser with the additional New button.

To save a Project:

1. Select File > Manage Projects > Save a Copy (**Figure 1.27**).

2. Browse to the directory where you want to store your Projects, give the Project an original name, and click Save (**Figure 1.28**).

✔ Tip

■ For the same reasons discussed in the previous section, it is recommended that you save your Project files in a directory *outside* the Liquid Edition installation folder.

To switch to a different Project:

1. Select File > Recent Projects, and then click whichever Project you want to return to (**Figure 1.29**).

   You will make this choice from a list of recent Projects; if you have picked original names for all of your Projects, the one you want will be easy to find.

2. Click the name of the Project you want to switch to, but be aware, there is no "are you sure prompt" here.

   The Project is loaded into Liquid Edition as soon as you make that click.

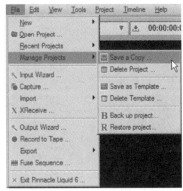

Figure 1.27 Saving a copy of the current Project.

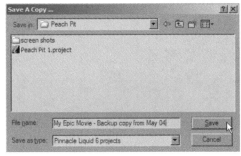

Figure 1.28 Save the Project to a safe location outside the Pinnacle folder.

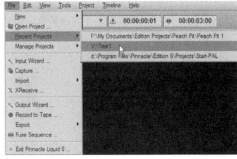

Figure 1.29 All recent Projects will be displayed here.

Switching between Projects in the Project Browser

It's also possible to access media clips stored in another Project while still remaining in the current Project. To do this, simply right-click the All tab in the Project Browser to bring up **Figure 1.30**.

You can now display any of the recent Projects and copy media clips to the current Project using the standard copy/paste commands (Ctrl+C/Ctrl+V). You can also use clips on the Timeline while they are stored in another Project, but this can make organizing your Project somewhat difficult.

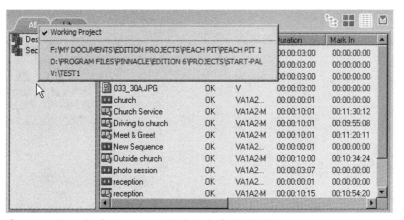

Figure 1.30 Swapping between recent Projects in the Project Browser.

Using Project Templates

A Project template is useful for setting up Liquid Edition to handle various different types of projects, perhaps with a standard intro.

For example, you may want a wedding video to have the tracks ordered as shown in **Figure 1.31**. Saving a Project template means you only have to set this up once and then load it back in whenever you need it.

Creating a Project template will save the layout of the Racks and Folders, any media clips placed in these folders, and any media clips that are on the timeline, but it won't save the toolbar buttons that you may have added to the interface.

To save a Project template:

1. Select File > Manage Projects > Save as Template (**Figure 1.32**).

2. Once the dialog box appears, choose a unique name and then click Save.

✔ Tip

■ Templates *must* be saved to the default template folder inside the Pinnacle program group (**Figure 1.33**). If you don't save them to this location, Liquid Edition can't see them.

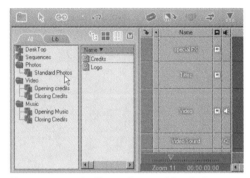

Figure 1.31 A typical layout for a wedding Project.

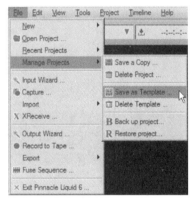

Figure 1.32 Saving a Project template.

Figure 1.33 The default location you must use when saving a Project template.

Figure 1.34 Opening a Project.

Figure 1.35 Choosing a template from the drop-down menu.

To open a Project template:

1. Select File > New > Project (**Figure 1.34**).

2. Browse to the Pinnacle directory where the Project template is stored, select the one you want, and click OK (**Figure 1.35**).

✔ Tip

■ If you can't see the template, you need to check if it has been saved in the default Pinnacle directory. If it hasn't, you can use Windows Explorer to locate the template and copy it to this location.

Using Project Backups

Using an original Project name for each and every production means that you can easily back up your work to a DVD, a zip file, or a network location.

To create a Project backup for export:

1. Select File > Manage Projects > Back up project (**Figure 1.36**).

   This brings up an interface with various options for you to choose from (**Figure 1.37**).

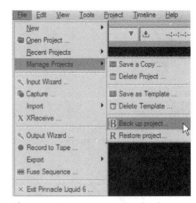

Figure 1.36 Creating a Project backup.

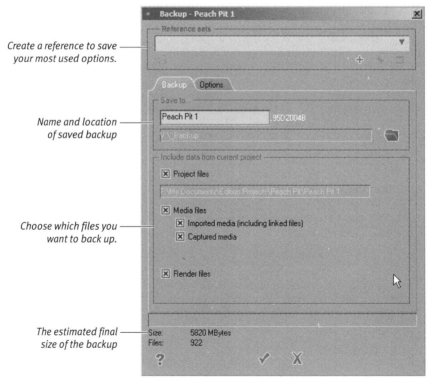

Create a reference to save your most used options.

Name and location of saved backup

Choose which files you want to back up.

The estimated final size of the backup

Figure 1.37 The Backup Options screen with various options that can be saved as a reference set.

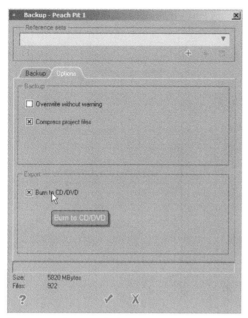

Figure 1.38 The second tab, Options, allows you to burn the backup directly to a DVD.

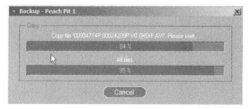

Figure 1.39 The backup process in action.

2. If you want to burn this to a DVD, click the Options tab and check the Burn to CD/DVD box (**Figure 1.38**).

3. Once you have decided which options to use, click the check mark to begin the process. Depending on the size of the project, this may take some time (**Figure 1.39**).

continues on next page

USING PROJECT BACKUPS

If you have checked the Burn to DVD box, then the DVD burn dialog will appear once the process is complete (**Figure 1.40**).

✔ Tips

- Liquid Edition does not support large projects spanning multiple DVDs. If your project archive is bigger than 4.7 GB (very likely), then you should create a folder on your hard drive and then use any DVD burning software that will support spanning. Instant CD/DVD version 7 from Pinnacle will do this, but others on the market also have this feature.

- Using the Project backup feature is a good idea if you are considering using the Delete Project option (**Figure 1.41**) Using this option deletes not only the Project files, but it can also be instructed to delete the media clips and the render files associated with that Project. If you delete a Project without backing it up, it's gone for good.

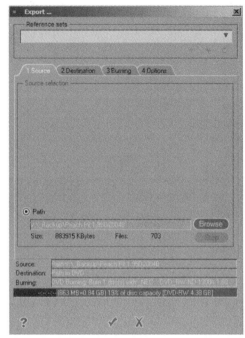

Figure 1.40 The DVD Burn dialog. For more details on this screen, see Chapter 12.

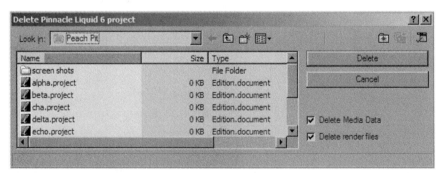

Figure 1.41 Deleting a Project makes it disappear for good, along with any media and render files if those boxes are marked.

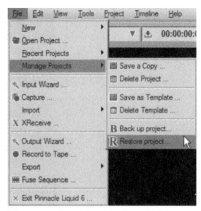

Figure 1.42 Restoring a backup Project.

To restore a Project from a backup copy:

1. Select File > Manage Projects > Restore project (**Figure 1.42**).

   This brings up the Restore screen.

2. Select which Project and which media to restore (**Figure 1.43**).

   The Options tab allows you to turn off any overwrite warning messages.

3. Click the check mark to begin the process.

   Depending on the size of the Project this may take some time.

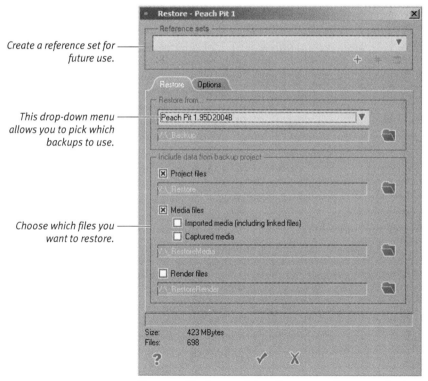

Create a reference set for future use.

This drop-down menu allows you to pick which backups to use.

Choose which files you want to restore.

Figure 1.43 The Restore dialog allows you to choose exactly what will be restored.

Navigating Using the Control Buttons

Liquid Edition is controlled by a combination of keyboard shortcuts, mouse control, and buttons. Running horizontally down the center of the Liquid Edition interface are the main control buttons (**Figure 1.44**).

Nothing is more frustrating than searching for some deeply hidden keyboard shortcut while you are in full creative flow, so Liquid Edition also allows you to add buttons to the interface.

Figure 1.44 The Timeline control buttons.

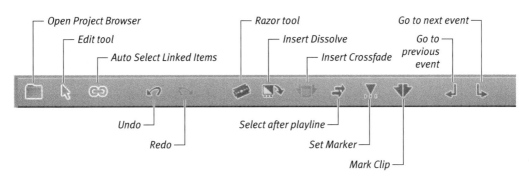

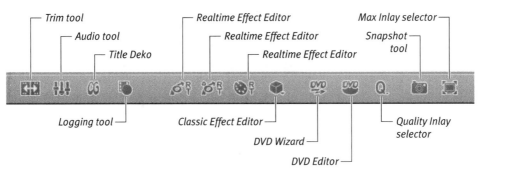

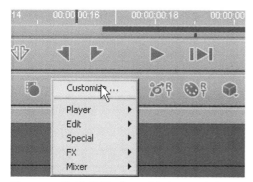

Figure 1.45 Right-clicking in any blank space between the buttons brings up the Customize option.

Figure 1.46 The Player Controls that can be added to the Timeline.

Customizing Liquid Edition

Liquid Edition is open to customization in pretty much all areas of the interface; in fact, it only takes a few mouse clicks to alter the interface to whatever style of workflow you are comfortable with.

Most users will want to customize one of four areas:

◆ The Timeline control buttons

◆ The keyboard shortcuts

◆ The Project Browser

◆ The Timeline tracks

To customize the buttons:

1. Right-click any blank space within the Button Control bar to bring up a selection menu (**Figure 1.45**) and then choose Customize.

   A small window with five tabs appears. The default tab houses the Player controls, but there are four other tabs to explore (**Figure 1.46**). Each tab contains a selection of buttons, many of which already exist on the Timeline.

continues on next page

2. Roll the mouse over the icons and a tool tip pops up and gives a brief description of each.

3. Buttons can be dragged and dropped from any of these tabs directly to the Timeline toolbar (**Figure 1.47**).

Move Build Container from here...

...to here.

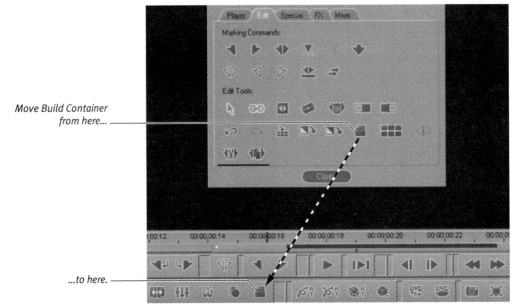

Figure 1.47 Here the Build Container button is dragged from the Edit tab to the Timeline next to the Logging tool.

Figure 1.48 Make room for more buttons by dragging the spacers off the toolbar and dropping them anywhere on the interface.

✔ Tips

- When you drag a new button to the Timeline, the other buttons will shuffle to the right and perhaps disappear from sight. To get them back, simply remove the blank spacer icons by dragging one anywhere off the interface and dropping it (**Figure 1.48**).

- If you see fewer than five tabs, you are clicking the interface directly below the Source window. This brings up a three-tabbed window (**Figure 1.49**).

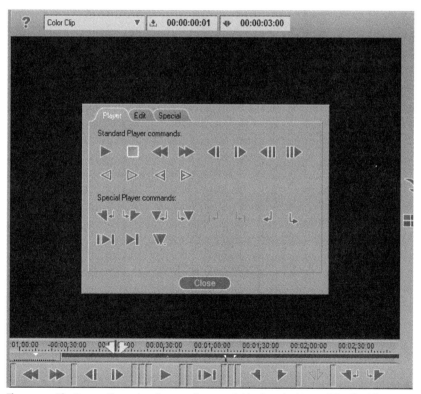

Figure 1.49 The Source Viewer has fewer options available than the Master/Timeline Viewer.

Customizing Keyboard Shortcuts

Figure 1.50 Opening the Control Panel in the drop-down menu.

Navigating the interface using buttons is one way of doing it, but many users find keyboard shortcuts to be much faster.

The list of shortcuts supported by Liquid Edition is formidable, but it doesn't stop there. Liquid Edition also allows all keyboard shortcuts to be customized, not only globally to support a keyboard shortcut across every interface, but also individually for each separate interface. This is particularly useful for avoiding the Press Alt+Ctrl+Shift+A type of scenario that leaves most users with fingers as twisted as their nerves.

To create a keyboard shortcut:

1. Select Edit > Control Panel (**Figure 1.50**).

2. If it is not already selected, click the User tab (**Figure 1.51**).

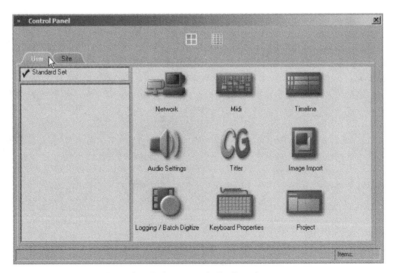

Figure 1.51 The Control Panel with the User tab displayed.

3. Double-click the Keyboard Properties button 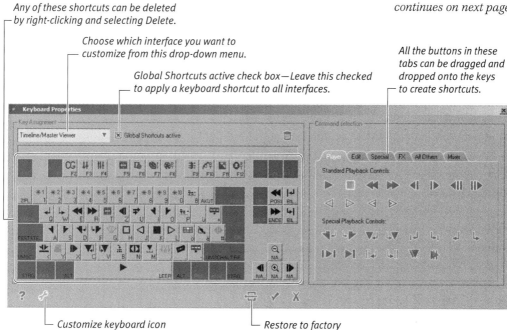 to bring up the Keyboard Properties interface.

4. Click the Customize keyboard icon to display the full interface (**Figure 1.52**).

5. If you want to add a global shortcut, make sure the Global Shortcuts active box is checked. If you want to add a tool to a specific tool and *no other*, make sure this box is not checked.

6. Drag any button from the right area over to the key to which you want it assigned (**Figure 1.53**).

continues on next page

Any of these shortcuts can be deleted by right-clicking and selecting Delete.

Choose which interface you want to customize from this drop-down menu.

Global Shortcuts active check box—Leave this checked to apply a keyboard shortcut to all interfaces.

All the buttons in these tabs can be dragged and dropped onto the keys to create shortcuts.

Customize keyboard icon

Restore to factory

Figure 1.52 The Keyboard Properties interface showing the command section on the right

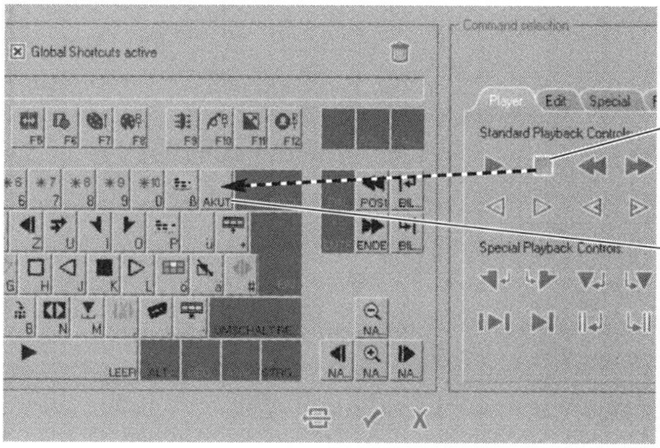

Dragging the Stop button from here...

...to here will assign that button to this key.

Figure 1.53 Dragging and dropping a button from the right area to the left to assign it to a key.

CUSTOMIZING KEYBOARD SHORTCUTS

7. To delete a shortcut, right-click any shortcut and select delete (**Figure 1.54**).

8. To exit this interface, *do one of the following:*

▲ Save your changes and close the tool by clicking the check mark.

▲ Click the "X" to close the tool without saving any changes you have made.

✔ Tip

■ Clicking the 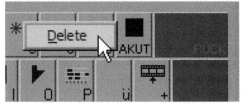 button will restore the keyboard settings to the installation default. Although you will lose all your customizations, it is sometime useful to do this if you have made a mess of the keyboard mapping.

Figure 1.54 Delete by right-clicking and selecting delete.

Classic Interface

Users of the Classic interface gain access to the Control Panel by clicking the Start button, moving the mouse up, and clicking once on the Control Panel icon.

After that, each operation is identical to those descriptions given in this chapter.

CUSTOMIZING KEYBOARD SHORTCUTS

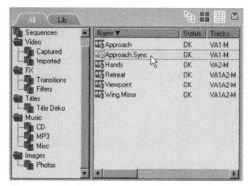

Figure 1.55 The Project Browser with Racks and Folders on the left and the media clips on the right.

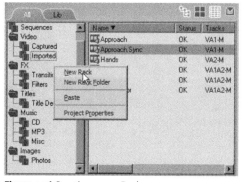

Figure 1.56 Creating a new Rack.

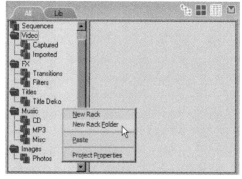

Figure 1.57 Creating a new Rack Folder.

Exploring the Project Browser

The Project Browser holds your media clips in Racks. A *Rack* is a virtual hook on which you hang your films, music clips, graphics, and titles. You can define as many Racks as you want, and you can even put these into a folder if you want to organize things further.

To create Racks and Folders:

1. Click the Open Project Browser button and you will see your Racks in the left window and any media you have displayed in the right window (**Figure 1.55**).

2. To create a new Rack, simply right-click the mouse inside the left window of the Project Browser and choose New Rack from the drop-down menu (**Figure 1.56**).

3. To create a Folder, right-click in the left window of the Project Browser and select New Rack Folder from the drop-down menu (**Figure 1.57**).

continues on next page

EXPLORING THE PROJECT BROWSER

4. Name your Racks and Folders. The default is always New Rack or New Rack Folder. If you make a typing mistake, just click the actual name and it will become highlighted so that you can change it (**Figure 1.58**).

✔ Tips

■ Racks can be dragged into folders in exactly the same way that files can be dragged around in the Windows environment. Using this method, it is easy to organize your media clips into this tidy easy-to-access workflow center (**Figure 1.59**).

■ If the Create Folder option is grayed out, make sure you are clicking inside a Folder and not inside a Rack.

Figure 1.58 Renaming a Rack or Folder by simply clicking the name.

Figure 1.59 The Project folder organized into well-named Folders and Racks. Media clips displayed in Picon View.

Premiere Translation

Racks are known to Adobe Premier users as Bins. Although the name is different, they function nearly the same way.

Right-click in the middle of the Project Browser.

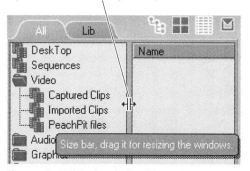

Figure 1.60 Click in the middle of the Project Browser...

Figure 1.61... to bring up another range of settings to adjust the angle of the browser.

Figure 1.62 The Project Browser with Racks on top, media clips below.

Using alternate Project Browser settings

By clicking the line that separates the left and right windows of the Project Browser (**Figure 1.60**) you can access another range of settings (**Figure 1.61**).

Clicking each one in turn will allow you to experiment (**Figure 1.62**), but to return to the default, check the Racks Left option.

EXPLORING THE PROJECT BROWSER

Customizing the Timeline

As with the rest of Liquid Edition, the Timeline is highly customizable, which allows you to set up the Timeline tracks to suit your own particular workflow. You can rename tracks to create more logical aliases than those assigned at start up and during the edit process. You may also find it useful to change the height of tracks, particularly when you're working with audio files, because doing so allows you to see the wave form a little better. You may also want to reduce the height of each track in order to fit more tracks onto the screen.

Figure 1.63 Selecting Rename to rename a track. It's that easy.

To rename tracks:

◆ Right-click the track and select Rename from the pop-up menu (**Figure 1.63**). A small outline box appears around the name into which you can type up to 31 characters (**Figure 1.64**).

✔ Tip

■ Clicking the New Sequence button in the top right corner of the interface will reset the names and heights back to their default values.

Figure 1.64 Up to 31 characters can now be entered.

To change track heights:

Do one of the following:

◆ To expand a clip, place the cursor over the bottom track line and drag it downward (**Figure 1.65**).

◆ Right-click the track and select Track Height from the pop-up menu (**Figure 1.66**). Then choose the height of your choice.

Figure 1.65 Drag a track to make it bigger...

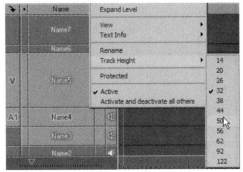

Figure 1.66 ... or right-click and use one of the preset values.

CUSTOMIZING THE TIMELINE

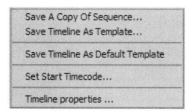

Figure 1.67 The Sequence Menu options.

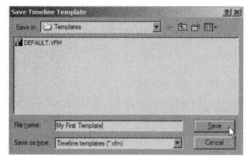

Figure 1.68 Save your Timeline template with a unique name.

To save a Timeline template:

1. Click the Sequence Menu icon in the upper-right corner of the interface.

2. Select Save Timeline As Template from the drop-down menu (**Figure 1.67**).

3. Browse to a folder where you want to keep this and give it a unique name before you save (**Figure 1.68**).

✔ Tip

■ Saving a Timeline template only saves those options that are available when you click the drop-down menu called Timeline, found at the top of the interface.

CUSTOMIZING THE TIMELINE

Templates—What Are They Good For?

Liquid Edition has three different templates (four if you include the keyboard mapping), which can be somewhat confusing for the beginner. To help smooth away this worry, I've condensed the three main templates, their function, and where they can be accessed into this easy-to-read sidebar.

- **Timeline template:** Saves only track heights, track names, and the position of any sub or matte tracks.

  Racks, Folders, and buttons are *not* saved in this template.

  The Timeline template is accessed via the Sequence Menu icon 📧 in the upper-right corner of the interface.

- **Project template**: Creates a template that includes the Racks and Folders and any material placed inside these folders and on the Timeline. It also saves the track names and heights.

  Timeline buttons are *not* saved.

  A Project template can be saved by selecting File > New > Save As Template.

- **User Templates**: This is the only way to save the position and customization of the toolbar buttons.

  To create a User Template you must create a new user. To do this:

  - ▲ Close Liquid Edition and select to log on as a different user from the Exit dialog (**Figure 1.69**).

  - ▲ Create a new user (**Figure 1.70**) and give it a logical, unique name (**Figure 1.71**); then click OK.

  Once a new user has been created, you will be presented with the User login screen every time you open Liquid Edition.

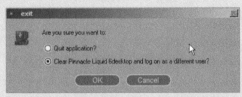

Figure 1.69 Logging on as a different user leads to...

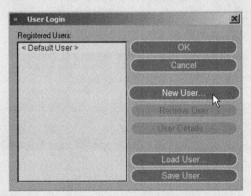

Figure 1.70... the Create New User screen.

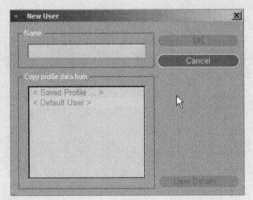

Figure 1.71 Here you can give your user a unique name.

LOGGING AND DIGITIZING

Once you have become familiar with Liquid Edition's interface, you are ready to begin creating your first production, and because every video production needs video footage, the first thing you'll need to do is digitize or import material into your computer. This chapter deals with the former, digitizing, often referred to by other NLE programs as capturing.

Digitizing your tapes is one of the more time-consuming and tedious parts of video editing, but Liquid Edition does have several tools to help alleviate this problem. In this chapter, I will cover capturing a complete tape, batch capturing just part of it, and how to detect the various scenes on a tape during the capture process.

Digitizing with Liquid Edition

With the right hardware, Liquid Edition has the ability to digitize the three basic video formats listed below. Using just a FireWire card and a Mini DV or high-definition (HDV) camera it's possible to capture either

Figure 2.1 A JVC HD10 High Definition (HDV) camera and a Sony Mini DV camera. Both use Mini DV tapes.

◆ AVI, from a Mini DV camera

or

◆ MPEG, from a HDV camera

With additional hardware, such as the Liquid MovieBox Pro or the Liquid Edition Pro AGP card, it's also possible to capture

◆ Analog, from VHS or similar sources

The DV/HDV option

Mini DV and HDV cameras use a digital format to record what is in front of the lens. This is then compressed by the camera into a space-saving form before being recorded as digital data to the tape (**Figure 2.1**).

The advantage of this is that when you digitize DV or HDV footage, you are in fact simply transferring digital data from the tape to your hard drive via a FireWire card. This is a relatively simple process and doesn't demand too much from the computer (**Figure 2.2**).

Figure 2.2 A Pinnacle FireWire card with FireWire lead.

The analog option

Using the MovieBox Pro or the two Legacy products—the Pro AGP card and the MovieBox Deluxe (**Figure 2.3**)—you will also have the option of digitizing from an analog source such as VHS or Hi-8. However, there is an important difference here in the way analog is captured.

While you are filming, the camera is recording an analog signal to the tape. When you try to transfer this to the computer, Liquid Edition must *convert* this analog signal to digital data for storing on the hard drive.

This will make great demands of your computer, and to do it successfully, you need a fast, well-optimized system. See the Appendix, "Troubleshooting," for help on this subject.

Figure 2.3 The MovieBox Pro (top-center), the Pro AGP card (bottom-left), and the MovieBox Deluxe all give Liquid Edition 6 analog capabilities.

DIGITIZING WITH LIQUID EDITION

HD or DV?

HDV or High definitionDV is a new TV standard that increases the picture quality from 704 horizontal pixels by 480 vertical pixels (Mini DV) (**Figure 2.4**) to 1280 horizontal pixels by 720 vertical pixels or 1920 pixels by 1080 pixels (HDV) (**Figure 2.5**).

Figure 2.4 An example of a Mini DV camera shot.

Figure 2.5 The same shot using an HD camera.

In a similar fashion to Mini DV, the HD camera converts what you are filming into data before recording it to tape. The major difference is the superior quality of the picture; also, MPEG encoding (the same standard used by DVDs) is used instead of AVI.

Capturing HD media clips is an identical process to capturing DV; the only difference is that you will be capturing in M2V format instead of AVI or DIF. This changes automatically once an HD camera is detected by Liquid Edition (**Figure 2.6**).

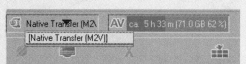

Figure 2.6 A native MPEG capture is automatically selected once an HD camera is detected.

Differentiating Between Logging and Digitizing

The naming convention Logging and Digitizing throws a lot of people because it is slightly different from the NLE norm, but in fact it's simple to understand.

◆ *Logging* enables you to create a log of what is on your DV/HD tape; this allows you to mark the sections of video you want to digitize.

◆ *Digitizing* is the process of transferring the video from the camera tape to the computer.

Both processes have their own unique place in video editing, and while you might favor using one over the other, inevitably you will end up using both.

✔ Tip

■ Logging is not possible with analog input because there is no device control between the analog device and the computer. BetacamSP cameras use an RS422 cable to overcome this, but such devices are relatively rare among home users.

Premiere Translations

Premiere refers to the process of transferring video from the camera to the computer as *capturing*. In Liquid Edition, this is called *digitizing*.

Premiere refers to the process of preparing a tape for batch capture as *creating a batch list*. Liquid Edition prefers to call this *logging* and creating a *logged* list.

This can be confusing for users migrating from Premiere, but really it is only the names that have been changed; the actual process is pretty much identical.

Touring the Logging Tool

The Logging Tool, though daunting when you first see it, is in fact easy to use and a powerful tool to exploit. However, you need to be aware of many submenus and various naming conventions to get the most out of this tool.

To open the Logging Tool:

1. Open the Logging Tool by clicking the Logging Tool button 🔘 or by pressing F6 (**Figure 2.7**).

2. Enter a unique name for the tape with which you are working.

3. Click the check mark in Figure 2.7 to display the complete Logging Tool (**Figure 2.8**).

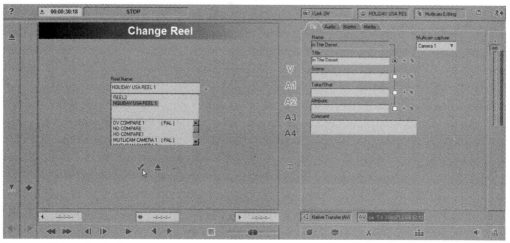

Figure 2.7 The Logging Tool.

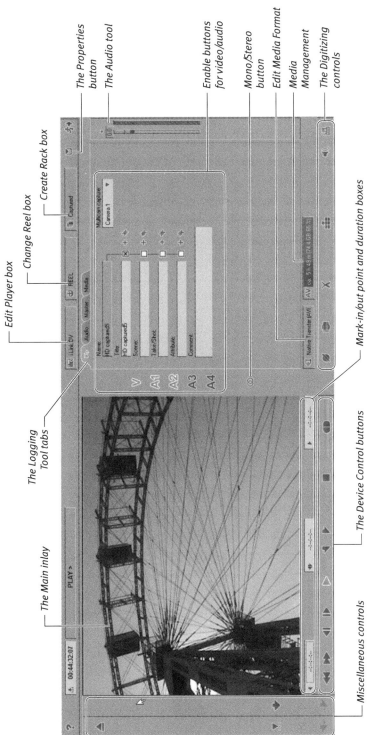

Figure 2.8 The Logging Tool open for business. Each of the components are described in the pages that follow.

Working with the Logging Tool

This section covers the components of the Logging Tool in more detail. Refer to Figure 2.8 for their location on the screen.

The Main Inlay

Here you will see your footage displayed. If this is black during playback, see the Appendix.

The Device Control buttons

These control your external DV device. Each button can be used to play the tape or move it forward or backward at a faster or slower rate. Using the arrow keys on the keyboard, you can step through the video frame by frame, although the accuracy of this will depend greatly on your DV camera.

To the far right of these controls is a Shuttle slider, which can be used to dynamically play the tape forward or backward at a variety of speeds. If the controls are grayed out and the message box at the top of the Logging Tool is flashing Device Not Ready, check that your camera is turned on, that you have it correctly connected, and that [i.link DV] is selected. If you still have problems, see the Appendix.

Mark-in/out point and duration boxes

If you are digitizing just a section of your tape, these information boxes will tell you the timecode for the mark-in and mark-out points and also the overall duration of the media clip.

Enable buttons for video/audio

Running down the center of the Logging Tool are five garish symbols: one V and four A's numbered 1 to 4. These allow you to choose what your digitized media clip will contain. By default, the V (for video) and the A's (for audio) 1 to 4 are highlighted. This means you will capture video and four channels of audio.

If you only require two channels of audio (and most people do), then click once on A3 and A4 to disable them. If you want to capture just video, you can disable all the audio channels, and if you want to just capture audio without the video, you can disable the video track by clicking the V.

✔ Tip

- Digitizing with four audio channels active will use up significantly more hard drive space than digitizing with just two. This is something to remember if your hard drive space is at a premium.

Figure 2.9 Choosing between Live capture and i.link DV.

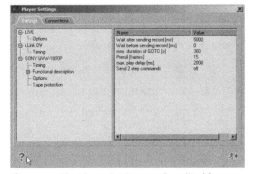

Figure 2.10 The Player Settings can be edited from here, but be careful when doing this.

Figure 2.11 Selecting a previously used Reel without leaving the Logging Tool.

Mono/Stereo button

Below the Enable buttons is the Mono/Stereo selection button. By default, the Mono button is displayed; it indicates that each audio track will be a mono sound track.

To switch each track to stereo, click once on this button to show two circles overlapping. This indicates that stereo will be captured.

Edit Player box

This allows you to switch between digitizing from a recorded source and digitizing from a live source by clicking the words i.link DV and selecting Live (**Figure 2.9**). This is necessary when you're capturing from an analog source.

Editing the camera properties is also possible by clicking once on the Edit Player button. Be careful here—there is no Restore to Default function (**Figure 2.10**).

Change Reel box

If you have already digitized several tapes in any one particular project, they will appear in this drop-down box when you click it (**Figure 2.11**).

You can also insert a new tape here without leaving the Logging Tool by clicking the Change Reel button.

Create Rack box

This drop-down box defaults to Sequence or the last Rack you were using when you open the Logging Tool, indicating that any clips you digitize will automatically be placed in that Rack. To change to another Rack, click once inside this box and select from the choices available (**Figure 2.12**). To create a new Rack without leaving the Logging Tool, click the Create Rack button ![icon].

The Properties button

Clicking here will allow you to alter various Logging Tool parameters. In general, you will use this if you are having problems with the Logging Tool. Be careful when adjusting these settings because the defaults are set to cope with the most likely digitizing scenarios and altering them may cause the Logging Tool to behave badly.

Full details of these options can be found in Chapter 6 of the Pinnacle Liquid Edition Reference manual.

Figure 2.12 Selecting in which Rack your digitized media clips will be stored.

Figure 2.13 The Multicam drop-down list displays 16 camera choices.

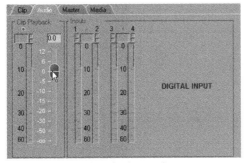

Figure 2.14 The Audio tab. Changes here are permanently written to the digitized media clips.

The Logging Tool tabs

This area of the Logging Tool contains four tabs that control the various options open to you while digitizing your videos. They all have a slightly innocuous look to them, but in fact, they contain some powerful functions. When used correctly, they will save you time and money.

◆ **The Clip tab** is open by default and allows you to name your clips prior to digitizing. (See Chapter 4 for a full explanation on this subject.) The information you provide in the various text fields will be available in the media clip's Properties box once it has been digitized. Place an "X" in the box directly to the right of those text boxes you want to use.

The Multicam capture option is also on this tab. This drop-down list (**Figure 2.13**) allows you to capture footage from up to 16 different cameras that you can match up later on the Timeline. This is a great function if you are editing a concert that was filmed with several cameras simultaneously. You'll find details on how to use this exciting feature later in this chapter.

◆ **The Audio tab** (**Figure 2.14**) allows you to adjust the sound settings before you capture the clip and also as you capture the clip. You can either preview the footage before you capture and set the slider to the appropriate point, or you can dynamically alter the sound levels as you capture. This alteration is known as a *destructive change* because the alterations are permanent to that media clip. If you want to alter the audio settings, you will have to digitize again.

◆ **The Master tab** (**Figure 2.15**) displays the contents of the current Timeline sequence. This is used when you want to digitize a media clip and send it directly to the Timeline. Using this tab, you can scroll along until you find the correct point on the Timeline where you want to insert the media clip.

◆ **The Media tab** is used to adjust the quality of the captured clip. Generally you won't need to adjust this, but you can find a full explanation of how to use it in Chapter 6 of the Pinnacle Liquid Edition Reference manual.

The Audio tool

This allows you to monitor the sound levels of a tape you are previewing or digitizing. If this goes into the red too often, you should consider using the Audio tool found in the Audio tab to reduce the level.

If you click the small button above the displayed numbers, you will reset the Audio tool to its default setting.

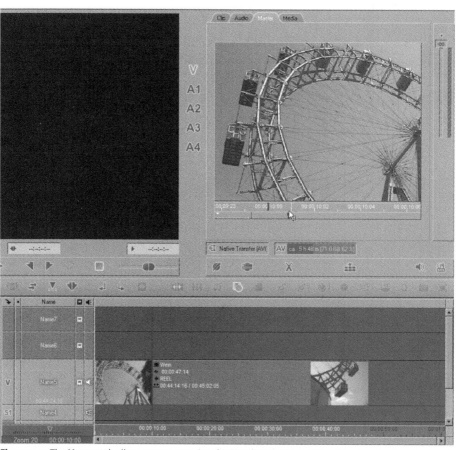

Figure 2.15 The Master tab allows you to examine the Timeline position without leaving the Logging Tool.

Figure 2.16 Two formats are available to Mini DV users.

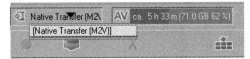

Figure 2.17 Only one format is available to HD camera users.

Edit Media format

This is used to choose into which format you will digitize your media clips. In fact, the choices with this version of Liquid Edition are fairly limited. If you have a Mini DV camera connected or if you are trying to capture from analog, then you will only be able to digitize using the AVI or DIF format (**Figure 2.16**). If you have an HDV camera attached (and it is set to MPEG output), then you will only be able to capture in the M2V format (**Figure 2.17**). Clicking the Edit Media Format button 🔳 will bring up some more choices, but without specialist hardware (available only to the Liquid Edition Silver and Chrome range), you will not be able to use any of them.

Logging and Digitizing Keyboard Shortcuts

The following keyboard shortcuts can be used when logging and digitizing media clips:

◆ **F6:** Opens and closes the Logging Tool

◆ **N:** Starts and stops the digitize process

◆ **B:** Logs a media clip

◆ **M:** Aborts the digitize process

These keys can be used to control a DV camera:

◆ **J:** Plays the tape backward increasingly faster each time the key is pressed

◆ **L:** Plays the tape forward increasingly faster each time the key is pressed

◆ **K:** Stops the tape

◆ **Spacebar:** Plays and also pauses the tape

◆ **Left and right arrow keys:** Moves the tape one frame forward or backward

◆ **Home key:** Fast rewind (no preview)

◆ **End Key:** Fast forward (no preview)

Media Management

Click once on the graphical representation of how much hard drive space you have remaining and you will be able to choose to which hard drive your media clips will be saved (**Figure 2.18**). If you only see one location, then you can add more by clicking the AV button **AV** to bring up the Media Management screen and then add a drive location from there. Full details on using this function are in Chapter 4.

This box also displays how much room remains on the current Media drive. This is displayed as

◆ A percentage

◆ The physical number of bytes remaining

◆ A measurement of time

These figures are always approximate and should be treated with caution. During the digitizing process, this display will dynamically decrease in value.

Figure 2.18 Select which drive or folder is the target for your digitized media clips.

The Digitizing controls

These six buttons control the actual digitizing of any media clips and what happens to them once they have been transferred from the camera to your computer.

◆ **The Log Clip button** : Every time you define a mark-in and mark-out point, you need to click this button to log the clip. You can create as many log entries as you like and then instruct the Logging Tool to digitize them all at a later stage. The keyboard shortcut is the letter B.

◆ **The Digitize button** : This magic button starts the digitize process and also stops it. Use it wisely. The keyboard shortcut is N.

◆ **Interrupt Digitizing button** : This button aborts the whole digitizing process. When you click it, no media is saved to the hard drive and playback is stopped. You must use this button only to abort the digitizing process. It is very important to understand this because many new users try to stop digitizing by using the Interrupt button and then wonder why they have no media on their hard drive. The keyboard shortcut is the letter M.

◆ **Send captured clips to the Timeline** : This will take a captured clip and insert it directly into the Timeline at the cursor's current position. You can use this feature to create a rough cut from a tape when you use it in combination with logging media clips.

◆ **Select Audio** : This button doubles up the function of the A1 to A4 buttons in the center of the interface.

◆ **Clip Link** : This button is used specifically with Sony DVCAM cameras. It allows you take advantage of the extra features this format offers. You can find complete details on this in your DVCAM camera manual.

Miscellaneous controls

Probably best described as sundry, this area comprises seven buttons that are used primarily to place markers on a clip prior to capture or to send the camera to a mark-in/out point you have created. You'll find full details of this later in this chapter.

✔ Tip

■ It is important to check that you have enough room before you begin digitizing. Try to avoid filling your hard drive beyond 90 percent of its total capacity as this may cause performance problems.

Which Format Should You Use—AVI or DIF?

Liquid Edition offers two formats with which to capture Mini DV and analog clips:

◆ **AVI:** The proprietary Windows format

◆ **DIF:** A proprietary format from Pinnacle

The DIF format was originally introduced by FAST, who later became part of Pinnacle. The format was used to help slower systems overcome problems when using the slightly less efficient AVI file format. In these days of fast processing power and cheap memory, DIF's place in NLE is limited.

It's also not a widely recognized format or a well-supported one, and for this reason alone, most users choose AVI. Doing so enables them to send their clips to other applications—Adobe's After Effects or Pinnacle's Commotion, for example.

FAT32 or NTFS?

Modern-day Windows systems use one of two types of file systems on their hard drives: FAT32 (File Allocation Table 32 bit), or NTFS (New Technologies File System).

Most Windows XP systems are shipped using NTFS because it is a more secure file format, but if you're adding a second hard drive just for capture, you will have a choice and you should always choose NTFS for this one simple reason.

◆ FAT32 has a maximum file length of 4 gigabytes (GB), about 18 minutes of DV.

   whereas

◆ NTFS has a maximum file length of 12 Terabytes (TB), more than a thousand hours of DV.

At the moment, no 12-TB drives are being sold (not this year anyway), but the obvious restrictions of FAT32 are plain to see. Digitizing a standard 60-minute tape to FAT32 will mean each clip can only be 4 GB, or 18 minutes long.

Your wedding scene is just a bit longer than this? Sorry, hard luck. You will have to capture it in two pieces and hope for a seamless join.

NTFS, on the other hand, can capture the whole tape (however long) in one continuous AVI. The only limitation is the available space on your hard drive. Serious editors will not choose anything other than NTFS.

DIGITIZING

Figure 2.19 Opening the Input wizard.

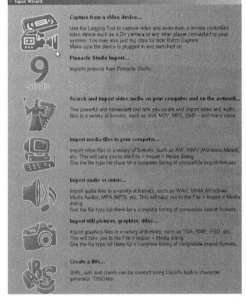

Figure 2.20 Once open, you can choose which type of import to make.

Using the Input Wizard to Digitize

Digitizing is the process of transferring the contents of a video tape—DV, HDV, or analog—to your computer's hard drive so that you can begin editing it.

This can be achieved by digitizing the whole tape in one go—while you make coffee, bathe the dog, phone your aunt—or by selecting individual clips from a tape and only digitizing the ones you want. This second option requires your presence pretty much 100 percent of the time.

If you feel the need to take life easy, then your best bet would be to use the Input wizard. New to version 6, this leads you down the road to digitizing nirvana.

To use the Input wizard:

1. Close the Logging Tool if it is still open and then select File > Input Wizard (**Figure 2.19**).

2. Click the top option, Capture from the video device (**Figure 2.20**).

continues on next page

Classic Interface

Wizards are not available when using the Classic interface.

USING THE INPUT WIZARD TO DIGITIZE

3. Choose in which Rack you want to store your media clips (**Figure 2.21**). You can also create a new Rack from this screen (**Figure 2.22**).

The Logging Tool opens and the wizard exits (**Figure 2.23**).

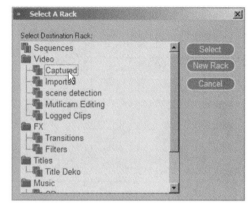

Figure 2.21 Choose the Rack in which you want to store your clips...

Figure 2.22 ...or create a new one.

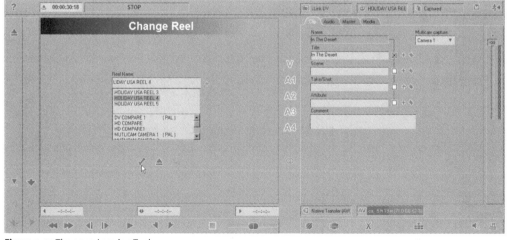

Figure 2.23 The open Logging Tool.

Digitizing an Entire or Part of a DV Tape

Digitizing a whole tape is easy enough and can be done by the computer while you do something else. The "something else" should be something not done with the computer because the digitize process likes to take full advantage of the computer resources and doesn't like to share. Trying to do something on the computer while digitizing is taking place may cause problems such as dropped frames or an aborted capture session.

You can also digitize part of a DV tape by defining which parts of the tape you want to capture; you can do this by adding mark-in and mark-out points with the Logging Tool.

To digitize an entire DV tape:

1. Open the Logging Tool by clicking the Logging Tool button [icon], by pressing F6, or by using the Input wizard (**Figure 2.24**).

2. Enter a unique name for the tape with which you are working.

continues on next page

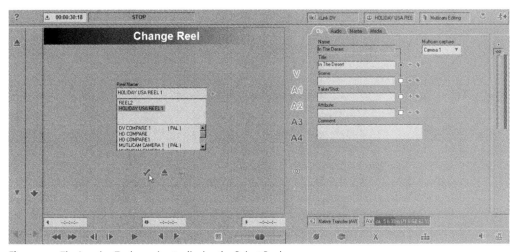

Figure 2.24 The Logging Tool opening to display the Select Reel screen.

3. Click the check mark to display the entire Logging Tool (**Figure 2.25**).

A unique tape name is very important when it comes to redigitizing clips, because the Logging Tool will prompt you for the correct tape.

4. To digitize the whole tape from beginning to the end, rewind the tape to the point where you want to digitize and then click the Digitize button or press the N key.

The Logging Tool will then begin digitizing from that point on, stopping when it reaches the end of the tape. If you want to stop the process before then, click once more on the Digitize button .

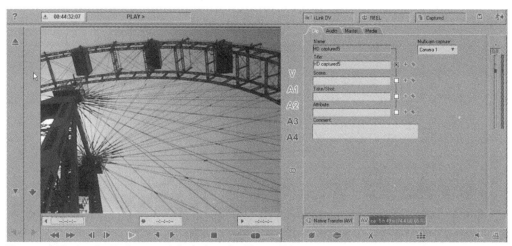

Figure 2.25 The Logging Tool open and displaying a feed from a DV camera.

DIGITIZING AN ENTIRE OR PART OF DV TAPE

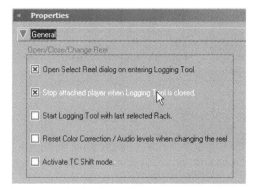

Figure 2.26 Altering the settings to stop your DV device once the tape ends to cut down on camera wear.

✔ Tips

- During the digitizing process, the media will be sent to the hard drive specified in the Media Management box and will appear in whichever folder is specified in the Create Rack box. To change either one, simply click the box and select from the given choices. See "Touring the Logging Tool" at the beginning of this chapter for further details.

- If you want your camera or DV device to turn off once capture is finished, click the Properties button once, select Properties from the drop-down list, open the General tab, and check the Stop attached player after Open End capture box (**Figure 2.26**).

To digitize part of a DV tape:

1. Click the Logging Tool button  or press F6 to open the Logging Tool (Figure 2.24).

2. Enter a unique name for the tape with which you are working. This is important when it comes to redigitizing clips because the Logging Tool will prompt you for the correct tape.

3. Click the check mark to display the entire Logging Tool (Figure 2.25).

4. Play the tape by pressing the spacebar, and preview the content until you find the point where you want to start digitizing.

5. Press the I key or click the Mark-In Point button.

   This sets a mark-in point and tells the Logging Tool that you want to begin digitizing from this point (**Figure 2.27**).

6. Continue to preview the tape until you reach the point where you want to stop recording. Press the O key or click the Mark-Out Point button.

   This sets a mark-out point and tells the Logging Tool to stop digitizing here. This also displays the overall duration of the media clips in the middle box (**Figure 2.28**).

7. Click the Digitize button or press N.

   The Logging Tool rewinds the tape to the mark-in point and then begins digitizing the tape until it reaches the mark-out point, where it will stop.

Figure 2.27 Setting a start or mark-in point for your digitizing.

Figure 2.28 Setting an end or mark-out point for your digitizing. The out point is the numerical value to the far left with the overall duration indicated by the numerical value in the middle.

✔ Tips

■ You can fine-tune the mark-in/out point by pressing the spacebar to pause the DV/HDV device and then by using the arrow keys on the keyboard to move one frame at a time forward or backward.

■ Stopping a capture session by clicking the Interrupt digitize/logging button ⊠ will abort the process completely; any media captured up to that point will not be stored.

Using Scene Detection for Long Media Clips

Getting the Logging Tool to digitize a long clip is all well and good, but you still end up with a large slice of media sitting on your hard drive. It will, at some point, need to be divided up so that it can be usefully manipulated.

This is done by

◆ Going through the clip and manually marking each scene yourself, creating subclips from these markers (see Chapter 14).

◆ Sending the media clips to the Clip Viewer and using the Scene Detection tool (see Chapter 14).

◆ Getting the Logging Tool to detect the scenes on the tape while digitizing takes place.

This last option is possibly the most elegant because it allows the Logging Tool to capture the whole tape, without you having to hold its hand. At the end, you are presented with a Rack full of media clips, each one representing a single scene on the tape.

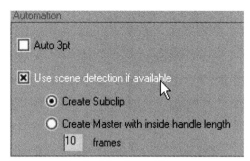

Figure 2.29 The check box for enabling scene detection, labeled "Use scene detection if available" is in the bottom-right corner in the Automation section.

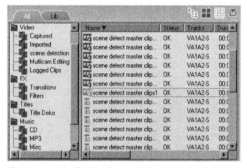

Figure 2.30 The finished result. The top sets of clips are examples of master clips; the bottom set of highlighted clips are examples of a master clip with its family of subclips.

To set up scene detection during capture:

1. With the Logging tool open, click the Properties button ⬚ and select Properties from the drop-down menu.

2. Open the General tab and check the box marked "Use scene detection if available" (**Figure 2.29**).

   There are two further choices here:

   ▲ Selecting Create subclip creates one long clip plus a number of subclips—reference clips to the master. This is useful if you decide you want to expand a particular clip or if you need to reference the whole tape at a later date.

   ▲ Selecting Create Master with inside handle length creates single media clips that are independent of any other. This is useful if you require a physically separate set of media clips for every scene.

   You'll need to experiment to see which suits your particular workflow.

3. Close the Properties box by clicking the check mark, and then follow the instructions given earlier for digitizing either the whole tape or part of it.

   When the digitizing process is finished, you should find a large number of subclips and/or master clips sitting in whichever Rack you defined (**Figure 2.30**).

✔ Tip

■ When creating master clips or subclips using scene detection, nothing will appear in your Project Browser until digitizing is finished. So don't be alarmed if at first nothing appears to be happening.

SCENE DETECTION FOR LONG MEDIA CLIPS

Digitizing Clips from Analog

The process of digitizing from an analog source has a number of caveats that you should be aware of before you attempt it. The actual process is fairly similar to that of digitizing a DV clip except that:

- When digitizing analog, the computer must convert the analog information stored on the tape to a digital format that can be stored on the hard drive.

  To do this, you need a fast CPU, a very quick hard drive, and a computer that has been optimized until it squeaks. If you don't have this enviable PC configuration, you will experience dropped frames, which means the media clips will appear to stutter during playback.

  The quality of the tape and the output quality of the camera or VHS recorder will also factor into this volatile equation. Cheap recorders from the local discount store are unlikely to give good results.

- You will not have any control over the playback functions of the analog camera or VHS recorder unless you use an RS422 control device such as a BetacamSP.

- You may see sound synchronization problems where the action on the screen does not match the audio. Sometimes this can be only a few frames out, but when this is applied to someone talking at the camera, the lack of lip synchronization is irritatingly obvious.

✔ Tip

- If you have the option, either capture the material to Mini DV first or pass the analog signal through a DV device and capture it via FireWire. The first of these options allows you to use device control and timecode; the second option will only filter the analog signal in an attempt to reduce problems with dropped frames and poor sound synchronization.

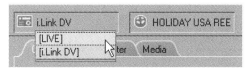

Figure 2.31 Selecting the Live setting in preparation for analog capture.

To digitize analog:

1. With the Logging Tool open, and after you have selected or typed in the name of a Reel, alter the input settings to accept analog by clicking the Edit player box once.

2. Select Live from the drop-down list (**Figure 2.31**).

   You are prompted to enter the name of the tape again.

3. Click the check mark.

   The timecode counter begins showing the Time of Day—this is a reference point for the editor only—and the status window shows the command Play (**Figure 2.32**).

4. Click once on the 🔳 button to bring up the Player Settings and open the Connections tab (**Figure 2.33**).

   continues on next page

Figure 2.32 Timecode is displayed as "Time of Day". This example shows 17:45 & 29 seconds & 5 frames.

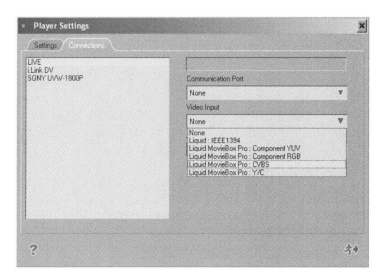

Figure 2.33 Depending on what hardware you have attached, you will see various input options here. These are the input options for the MovieBox Pro.

5. Alter the video and audio inputs to those available in the drop-down box and close the dialog box by clicking the Running Man button .

6. Press play on your camera or VHS recorder.

   The Inlay should display the contents of your tape.

7. Click the Digitize button or press N and the Logging Tool will begin digitizing until you click the Digitize button or press N again.

✔ Tips

■ During this process, the media will be digitized to the hard drive specified in the Media Management box and will appear in whichever folder is specified in the Create Rack box .

   To change either one, simply click the box and select from the choices given. See "Touring the Logging Tool" at the beginning of this chapter for further details.

■ If the Inlay is black or the Digitize button remains gray, you may have to check your player settings to see if they are correct and that the cables are correctly connected between your analog source and the computer.

Logging a Tape

Logging is a way of creating a list of what is on the Reel, allowing you to batch digitize only those clips you really want or to digitize a tape at a later date. You can perform either of these logging processes without having to sit there while the computer does the actually digitization; but of course, you must first create a logged list.

It works like this: You preview a tape, probably not in real time, fast forwarding to events that interest you and that you want to digitize. By marking these files with mark-in and mark-out points and then by clicking the Log Clip button 🖉, you create a list of reference points that the Logging Tool can use to digitize the tape while you go and do something less boring.

DV Timecode

All DV cameras create a type of timecode on the tape, although this is more of a recording of the tape's position than what is regarded as timecode by the video industry. The differences are important.

Image the timecode on a DV tape as being similar to the counter on an old tape player—the type that counts up to 999 as the tape is played back and has a small button that resets the counter to zero.

Now here's the problem:

◆ If you take the DV tape out of the camera, for whatever reason, then put it back in again and start recording with a small gap between the last clip and the next, the timecode will reset to zero.

Why is this a problem?

◆ To create a log of the clips on a tape, the Logging Tool uses the DV timecode as a reference point. If it discovers two points on the tape with the same timecode, it will always refer to the first one, thus making it impossible to log or batch capture the whole tape.

To avoid this problem, you can do two things:

◆ Record blank footage to every tape before you use them. This is called stripping a tape.

◆ Always record at least 15 to 20 seconds of spare footage on the tape before you take it out and make sure you rewind to somewhere in the middle of this section.

If you do have a gap in your timecode, you will have to manually capture it by positioning the tape after the timecode break and then pressing the Digitize button 🖾. If that doesn't work, you should try using the Live setting and capturing without device control.

To log a tape:

1. Click the Logging Tool button 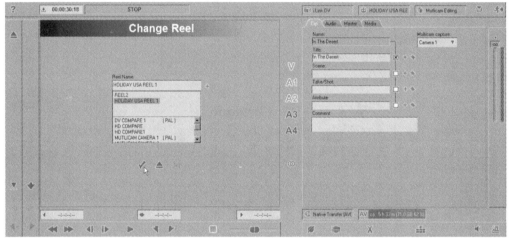 or press F6 to open the Logging Tool (**Figure 2.34**).

2. Enter a unique name for the tape with which you are working.

   This is important when it comes to redigitizing clips because then the Logging Tool can prompt you for the correct tape.

3. Click the check mark to display the entire Logging Tool (**Figure 2.35**).

Figure 2.34 Entering a Reel name.

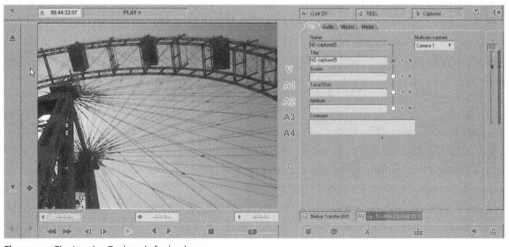

Figure 2.35 The Logging Tool ready for business.

4. Select which Rack you would like to eventually use by clicking the Sequences box and making a choice from the selection available. If you make no choice, the Logging Tool will default to the Sequences Rack or the last Rack you used.

5. Start the tape playing and when you see the rough point where you want your media clips to begin, press the spacebar to pause the tape; then use the left and right arrow keys to fine-tune this position.

6. Once you are happy with this position, press the I key or click the Mark-In Point button ◀ to set the start position—the mark-in point.

7. Start the tape again by pressing the spacebar and look for your end point— the optimum point where the media clip should end.

8. Press the spacebar again to pause the playback and use the arrow keys to fine-tune this position.

9. Once you are happy with this position, press the O key or click the Mark-Out Point button ▶ to set the end position—the mark-out point.

continues on next page

LOGGING A TAPE

10. Now that you have a mark-in and mark-out point defined for this particular media clip, you can log it by clicking the Log Clip button ▨ or by pressing B.

A logged clip appears in the Rack you selected in Step 3 (**Figure 2.36**).

▲ When in Detail view, the logged clip will look like this 🦋, a small icon of a filmstrip with a butterfly in the top-left corner.

▲ When in Picon view, it will look like this ▮, a black screen or the first frame of the media clip with a small white exclamation mark in the left-hand corner.

11. Repeat Steps 4 to 7 until you have finished logging the entire tape, or at least until you have finished the part you are interested in.

You should now have a Rack that looks something like **Figure 2.37**.

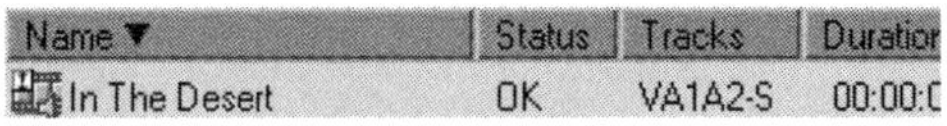

✔ Tips

■ Use the keyboard shortcuts I and O to define mark-in and mark-out points, then use B to log the clip.

■ If you aren't too bothered about fine-tuning the mark-in and mark-out points of your batch list, you can use the I, O, and B keyboard combination without pausing the tape or even stopping it.

Name ▼	Status	Tracks	Duration
In The Desert	OK	VA1A2-S	00:00:0

Figure 2.36 A logged clip shown here in Detail view.

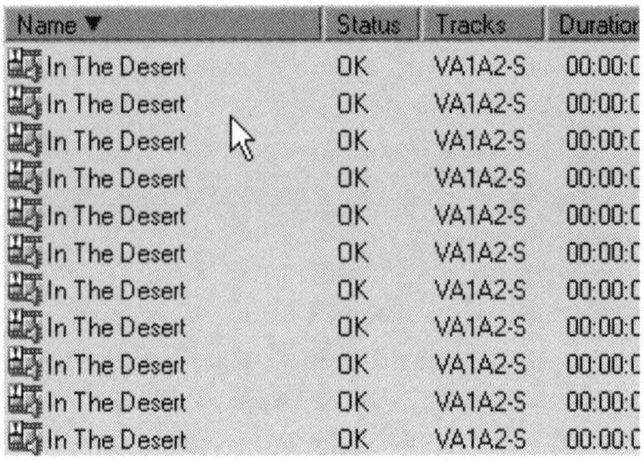

Name ▼	Status	Tracks	Duration
In The Desert	OK	VA1A2-S	00:00:0
In The Desert	OK	VA1A2-S	00:00:0
In The Desert	OK	VA1A2-S	00:00:0
In The Desert	OK	VA1A2-S	00:00:0
In The Desert	OK	VA1A2-S	00:00:0
In The Desert	OK	VA1A2-S	00:00:0
In The Desert	OK	VA1A2-S	00:00:0
In The Desert	OK	VA1A2-S	00:00:0
In The Desert	OK	VA1A2-S	00:00:0
In The Desert	OK	VA1A2-S	00:00:0
In The Desert	OK	VA1A2-S	00:00:0

Figure 2.37 The Rack full of logged clips. Note the small butterfly in the top-left corner of the icons.

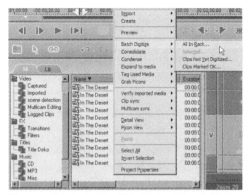

Figure 2.38 Select either All In Rack or Clips Not Yet Digitized.

Figure 2.39 A batch list includes those clips that will be digitized.

Digitizing Logged Clips

Once an entire Reel is logged, you can instruct the Logging Tool to capture either the whole thing or just those logged clips you are interested in.

This is important: To digitize logged clips, you must first exit the Logging Tool. This is one of those irksome personality issues that Liquid Edition suffers from, and if exiting the Logging Tool to begin digitizing makes no sense to you, join the club.

To digitize all the clips in a Rack:

1. Make sure the Logging Tool is closed, then in the Project Browser, if it is not already open, select the Rack that contains your logged clips.

2. Right-click inside the right window of the Project Browser and select Batch Digitize from the pop-up menu.

3. Select All In Rack (**Figure 2.38**).

4. If there are clips in the Rack that have already been digitized, select Clips Not Yet Digitized.

    The Logging Tool opens, displaying the batch digitizing interface and a list of all the clips you have logged, along with details on mark-in and mark-out points and the Reel name they were taken from (**Figure 2.39**).

    The Audio and Media tabs have the same function here as they did when you were digitizing. See "Digitizing a DV tape" for details. The two options at the top are specialist options for batch digitizing. Details on this can be found in Chapter 8 of the Pinnacle Liquid Edition Reference manual.

continues on next page

5. Check that you have the correct hard drive selected in the Media Management box and then click the Digitize button to begin the process.

6. Confirm that you are using the right tape by clicking the check mark.

   The Logging Tool rewinds the tape to just before the mark-in point of the first clip and then it starts to play (**Figure 2.40**).

   When it reaches the mark-in point, it begins to digitize; when it reaches the mark-out point, it stops digitizing and fast forwards to the next mark-in point. This continues until all the clips have been digitized.

✔ **Tip**

■ You may want to turn Scene Detection off when digitizing from a batch list; otherwise, your batched clips will be subdivided up into their individual scenes.

Figure 2.40 A list of batched clips being digitized.

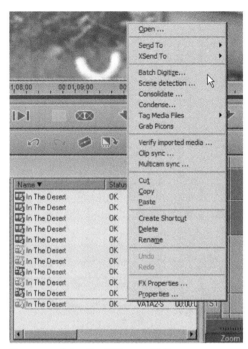

Figure 2.41 Using the Ctrl key and left mouse, you can selectively pick which clips to digitize.

To digitize a selection of clips in a Rack:

1. Hold down the Ctrl key and then left-click each of the logged clips you are interested in.

2. Click any of these clips and choose Selected from the Batch Digitize options (**Figure 2.41**).

Multicam Capture

New to version 6 is the ability to capture several tapes with identical timecodes and match them up later on the Timeline using a picture in Picture Effect. This allows you to edit all the cameras at the same time, in real time (**Figure 2.42**).

Full details on how to edit with Multicam media clips can be found in Chapter 14.

✔ Tip

- Clips that are not captured using the Multicam Capture feature can still use this feature by using Multicam Sync. For complete details, refer to Chapter 14.

Figure 2.42 An example of Multicam. Note the inserted keyframes at each camera change.

The rules for Multicam Capture

To use this feature you must be aware of the following rules:

◆ Only Camera 1 will contain any audio, so obviously, this should be the tape to which you want to sync audio.

◆ The timecode of all the tapes used must be the same.

◆ The timecode of all the tapes must not contain any breaks.

Once you have confirmed that your tapes fall in line with these rules and you have decided which tape to use, you can start to use Multicam Capture.

✔ Tips

■ If there is a problem with timecode, capture all tapes as normal, then align them later using the Multicam Sync feature. See Chapter 14 for details.

■ Multicam Capture is an advanced capture technique, and as a result, you should be aware of how to use the basic capture techniques and be aware of how to set mark-in and mark-out points before attempting this task.

■ Scene Detection should be turned off when using Multicam Capture.

MULTICAM CAPTURE

To digitize using Multicam Capture:

1. Label each of your tapes clearly and then insert the first one.

2. Open the Logging Tool as described in the previous sections, and name your Reel "Project Name camera 1", where "Project Name" is the name of your project (**Figure 2.43**).

3. Set a mark-in and mark-out point for |this media clip and give it a unique title, preferably ending with "camera 1" (**Figure 2.44**).

4. Now click the Digitize button 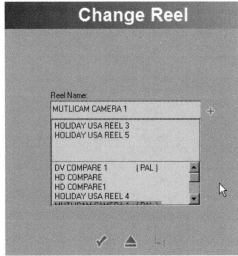 , and the media clip for camera 1—the "Master Camera" clip—is digitized, at the same time creating a template for all the other tapes you have.

Figure 2.43 It's important that your Reel name is totally unique when you are attempting a Multicam capture.

MULTICAM CAPTURE

Figure 2.44 The media clips should also have a unique name ending with the camera number so that you can make sense of it later.

5. Once the digitize process is complete, you can insert a new tape by opening your camera. Do not exit the Logging Tool while you are doing this.

Note that when you open the camera, the Logging Tool will reset and ask you for the name of this Reel. *Do not* enter a new Reel name; use the Reel name you used in Step 2, and make sure the Auto increment has not changed or added a number onto the end of the Reel name (**Figure 2.45**).

6. With the new tape inserted, check again that the Reel name has not changed, and then click the check mark.

7. Drag the media clip captured using the camera 1 setting up and into the Logging Tool Inlay (**Figure 2.46**).

The mark-in and mark-out points from this media clip are cloned and automatically appear in the Logging Tool to match the Master Camera clip.

continues on next page

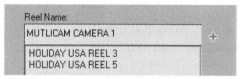

Figure 2.45 Check that the Reel number has stayed the same.

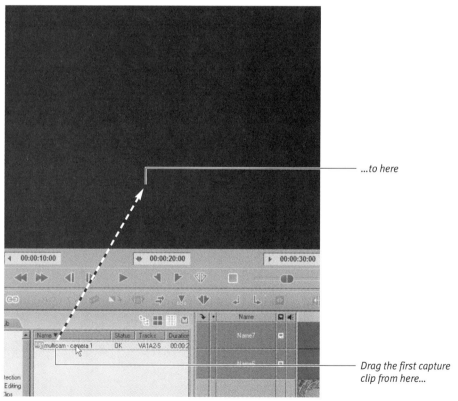

...to here

Drag the first capture clip from here...

Figure 2.46 Drag the master camera clip up into the logging window to clone the mark-in and mark-out points.

MULTICAM CAPTURE

8. Select Camera 2 from the drop-down list (**Figure 2.47**), then name the clip again. Finish the name off with "camera 2" (**Figure 2.48**).

9. Click the Digitize button 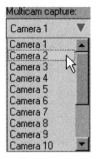 ; this media clip will now be digitized and synchronized with the media clip captured using the camera 1 settings.

10. Repeat steps 5 to 9, increasing the camera setting each time and paying strict attention to the naming convention for each of your media clips.

It's important to remember that you must always use the same Reel name for each tape you insert. Change this and the whole thing falls apart.

✔ Tips

■ Up to 16 Reels can be synchronized together like this; but remember, only the first one can have any audio.

■ Media clips that have already been captured using the camera 1 setting can be turned into Multicam media clips using the Multicam Sync function. See Chapter 14 for complete details.

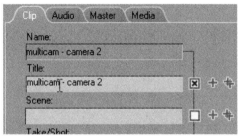

Figure 2.47 Select Camera 2 from the list.

Figure 2.48 Alter the camera number for the media clips.

Using Multicam to edit media clips

Comprehensive instructions on how to edit Multicam media clips are in Chapter 14, but it seems unfair not to show you the basics after you have been through so much to capture the clips in the first place.

To edit Multicam media clips:

1. Send the first clip (the one captured with the camera 1 setting) to the Source Viewer by dragging and dropping the clip. It must be this first clip; none of the others will achieve the same effect.

   This brings up a multiwindow display showing you all the Multicam media clips. A number in the bottom-right corner of each indicates to which camera it belongs (**Figure 2.49**).

2. Navigate through the Source Viewer's Timeline where you can select which clips you want to be displayed and when by clicking directly on the camera represented by that square.

   This creates keyframes along the Source window's Timeline.

3. Send the edit to the Timeline by clicking the Insert to Timeline arrow between the two windows. Then play through the clip to see the camera changing on each of your clicks.

This is the quick and dirty version of how to use this feature, but I've only described it here to give you a taste of what is to come. To find out more, go to Chapter 14 and read the section on Multicam editing.

Figure 2.49 An example of Multicam at work. When it is sent to the Timeline, the Multicam edit looks like this.

MULTICAM CAPTURE

IMPORTING MEDIA CLIPS

The alternative to using the Logging Tool is to directly import media into your computer. It is the most direct way you have of bringing media clips such as pictures, music, animations, and other media types into your project. Here is a list of supported file suffixes:

*.bmp, *.png, *.tga, *.tif, *.pcd, *.psd, *.pcx, *.bsi, *.jpg, *.avi, *.dif, *.dv, *.dvd, *.m2v, *.yuv, *.mxf, *.dvsd, *.2vuy, *.mpeg; *.mpg; *.ts, *.vob, *.mov, *.wmv, *.mpa, *.mp3, *.wma, *.wav

As you can see, the list is quite extensive, with most common types of media supported. However, the types of imports you are most likely to make will fall under one of these categories:

- Picture formats including JPEG, TIFF, BMP and others.
- Music formats such as WAV.
- MP3 files and CD tracks ripped using Windows Media Player (WMV files).
- Windows Video standard (AVI files); this includes DivX and other encoded clips, although the relevant codec must be installed.
- Apples Movie standard (MOV files) and MPEG files such as the VCD and SVCD MPEG formats.
- Video object (VOB) files from a DVD.

Any number of clips can be imported at any one time, and there is no physical size restriction either, although extra big files will make your Timeline extra slow to update.

Touring the Import Media Window

Importing a media file is essentially the same process no matter what type it is—the exceptions being S/VCD and VOB files, which have an extra preview feature. For all other media files, Liquid Edition uses the same interface—the Import Media window—to suck them into your projects.

✔ Tip

■ Liquid Edition refers to any type of media—image, video, or sound—as a media clip, regardless of its format or its content.

To Open the Import Media window:

1. Select File > Import > Media (**Figure 3.1**). This Import Media window is fairly uncomplicated with only limited options to choose from (**Figure 3.2**).

2. To exit the Import Media window without importing anything, click Cancel.

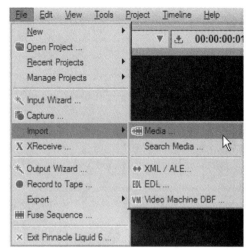

Figure 3.1 Opening the Import Media window using the drop-down menu system.

Elements of the Import Media window

The following list describes the various feature of the Import Media window.

◆ **The file location selection area:** All windows commands are supported here including Create New Folder and browsing directories. The last icon on the list can select Thumbnails, Titles, Icons, Details, or List View just as you would do when using Windows Explorer.

◆ **The file selection area:** As a rule, if it appears in this window, then you can probably import it into the Project Browser.

◆ **File name:** Once the file is selected, the filename appears here.

continues on next page

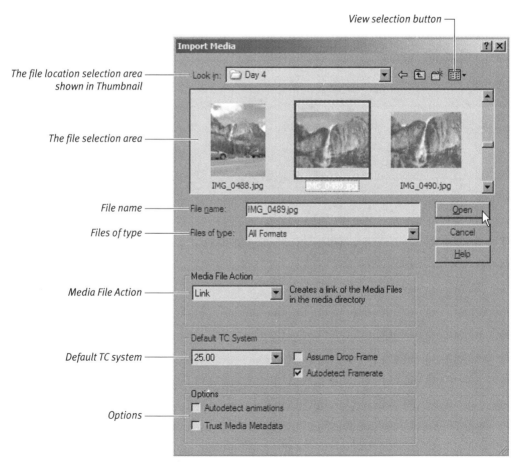

View selection button

The file location selection area shown in Thumbnail

The file selection area

File name

Files of type

Media File Action

Default TC system

Options

Figure 3.2 The Import Media window viewed here as thumnails.

TOURING THE IMPORT MEDIA WINDOW

- ◆ **Files of type:** If you want to filter the files, you can subdivide the media clips into their different categories (**Figure 3.3**).

- ◆ **Media File Action:** Here you decide what method of import to use for each media clip. There are three choices (**Figure 3.4**).

    - ▲ **Link:** This creates a simple link between the original media clip and Liquid Edition; a new file is not created. This type of import is quick because no new media is created; Liquid Edition merely notes where the original media clip is and makes use of the file from that location. If a media clip is on a local hard drive, in a place where it is unlikely to be moved (for example, on your media drive), then you could safely use Link and enjoy the speed benefits this offers.

    - ▲ **Copy:** This copies the original media clip to whichever hard drive you have specified as your media drive. This is the best option to use if you are importing MP3 or WAV files from a CD or video files from SVCD or DVD sources.

    - ▲ **Move:** This physically moves the original media clip to the media drive.

Both Copy and Move require some kind of file transfer, which will create a slower import than the Link method. If, however, the media clip exists on a network or removable drive, then you will probably want to copy or move it so that you can guarantee access to it in the future.

Copy is the safest option since Move will physically remove the media clip from wherever it was originally stored.

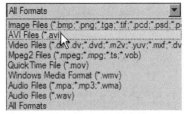

Figure 3.3 You can filter which files you import by selecting them from this drop-down list.

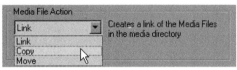

Figure 3.4 The three choices available from the Media File Action menu.

TOURING THE IMPORT MEDIA WINDOW

◆ **Default TC system:** This is only used when importing a video clip and with a frame rate that is not standardized. See Chapter 6 of the Pinnacle Liquid Edition Reference manual for complete details.

◆ **Options:** Here you have two check boxes:

▲ **Autodetect animation:** This is used to import animation files so that only one file, a reference file, appears in the Project Browser. See the "Importing Animations" sidebar for details.

▲ **Trust Media Metadata:** This is used by another version of Liquid Edition called Liquid Blue.

Importing Animated Sequences

To import an animated sequence, you must mark the Autodetect animations options box in the import media box (Figure 3.2), select the first frame from the animation, and click Open or press the Enter key on your keyboard (**Figure 3.5**).

This will create a single clip in the Project Browser (**Figure 3.6**). When dragged to the Timeline, this single clip will be associated with the rest of the animated files stored on the hard drive and will display the animation on the Timeline or in the Source Viewer.

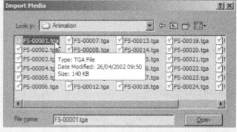

Figure 3.5 The first frame of a TGA animation highlighted. This example can be found in the media file inside the Pinnacle directory.

Note that this technique will only work with animated sequences—animations that exist as a series of individual images, not as a single compiled file.

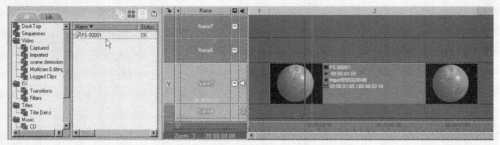

Figure 3.6 The animated clip in the Project Browser and also on the Timeline.

Using the Input Wizard

To help users gain a quick understanding of the Liquid Edition workflow, version 6.0 introduces a wizard to assist with the import process. If you have never imported a media clip before, it's well worth running the wizard at least once just to see the workflow in action.

To import a media clip using the wizard:

1. Select File > Input Wizard (**Figure 3.7**). This opens the Input wizard (**Figure 3.8**).

2. Choose which media type you want by clicking the appropriate icon.

   You are asked to select the Rack to which you want to import the media file (**Figure 3.9**).

Figure 3.7 Selecting the Input wizard.

Importing Studio 9 Projects

New to Liquid Edition 6 is the ability to import a Project created in Pinnacle Studio 9. You must be using the latest patched version of Studio 9 and the media files must be accessible by Liquid Edition 6.

Studio projects can be imported by selecting File > Import > XML/ALE, and importing the relevant *.STE file.

Although, Clip effects (filters) are not imported and all Transition effects are transformed into simple dissolves. DVD menus and other DVD-related objects are also not imported.

Classic Interface

Wizards are not available when using the Classic interface.

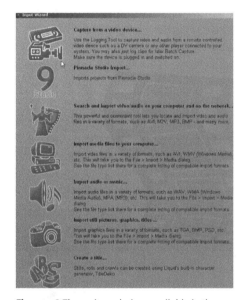

Figure 3.8 The various choices available in the Input wizard.

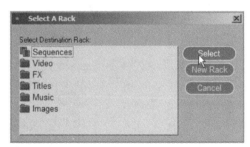

Figure 3.9 Choose a Rack or create a new one from here.

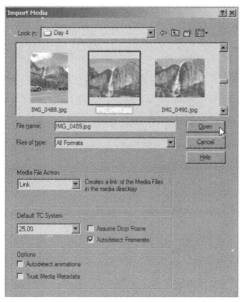

Figure 3.10 The Import Media window. See the start of this chapter for a detailed tour of this window.

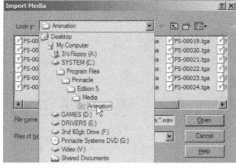

Figure 3.11 Find your file using the standard Windows functions.

3. Make your choice, click Select, and the Import Media window will open from which you can pick your file (**Figure 3.10**).

4. Browse to the file using the normal Windows functions (**Figure 3.11**).

5. When you have located your chosen file, click once to select it, and then click Open or press Alt+O.

The clip takes a moment to import and appears in the Rack you selected in step 4.

Once inside Liquid Edition, you can alter the media clip anyway you like without altering the original. Remember: Liquid Edition is a nondestructive editor.

✔ Tip

■ Just as you can in Windows, you can select more than one file at a time. Multiple clips are selected by holding down the Shift key to select neighboring clips or by holding down the Ctrl key to select individual clips. Clicking once inside the file selection area and then pressing Shift+A will select all of the clips in the folder. Unsupported clips (operating system files) are not seen by Liquid Edition and will not be selected.

Search Media

New to version 6 is the Search Media option, the third icon in the Input wizard .

This is a useful tool for tracking down those hard-to-find media clips that exist on your computer. The interface contains many filtering options that you should use to stop a search from taking too long and to pinpoint the results with a little more accuracy.

The window in **Figure 3.12** has been set up to search just the F drive for images. The results of that search are displayed in the top-right window.

continues on next page

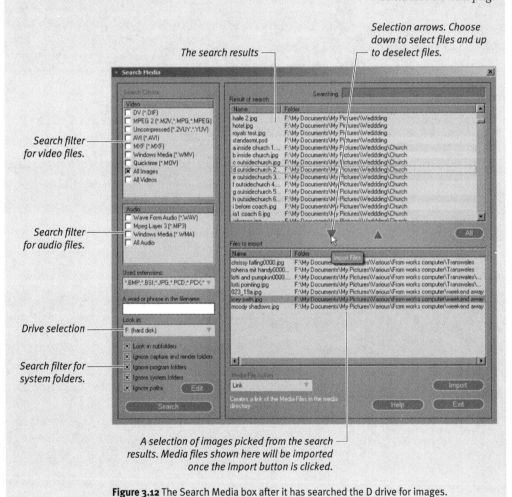

Selection arrows. Choose down to select files and up to deselect files.

The search results

Search filter for video files.

Search filter for audio files.

Drive selection

Search filter for system folders.

A selection of images picked from the search results. Media files shown here will be imported once the Import button is clicked.

Figure 3.12 The Search Media box after it has searched the D drive for images.

Search Media *continued*

By highlighting those images you want (using Ctrl+left-click and Shift+left-click) and then pressing the Down arrow, you can quickly select which images you want to import.

Clicking the Import button finishes this process and places your imports into a specially created Folder and Rack (**Figure 3.13**).

Audio, video, and images racks are automatically created during the import stage using the Search Media method, creating a pretty neat and quick method of collating your imports.

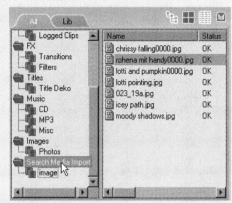

Figure 3.13 The new Search Media Folder containing the imported files.

Manually Importing a Media Clip

Importing a media clip without the wizard is an identical process, but without the hand-holding. This means that you must choose which Rack you want your import to be stored in before you begin. It's not a big step, and once you understand the import process, you will probably want to stop using the wizard completely.

To import a media clip:

1. Check to make sure you have selected the correct Rack in the Project Browser. (By default, media clips will always be imported into the last selected Rack.)

   You select a Rack by simply clicking it in the left window of the Project Browser.

2. *Do one of the following:*

   ▲ Click inside the right window of the Project Browser and select Import from the pop-up menu (**Figure 3.14**).

   ▲ Select File > Import > Media (**Figure 3.15**).

   This will bring up the Import Media dialog (**Figure 3.16**). For full details of the Import Media box see Figure 3.2.

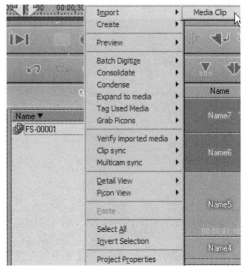

Figure 3.14 Open the Import Media window by right-clicking in the Project Browser...

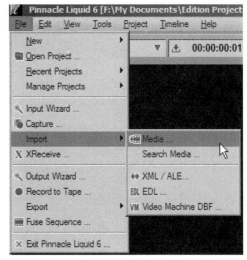

Figure 3.15 ...or use the drop-down menu.

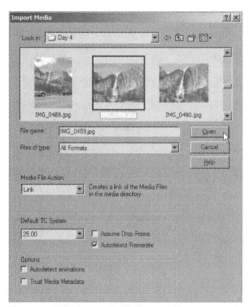

Figure 3.16 The Import Media box; see figure 3.2 and the accompanying text description in the section "Elements of the Import Media window" for full details.

3. Use the Windows browser to locate the file you want to import.

4. Highlight the media clip you want, and then click the Open button or press Enter.

The media clip will now import into the Rack you have selected in step 1.

✔ Tips

■ Just as you can in Windows, you can select more than one media clip to be imported at a time. Select multiple media clips by holding down the Shift key to select neighboring clips or by holding down the Ctrl key to select individual clips. By clicking once inside the file selection area and then pressing Shift+A, you can select all of the clips in this folder. Unsupported clips (operating system files) are not seen by Liquid Edition and will not be selected.

■ Liquid Edition also allows you to drag and drop clips from Windows Explorer into the Project Browser.

MANUALLY IMPORTING A MEDIA CLIP

Importing S/VCD and VOB Files

If you try to import a VCD/SVCD or VOB file, a dialog will appear displaying the available audio and video tracks (**Figure 3.17**). VOB files may display more than one audio file; this will probably contain the different language versions built into the DVD.

Once you have decided which audio track to use, click Preview to bring up a small inlay window inside which the VCD/SVCD or VOB file will play (**Figure 3.18**). Click Import to import the files.

Although you can import a VOB file (video object—MPEG-2 compliant files found on a DVD) into Liquid Edition, because of copyright restrictions, you must first copy it to your hard drive. You can acquire many popular tools on the Internet to do this.

You must also have an AC3 codec installed on your computer to use the audio in a VOB file. Codecs are freely available from http://ac3filter.sourceforge.net.

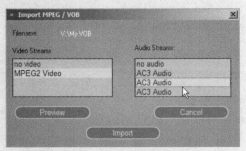

Figure 3.17 If you choose to import an SVCD or VOB file using this screen, you will be able to preview the file before you finish importing it.

Figure 3.18 The Preview window open under the selection screen once the Preview button is clicked.

Figure 3.19 The original digital snapshot, reduced in size to fit in this book.

Dealing with Image Import Problems

Although Liquid Edition can import pretty much anything, some imports may throw up unexpected results. Images from digital cameras and scanners are particularly prone to problems.

Most imported images will have been taken by digital cameras and will have frame and image sizes that vary to the moon and back. That's not a problem for Liquid Edition to import, but it can be a problem if you want them to display correctly on the Timeline.

Figure 3.19 shows a picture taken with a 2 MB digital camera. When imported into Adobe Photoshop, this picture has an image size of 1600 pixels by 1200 pixels. This is a big picture but not uncommonly big in the digital camera world. When this picture is displayed in the Source Viewer, the image only shows a zoomed-in section; on the Timeline the effect would be the same (**Figure 3.20**).

Figure 3.20 The same digital photo placed in the Source Viewer and on the Timeline.

Why does this happen?

Video editing systems have a resolution that is linked to the TV standard used in each country. For example,

- In the U.S., the National Television System Committee (NTSC) standard uses a screen resolution of 720 pixels by 486 pixels.

- In Europe, the Phase Alternating Line (PAL) standard uses a screen resolution of 720 pixels by 576 pixels.

To display an image correctly, you must scale it to fit one or the other of these sizes or convert it from an oversized image to one that is the correct size.

Converting your pictures to the size you want requires time and a photo manipulation program. This means that every photo you want to import into Liquid Edition needs to be altered in this way. This is a laborious process if you have a lot of photographs to convert.

The solution is to let Liquid Edition scale each photograph to fit the resolution being used by Liquid Edition. See the section, "Resizing Images" later in this chapter, for details.

Files that won't import correctly

If you do come across a media clip that is not one of the recognized file types, or you have one that does show up in the Liquid Edition file browser but will not import, then you will have to convert it before you try to import it.

Usually Liquid Edition gives an error message telling you why it can't import the file and you can use this information to help you find a conversion program. The popular program TMPGEnc (www.tmpgenc.com) is good place to start, but other conversion programs are only an Internet search away.

Files that won't display correctly

Video files, particularly those downloaded from the Internet, are encoded with a variety of different codecs to help reduce their overall size. Some, like DivX, have become standard codecs, but others are not as well known and you may end up importing a media clip and then only seeing a blank screen when you try to play it back. If your system is working correctly, there are only two reasons for this:

- **The clip needs to render before it can play back.** Check this by clicking the Render icon Σ to see if the clip is rendering and how long this will take.

- **The clip uses a codec that is not installed on your computer.** Check this by trying to play the clip in Windows Media Player. Media Player will give an error message if it doesn't recognize the codec. If you are very lucky, Media Player will download the correct codec automatically. But only if you are very lucky—in the real world this rarely works.

Figure 3.21 Selecting the Control Panel.

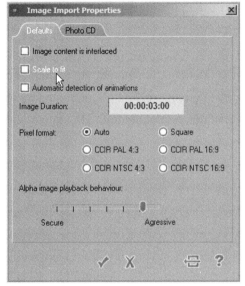

Figure 3.22 The Image Import Properties box.

Resizing Images

Converting images can be achieved at three different times:

◆ During Import

◆ While it is in the Project Browser

◆ When it has been placed on the Timeline

To resize during Import:

1. Select Edit > Control Panel (**Figure 3.21**).

2. Click Image Import ▨.

   This brings up the Image Import Properties box (**Figure 3.22**).

   Most of the settings here are for various specialized image-related problems and configurations. Details on this can be found in Chapter 6 of the Pinnacle Liquid Edition Reference manual.

   The two areas of greater interest are

   ▲ **Scale to fit:** When checked this will import images to the current TV standard.

   ▲ **Image Duration:** This defaults to 3 seconds, but most editors prefer a minimum duration of at least 10 seconds. You can set this here and dynamically resize it later if you need to.

continues on next page

RESIZING IMAGES

3. Check the Scale to fit box.

4. Close the Image Properties box and import your photograph.

Figure 3.23 shows the original photograph imported with this setting. Don't worry too much about the black border running around the outside of the screen; remember, not all of the Inlay will be shown on most TV screens. You'll need to practice trial and error here to see what works for you.

✔ Tip

■ The Lizard JPEG is one of the sample files that can be downloaded from www.peachpit.com/liquid6vqp.

Figure 3.23 The original photo reimported using the new settings.

Classic Interface

Users of the Classic interface gain access to the Control Panel by clicking the Start button, moving the mouse up, and clicking once on the Control Panel icon.

After that, each operation is identical to those descriptions given in this chapter.

Figure 3.24 Accessing the media clip's properties.

To resize in the Project Browser or on the Timeline:

1. If you have already imported your images and you now want to resize them, right-click the image in the Project Browser (or on the Timeline) and select Properties from the pop-up menu (**Figure 3.24**) to display the Properties of that image (**Figure 3.25**).

2. Click the V tab to display the visual settings (**Figure 3.26**).

continues on next page

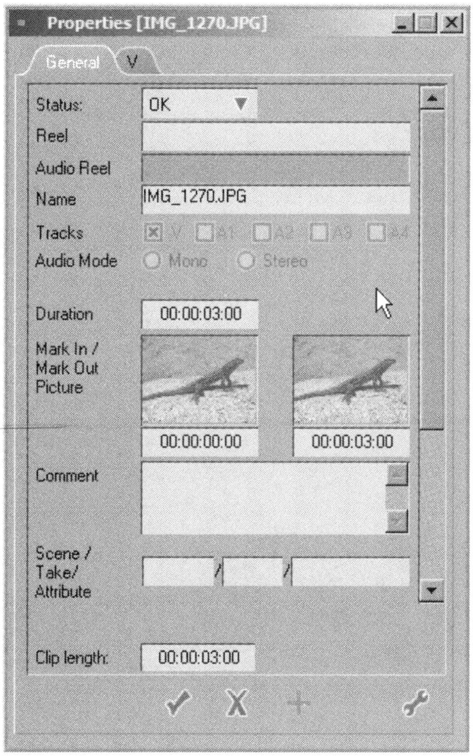

Figure 3.25 The media clip Properties box.

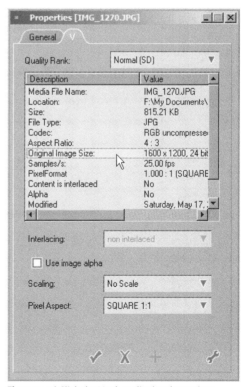

Figure 3.26 Click the V tab to display the options.

RESIZING IMAGES

3. At the bottom are three drop-down menus. Click the middle one, Scaling, and select Fit largest - Keep Aspect (**Figure 3.27**).

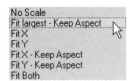

Figure 3.27 Select Fit largest - Keep Aspect from the drop-down list.

4. Click the cross button  to apply this, and then click the check mark button to exit the Properties box.

Figure 3.28 shows the photograph in the Source Viewer using this setting.

Figure 3.28 The photograph after it is has been adjusted.

Which One Is Best for You?

This will depend on the original physical dimensions of the image, but because NLE is non-destructive, you can freely experiment to find out which setting works best for each photograph.

Figure 3.29 shows the six different options you have for stretching a picture with the original image at top center.

◆ **Fit largest - Keep Aspect:** Stretches each side equally

◆ **Fit X:** Stretches only the vertical aspect and ignores the horizontal aspect ratio

◆ **Fit Y:** Stretches only the horizontal aspect and ignores the vertical aspect ratio

◆ **Fit x - Keep Aspect:** Stretches the vertical to fill the screen but keeps the horizontal aspect ratio correct

◆ **Fit Y - Keep Aspect:** Stretches the horizontal to fill the screen but keeps the vertical aspect ratio correct

◆ **Fit Both:** Stretches all sides, ignoring both aspect ratios

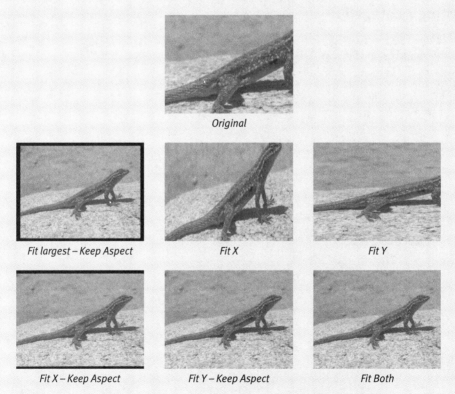

Figure 3.29 The six different options for adjusting an image after it has been imported.

RESIZING IMAGES

Creating Media Files

Although it is true that media files need to either be imported or digitized to be used in Liquid Edition, the exceptions are certain types of media you can create in Liquid Edition.

These fall into four categories:

◆ Creating a color clip

◆ Creating a signal clip

◆ Creating a DVD menu

◆ Creating a title

I deal with creating a DVD menu in Chapter 12 and creating a title in Chapter 10, but I detail how to create color and signal clips in the following sections.

Creating a color clip

You'll often create a color clip to function as the background in an effect or to be used for the lead-in to start a video or the lead-out to end it.

To create a color clip:

1. Select the Rack you want to create the clip inside, and right-click in the right window of the Project Browser.

2. From the pop-up menu, select Create > Color Clip (**Figure 3.30**).

   This brings up the Color Matte Clip box.

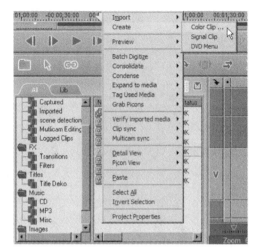

Figure 3.30 Accessing Create > Color Clip.

3. On the right side of the box, choose from three settings:

Single color: A standard color clip made from the color of your choice (**Figure 3.31**).

A Linear Gradient: Uses two colors and creates a gradual fade from one color to the next in a straight line from left to right (**Figure 3.32**).

continues on next page

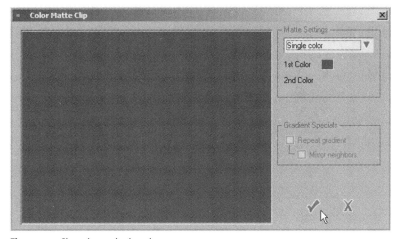

Figure 3.31 Choosing a single color.

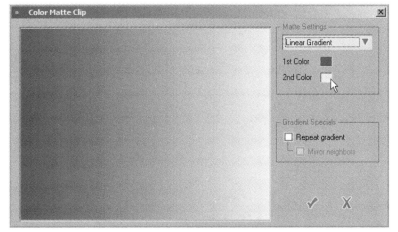

Figure 3.32 A linear gradient color clip.

Circular Gradient: Uses two colors and creates a gradual fade from one color to the next in a circular pattern from the top-left corner (**Figure 3.33**).

4. Choose which color you want by clicking the small colored rectangle to bring up the color picker (**Figure 3.34**).

5. Once you have decided on a color, click the check mark to exit the color picker.

6. Click the check mark to exit the Color Matte Clip box.

   A color clip is created in the Rack you have selected.

   You can insert this new media clip into the Timeline or the Source Viewer and use it just like any other media clip (**Figure 3.35**).

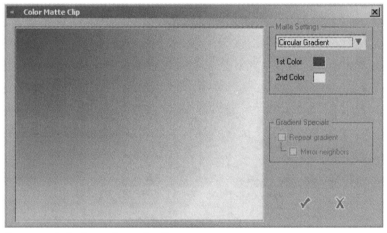

Figure 3.33 A circular gradient color clip.

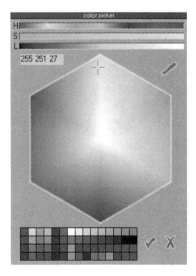

Figure 3.34 The color picker tool.

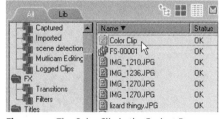

Figure 3.35 The Color Clip in the Project Browser.

Creating a signal clip

The use of a signal clip is somewhat esoteric; all you actually create is a WAV file with a single beep inside it. Some editors use this to give the end of scenes an audio mark or to create an audio queue that they can use as a guide. The rest of us will find its functionality less remarkable.

To create a signal clip:

1. Right-click inside the right window of the Project Browser.

2. From the pop-up menu, select Create > Signal Clip.

   The signal clip is created inside the Rack you have selected.

MANAGING YOUR MEDIA

Much of the magic behind Liquid Edition, the method by which it creates such spectacular effects with ease, is a simple matter of smoke and mirrors. In other words, it all happens behind the scenes and is controlled by the Media Management system. This is a complex system of file associations and file structuring, but if this means nothing to you, that's okay, because most of the time you won't even need to worry about what's happening and how it all works.

Every now and then, however, you will have to get your hands a little dirty with Media Management, and that's where the problems can start.

Every program has its own way of organizing the data with which it needs to work. Liquid Edition's method is no more complex than any other, but it can be a problem area for beginners. In this chapter, you'll learn how and where Liquid Edition stores its media clips, and also how these locations can be easily switched around at will.

Finding Your Media

Anything digitized by the Logging Tool is stored inside a media folder; this is usually the folder you picked during the install process. If you look inside this folder using Windows Explorer, you'll see a folder called Reels. Look in here and you will find a number of folders that will all have the same names as the Reels used when working with the Logging Tool (**Figure 4.1**).

So far so easy, but look inside any of these Reel folders and you'll see a confusing array of files with 20-digit names of seemingly random numbers and letters (**Figure 4.2**).

Deciphering filenames

These numbers do actually mean something. The first eight numbers represent the clip-in point of the media file; the second set of eight numbers represent the clip-out point. This is displayed in the format of hours:minutes: seconds:frames and the letter at the end tells you if it is a video (V) or an audio (A) track.

The other files in this folder are associated Media Management files that tell Liquid Edition what you have been doing with this clip and to which sequences it belongs. Try to think of the contents of this folder as being the complete sum of its parts. None of these files can be separated from any of the others for Liquid Edition to be able to work with them. They must stay together.

This is the Media Management file system in action, and although it may look confusing, don't worry—all the Media Management tasks are and should be controlled from within Liquid Edition. Users who ignore this "rule" will find themselves encountering problems.

Figure 4.1 A folder created by the Logging Tool. The first part of the name is created by the user when capturing.

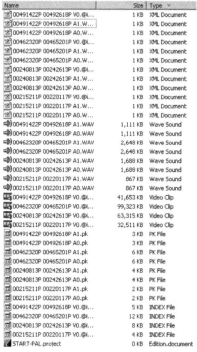

Figure 4.2 The contents of a folder created by the Logging Tool. All these files are important.

Clip-In vs. Mark-In

Reference is often made to a media clip having a clip-in/out point and a mark-in/out point. The differences are important.

A clip-in/out point marks the start and end of the media *file* on the drive. These two points cannot be changed, and if they are, then a new media *file* is created.

A mark-in/out point marks the start and end point of a media *clip*. The points can be changed inside Liquid Edition without altering or creating a new media clip.

✔ Tips

■ If you need to import a media clip from a Reel folder, then you can select thumbnails from your Windows settings (**Figure 4.3**). You will see the first frame of the clip displayed, which at least gives you a clue as to the clip's contents. You can also open the clip inside Media Player by double-clicking it.

■ When importing a video clip from the Media folder, you only need to select the video track; the associated audio will be imported automatically.

Figure 4.3 Selecting thumbnails in Windows Explorer makes it easier to identify clips.

Working with the Media Drive

When Liquid Edition was installed, the wizard asked for a suitable location to store media that is either captured or imported. It's here that you will find the directories used by the Media Management system.

However, you are not restricted to using just this drive or just this folder; it is also possible to add another drive or folder anytime.

To add a new media drive or folder:

1. To open the Control Panel, *do one of the following:*

   ▲ Select Edit > Control Panel (**Figure 4.4**).

   ▲ Click the Classic interface's Start button and select Control Panel from the list (**Figure 4.5**).

2. Once the Control Panel is open, click the Site tab (**Figure 4.6**).

Figure 4.4 Accessing the Control Panel from the drop-down menu.

Figure 4.5 Accessing the Control Panel from the Start button when using the Classic interface.

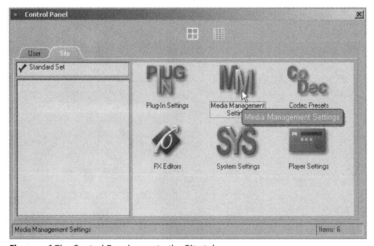

Figure 4.6 The Control Panel open to the Site tab.

3. Double-click the Media Management button 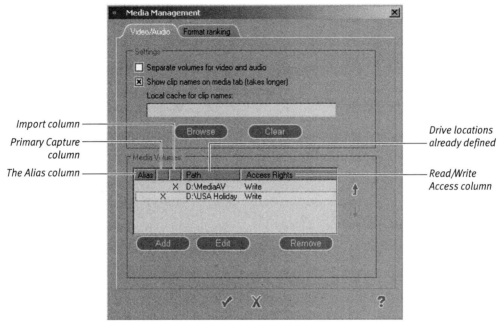 to open the Media Management interface (**Figure 4.7**).

continues on next page

Import column

Primary Capture column

The Alias column

Drive locations already defined

Read/Write Access column

Figure 4.7 The Media Management interface.

WORKING WITH THE MEDIA DRIVE

4. Click the Add button at the bottom of the screen.

A Windows browser pops up (**Figure 4.8**).

5. Browse to the drive you want and either create a new folder or use one that already exists.

6. Click the OK button.

The new Media Drive is created (**Figure 4.9**).

To move a Media Drive:

◆ You can alter this drive location by simply clicking the Edit button and browsing to a new location. Doing this will not affect your Project or your sequences because Media Management will always be tracking where each media clip is stored.

If you find yourself running short of hard drive space, this new location can be on a totally new hard drive without Liquid Edition losing track of any files.

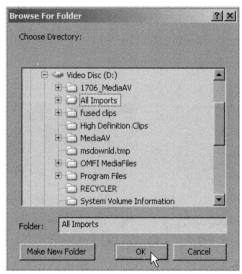

Figure 4.8 Browse to the folder you want or create a new one.

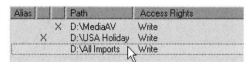

Figure 4.9 The new media location added to the Media Management interface.

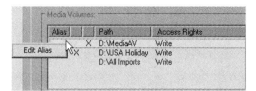

Figure 4.10 Editing the alias by clicking in the first column.

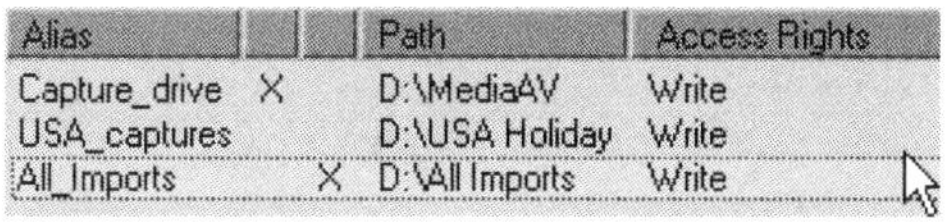

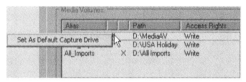

Figure 4.11 All three drives now have an alias that can be recognized.

Figure 4.12 The second column is used to set the primary volume...

Figure 4.13 ...which is marked by a large X in this column.

Organizing Your Media Drives

Once created, the Media Drive can be organized to further streamline your workflow by adding an alias to the drive for easier identification. It's also possible to nominate which drive or folder will be the default for capture and which will be the default for import.

✔ Tip

■ Drives used for capture or import should always be separate from the drive that holds Windows XP. It should also be a large drive with a spin speed of 7200 rpm. See the Appendix for more details.

To create an alias:

1. With the Media Management interface open, select a drive from the list by clicking it once.

2. Right-click that drive in the Alias column (the first column in that row).

3. Click the Edit Alias pop-up menu (**Figure 4.10**).

   A text cursor appears inside the Alias area.

4. Enter your text.

   This box will grow to accommodate large strings, but it will push the others off the screen (**Figure 4.11**). This interface cannot be resized.

To select the default capture drive:

1. With the Media Management interface open, select a drive from the list by clicking it once.

2. Right-click under the Primary Volume column (the one next to the word "Alias").

3. Click Set As Default Capture Drive (**Figure 4.12**).

   A large X appears in this column to indicate that this is now the default capture drive (**Figure 4.13**).

To select the default import drive:

1. With the Media Management interface open, select a drive from the list by clicking it once.

2. Right-click under the Import Volume column (the one to the left of the Path column).

3. Click Set As Import Drive (**Figure 4.14**). A large X appears in this column to indicate that this is now the default import drive (**Figure 4.15**).

✔ Tip

■ Both the Primary and Import Volume columns are blank by design. The boxes are apparently too small to fit text into.

To alter the access rights:

1. With the Media Management interface open, select a drive from the list by clicking it once.

2. Right-click under the Access Rights column.

3. Click either Read or Write to set the access rights for that drive (**Figure 4.16**). The word Write or Read appears in this column depending on which you selected (**Figure 4.17**).

   You change the access rights to Read to protect a Media Drive from being altered once a project is completed, but you will need to switch it back to Write if you need to perform any more editing.

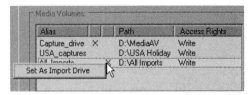

Figure 4.14 The third column is used to set the import volume...

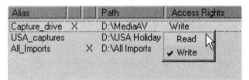

Figure 4.15 ...which is marked by a large X in this column. Without it, all imports default to the primary volume.

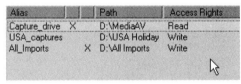

Figure 4.16 The last column is used to set the read/write access rights.

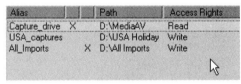

Figure 4.17 Here the primary capture volume has been changed to Read, protecting it from alteration.

To delete a Media Drive:

1. With the Media Management interface open, select a drive from the list by clicking it once.

2. Click once on the Remove button and the drive vanishes.

There is no second warning with this feature and you will not be prompted with an "Are you sure?" message. The drive location will simply be deleted. Make sure you have the right drive selected before you do this.

However, remember that you are only removing it from the Media Management system; you are not deleting it from your hard drive. If you delete the wrong one, then simply bring it back in again using the instructions on page 114.

✔ Tip

■ Any of the above alterations can be changed on the fly. However, be cautious when deleting a Media Drive because Liquid Edition will no longer be able to use any files stored at that location.

Physically Moving Your Media Around

Liquid Edition's unique file structure means that you have to exercise some care when moving files around using the Windows Explorer. Physically removing a file from a folder and transferring it to another can cause the Timeline render marker to go dark red—a sign that the media can't be located and can't be worked with. Restoring this can be difficult, and in some cases, impossible.

However, if you need to switch the location of your media files using Windows Explorer, then you need to understand the following rule:

◆ When searching for media clips, Liquid Edition is looking for a folder called Reels. This folder can be anywhere in the directory tree, but it must be the folder that contains the video clips and *all* the associated files.

To physically move the location of a media file:

1. Open Windows Explorer and create a new folder, giving it a unique name that is associated with the project you are working on—for example, USA-Holiday-Tape 1 (**Figure 4.18**).

2. Open this new folder and create another folder inside this one called Reels (don't forget the "s").

3. Browse to the original Media folder and locate the original Reels folder.

   Inside you will find the names of all the Reels you have captured to this location.

4. Once you've located the correct folder, right-click it and select Copy (**Figure 4.19**).

   Remember, it's the whole folder you are copying, not just the one video and

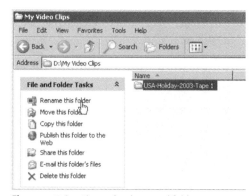

Figure 4.18 Creating a clearly named folder at a new location.

Figure 4.19 Copying the *entire* folder from the original location.

accompanying audio files. Everything in that folder must be copied, so it is far easier to copy the folder itself.

5. Browse back to the new Reels folder you created in Step 1, right-click, and select Paste.

   Make sure you are pasting inside the new Reels folder; if you do not, then Liquid Edition will not be able to find it.

6. Open the Media Management interface and then add this new location following the instructions in the "To add a new media drive or folder" section earlier in this chapter. You only need to select the folder in which the new Reels folder has been created. In this example, the folder USA-Holiday-Tape 1 is added.

   Once it has been added, Liquid Edition will automatically look inside this new location for the Reels folder. Once it finds this, it will scan the contents and reassociate any clips it has in the Project Browser with any clips that are stored in this new location.

✔ Tip

- The secret here is to remember that the folder called Reels (don't forget the "s" on the end) must be the folder that contains your media clips. No Reels folder, no media clips. It's that simple.

When Moving Media Goes Bad

There can be times, particularly when you're using removable hard drives, that it all goes wrong and you end up with all the render slices turning dark red. This is Liquid Edition's way of telling you it can't find the file. If this happens, do the following:

- Right-click inside the right window of the Project Browser and select Verify Imported Media. Then chose All In Rack or Selected. Follow the prompts and Liquid Edition will search the Media folders looking for these associated clips.

  If it cannot find the files, then make sure the drive they are stored on appears in the Media Volume area of the Media Management interface.

Deleting and Restoring Media Clips

Like everything else under the Media Management system, deletion should be done with the Project Browser because physically removing files using Windows Explorer isn't easy or safe—particularly because the filenames do not immediately allow you to identify a file.

To delete a media clip:

1. Select the media clip in the Project Browser and press Delete on the keyboard.

   A Delete dialog pops up asking if you want to delete the clip and also the corresponding media.

2. *Do one of the following:*

   ▲ To delete the clip and any parent clip that belongs to it, select both in the dialog. If this clip is one of several Subclips, then all clips will be deleted.

   ▲ To remove just the clip from your Project Browser, select Delete Media in the dialog. The clip remains on your hard drive.

To restore a media clip:

1. Click the Eye icon in the Liquid Edition taskbar (**Figure 4.20**).

2. Switch to Storyboard view by clicking the second icon up on that column (**Figure 4.21**). If you are using a dual screen setup, the Trash can will already be displayed on one of your monitors and, in this case, you obviously won't need to switch your view.

   The Edition Desktop is displayed with the Trash can in the upper-left corner (**Figure 4.22**).

Figure 4.20 The Eye icon used to switch between interfaces.

Figure 4.21 The Storyboard icon is second from the bottom.

Figure 4.22 The Edition Desktop and the Trash can.

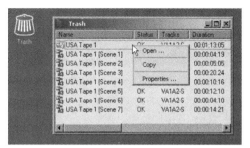

Figure 4.23 The contents of the Trash can.

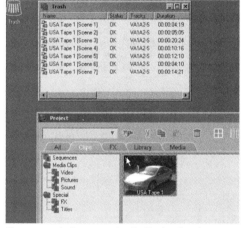

Figure 4.24 A clip restored to its Rack using drag and drop.

3. Right-click the Trash can and select Open from the list (**Figure 4.23**).

This displays a list of those files recently deleted.

4. Select the file you want to restore and drag it back to the Rack it came from (**Figure 4.24**).

This restores the file not only in the Project Browser, but also on the Timeline if it was used there.

✔ Tips

- Any media clips that are present on the Timeline but are deleted from the Project Browser will not be removed, but they will display a black screen with an "!" to indicate the associated media is missing.

- You can also use copy and paste to restore files from the Trash to a Rack.

Render Files

Render files are also covered by the Media Management system. They represent the magical part of the smoke and mirrors by creating the effects in real-time previews and keeping the show running smoothly.

This location was also selected during the install, but it can be changed at any time. However, any render files you have associated with the current Project will need to be rerendered.

You should also be aware that the Render drive can only be moved, and unlike the Media Drive, you can only have one Render drive at any one time.

Figure 4.25 Accessing the Control Panel from the drop-down menu.

Figure 4.26 Accessing the Control Panel from the Start button when using the Classic interface.

To move the Render drive:

1. Open the Control Panel by *doing one of the following:*
   - ▲ Select Edit > Control Panel (**Figure 4.25**).
   - ▲ Click the Classic interface's Start button and select Control Panel from the list (**Figure 4.26**).
2. Click the Site tab (**Figure 4.27**).

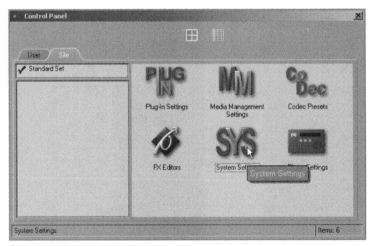

Figure 4.27 The Control Panel open to the Site tab.

3. Double-click the System Settings button
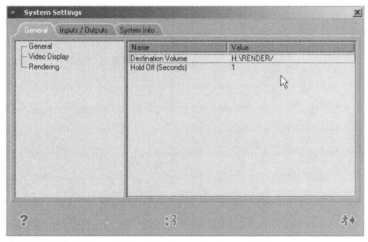 to open the System Settings interface.

4. Locate and click the word Rendering in
the General tab (**Figure 4.28**).

This displays the render location in the
right window.

continues on next page

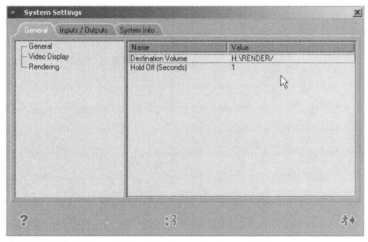

Figure 4.28 The System Settings interface on the General tab.

5. Double-click directly under the Value column to display a small button containing three dots. This is the Browse button (**Figure 4.29**).

6. Click the Browse button to display the directory tree. Browse through this in the normal way until you have selected a new location for your render folder.

7. Click the OK button and then the Running man 🏃 to close the editor. All render files are now directed to this new location.

Name	Value	
Destination Volume	H:\RENDER\	...
Hold Off (Seconds)	1	

Figure 4.29 Changing the render folder location.

Render Files That Grow

Some types of render files can grow to enormous sizes. For instance, if you imported a DivX movie that was an hour long, Liquid Edition would have to render this before it could be played in the Source Viewer or on the Timeline. Typically this would create a file size larger than 12 gigabytes. This isn't massive by today's standards, but it may still be troublesome if you are running short of space. In cases such as this, you would be well advised to move the render file location—at least temporarily.

DVD render files can also grow to eye-watering sizes, but with these, location can be predefined before rendering or burning takes place. See Chapter 12 for more details.

Figure 4.30 The Eye icon used to switch between interfaces.

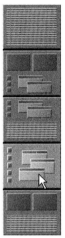

Figure 4.31 The Storyboard icon is second from the bottom.

Deleting unwanted render files

During the edit process, Liquid Edition will create a large number of render files, some of which you'll later discover you don't need, or you'll find that they were used by another sequence and are taking up space you now badly need.

Liquid Edition allows you to delete these unwanted files in a selective manner so that you can reclaim wasted space without jeopardizing the project you are working on.

To delete render files:

1. Click the Eye icon in the Liquid Edition taskbar (**Figure 4.30**).

2. Switch to Storyboard view by clicking the second icon up on that column (**Figure 4.31**) or press Shift+F3 on the keyboard. If you are using a dual screen setup, the Trash can will already be displayed on one of your monitors and, in this case, you obviously won't need to switch your view.

    This displays the Edition Desktop with the Trash can in the upper-left corner.

3. Right-click the Trash can and select Delete Render Files Of Project.

continues on next page

RENDER FILES

4. Choose one of the following from the list (**Figure 4.32**):

▲ **All:** To delete all render files associated with this project and all previous projects.

▲ **Not Used By Current Sequence:** To delete all the render files but not the ones you are currently using.

▲ **Not Used By Any Sequence In This Project:** To delete any render files left over from previous Projects but retain the current ones.

▲ **Not Used By Selected Sequence(s) In Project Window:** To delete any render files from sequences you have not highlighted before right-clicking the Trash can.

Once you have clicked your choice, those render files will be deleted. There is no "Are you sure you want to do this?" question, so be absolutely sure before you click.

Cleaning and diagnosing a Project

The Trash can has two further uses:

◆ **Cleaning up a Project:** Used to clear Undo information and any redundant objects no longer associated with this Project.

◆ **Diagnose a Project:** Used to repair damaged files created inside the Trash can in the event of software crash. Theoretically it is possible to restore files from here.

Both functions are accessed by right-clicking the Trash can and selecting either one.

Figure 4.32 The Trash can with all the render options displayed.

THE FIRST ASSEMBLY— STORYBOARDING

5

Every video production is essentially a story with a beginning, a middle, and an end. Special effects, titles, and voice-overs can all be added later in the process, but the first step is to get the order of your story right so that it actually has these three story elements.

To get this right, people in the film industry use sketches of each scene to help them visualize how the film will eventual look. Historically, this actually meant sticking hand-drawn sketches on a wall and shuffling them about to create a basic visualization of the story for the producer, director, and writer. This technique is called *storyboarding* and it is essential for video productions of any significant length. Nothing saves time— and money—like preparation!

By using the storyboarding technique, you can visualize the first layout of the video with a few simple mouse clicks, experimenting with the order of scenes or just figuring out which take works best. This is called creating a *first assembly*, and its importance should not be overlooked, because this type of workflow can be much quicker than using the Timeline—especially in the initial stages of the project. It does carry a disadvantage in that you can't add titles and certain effects, but you don't really need these items at this stage. Much more important is making sure you have a coherent story. Remember: all the special effects in the world will not keep your video alive if you fail to provide a good story.

The Storyboard Interface

Liquid Edition has two main interfaces: the Timeline and the Storyboard. The default interface is the Timeline, but by swapping to the Storyboard, you can begin an assemble edit of your project. With most NLE programs with less sophisticated storyboard functions, you might be tempted to head directly to the Timeline after capture in order to start editing right away, especially when the storyboard seems like an extra step. However Liquid Edition's storyboard is much more efficient and an easier way to visualize the first step. And since you can drag and drop, or send the storyboard results directly to the Timeline, it's not an extra step after all. If you are serious about creating a project that is polished in appearance then the storyboard should be your next stage after you have captured or imported your footage.

Users of dual-screen displays should read the information in the "Dual-Screen Users" sidebar as all the examples here are for a single-screen display.

To open the Storyboard interface:

1. Click the Eye button to open the various view options (**Figure 5.1**).

2. Click the Storyboard icon (**Figure 5.2**) so that your Liquid Edition desktop looks like **Figure 5.3**.

✔ Tip

■ The keyboard shortcut for opening the Storyboard interface is Shift+F3. To return to the Timeline use Shift+F2.

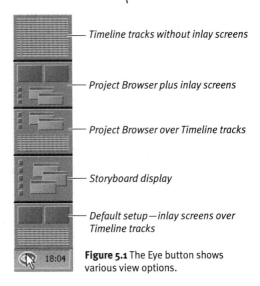

Timeline tracks without inlay screens

Project Browser plus inlay screens

Project Browser over Timeline tracks

Storyboard display

Default setup—inlay screens over Timeline tracks

Figure 5.1 The Eye button shows various view options.

Figure 5.2 Click this icon to open the Storyboard layout.

THE STORYBOARD INTERFACE

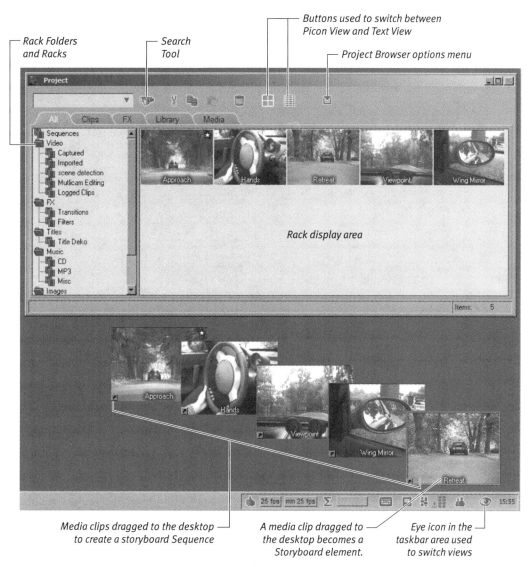

Rack Folders and Racks

Search Tool

Buttons used to switch between Picon View and Text View

Project Browser options menu

Rack display area

Media clips dragged to the desktop to create a storyboard Sequence

A media clip dragged to the desktop becomes a Storyboard element.

Eye icon in the taskbar area used to switch views

THE STORYBOARD INTERFACE

Figure 5.3 The Storyboard layout shows the Liquid Edition desktop with five Storyboard elements and their master clips contained in the Project Browser.

Dual-Screen Users

If you have a dual-screen display, the Eye icon button will display the dual-screen range of options (**Figure 5.4**).

To see the various options in action, simply click each one. The second icon from the bottom will probably be the one you'll want to use the most. This places the Storyboard on the right monitor and the inlay screens and Timeline on the left monitor (**Figure 5.5**).

Some graphics cards will not support an overlay on the secondary monitor; users with this type of card will need to use the option shown in figure 5.5; otherwise, they will see a blank inlay when playing clips.

continues on next page

Figure 5.4 The dual-screen view options.

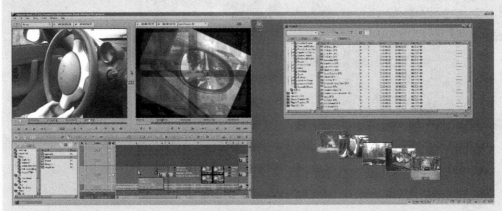

Figure 5.5 If you have no inlay on your secondary monitor, use this layout.

THE STORYBOARD INTERFACE

Dual-Screen Users *continued*

The main advantages of having a dual-screen setup are:

◆ You will be able to display a much longer Timeline (**Figure 5.6**).

◆ You can display both the Storyboard and the Timeline at the same time (Figure 5.5).

◆ You can display the full library of FXs without having to constantly switch screens (**Figure 5.7**).

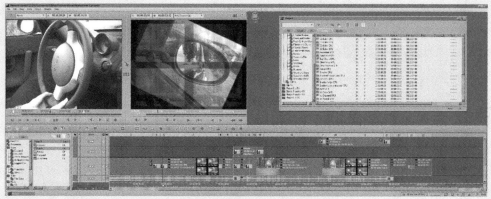

Figure 5.6 The Timeline extended across both monitors on a dual-screen setup.

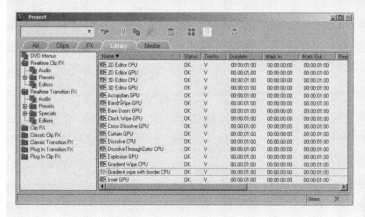

Figure 5.7 If the Timeline is restricted to the left monitor, it is then possible to give the Project Browser even more room. Here the real-time transition editors are displayed.

Editing Using the Storyboard

Using the Storyboard involves three main stages: preparation, creation, and previewing. In this section, you'll learn how to tackle each of these and you'll also become familiar with a couple of tricks that will speed up your workflow. These stages contain substages that cover how to edit media clips, how to add simple effects, and how to alter the playback order. Once you have worked your way through this section, you should be able to create a complete Storyboard Sequence and make it ready for further editing on the Timeline.

Once a Storyboard Sequence is complete, it must be sent to the Timeline so that you can add titles, music, and certain effects. This task is explained fully in the last section of this chapter.

Definitions Used in This Chapter

◆ **Master, subclip, or media clip:** Any clip in the Project Browser.

◆ **Storyboard element:** Any clip that has been dragged to the Liquid Edition desktop.

The term Storyboard element is unique to this book and is used here to define the difference between a clip stored in the Project Browser and a clip that has been dragged to the Liquid Edition desktop.

◆ **Storyboard Sequence:** Any collection of Storyboard elements existing on the Liquid Edition desktop.

◆ **A Picon**: Media clips can be displayed in the Project Browser as text or as thumbnails. Liquid Edition refers to a thumbnail as a Picon (Picture-Icon).

Create a new sequence by clicking here

Figure 5.8 The New Sequence button creates a new Timeline Sequence.

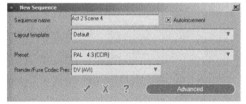

Figure 5.9 Pressing the New Sequence button allows you to name the sequence and select its properties.

Preparing the Storyboard

The first stage, preparation, is simple enough; it requires you only to create and name a Timeline Sequence. The effective use of a Timeline Sequence is covered in Chapters 6 and 14, but in this section, the examples show a sequence called "Act 2 Scene 4"; which should give you a clue as to the function of this incredibly powerful feature.

To prepare the Storyboard:

1. On the main interface, click once on the New Sequence button in the top-right corner of the interface (**Figure 5.8**).

2. When the New Sequence dialog appears, enter a unique sequence name in the top box (**Figure 5.9**).

   The other settings are explained in Chapter 6.

3. Check that the Timeline cursor is placed where you want to insert your clips. This may be at the beginning of the Timeline, but it may also be just after the last sequence you worked on.

✔ Tip

■ If you have a dual-screen setup, then you don't need to worry about placing the Timeline cursor because you will have the option of dragging your clips from the Storyboard monitor to the Timeline. Single-screen users don't have this luxury and must always plan ahead.

Creating the Storyboard

Creating a Storyboard Sequence is wonderfully and refreshingly easy. It's just a matter of drag and drop.

The big advantage of the Storyboard is that any of these clips can be dragged to the desktop and sorted into any play order you like. The clips can even be shuffled around inside the Project Browser by simply dragging and dropping them.

✔ Tip

■ The five clips used in this chapter are available for download from www.peachpit.com/liquid6vqp. Although, you can also use your own clips to complete the next set of tasks.

To create a Storyboard Sequence:

1. If you are using a single screen monitor, open the Storyboard as described earlier and click the All tab if it is not already displayed.

   This displays your clips on the right with the Rack Folders and Racks on the left (**Figure 5.10**).

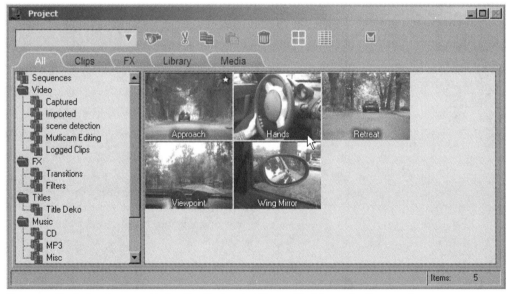

Figure 5.10 The Project Browser with the clips displayed as Picons. All of the media clips stored on your computer can be accessed from here.

2. Drag your clips onto the desktop in the order you want to be played.

Figure 5.11 shows a sequence with a car approaching the viewer; a cut to the hands steering the car; another cut to the viewpoint of the driver; a cut of the mirror; and finally, a cut to the car retreating. This is the beginning, middle, and end of the story, or scene, in this case.

✔ **Tip**

■ The examples in this section show you how to create a project in small, manageable building blocks, rather than trying to assemble an epic film that is one very long timeline. Imagine *Lord of the Rings* sitting on your Liquid Edition Timeline. Tracking the changes and even finding individual scenes would become time consuming and frustrating. A much easier and more logical approach would be to split the job up into bite-sized sequences that could be assembled into an epic later.

For more details on creating and using Sequences, see Chapter 6.

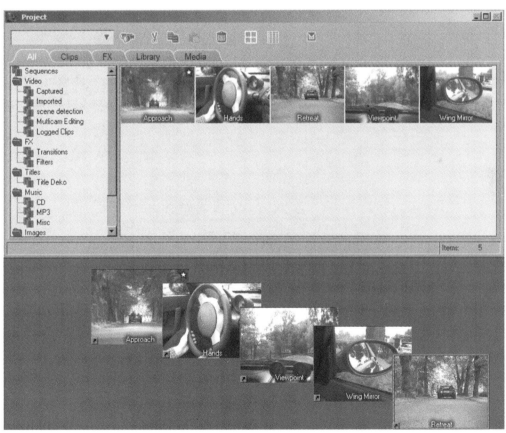

Figure 5.11 Five clips have been dragged onto the desktop creating five overlapping Storyboard elements. This overlapping order is how playback order is determined.

CREATING THE STORYBOARD

Show the First and Last Frames

A Picon can also be set to display the first and last frame of a clip. This is known as displaying the Head and Tails.

If you hold down the Alt key and left-click this clip, the media clip will play inside this Picon.

Right-click a Storyboard element and select Picon View > Mark In/Out Large (**Figure 5.12**).

This displays the element as shown in **Figure 5.13**.

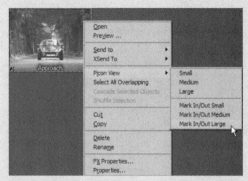

Figure 5.12 The Picon View allows you to set the size of the Picon and its display properties.

Figure 5.13 Here the Picon's display properties have been altered to show both the start and finish point of the clip.

Previewing in the Storyboard

Once you are happy with the Sequence, you'll want to preview it so that you can see if any changes need to be made.

To play a Storyboard Sequence:

1. Do one of the following:
   ▲ Using the left mouse button, drag a lasso around all the clips to highlight them (**Figure 5.14**).
   ▲ Right-click the last clip in the pile and choose Select All Overlapping to highlight all the clips (**Figure 5.15**).

continues on next page

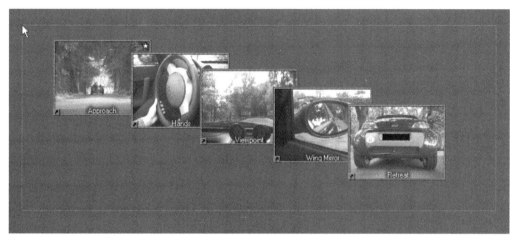

Figure 5.14 Dragging a lasso around the clips will mark each one with a golden frame. This means all the clips have been selected...

Figure 5.15 ... or you can right-click the last clip in the pile and choose Select All Overlapping to highlight all the clips.

2. Once the clips are selected, right-click the last clip in the sequence (don't click any of the others) and select Preview from the pop-up menu (**Figure 5.16**).

3. Once the Clip Viewer is displayed (**Figure 5.17**), press the spacebar or press the Play button to play the sequence back from beginning to end. If the playback order is not correct, read on.

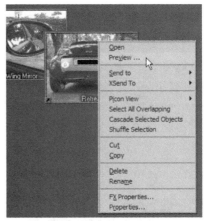

Figure 5.16 Previewing a selection requires you just to right-click the last clip in the pile and choose Preview from the pop-up menu.

Figure 5.17 The Clip Viewer displayed here has been customized with extra buttons to increase its functionality.

Playback order

The order in which Liquid Edition plays the Storyboard elements is determined by the order in which you click them.

◆ The last element clicked is the last one played back.

◆ The first one clicked is the first one played back.

In **Figure 5.18**, you can see that the Storyboard element called Viewpoint has been clicked last and is now on top of the others. The Viewpoint clip will now play last after the Retreat clip, thus ruining the play order.

✔ Tip

■ If one of your clips plays out of sequence, you can reassemble the order by clicking each element once in turn from the first to the last.

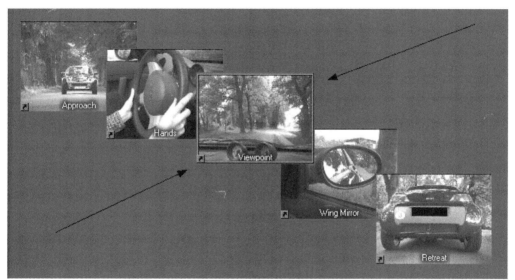

Figure 5.18 In this example, the middle clip (Viewpoint) has been clicked last and is now on top of the pile.

Trimming Clips in the Storyboard

After playback, you may find that some clips have too much footage either at the beginning or the end of the clip. To fix this, you need to use the Clip Viewer to trim off the unwanted material (**Figure 5.19**).

The Clip Viewer is a powerful part of the Storyboard interface with a number of interesting features including color correction, scene detection, and audio level adjustment. It is a good idea to explore the potential of this tool even though it might not look that exciting.

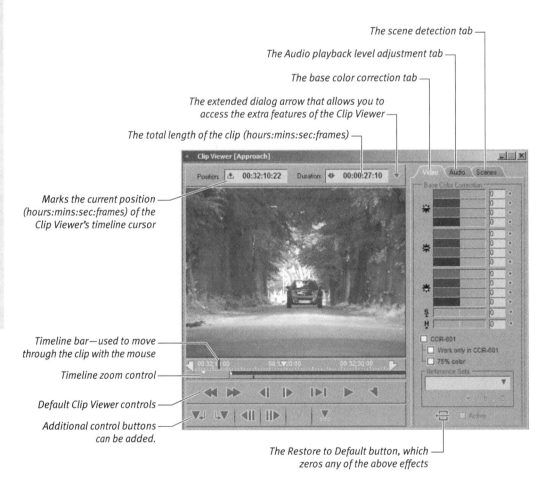

The scene detection tab

The Audio playback level adjustment tab

The base color correction tab

The extended dialog arrow that allows you to access the extra features of the Clip Viewer

The total length of the clip (hours:mins:sec:frames)

Marks the current position (hours:mins:sec:frames) of the Clip Viewer's timeline cursor

Timeline bar—used to move through the clip with the mouse

Timeline zoom control

Default Clip Viewer controls

Additional control buttons can be added.

The Restore to Default button, which zeros any of the above effects

Figure 5.19 The Clip Viewer is used extensively in the Storyboard area to trim unwanted footage from individual clips. The Clip Viewer shown here has been customized with additional tool buttons.

Figure 5.20 The left side of the Clip Viewer shows the Mark-In point that has been added to the clip.

Figure 5.21 The right side of the Clip Viewer shows the Mark-Out point that has been added to the clip.

To open a clip in the Clip Viewer:

Do one of the following:

◆ Double-click a clip in the Project Browser to open it up inside the Clip Viewer.

◆ Right-click and select Open.

If this sends the clip to the Source Viewer, then you are probably using a dual-screen display. For advice on this, see the sidebar "Sending a Clip to the Clip Viewer When in Dual-Screen Mode," later in this chapter.

To set mark-in and mark-out points in the Clip Viewer:

1. Once the clip is loaded into the Clip Viewer, use the mouse or the arrow keys to look for the best place for your clip to start—your new in point.

   This is called scrubbing and is discussed in the sidebar "Scrubbing Explained," on the next page.

2. Once you have found the ideal start to your clip—the in point—press the I key on the keyboard or click the Mark-In Point button.

   You will see that a small Mark-In Point icon has now been added to the Timeline of the Clip Viewer (**Figure 5.20**).

3. To select a point where you would like your clip to finish—the out point—scrub through the clip again until you find the optimal point, and then press the O key or click the Mark-Out Point button.

   A small Mark-Out Point icon has now been added to the Timeline of the Clip Viewer (**Figure 5.21**).

continues on next page

TRIMMING CLIPS IN THE STORYBOARD

4. Use the Zoom tool to reduce the view if you can't see both the mark-in and the mark-out points on the Timeline display (**Figure 5.22**).

5. Right click the Clip Viewer toolbar and select Player>Play In to Out to play back the clip from the new points you have just defined.

6. You can set a different mark-in or mark-out point simply by moving the cursor to a new point and pressing the I or the O key again.

✔ **Tip**

■ The Play In to Out button ▶ is not present by default and must be added to the Clip Viewer toolbar. See Chapter 1 for details on customizing interfaces.

Figure 5.22 The Zoom tool in the bottom left of the illustration can be used to scale the Timeline. When the cursor is placed over the Zoom tool, a magnifying glass appears next to it.

TRIMMING CLIPS IN THE STORYBOARD

Scrubbing Explained

Scrubbing is a term used when the Timeline cursor is moved manually through each frame, rather than being played back. Scrubbing can be performed using either the mouse or the keyboard.

To move the Timeline cursor quickly to the point you want, use the mouse by:

1. Placing the white arrow onto the Timeline of the Clip Viewer

2. Holding down the left mouse key

3. Moving the mouse to the left or right

If your mouse is equipped with a wheel, this too can be used to step forward or backward one frame at a time.

If you want to move the Timeline cursor with a little more accuracy, then use the keyboard arrows. This allows you to step through each frame one at a time. Holding down the arrow key will move the clip forward or backward at speed.

The J, K, and L keys can also be used with the Clip Viewer. K stops playback, L plays the clip forward a little faster each time it is pressed, and J plays the clip backward a little faster each time it is pressed.

✔ Tips

- Hitting Home or End will take you to the first or last frame of your clip. However, if this is a Subclip, then hitting the Home or End key will take you to the mark-in and mark-out points of the master clip, not the Subclip.

- The extended dialog arrow is always grayed out if you open a Storyboard element in the Clip Viewer. To use the advanced features of the Clip Viewer, you must double-click a clip inside the Project Browser. This is because a Storyboard element is a copy of the original clip, and as a result, you can only alter its mark-in and mark-out points.

Sending a Clip to the Clip Viewer When in Dual-Screen Mode

When you are in dual-screen mode, a clip is sent to the Source Viewer instead of the Clip Viewer. To overcome this, right-click inside the right window of the Project Browser and select Project Properties from the list. This brings up the Project Properties screen. The center section of this screen gives you the option of what Liquid Edition should do when you double-click a clip. Change this from the default to Load Clip into Clip Viewer. You can change this back again at any time.

Mark-In and Mark-Out Points

Mark-in and mark-out points are the basic currency of any nonlinear editing program, and it is important to understand the concept.

Remember: adding either a mark-in or mark-out point does not physically alter the original clip. It merely tells the program to ignore any material that falls outside of these two points.

For a further explication of nonlinear editing, see Chapter 1.

Trimming a Storyboard element

You can also directly trim a clip (or Storyboard element) without opening the Clip Viewer. While this has limited potential for editing, it does create a very quick way of previewing a clip.

To open a media clip without using the Clip Viewer:

1. Make sure the Project Browser is displaying the clips in Picon View and then select the Picon you want to view by clicking it once.

2. Hold down the Alt key and double-click the element.

   The Picon plays inside its own little thumbnail (**Figure 5.23**) and a small Timeline appears underneath it.

To trim a clip inside its own Picon:

1. Press the spacebar once to stop playback.

   It's now possible to move the clip backward and forward, either frame by frame using the left and right arrow keys, or quickly using the mouse.

2. Pressing the I key on the keyboard will set a mark-in point inside the Picon. Pressing O on the keyboard will set the mark-out point.

Figure 5.23 A Storyboard element playing inside its own picon.

Other Uses for the Storyboard

In addition to creating your Storyboard Sequence, you can achieve a number of other tasks while still in the Storyboard interface. You'll accomplish most of these tasks using the advanced features of the Clip Viewer, but you can also add various filters to each clip, creating some basic visual effects without leaving the Storyboard. You accomplish this using the FX library.

Adding filters and other FX

In truth, adding a filter to a Storyboard clip has limited value and this operation is probably best left until the clip is on the Timeline. However, if you want to use a simple effect, such as zooming in on a picture or adding a Lens Flare effect, then it is possible to do this from within the Storyboard.

✔ Tip

- Transitions can't be added to clips in Storyboard mode. You must move to the Timeline to use them.

To add a clip FX filter to a Storyboard clip:

1. With the Storyboard interface open, click the Library tab and select the Editors Rack in the Realtime Clip FX folder in the right window of the Project Browser (**Figure 5.24**).

   This displays all the video filters available to you.

2. To display the filters as in Figure 5.24, click once on the Name tab.

3. Select a simple filter (in Figure 5.24 the 2D Editor CPU has been selected), and double-click it.

   This opens the Effect Editor interface.

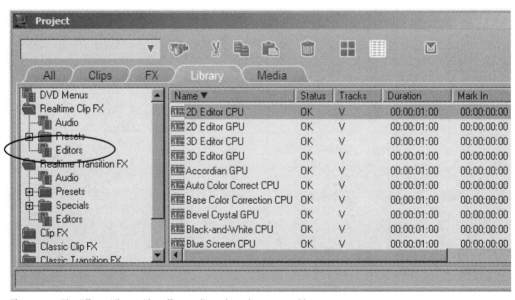

Figure 5.24 The Effects Library. The effects editors have been sorted by name.

OTHER USES FOR THE STORYBOARD

4. Click the All tab to display your clips if they are not already displayed (**Figure 5.25**).

5. Click once on any one of your clips inside the Project Browser.

A white star appears in the clip's top-right corner, and the clip itself is displayed inside the editor.

continues on next page

Figure 5.25 The 2D Editor window opens and the Project Browser automatically moves to the bottom of the screen.

6. You can now alter the effect in any way you choose. In **Figure 5.26** the clip has been flipped horizontally to give the illusion of a right-hand drive car.

7. When you have finished editing, click the Running Man button 🏃 in the top-right corner of the editor.

✔ Tip

■ When you exit the editor, you will be presented with half a Storyboard interface hidden behind the Source and Timeline windows. Return to a full-sized Storyboard interface by clicking the Eye icon and selecting the Storyboard layout. Or press Shift+F3 on the keyboard.

Figure 5.26 Here, the Mirror tab has been opened (the small triangle next to the word Mirror was clicked), and the Flip Horizontal box has been checked.

Figure 5.27 Right-clicking a clip displays this pop-up menu. At the very bottom is the FX Properties selection.

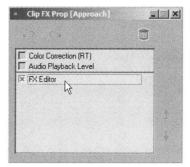

Figure 5.28 The Clip FX Prop window. Here you can deselect an effect by clicking the X or by highlighting the effect and clicking the Bin button.

To remove an effect from a clip:

1. Right-click any clip with a white or blue star in the top right corner and select FX Properties from the pop-up menu (**Figure 5.27**).

   The Clip FX Prop window appears (**Figure 5.28**).

2. *Do one of the following:*

   ▲ Deselect the effect by clicking the X.

   ▲ Delete the effect by clicking once on the name of the effect and then click the Bin button ⬛ in the top-right corner.

✔ Tip

■ The advantage of deselecting the effect is that later you can add it back again by simply putting the X back in the box. Clicking the Bin button means it is gone forever.

Advanced features of the Clip Viewer

The Clip Viewer has an extended dialog arrow that gives you access to the Base Color Corrector, the Audio Playback tool, and the Scene Detection tool. Their use within the Storyboard is limited; however, the main features are listed below.

- The Base Color Corrector can be used to quickly correct basic color problems, to add a color cast to a clip (for example, blue for a night effect), or to turn a clip to black and white quickly by turning the saturation down to –255.

- The Audio Playback tool can be used to quickly adjust clips with too much noise, such as those of a running car.

- The Scene Detection tool is probably the most useful of the three. In Storyboard mode, you can use it to divide up long clips quickly and easily.

All of these features are discussed in greater depth throughout this book. Refer to the index for their location.

Sending to the Timeline

Once you have created the first assembly of your sequence, it is time to send the whole thing to the Timeline so that you can add titles, apply special effects, and make other alterations that are beyond the ability of the Storyboard editor.

✔ Tip

■ Before you send the Storyboard to the Timeline, switch back to the Timeline view (Shift+F2) and check the position of the Timeline cursor. Ideally this should be at the beginning of the Timeline, but you may want it somewhere else.

To send to the Timeline:

1. Do one of the following:
   ▲ Drag a lasso around all your clips (**Figure 5.29**).
   ▲ Right-click the last element and click Select All Overlapping (**Figure 5.30**).

2. Right-click the last element in the sequence and select Send To > Timeline from the pop-up menu (**Figure 5.31**).

continues on next page

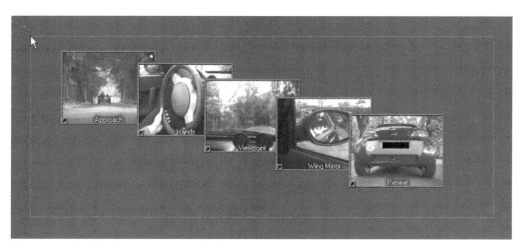

Figure 5.29 A Storyboard Sequence surrounded by a dragged lasso.

Figure 5.30 An alternative method of highlighting all the clips in a Storyboard Sequence is to right-click the last clip and choose Select All Overlapping.

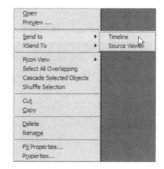

Figure 5.31 The Send to > Timeline option will send the sequence to the Timeline cursor's current position.

3. Switch to the Timeline view by selecting the Eye button  or by pressing Shift+F2 on the keyboard.

Your sequence is now on the Timeline (**Figure 5.32**).

✔ Tip

■ In the preceding example, the clips were sent to the default track Name 5; however, it is possible to send them to the track of your choice. For more details on this process, called track mapping, see Chapter 6.

Figure 5.32 The Storyboard Sequence after it has been sent to the Timeline. Mission accomplished.

FINE-TUNING YOUR EDIT

The Timeline view is the center hub of Liquid Edition. Once the media clips have been digitized or imported, organized into racks and folders, and, perhaps, roughly assembled in Liquid Edition's Storyboard mode, it's time to fine-tune the edit and prepare it for any special effects you might want to add.

In Chapter 5, you learned how to use the Storyboard mode to create a basic sequence that you then arranged into the rough order you needed. Then, in the last step, you sent this sequence to the Timeline for further editing. This chapter covers the various techniques you'll need to accomplish this fine-tuning and also those techniques you'll need to get the most from the interface, thus increasing your workflow and your productivity. You'll learn how to navigate the Timeline and insert media clips, but one general tip that you should learn right now is that a single right-click can go a long way in Liquid Edition, whichever interface you are working on. A simple right-click can expose a myriad of shortcut menus, allowing you to burrow quickly and deeply into the core power of Liquid Edition.

Opening the Timeline

If you have just finished Chapter 5, your interface will probably still be in Storyboard view. This needs to be changed to Timeline view in order to progress with the next section of task-based instructions.

✔ Tips

■ If you are still in the Storyboard view, don't forget to send your Sequence to the Timeline by following the instructions at the end of Chapter 5 before swapping over to Timeline view.

■ If you are using a dual-screen setup, both Storyboard and Timeline will already be visible and this task will not be necessary.

To open the Timeline interface:

1. Click the Eye button 👁 to open the various view options (**Figure 6.1**).

2. Click the Timeline icon (**Figure 6.2**) so that your Liquid Edition desktop looks like **Figure 6.3**.

✔ Tip

■ Single-screen users can also access the Timeline interface by pressing Shift+F2.

Figure 6.1 View options for single-screen users. Dual-screen users, see Chapter 5.

Figure 6.2 Icon to select the Timeline view.

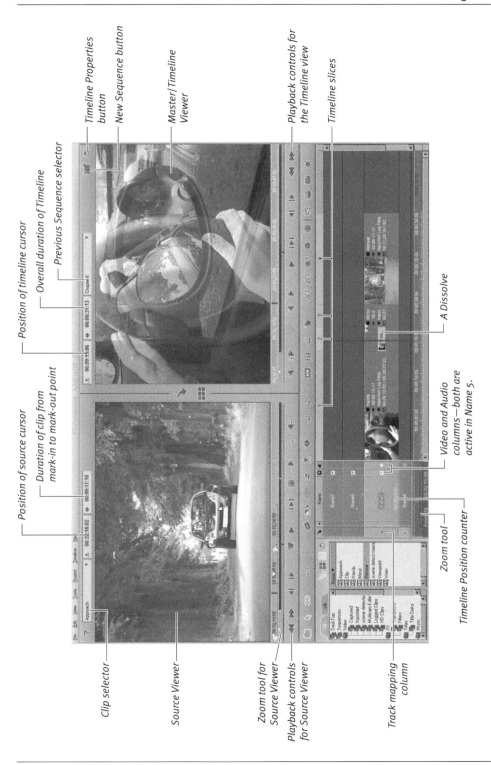

Figure 6.3 The Timeline view showing the Project Browser and the Sequence constructed in Chapter 5.

OPENING THE TIMELINE

Clip selector

Position of source cursor

Duration of clip from mark-in to mark-out point

Source Viewer

Zoom tool for Source Viewer

Playback controls for Source Viewer

Track mapping column

Zoom tool

Timeline Position counter

Position of timeline cursor

Overall duration of Timeline

Previous Sequence selector

Timeline Properties button

New Sequence button

Master/Timeline Viewer

Playback controls for the Timeline view

Timeline slices

A Dissolve

Video and Audio columns—both are active in Name 5.

Navigating the Timeline

The rules for moving around the Timeline are the same as those you learned when you were dealing with the Clip Viewer in Chapter 5, but if you skipped that chapter, the concepts of scrubbing, zooming, and undoing your mistakes are covered here. Remember, it is very important that you learn to use the mouse and keyboard shortcuts effectively.

Scrubbing the Timeline

Unlike with the Source Viewer, you can scrub the Timeline from two places: directly under the clips, or directly under the Master/Timeline Viewer.

To scrub the Timeline:

1. Make sure the Master/Timeline Viewer has a red border indicating that it is selected.

2. Scrub by doing one of the following:

   ▲ Click the Timeline bar, hold down the left mouse button, and drag the cursor left or right (**Figure 6.4**). If your mouse is equipped with a wheel, use it to step forward or backward one frame at a time.

   ▲ Hold down the Alt key and hold down the left mouse button and drag the cursor anywhere over the Timeline clips.

   ▲ Use the keyboard arrows to step through each frame, one at a time. To move the clip forward or backward faster, hold down the left or right arrow key. To go even faster, hold down the Shift key at the same time.

   ▲ Use the J, K, and L keys on your keyboard. K stops playback; L plays the clip forward a little faster each time it is pressed, and J plays the clip backward a little faster each time it is pressed.

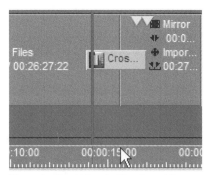

Figure 6.4 Scrubbing the Timeline with the mouse.

Figure 6.5 Magnification at Zoom 1 will display one frame per Timeline mark.

Figure 6.6 Magnification at Zoom 37 will show a two-hour Timeline (approximately) completely on a single monitor.

Two Cursor Lines when in Zoom 1

When the Zoom tool has been expanded to the Zoom 1 setting, the cursor displays a bold red line followed by a faint red line (**Figure 6.7**).

The gap between these two lines is a single frame and will always be the one being displayed in the Master/Timeline Viewer. Any cuts or insertions you make will occur on the dark red line, not the faint red line.

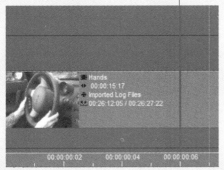

The dark red line at the start of the frame being displayed.

Figure 6.7 At Zoom 1, the timeline cursor brackets which frame is currently being displayed.

✔ Tips

- By using the arrow keys and/or the mouse wheel, you can be frame perfect when scrubbing the Timeline.

- When scrubbing the Timeline, you won't hear any audio; this is because, by default, audio tracks are ignored at all times except when you are previewing. Details on activating audio so you can hear the media clip during scrubbing can be found in Chapter 7.

Using the Zoom tool

To display more detail on the Timeline, or to see a whole hour-long project in one screen, you'll need to use the Zoom tool.

To use the Zoom tool:

- ◆ Using the mouse, place the arrow pointer over the Zoom tool and drag it to the left to show a higher degree of magnification (**Figure 6.5**) or to the right to show a decreased level of magnification (**Figure 6.6**).

✔ Tip

- Pressing the up and down arrows on the keyboard will also cause the Timeline to zoom in and out. You can do this while the Timeline is playing.

Using Undo/Redo

Undo in Liquid Edition has the universally recognized shortcut Ctrl+Z. However the Undo command has some restrictions that can seem confusing to the beginner. The basic rule for the Undo command is that it only affects certain elements on the Timeline— namely, *the position, duration, and existence of either a media clip or a transition.*

Other elements, such as filters, Timewarp, and any audio alterations are not affected by the Timeline Undo because they have their own integral Undo functions. See Chapters 7 and 9 for full details on how to undo these elements.

✔ Tips

- If you are unsure what effect using the Undo command will have, you can look at a complete Undo history by Ctrl+Shift+left-clicking the Undo button  (**Figure 6.8**). Press Escape (Esc) to exit the Undo History screen.

- The Redo command also performs as expected, taking the user one step forward.

- Double-clicking any of the Undos or Redos displayed in the history will undo or redo that particular command.

Figure 6.8 The complete Undo history for this Sequence. This history shows 61 possible Undos, which can be selected in any order.

Moving Clips Around the Timeline

Once a media clip is on the Timeline, it can be manipulated separately from its Project Browser parent. That means you can copy and paste the media clip to other parts of the Timeline, drag existing clips around the Timeline, trim the clip's mark-in and mark-out points, or cut the clip into separate media clips live on the Timeline with the razor blade.

Audio Grouping

The examples in this chapter show clips that are grouped—the audio has been folded inside the video clip so that only the video clip is shown. This is known as *embedded audio* and is explained in greater depth in Chapter 7.

To better and more easily understand the concepts outlined in this chapter, you should enable audio grouping and thus display your own samples using the embedded format; as opposed to the default which is disbanded audio and displays the audio on a separate track to the video.

To use embedded audio, simply right-click the small arrow at the top of the Name column and select Insert Grouped (**Figure 6.9**). Insert Grouped needs to be selected each time you start a new sequence. This automatically deactivates the audio tracks and causes all audio to become embedded.

The advantage of embedded or grouped audio is that you are less likely to send the audio out of sync while editing. When you first start to use Liquid Edition, you will find that this one setting is invaluable in that it helps you avoid the stress of accidentally sending your clips out of sync.

Click here to bring up the Grouping menu.

Figure 6.9 Selecting grouped audio tracks to force audio embedding.

Copy/cut and paste

These actions follow the Windows convention—you copy a clip into the clipboard (a temporary scratch area) before pasting it somewhere else. It's also possible to cut a clip so that it is removed from its present position and relocated elsewhere.

The Windows shortcuts keys Ctrl+X, Ctrl+C, and Ctrl+V are fully supported when you are using this method.

To copy/cut and paste a clip(s):

1. Select one media clip by clicking it, or select several by holding down Ctrl and clicking as many as you like (**Figure 6.10**). You can also drag a lasso around all the clips you want to select (**Figure 6.11**).

Figure 6.10 Use the Ctrl key to selectively highlight those clips you want...

Figure 6.11 ...or drag a lasso around those that you want.

Figure 6.12 Selected clips are copied into a temporary area for transferring via...

2. Press Ctrl+C or right-click the clip(s) and select Copy > Selected Clips (**Figure 6.12**).

It is also possible to use Ctrl+X to delete the clip and paste it elsewhere. But you can only cut one media clip at any one time.

3. Move the timeline cursor to the position to which you want these clips copied and press Ctrl+V, or right-click and select Paste (**Figure 6.13**).

continues on next page

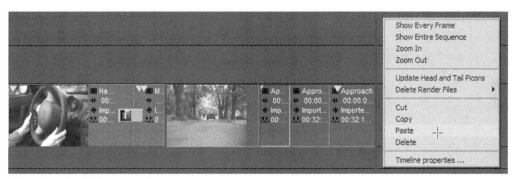

Figure 6.13 ...the Paste command.

✔ Tip

■ You can also copy a media clip by selecting the clip(s), holding down the Ctrl key, and dragging the clip from wherever it was on the Timeline (**Figure 6.14**) to its new position (**Figure 6.15**).

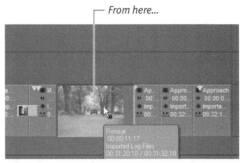

Figure 6.14 By holding down the Ctrl key, you can create an exact copy of a clip...

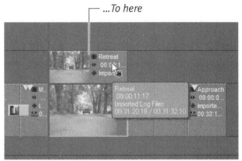

Figure 6.15 ...and drag it to anywhere on the Timeline.

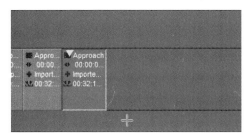

Figure 6.16 Highlight a clip by clicking it once...

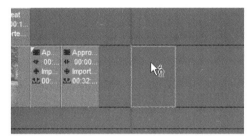

Figure 6.17 ...then drag it to a new position.

Dragging a clip

You can move every element on the Timeline to another location by clicking the media clip and dragging it to a new location. Be careful when doing this because you could accidentally force audio tracks out of sync, if you are using disbanded audio.

The moral of the story is don't ever let your mouse cursor stray far from your Undo button.

To drag and drop a media clip:

1. Click the media clip so that it becomes highlighted (**Figure 6.16**).

2. Hold down the left mouse button and drag the media clip to its new position (**Figure 6.17**).

3. Once you are happy, release the mouse button to drop the clip.

✔ Tips

- Multiple clips can be selected using Shift+Ctrl, or by dragging a lasso around them.

- Clicking the Select after playline button will highlight all those clips to the right of the Timeline, enabling you to move them all at the same time.

- As you drag the clip, it will try to latch onto marker points or the mark-in and mark-out points of other clips. Toggle this action off by holding the Shift key down while dragging a media clip around.

MOVING CLIPS AROUND THE TIMELINE

Using magnets

When you drag a clip on the Timeline, it automatically tries to align itself with any neighboring clip using magnets. The magnet symbol appears by default on the left side of the mark-in point of the media clip you are dragging. It will be attracted to any mark-in or mark-out point of a clip already on the Timeline, either on the same track as the one on which you want to place your clip (**Figure 6.18**), or on a track directly above or below it (**Figure 6.19**).

Sometimes it may not be convenient to align your clip to this point; in this case, you can change the magnet's polarity on the fly.

To change the magnet's polarity:

1. After making sure you have at least one other clip on the Timeline, drag a clip from the Project Browser toward it (**Figure 6.20**).

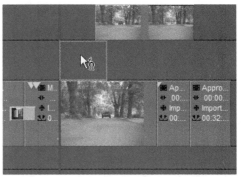

Figure 6.18 The magnet has latched onto the mark-in point of the clip underneath it...

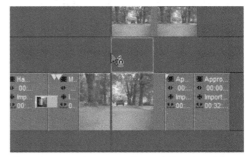

Figure 6.19 ...and now onto the mark-in point of the one above.

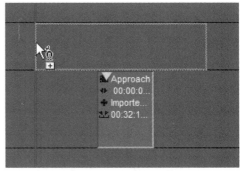

Figure 6.20 The default polarity for the clip magnet is the media clip's mark-in point.

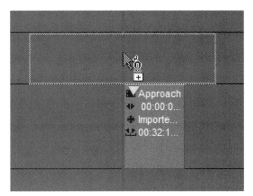

Figure 6.21 Pressing the Alt key once will change this polarity to the exact middle of the clip.

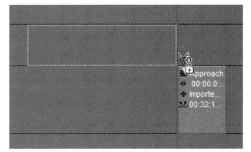

Figure 6.22 Pressing Alt again will shift the polarity to the media clip's mark-out point.

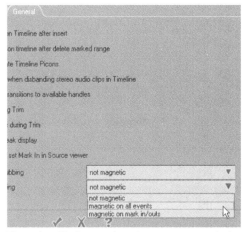

Figure 6.23 The bottom drop-down menu controls the behavior of the clip magnets.

2. Still holding down the left mouse button, press Alt once.

   The magnet shifts polarity to the center section of the clip (**Figure 6.21**).

3. Still holding down the left mouse button, press Alt again.

   The magnet shifts polarity to the right side, or mark-out of the clip (**Figure 6.22**).

   Once a clip is released, the magnetic polarity defaults back to the mark-in point of the clip.

To turn the magnet off:

Do one of the following:

◆ Right-click the Timeline and select Timeline Properties. Then select the General tab and change the selection in the Default magnet for editing drop-down list to suit your needs (**Figure 6.23**). Click the check mark to apply this change.

◆ Hold down the Shift key while dragging; this temporarily toggles the magnets off for as long as you are holding the key down. You'll find this option particularly useful if you are dragging a media clip onto a very complex Timeline. This is because the mark-in point will try to latch onto every single event it passes, which will make the drag-and-drop process frustratingly slow.

✔ Tip

■ A clip that is already on the Timeline will switch to a right-side polarity the first time you hit the ALT key and the middle polarity on the second time you hit the ALT key.

Trimming Clips

The process of getting rid of unwanted material either at the beginning or end of a clip is called *trimming*. In Chapter 5, you accomplished this using the Clip Viewer, but it's also possible to trim a clip in the Source Viewer or on the Timeline using the Trim Editor.

Trimming on the Timeline

This is a quick and dirty method and is only really useful when you see a clip that you can quickly and simply adjust on the Timeline. This method lacks sophistication and can lead to alignment problems if you are using Film Style (see the "Edit Styles" sidebar for details on Film Style and Overwrite Style), but any errors you make are only an Undo key away from being fixed.

To trim a clip on the Timeline:

1. Select the clip you want to trim by clicking once on its mark-in or mark-out point.

   If you are in Overwrite Style, a red handle appears on the clip (**Figure 6.24**); a yellow one appears if you are in Film Style (**Figure 6.25**).

2. While holding the left mouse button down, drag the clip to the left or to the right.

   If you are in Overwrite Style, a gap appears (**Figure 6.26**).

   If you are in Film Style, any neighboring clips to the immediate right shuffle up or down the Timeline depending on which way you are dragging the mark-in or mark-out point (**Figure 6.27**).

Figure 6.24 A red handle on the mark-out point of a media clip indicating Overwrite Style.

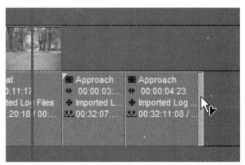

Figure 6.25 A yellow handle on the mark-out point indicating Film Style is toggled on.

Mark-out point trimmed in this direction

◄ -

Figure 6.26 In Overwrite Style, a gap is left when a mark-out point is dragged down the Timeline.

Neighboring clip moves up the Timeline.

- - - - - - - - - - - ➤

Figure 6.27 In Film Style, no gap is left because the neighboring clips follow the trim down the Timeline.

Figure 6.28 The Trim tool activated by holding down the Ctrl key and pressing an arrow key.

3. You can now drag this clip in or out depending on whether you want to increase or decrease its length. However, you can only increase the clip to its clip-in point where the physical length of the media ends.

Unless there is a non-real-time filter on the clip, as you drag it, the result is displayed in realtime in the Master/Timeline Viewer.

4. When you are happy with the result, release the mouse key.

✔ Tips

- If you hold down Ctrl and use the keyboard arrows, you will be able to trim the clip one frame at a time (**Figure 6.28**).

- If you are seeing performance problems when trimming clips on the Timeline, see the sidebar, "Automatic Picon Update" later in this chapter for a possible solution.

TRIMMING CLIPS

Edit Styles

Liquid Edition has two edit styles that affect the way clips behave on the Timeline: Overwrite Style and Film Style. You can change between these by clicking once on the toggle button that sits between the Source and Master/Timeline Viewers.

 Overwrite Style: This is the default setting when Liquid Edition is launched. It does pretty much what it says on the box—any clip you send or drag to the Timeline will overwrite the clip(s) at the timeline cursor's position.

Figures 6.29 and **6.30** show a new clip, Entering car. It is brought into the Timeline and overwrites the first few seconds of the Approach clip.

This is the default editing style. Clips sent to the Timeline do not affect the order or (more importantly) the audio synchronization of the other clips.

continues on next page

Figure 6.29 A new clip dragged onto and over the first clip on the Timeline.

This clip has now overwritten...   ...the beginning of this clip.   All other clips do not move.

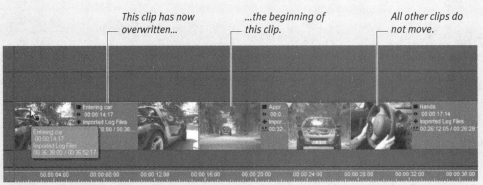

Figure 6.30 Once the media clip is dropped, the beginning of the original Timeline media clip is overwritten.

Edit Styles *continued*

Film Style: This mode is slightly more complex, and using it on a crowded Timeline is slightly risky. Primarily, you'll use Film Style to insert a clip without losing any footage from any clips already on the Timeline. However, because added clips will move any existing clips to the right (or "up" the Timeline), to make room for any new clips, you can lose audio sync if not all of the tracks are active (see the "Audio Sync Issues" sidebar for details).

Figure 6.31 shows the Entering car clip dragged to the mark-in point of the Approach clip. Once it is placed here, all other clips to the right move up the Timeline.

Figure 6.32 shows what happens if the same clip is sent to the start of the Timeline. When you release it, all the clips move up to make room for this new clip, but a gap is also created. This is because gaps are also included in the Timeline when you are using Film Style.

continues on next page

New clip inserted here...

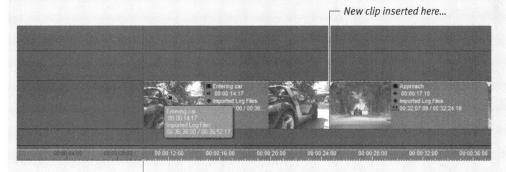

...*existing clip moves up to here*

Figure 6.31 In Film Style, all other clips will move when a new clip is placed on the Timeline.

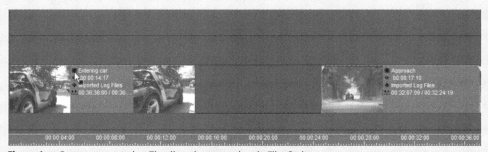

Figure 6.32 Gaps are counted as Timeline elements when in Film Style.

Edit Styles *continued*

If you try to close this gap by dragging one clip toward the other, you will see a No Entry symbol (**Figure 6.33**) indicating that this is not allowed. In fact, you can only drag clips "down" the timeline when you're in Film Style. To move them the other way, you have to switch back to Overwrite Style.

Figure 6.33 Dragging a clip up the Timeline toward other clips is not allowed in Film Style.

Audio Sync Issues

As discussed earlier, all the examples in this chapter show clips that have embedded audio—audio that is included inside the video track—for a very good reason. When clips have embedded audio, they are in the safest format for being trimmed and manipulated in Film Style. This is because a media clip with an embedded audio track will not be affected by a clip inserted in Film Style. It will always remain in sync.

Figure 6.34 shows a clip dragged onto a part of the timeline containing a clip that has its audio track disbanded (the opposite of embedded). If you compare the marker on the Approach clip to the marker on the audio track, you can see that they are now badly out of sync because the new clip has pushed the old video clip up the Timeline while leaving the audio track untouched.

For more details on audio options when you are editing the Timeline, see Chapter 7. But at least for the rest of this chapter, I recommend that you work only with embedded audio.

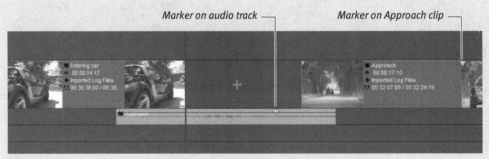

Figure 6.34 When not embedded, audio can be sent out of sync when using Film Style.

Trimming with the Trim Editor

The Trim Editor is an area that some users find challenging, partly because of Liquid Edition's single-track Timeline, and partly because visualizing the final trim can cause some confusion. However, the problems only really occur once transitions are used; I deal with this problem more fully in Chapter 8. For the moment, we'll restrict this part of the tutorial to looking at trimming a hard cut.

To use the Trim Editor:

1. Make sure the timeline cursor is approximately over the point where the two clips meet on the Timeline. The Trim Editor always opens to the nearest cut, and that might not always be the one you think it is, so check first.

2. Open the Trim Editor by clicking the Trim Editor button 🔳 or by pressing F5. The Trim Editor opens displaying the left clip—the outgoing clip—in the left window and the right clip—the incoming clip—in the right window (**Figure 6.35**). By default, both the left and right windows have a black selection bar directly underneath them. This means that both clips will be trimmed at the same time.

3. Press the right arrow key. Both clips advance one frame up the Timeline; the left one (the outgoing clip) will get longer if it can, the right one (the incoming clip) will get shorter.

continues on next page

Preparing the Timeline for the Next Task

In order to better understand the Trim Editor, prepare your Timeline by placing a short clip on the Timeline, and then by dragging the timeline cursor to about the half-way point of this clip. Insert a cut by pressing the Add Edit button 🔳 or by pressing the Period key (.) on the keyboard.

This needs to be done because clips cannot be trimmed beyond their own physical length; however, a clip that has been cut using the method above will not suffer this limitation and will help you to better understand how the Trim Editor functions.

Figure 6.35 The Trim Editor

Restore button

Outgoing selection bar

Slip Trim tool

Play controls

Frames plus or minus

Incoming selection bar

Outgoing clip

Duration of outgoing clip

Position on Timeline

Duration of incoming clip

Incoming clip

4. Press the left arrow and the opposite will happen.

In both cases, any neighboring clips to the immediate right are not affected by the changes made here (**Figure 6.36**).

In both cases the Frames counter increases in the positive direction for each clip.

Outgoing clip is now 10 frames longer.

Incoming clip is now 10 frames shorter.

The neighboring clip retains its position.

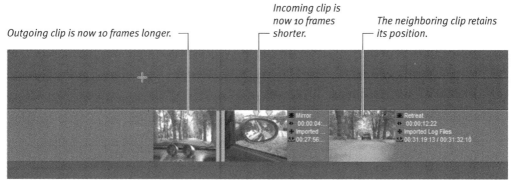

Figure 6.36 A simple trim of both clips at the same time.

Trimming only one clip

The previous example trims both clips together, but you may only want to make one of these clips longer or shorter. To do this, you simply activate either the Outgoing or the Incoming selection bar (see Figure 6.33). However, when you trim only one clip at a time, the neighboring clips to the right will shuffle up or down the Timeline, depending on which way you trim your clip.

This is similar to the Film Style edit detailed in the "Edit Styles" Sidebar earlier in this chapter.

To adjust just one clip using the Trim Editor:

1. Open the Trim Editor by pressing F5.

2. Press the P key once to switch the black bar to the right window.

   This selects the incoming clip to be trimmed (**Figure 6.37**).

3. Press the P key twice to switch the black bar to the left window.

   This selects the outgoing clip to be trimmed (**Figure 6.38**).

4. To decrease the size of the clip by one frame, press the right arrow now.

   Any neighboring clips to the immediate right shuffle down the Timeline so that no gap is created.

   Pressing the left arrow does the opposite.

✔ Tips

- Clicking the Play preview button ![icon] in the center of the clip will play approximately 2 seconds of the incoming clip followed by 2 seconds of the outgoing clip in a continuous loop.

- Clicking the cursor in the middle of both windows will highlight both selection bars.

- The buttons ![icon] ![icon] will jump the trim 10 frames forward or backward.

- You cannot trim beyond the physical length of a clip.

Figure 6.37 The black bar on the right means only the incoming clip will be trimmed.

Figure 6.38 The black bar on the left means only the outgoing clip will be trimmed.

Editing with Slip Trim

If you want to trim a clip on the Timeline but you don't want all the neighboring clips moving up or down, you must use the Slip Trim tool. This allows you to edit both the mark-in and mark-out points of a clip or clips at the same time.

To edit with Slip Trim:

1. Open the Trim Editor by clicking the Trim Editor button ▣ or by pressing F5.

2. Select which clip you want to trim by pressing the P key to move the selection bar. By default, you will edit both clips at the same time (**Figure 6.39**).

3. Click the Slip Key button ◉.

   The mark-in and mark-out points for the selected clip(s) become highlighted.

4. Press the left or right arrow key to adjust the clips down or up the Timeline respectively.

   Because both mark-out points are being adjusted by an equal amount to the mark-in point, any neighboring clips to the immediate right are not affected by the changes made here.

✔ Tips

- This procedure is identical when selecting just the incoming or just the outgoing clip and the results are the same. Only those clips being trimmed will be affected; the rest of the Timeline will remain intact.

- Again, you cannot trim beyond the maximum length of a clip.

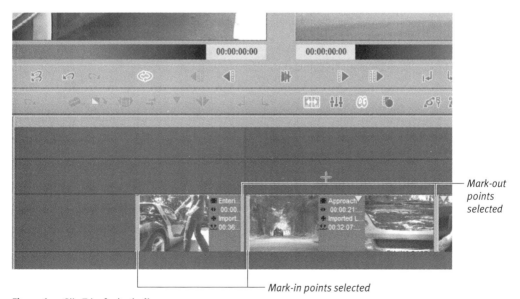

Mark-out points selected

Mark-in points selected

Figure 6.39 Slip Trim for both clips.

TRIMMING CLIPS

Automatic Picon Update

By default, Liquid Edition updates the heads and tails of each clip automatically. If you have a slightly slower system, this may cause you considerable performance problems when you're trimming a clip on a particularly crowded Timeline.

To turn off the automatic updates, simply right-click anywhere in the Timeline and select Timeline Properties from the pop-up menu. Then, switch to the General tab and uncheck the Automatically update Timeline Picons box (**Figure 6.40**).

Once this has been set, you will need to manually update the Picons each time you trim a clip. To do this, simply right-click anywhere in the Timeline and select Update Head and Tail Picons from the pop-up menu (**Figure 6.41**).

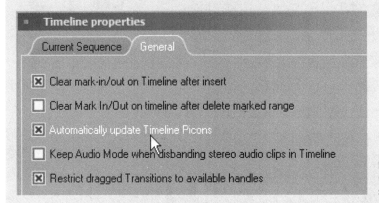

Figure 6.41 Automatic update of Timeline Picons is shown here as toggled on.

Figure 6.40 Manually updating the heads and tails.

TRIMMING CLIPS

Cut created here.

Figure 6.42 The razor blade can divide a clip in two.

Cutting Clips

A cut is created on a media clip usually for one of two reasons: the clip contained two scenes and both require individual trimming, or the middle of the clip is not wanted and needs to be deleted.

Liquid Edition uses the razor blade tool to cut a clip.

To cut a clip:

1. Scrub through the media clip until you find the place where you want to create a cut. You can make the cut accurate by using the arrow keys to step through one frame at a time.

2. Click the Razor button [img] or hit the period (.).

A cut is created, dividing the clip into two pieces (**Figure 6.42**).

Active, Inactive, and Protected Tracks

Each track in Liquid Edition has three natural states: Active, Inactive, and Protected.

Only those tracks that are active can be affected by the razor blade. Active tracks are, by default, Name 5, Name 4, and Name 3.

Active tracks are always light blue; Inactive tracks are dark gray (**Figure 6.43**). You can change their state by simply clicking directly on the name track to change the color.

Clips can be dragged to either an Inactive or Active track, but the razor blade and the insertion of Dissolves (see Chapter 8) and Cross Fades (Chapter 7) will not affect or be applied to Inactive tracks.

A Protected track is one that can no longer be edited. To protect a track, right-click the

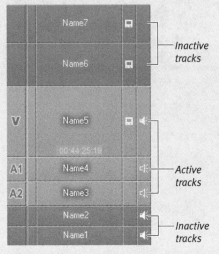

Figure 6.43 Name 5, 4, and 3 are active; the rest are inactive.

track's name and select Protect from the list of choices. This turns the whole track—including the clip(s) on the Timeline—light gray and indicates that the clips are now fixed and cannot be altered or added to in any way (**Figure 6.44**).

To unprotect a track, right-click the name again and deselect Protect by clicking it.

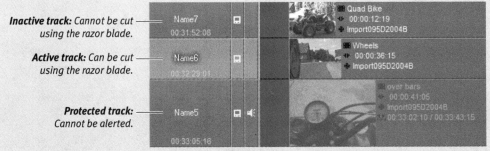

Inactive track: Cannot be cut using the razor blade.

Active track: Can be cut using the razor blade.

Protected track: Cannot be alerted.

Figure 6.44 A Protected, an Active, and an Inactive track.

CUTTING CLIPS

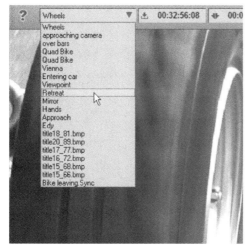

Figure 6.45 The media clip selection menu.

The Source Viewer

You'll use the Source Viewer primarily for previewing clips when you're in the Timeline view. It's a very simple interface that contains a number of useful tricks including the trimming and insertion of media clips.

Once you have assembled your edit and trimmed your clips, you will probably need to trim and insert new material such as images or other media clips. You do this via the Source Viewer, where you can preview a clip, trim it by adjusting mark-in and mark-out points, and insert it into the Timeline via drag and drop or by creating a three-point or four-point edit at the Timeline cursor position.

To send a clip to the Source Viewer:

Do one of the following:

◆ Double-click the media clip inside the Project Browser.

◆ Right-click the media clip and select Send to Source Viewer.

◆ Drag the clip from the Project Browser and drop it into the Source Viewer.

◆ Click the media clip selection menu and select one of the clips from there (**Figure 6.45**).

Tool Buttons That Should Be Added to the Source Viewer

The Source Viewer is already fairly crowded, but you should add these four buttons to your interface if they are not already there. Chapter 1 contains complete details on how to add a button to any of the Liquid Edition interfaces.

◆ **Go to Next Event** : Used to navigate both mark-in/mark-out points and also markers.

◆ **Open Marker List** : Can be used to edit, rename, and navigate to markers.

◆ **Delete Marker** : Used to delete the currently selected marker.

◆ **Play from Mark-In to Mark-Out** : Used to play a clip from its mark-in to mark-out point rather than its clip-in to clip-out point.

The Zoom tool

Once you have a clip inside the Source Viewer, you can use the Zoom tool to adjust how big the Timeline indicators are.

To use the Zoom tool:

◆ Place the mouse cursor over the Zoom tool so that it turns into a magnifying glass; then left-click and drag it to the left to show a higher degree of magnification or to the right to show a decreased level of magnification (**Figure 6.46**).

✔ Tip

■ Directly to the right of the Zoom tool is a black horizontal line. This indicates how much of the clip you can currently see in the Source Viewer's Timeline. The red mark below this indicates the position of the cursor.

Zoom tool

Black bar indicates visible area.

Figure 6.46 The Zoom tool in action.

Timeline cursor position

Scrubbing a Media Clip

Scrubbing is a term used to describe the timeline cursor being moved manually through each frame rather than being played back. It's primarily used to find an exact position on the Timeline for either placing a special effect or inserting a new clip.

Scrubbing can be performed using either the mouse or the keyboard, or more likely, a combination of both.

You can scrub the Timeline using any of the following methods:

◆ Hold down the left mouse button and move the mouse to the left or right. If your mouse is equipped with a wheel, you can also use this to step forward or backward one frame at a time.

◆ Press the left or right arrow to move the timeline cursor one frame at a time. Holding down the arrow key moves the clip forward or backward at speed.

◆ Use the J, K, and L keys to play the clip back at various speeds. K stops playback; L plays the clip forward a little faster each time it is pressed; and J plays the clip backward a little faster each time it is pressed.

When scrubbing the Timeline, you won't hear any sound. This is the default setting for Liquid Edition; it's set this way to enhance performance during scrubbing. For information on activating audio scrubbing and the restrictions that apply to this, see Chapter 7.

THE SOURCE VIEWER

Trimming a clip in the Source Viewer

You can trim dynamically in the Timeline to adjust your clips the quick and dirty way. The more refined method is to use the Source Viewer to trim the clip. Once the clip is in the Source Viewer, your first job is to preview and look for anything that might need to be cut out from the start or the end. In fact, you might decide just to use a few seconds from the middle of the clip. You can do all of this by adding mark-in and mark-out points to the clip.

To add a mark-in or mark-out point in the Source Viewer:

1. Once the clip is loaded into the Source Viewer, use the mouse or the arrow keys to look for the best place for your clip to start.

   This is called *scrubbing* and is discussed earlier in this chapter.

2. Once you have found the ideal place to start your clip—the mark-in point—press the I key or click the Mark-In Point button .

   A small Mark-In Point icon has now been added to the Timeline of the Clip Viewer (**Figure 6.47**).

Figure 6.47 A mark-in point added to the Source Viewer.

3. To select a point where you would like your clip to finish—the mark-out point—scrub though the clip again until you find the optimal point; then press the O key or click the Mark-Out Point button ▶ .

A small Mark-Out Point icon has now been added to the Timeline of the Clip Viewer (**Figure 6.48**).

4. Use the Zoom tool to reduce the view if you can't see both the mark-in and the mark-out points on the Timeline display.

5. Click the Play from Mark-In to Mark-Out button ▶▶ to play back the clip from the new points you have just defined.

6. If the new mark-in and mark-out points don't suit your needs, you can set different points simply by moving the cursor to a new point and pressing the I or the O key again.

Remember: adding either a mark-in or mark-out point does not physically alter the original clip. It merely tells the program to ignore any material that falls outside these two areas. For a further explication of nonlinear editing, see Chapter 1.

✔ Tips

■ Pressing Home or End will take you to the first or last frame of your clip. However, if this is a Subclip, then pressing the Home or End key will take you to the clip-in or clip-out point of the clip.

■ When the Source Viewer is selected, it is surrounded by a red border.

Figure 6.48 A mark-out point added to the Source Viewer.

Sending a Clip to the Timeline

Once you've adjusted the mark-in and mark-out points of the media clip and added any markers, it's time to send the clip to the Timeline. In Chapter 5, I showed you how to send a Storyboard Sequence to the Timeline, but when you're using the Source Viewer to send the clips, you have several options open to you that involve using the Insert Source into Master button or drag and drop, or creating a three- or four-point edit.

Sending to an empty Timeline

Placing a clip on an empty Timeline or at the end of the current Sequence is relatively simple, and once you have trimmed your clip in the Source Viewer, you are ready to go.

To send a clip to an unoccupied part of the Timeline:

1. Place the timeline cursor where you want the clip to land by either using the navigation keys or the mouse.

2. Check that the correct clip is loaded into the Source Viewer and that the mark-in and mark-out points have been set as required.

3. To send the clip to the Timeline, *do one of the following:*

   ▲ Click once on the Insert Source into Master arrow ![icon]. The clip is now sent from the Source Viewer to the current Timeline position (**Figure 6.49**).

   ▲ Hold down the Ctrl key and drag the clip from the Source Viewer to the Timeline by holding down the left mouse key.

✔ Tip

■ Dragging and dropping allows you to dynamically place the clip at any point on the Timeline, but the rules of Overwrite Style and Film Style will be obeyed.

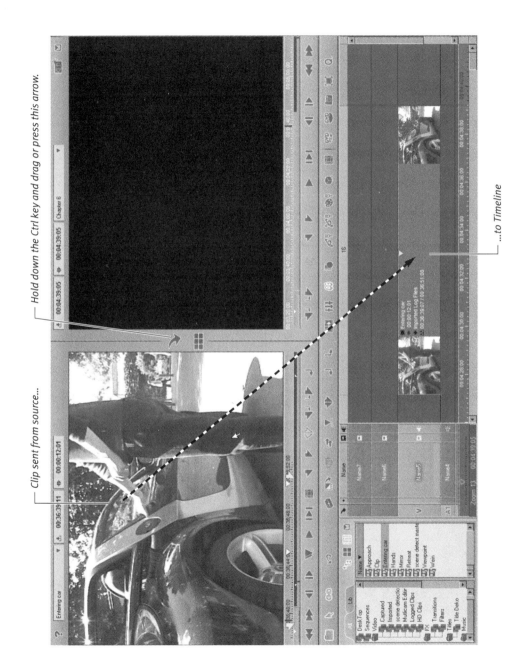

Hold down the Ctrl key and drag or press this arrow.

Clip sent from source...

...to Timeline

Figure 6.49 The media clip is sent from the Source Viewer or dragged with the mouse.

Sending a Clip to the Timeline

Sending to an occupied Timeline

Sending to a Timeline that already contains clips is basically the same process as sending to an unoccupied Timeline; however, here the Overwrite Style and Film Style rules need to be observed more carefully.

As you will recall from the "Edit Styles" sidebar earlier in this chapter the basic difference between these two styles is that Film Style shuffles the already existing clips up to make room for any new clips you insert, while the Overwrite Style simply writes over the existing clips. Which one you use will depend on what exists on the Timeline.

✔ Tip

■ Remember to work only with grouped clips where possible.

To insert a clip in Overwrite Style:

Do one of the following:

◆ Place the timeline cursor on an empty part of the Timeline but with a clip directly to the right and click the Insert Source into Master button ⬂.
Clicking this button places the clip at your chosen position; the clip on the right moves up to make room for the new clip (**Figure 6.50**).

◆ Place the timeline cursor on a clip that is already on the Timeline and click the Insert Source into Master button ⬂.
This action cuts the original clip at the cursor position and then places the Source Viewer clip there, thus overwriting the original clip and any other clips to the right for the duration of the newly inserted clip (**Figure 6.51**).

Inserted clip   *Existing clip shuffles up the Timeline.*

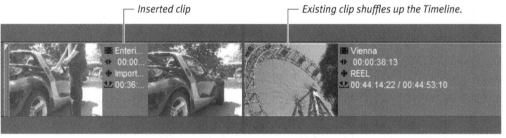

Figure 6.50 Inserting a clip at the start of the Timeline.

Inserted clip cuts the original clip at the timeline cursor...   *...and overwrites the original clip and any other clips to the right (up the Timeline).*

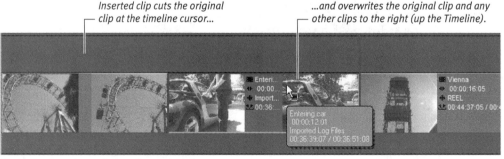

Figure 6.51 Inserting a clip into the another.

To insert a clip in Film Style:

1. Check to make sure the appropriate audio and video tracks are active.

2. Toggle Film Style on and then *do one of the following:*

   ▲ Place the timeline cursor on an empty part of the Timeline but with a clip directly to the right and click the Insert Source into Master button 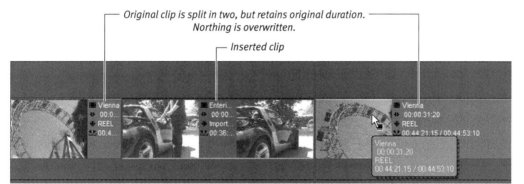.

   This places the clip at your chosen position while respecting both the mark-in and mark-out points of the clip. However, the clip on the right moves up to make room for the new clip. In all respects, this performs the same as when you use Overwrite Style.

   ▲ Place the timeline cursor on a clip that is already on the Timeline and press the Insert Source into Master button.

   This cuts the original clip at the cursor position, moves everything to the right, cuts up the Timeline, and then places the Source Viewer clip there. The original clip stays the same length and is not overwritten but is split on either side of the inserted clip (**Figure 6.52**).

Original clip is split in two, but retains original duration.
Northing is overwritten.

Inserted clip

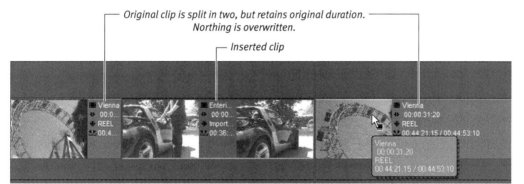

Figure 6.52 Inserting a clip in Film Style.

SENDING A CLIP TO THE TIMELINE

Creating the Three-Point Edit

The three-point edit is used to insert a clip into a point on the Timeline using specific reference points. The three points referred to are the In and Out-points defined in the Source Viewer and a final In-Point (or insertion point) that is placed on the Timeline.

The process is pretty much the same as what happens if you either drag a clip from the Source Viewer to a specific point on the Timeline, or if you simply place the timeline cursor there and click the Insert Source into Master button .

Usually a clip already occupies the point where you want to insert your clip and you want to overwrite it, and perhaps keep the audio track underneath. The three-point edit is often used for cutaway shots where the narration or the interview continues uninterrupted, but another image is displayed. For example, a journalist may be talking into the camera about a politician. At some point, the image may cut away to show a soundless clip of the politician who is being referred to before it cuts back to the journalist. This is known as a *cutaway*.

The advantage of placing a mark-in point on the Timeline is that it is simply more accurate to use your third point to carefully define the exact insertion point of your clip.

To create a three-point edit:

1. If you want to retain the audio for the clip on the Timeline you will be overwriting, prepare it by right-clicking the clip and selecting Disband Clip(s) from the drop-down list (**Figure 6.53**).

Figure 6.53 Selecting Disband Clip(s) if you don't want the original audio being overwritten by the inserted clip.

CREATING THE THREE-POINT EDIT

Now that audio is disbanded, make sure the audio track is inactive by clicking it once to turn it gray. The audio track for this clip will now be unaffected by the added media clip.

If you don't need to retain the audio, you can ignore this step.

2. Load a media clip into the Source Viewer and define the mark-in and mark-out points of this clip.

These are the first two points of your edit (**Figure 6.54**).

3. Now scrub the Timeline until you find a suitable place to insert the clip; then click the Mark-In Point button .

This creates the third point of your edit (**Figure 6.55**).

continues on next page

Figure 6.54 Mark-in and mark-out points set for Source Viewer.

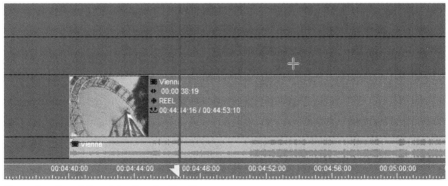

Figure 6.55 A mark-in point set on the Timeline.

CREATING THE THREE-POINT EDIT

4. Click the Insert Source into Master
button .

The clip appears at this point in the
Timeline, overwriting the existing clip
(**Figure 6.56**).

✔ Tip

■ More information on disbanding audio
can be found in Chapter 7.

Clip sent from here...

*...to here.
Audio of
original clip
is retained.*

Figure 6.56 Clicking the Insert Source into Master button sends the clip to the Timeline.

Unwanted Audio Tracks

In this three-point edit example, the original audio was disbanded and was not overwritten. However, you may now have inserted a media clip containing audio that you don't want.

To turn this off, you need to right-click the media clip in the Timeline, select Properties, and deselect any audio boxes that are not grayed out.

Figure 6.57 shows the properties for Entering car with the audio tracks A1 and A2 deselected.

Cutting out the audio in this way is clean and effective; it also leaves the original media clip in the Project Browser untouched.

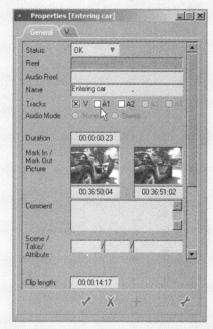

Figure 6.57 The media clip's Properties screen with audio tracks deselected.

Creating the Four-Point Edit

The four-point edit functions in a similar fashion to the three-point edit, and it is also used to either create cutaway shots or to replace the existing clip completely. However, it has an extra trick up its sleeve in that it also adjusts the mark-out point of the inserted clip to suit the gap you want the clip to fit into. You can do this by adjusting the overall speed of the clip; either to slow it down or to speed it up, making the clip fit inside the two points you have defined on the Timeline.

To create a four-point edit:

1. To retain the audio for the clip on the Timeline, prepare it by right-clicking the clip and selecting Disband Clip(s) from the drop-down list.

Now that audio is disbanded, make sure the audio track is inactive by clicking it once to turn it gray. The audio track for this clip will not be unaffected by the added media clip.

If you don't need to retain the audio, you can ignore this step.

2. Load a clip into the Source Viewer and define its mark-in and mark-out points.

   These are your first two points.

3. Now scrub the Timeline until you find a suitable place to insert the clip; then click the Mark-In Point button ◀.

   This creates your third point.

4. Now scrub the Timeline again until you find a suitable place for your mark-out point and click the Mark-Out Point button ▶.

   This creates your fourth point (**Figure 6.58**).

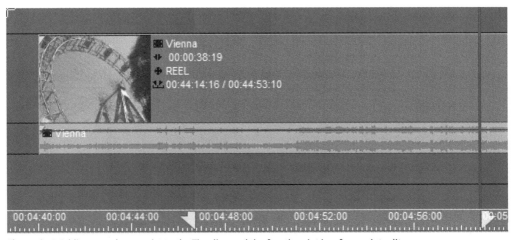

Figure 6.58 Adding a mark-out point to the Timeline and the fourth point in a four-point edit.

5. Click the Insert Source into Master button 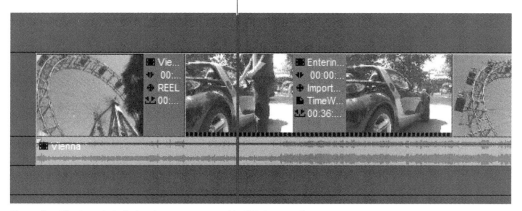 and the clip will appear at the mark-in point in the Timeline, overwriting the existing clip. A dynamic Timewarp is added to the clip to make it fit inside the points you have defined (**Figure 6.59**).

✔ Tips

- Dynamic Timewarp is a non-real-time effect that must be rendered before it can be viewed. Clips with this effect applied to them will have a speckled black and purple band running along the bottom of the video section. More details on Timewarp can be found in Chapter 9.

- If you want to retain the audio of the clip you are overwriting, you will need to disband the audio first. See Chapter 7 for details.

- The inserted clip will retain audio up to a maximum of 200 percent and a minimum of 50 percent Timewarp, although the video is not limited to these speeds.

Clip inserted at mark-in point.

Figure 6.59 The inserted clip has been compressed to fit into a smaller gap.

Filling a Gap

Trimming a media clip to close a gap on the Timeline is one way to stop your video from having lots of embarrassing black gaps in it. But what happens if the clip is not long enough to fill the gap and the rest of the Timeline cannot be moved down?

Again, this is where Timewarp can help.

1. Right-click the clip you want to stretch and select Linear Timewarp from the menu.

2. Check the Fit to fill (dynamic speed) box (**Figure 6.60**) and then click the check mark.

The speed of the clip is automatically adjusted to fit the gap between the clip you are applying this Timewarp to and the nearest clip on the right.

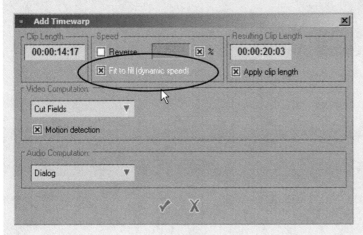

Figure 6.60 The Timewarp Fit to fill function.

CREATING THE FOUR-POINT EDIT

Inserting a Clip: Other Methods

Of course, some clips don't need to be trimmed or inserted using any of the more complex methods just discussed. For instance, you can bring photographs into the Timeline without trimming; as trimming a photograph (effectively, a single video frame) would achieve nothing.

To allow true creative flow, Liquid Edition allows you insert a clip in a variety of different ways, but of course the rules of Overwrite Style and Film Style still apply to each of the methods detailed here.

To simply insert a clip:

Do one of the following:

- Drag and drop a clip from the Source Viewer by holding down the Ctrl key.

- Drag and drop a clip from the Project Browser by simply selecting the clip, holding down the left mouse button, and dragging it into position.

- Right-click the clip in the Project Browser and select Send to Timeline from the pop-up menu.

✔ Tip

- When you send clips from the Project Browser, you can use the common Windows file selection conventions. You can select multiple clips using the Shift or Ctrl key and the left mouse button. These clips will be placed on the Timeline in the order in which they appear inside the Project Browser.

Mapping the Timeline

Each of the examples just discussed (except for drag and drop) will send the video by default to the Name 5 track. This is because that track has been designated, or mapped, to receive all video files. You can determine if this is the case if you see the large V that sits in the first column (**Figure 6.61**) or VA if the "grouped" or Embedded option is selected.

Figure 6.61 The V indicates that this track is mapped for video.

Designating tracks in this way is known as mapping. Mapping tracks can be altered on the fly to suit your workflow.

To map the video track:

Do one of the following:

Figure 6.62 The Mapping selection box.

- ◆ Right-click in the Mapping column to which you want to map the video, and select V or VA from the pop-up box (**Figure 6.62**).

- ◆ Left-click the actual V and drag it up to the column to which you want to map the video (**Figure 6.63**).

✔ Tip

- ■ If you are using the Insert Grouped option discussed earlier in this chapter, the V will be displayed as VA to indicate that it contains video and audio.

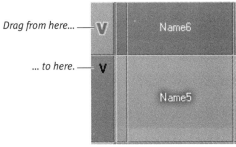

Figure 6.63 Manually setting the video mapping.

To map the audio track:

Do one of the following:

- ◆ Right-click in the Mapping column to which you want to map the audio, and select S1 or A1 from the pop-up box.

- ◆ Left-click the actual S1 or A1 and drag it down to the column to which you want to map the audio.

✔ Tip

- ■ Further details on S1 and A1 audio mapping can be found in Chapter 7.

Adding Markers

Adding markers to a clip allows you to have visual clues as to when a specific event is going to occur. This is important because when a clip is added to the Timeline, only the start frame and end frame (the heads and tails) are displayed. The rest of the clip is one long piece of blue. The Film Strip mode found in Adobe Premiere is unfortunately not an option in Liquid Edition.

✔ Tips

- Markers can be added to any media (audio, image, or video). Adding markers to the tempo—the rhythm of a tune—is a good example of why markers are used. But you can also use them to mark key sections of a Sequence to which you want to attach buttons during DVD authoring. See Chapter 12 for more on this.

- Markers are also visible in all of the FX editors, including Timewarp.

To set a marker:

1. With a clip open in the Source Viewer, scrub through until you see a place where you want to add a marker.

2. Hit the M key on the keyboard and a small gray triangle appears on the Source Viewer's Timeline.

   When the cursor is on this point, a triangle also appears in the top center of the Source Viewer (**Figure 6.64**).

   In this example, a marker has been added to indicate when the car door is about to close. You could then use this marker later to add the sound effect of a door closing. Preparation like this can save you time when you're editing long, complex Timelines.

✔ Tips

- Extra buttons, such as Go to Next Event and Open Marker list, need to be added to the toolbars (Timeline, Source, and Clip Viewers) in order to fully exploit the full functionality of Markers. See the "Tool Buttons That Should Be Added..." sidebar that appears in this chapter for details. Also, see Chapter 1 to learn how to add a button to an interface.

- Markers can be added using the Clip Viewer. They can also be added directly to the Timeline, which helps you mark out possible DVD chapter points.

Figure 6.64 A marker added just as the car door was closing.

To navigate the markers in a clip:

Do one of the following:

◆ Use the Go to Next Event buttons.

◆ Use the Open Marker List button to open the makers list, and double-click the marker you want (**Figure 6.65**).

✔ Tip

■ The Open Marker list does not appear on the toolbars by default. See Tip on previous page.

To rename a marker:

Do one of the following:

◆ Double-click the marker and a small dialog box will open into which you can enter your text (**Figure 6.66**).

◆ Click the Open Marker List button and then right-click and select Rename (**Figure 6.67**).

To delete a marker:

1. Open the list of markers using the Open Marker List button.

2. Highlight the marker(s) you want to delete.

3. Right-click any of the highlighted markers and then select Clear Selected Markers or Clear All Markers (**Figure 6.68**).

To move a marker:

◆ Hold down the Alt key and place the mouse cursor over the marker. The cursor turns into a crosshair pointer and you can drag this marker to its new position by holding down the left mouse button. This works only in the Master and the Source Window.

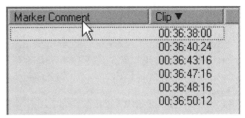

Figure 6.65 Open Marker List button displaying all the Source Viewer markers.

Figure 6.66 Directly naming a marker.

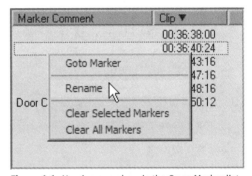

Figure 6.67 Naming a marker via the Open Marker list.

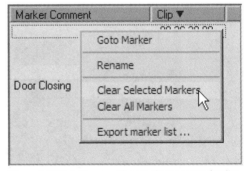

Figure 6.68 Deleting a marker via the Open Marker list.

Understanding Timeline Slices

As you've been adding clips to the Timeline, you've probably noticed a number appearing above them (**Figure 6.69**).

This is called a *Timeline slice* and it's part of the media management system's way of keeping track of what's on the Timeline. Every time you add a clip and every time you use the razor blade, a new slice is created. Each slice can be manipulated independently.

✔ Tip

■ The more slices that exist on the Timeline, the slower Liquid Edition will respond to your commands. Once you reach a Timeline that contains many hundreds of slices (easily done on an hour-long project), you will see a significant lag when you add clips or trim clips. You can avoid this by making sure you create a new Sequence for every separate part of your Project. This will at least cut down on the slice count while you are editing. During the final assembly, there is no way to avoid a high slice count, but at that stage, most of your fine-tuning should have been completed.

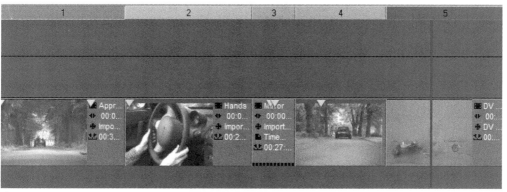

Figure 6.69 Timeline slices appear as each clip is added or as the razor blade is used. *(See color insert.)*

The Color of Slices

Timeline slices come in five colors; each one represents the state of the clips directly below that slice.

◆ **Gray:** The normal state for a clip. The clip has no special effects attached to it and no rendering is required.

◆ **Yellow:** A real-time FX has been added to the clip. The FX will preview without rendering, but the slice will need to be rendered before it is taken out to DVD or tape.

◆ **Red:** A non-real-time FX has been added to the clip. The FX must be rendered to be viewed. This normally occurs during background rendering.

◆ **Green:** Real-time and non-real-time FX have been rendered. Normally the change from red to green is gradual so that you can see how much of the clip has yet to render. Any part of the slice that is green can be played back while you are waiting for the rest of the clip to render. This rule does not apply to yellow slices. For various technical reasons, some machines do not show a gradual change from red to green but rather a change once the render is complete.

◆ **Dark Red:** This means the clip directly under this slice cannot be found by the media management system. See Chapter 4 for details.

Background Rendering

All rendering in Liquid Edition (yellow or red slices) is carried out in the background. In practical terms, this means you can carry on using the program, opening new clips to edit, creating new titles, opening other FX windows, and so on, while the program carries on rendering anything you have already worked on.

To see the progression of the background rendering, click once on the Sigma icon in the Liquid Edition taskbar ![Σ]. This will bring up the Render View dialog (**Figure 6.70**).

Here you can turn rendering on or off and you can also check the Include yellow slices box to render your real-time FXs.

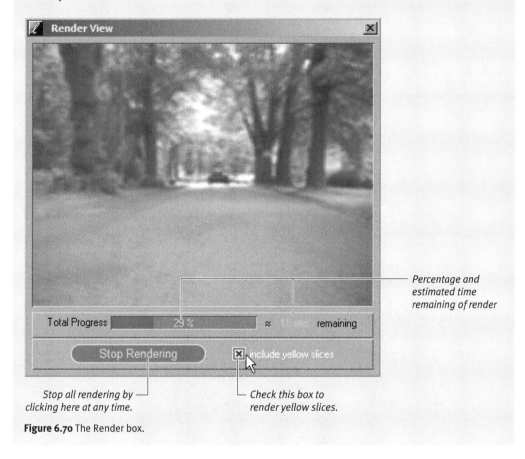

Percentage and estimated time remaining of render

Stop all rendering by clicking here at any time.

Check this box to render yellow slices.

Figure 6.70 The Render box.

Previewing Your Sequence

During the edit process, you will want to constantly preview your media clips and the adjustments you have made. You can do this by manually controlling the timeline cursor—place the cursor at the start of where you want to preview, press the space-bar to play, and press it again to stop.

It is also possible to play a section of the Timeline in a continuous loop so that you can quickly preview whether or not a particular set of clips works together or if a Dissolve needs tweaking.

To create a continuous playback:

1. Position the timeline cursor at the start of the area you want to preview, and press I to add a mark-in point to the Timeline.

2. Position the timeline cursor at the end of the area you want to preview, and press the O key to add a mark-out point to the Timeline (**Figure 6.71**).

3. Click the Play from Mark-In to Mark-Out button ▶️ and the Timeline plays in a continuous loop until you click the button again.

Figure 6.71 A section of the Timeline marked out for playback.

✔ Tip

- You can add a mark-in and a mark-out point to the Timeline by selecting the slices above the area you want to preview, right-clicking, and selecting Set Mark In/Out For Edits *x* -> *y*. Multiple slices can be selected using the Shift key (**Figure 6.72**).

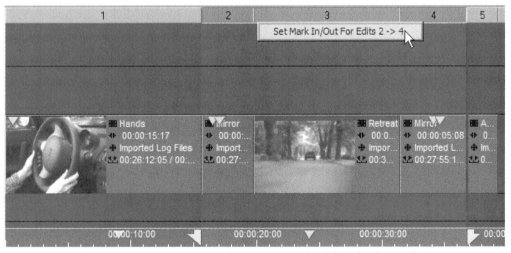

Figure 6.72 A mark-in and mark-out point added to the Timeline via right-clicking the slice numbers.

Working with Audio

Audio isn't just the other half of video editing; it's the greater part of the whole production. Because the ear—unlike the eye—is hard to fool and is often subconsciously able to register any errors, problems, or distractions within, audiences are apt to pick up audio mistakes far more quickly than visual errors. How good (or bad) your audio editing is contributes to your audience's visual enjoyment; without good audio they will miss vital clues as to what is going on.

With these scary factors in mind, you need to take audio very seriously indeed. That's why this chapter appears after the chapter that covered how to fine-tune your Timeline Sequence and before the chapter that covers adding effects and titles. You must make sure your sound is correct early on in the edit process and not shuffle it over to the "do it later" section of your life.

In this chapter, you will learn how to adjust audio levels, disband stereo tracks, add sound filters, and lastly, play around with the new and exciting 5.1 surround sound feature. By the time you've conquered all the skills in this chapter, your audio files should sound as good as your video looks. Fail, and the eye will almost certainly be distracted by the ear.

Editing with Audio—Concepts and Consequences

Audio in Liquid Edition comes from just two sources.

◆ Video you either captured or imported

◆ Music you imported in any of the supported formats

However, although Liquid Edition supports many formats, audio is always converted to WAV format during import. This conversion makes little difference to your editing experience, but it does make Liquid Edition's life a little easier. Also, you'll find that you're able to use your files in more applications (more on this in Chapter 13).

Once you've imported the audio file into Liquid Edition, you should treat it just like another media clip. You can trim it in the Source Viewer, on the Timeline, and in the Clip Viewer. You can copy it across your Project countless times, and you can adjust it either simply to alter the volume level, or using more complex filters to clean up and adjust the sound.

WAV = Waveform Audio

Don't get too hung up on what all these three letter acronyms (TLAs) actually mean. But for those of you with a burning curiosity to know, a WAV file is a Microsoft propriety file system used for audio. It is widely supported by many applications both on the PC and the Mac.

Copyright?

You can't legally use music under copyright (anything owned by some else; like Sony, for example) in your own video productions. No legal rule says, "If you only use this song for your holiday DVDs, then that's okay"; if you use it, then you have broken the copyright agreement. It's that simple.

Having said that, the chances of men in black turning up at your house with baseball bats and a subpoena are slim. However, the chances of you getting into a copyright wrangle increase if your video Project gains any kind of exposure.

So, if you create a wedding video that will probably only ever be played by the Happy Couple in front of unwillingly guests, then you probably can include that much needed "Lady in Red" track.

If you are producing a video brochure for a product you want to sell, then you should be aware that you may not be looked on favorably by the copyright owners. In this case, use copyright-free music; it is just an Internet search away.

Grouped and embedded audio

In Chapter 6, my advice was to use embedded audio; that is, audio wrapped up inside the video and displayed on the Timeline as one item (**Figure 7.1**).

The reason for this is simple; once audio is separated from the video clip, it becomes vulnerable to synchronization problems caused by adding a new media clip into an occupied area of the Timeline. When an audio synchronization problem occurs, it can be dramatic—the sound may disappear for a few seconds—or it can be subtle—lip movements do not match the words being spoken.

Remember, the eye can be fooled, but the ear cannot. A lip sync problem is the nemesis of video editing; once you have one, it can be very difficult to get rid of it and put things back in sync again.

A much neater way is simply to avoid the problem altogether by using embedded audio at all times and only disbanding the audio clip when you really, absolutely have to.

✔ Tips

- You can find a section—Keeping Audio and Video in Synch—dealing with synchronization problems that occur with disbanded audio later in this chapter.

- Whenever possible, try to keep the tracks Name 4 and 3 unoccupied so that disbanding clips have somewhere to go.

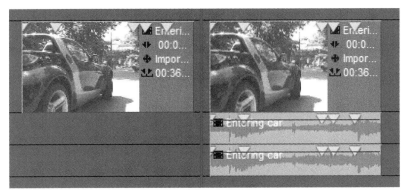

Figure 7.1 The clip on the left is embedded audio; the clip on the right is disbanded audio.

To use embedded audio:

Do one of the following:

◆ Click the Timeline drop-down menu at the top of the interface and select Insert Grouped (**Figure 7.2** left).

◆ Right-click the small arrow at the top of the Name column and select Insert Grouped (**Figure 7.2** right).

This automatically causes all audio to become embedded when the Source Viewer sends it to the Timeline.

To disband audio on the Timeline:

1. Select the clip you want to disband.

2. Right-click and select Disband Clip(s) from the menu (**Figure 7.3**).

The disbanded audio appears directly under the video clip.

Click here to access this menu.

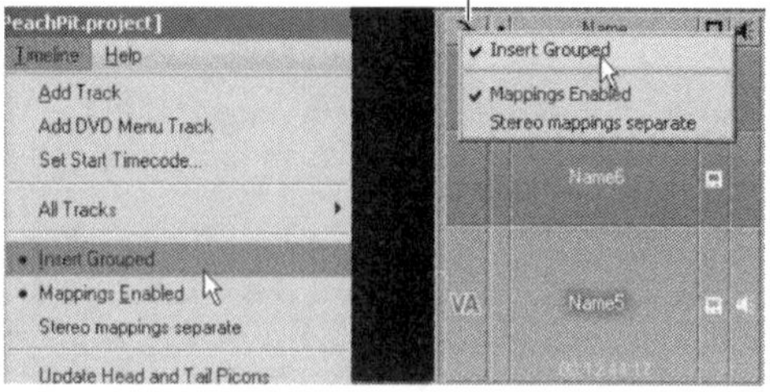

Figure 7.2 Two methods of selecting embedded audio.

Figure 7.3 Right-clicking a clip allows you to select Disband Clip(s).

Stereo or Mono

When a clip is disbanded, it can appear either with both stereo tracks on one Timeline track or with the left and right channels occupying a track each.

You set the option in the actual media clip by right-clicking the track before you disband the audio and then selecting Properties (**Figure 7.4**). Here you can select Mono or Stereo for the audio mode.

Figure 7.4 Selecting Stereo in the clip's properties.

◆ Stereo causes both the left and right track to appear on one Timeline track (**Figure 7.5**).

◆ Mono allows the left and right track each to occupy a separate track (**Figure 7.6**).

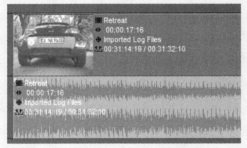

Figure 7.5 Stereo occupies one Timeline track...

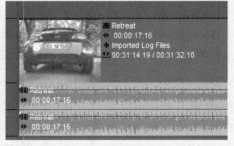

Figure 7.6 ...whereas Mono occupies a track for each channel.

An alternative method involves right-clicking again on the audio after you have disbanded it. This causes a stereo track to disband into two mono tracks. After that, the disband option is grayed out (**Figure 7.7**).

This method works on imported audio tracks as well as the audio from a video clip (**Figure 7.8**).

Figure 7.7 Stereo audio clip on the left, disbanded to mono on the right.

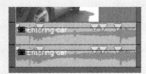

Figure 7.8 Video disbanded.

Opening the Audio Editor

The process of volume adjustment is identical for embedded and disbanded audio. Liquid Edition allows you to freely alter the audio of either display using a variety of tools that lets you set the pace of your own workflow. At the same time, you can visualize the volume settings by displaying a volume line on an embedded or disbanded clip.

Totally rewritten for version 6, the Audio Editor is the heart and soul of audio editing in Liquid Edition. It's also remarkably simple to use.

✔ Tip

■ If the Audio Editor is not open, then some of the tasks here—for example, adding audio keyframes, adjusting the volume level, and undoing audio keyframes—will not be possible. If what you are trying to do will not work, the first thing you need to check is whether the Audio Editor is actually open.

To open the Audio Editor:

◆ Click the Open Audio Editor button ▦ of press F4 on the keyboard.
This opens the Audio Editor (**Figure 7.9**).

✔ Tip

■ During playback the VU meters show yellow when the audio is in a safe range. When it peaks into red, the sound can become clipped, or it may drop out entirely. This is the digital equivalent of distortion, and you should monitor your VU meters carefully to make sure they stay out of the red.

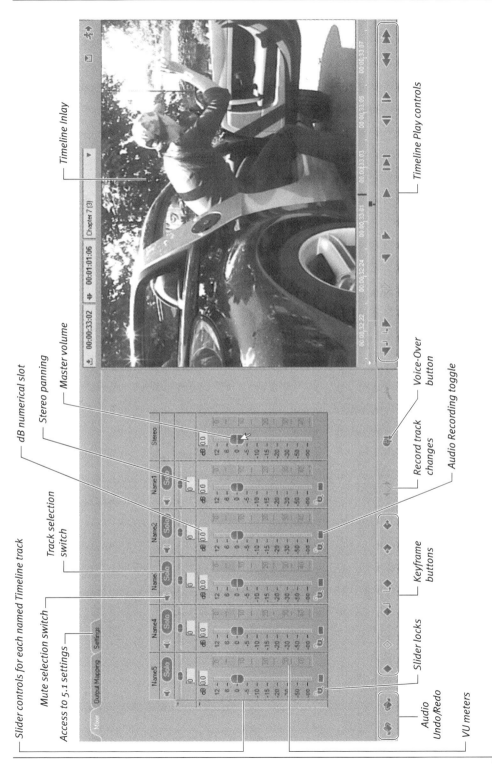

Figure 7.9 The Audio Editor.

Slider controls for each named Timeline track

Access to 5.1 settings

Mute selection switch

Track selection switch

dB numerical slot

Stereo panning

Master volume

Timeline Inlay

Timeline Play controls

Record track changes

Voice-Over button

Audio Recording toggle

Keyframe buttons

Slider locks

Audio Undo/Redo

VU meters

Understanding Audio Tracks

The top row of the Audio Editor contains the names of all your tracks; the one on the left is normally Name 5 (unless you have renamed it), and it contains your media clip.

To add or remove a track to/from the Audio Editor:

◆ Click once on the speaker icon column.

The track name appears or disappears in the Audio Editor (**Figure 7.10**).

✔ Tip

■ To select all tracks, right-click the small speaker at the top of the column and select Audio Playback On (**Figure 7.11**).

Clicking here...

...causes a track to be added here.

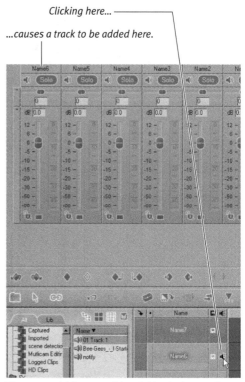

Figure 7.10 Adding a track by clicking in the speaker column.

Figure 7.11 Selecting all tracks.

Figure 7.12 When you select Show Volume...

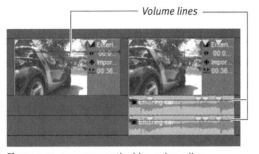

Volume lines

Figure 7.13 ...you can see the blue volume line.

Showing the Volume Level

Liquid Edition displays the volume level as a thin blue line that runs the length of the clip. When you adjust the audio level, this line moves up and down to reflect these changes.

However, by default, this graphical representation of the volume is not shown, and without this, you might have trouble visualizing exactly what you are doing.

To show volume with the volume level:

◆ Right-click the small speaker at the top of the audio row and select Show Volume (**Figure 7.12**).

A small blue line appears near the top of all video and audio clips (**Figure 7.13**).

Keyframes

Each time you adjust the audio levels, a number of small blue diamonds appear (**Figure 7.14**).

These diamond marks are called *keyframes* and are part of the magic behind the NLE system.

A keyframe does pretty much what it says on the box: It creates a key point around which certain actions occur.

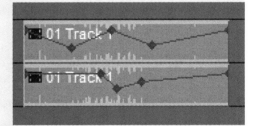

Figure 7.14 The small blue diamonds indicate keyframes.

With audio editing, keyframes are created every time you make an adjustment to the audio levels. In Figure 7.14, you can see that multiple changes have been made, creating multiple blue diamonds—keyframes—that control the level of audio.

Once created, these keyframes can be manipulated, moved, or deleted at will, which is the true power of a keyframe. However, the Audio Editor must be open to be able to adjust audio keyframes.

Keyframes are also used extensively in Liquid Edition to control visual effects. You can find more on keyframes and their uses in Chapters 8 and 9.

Dynamically Adjusting the Audio

Once you can see a volume line, you can adjust it using the mouse or the sliders in the Audio Editor. If you use the mouse to directly alter a key and add keyframes, you have the advantage of being able to match keyframes with significant events on the Timeline. But this way of doing things does lack accuracy; for that, you need to use the sliders.

✔ Tips

- Remember, the Audio Editor *must be open* for you to adjust an audio track on the Timeline. If it is not open, you won't be able to access the keyframes with the mouse.

- Keyframes—like media clips—are magnetic. This means you can toggle them off by holding down the Shift key.

To adjust the volume with keyframes:

1. Open the Audio Editor by pressing F4 on the keyboard.

2. Place the mouse pointer over the blue volume line so that it turns into a small hand (**Figure 7.15**).

3. Hold down the left mouse button to create a keyframe that you can drag up or down, thus raising and lowering the volume (**Figure 7.16**).

   You can also drag this keyframe horizontally along the length of the clip (**Figure 7.17**).

✔ Tips

- Once you've defined a keyframe, you can control it using the slider.

- Moving a slider automatically creates a keyframe.

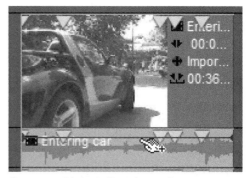

Figure 7.15 With the Audio tool open, the mouse cursor appears as a hand when placed near a volume line.

Figure 7.16 Dragging the volume down with the mouse.

Figure 7.17 Adjusting the keyframe's point with the mouse.

Drag a Keyframe off
the clip to delete it.

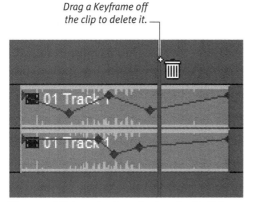

Figure 7.18 Delete a keyframe by dragging it off the audio clip.

Audio Undo/Redo

Liquid Edition has several areas of Undo, each one operating independently from the others. In Chapter 6, you saw how the main Undo command (Ctrl+Z) undid the last movement on the Timeline. However, this Undo command does not affect keyframes applied to audio clips.

To demonstrate this, place an audio clip on the Timeline and then add a keyframe to the volume using the instructions in the "To adjust the volume with keyframes" task earlier in this chapter. Now click the Undo button or press Ctrl+Z. Instead of the keyframe vanishing, the audio clip is removed from the Timeline.

If you need to undo a keyframe on an audio track, you must use the Audio Undo/Redo buttons at the bottom left of the Audio Editor or their keyboard shortcut—Ctrl+Shift+Z. These buttons operate in the same fashion as the normal Undo/Redo commands, but the audio track must be selected for them to work and the Audio Editor must be open.

Controlling Keyframes

It is vital that you learn to control keyframes if you want to work with any kind of fluidity. Fortunately, the concept and the actualities are very simple. Moving a keyframe is a simple matter of clicking it and dragging it somewhere else, but deleting a keyframe is slightly more involved.

To delete a keyframe:

Do one of the following:

◆ Click the keyframe and drag it anywhere off the clip. A small trash can symbol appears to let you know this is going to be deleted (**Figure 7.18**).

◆ Use the Go to Next/Go to Previous buttons , which are under the Audio Editor, until you reach the keyframe you want to delete. Then press the Delete Keyframe button .

◆ If the keyframe you want to delete was the last one you placed, make sure you select the audio clip and click the audio Undo key .

✔ Tip

■ You must have the Audio Editor open to delete an audio keyframe.

Adjusting the Volume on the Fly

The sliders represent a visualization of what most professional editors would see on a physical audio editor, except in this case, they are controlled by the mouse.

Altering the volume level of a clip isn't just a simple matter of sliding the controls up or down as the clip plays back. You need to make certain preparations before you can adjust a clip live.

To adjust the volume during play:

1. Place a mark-in and a mark-out point on the Timeline around the area you want to adjust.

   This can be the whole Timeline if you want, or just a section of it but the Mark-in and Mark-out point must be on the Timeline and not on the actual clip itself. (**Figure 7.19**).

2. Open the Audio Editor by pressing F4.

3. Click once on the Audio Recording lights to turn them red if they are not already activated (**Figure 7.20**).

4. Click the Record Audio Mix button when everything is ready.

   The time cursor jumps 5 seconds behind the mark-in point and begins to play.

5. Alter the sliders as you see fit during playback.

   A line is drawn over the audio clip describing your actions with the sliders (**Figure 7.21**).

   Once the mark-out point is reached or if you click the Record Audio Mix button again, the audio mix stops.

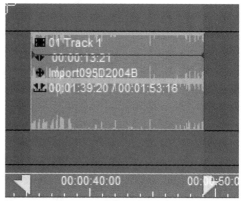

Figure 7.19 Place a mark-in and a mark-out point around the section you want to alter.

Figure 7.20 Activate the recording lights for each track you need to work with.

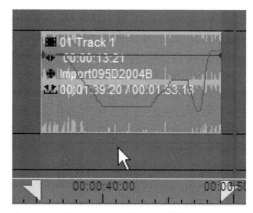

Figure 7.21 The squiggle left by the sliders.

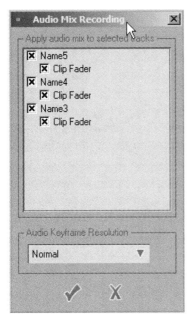

Figure 7.22 Click the check mark to accept the changes...

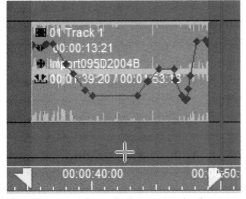

Figure 7.23 ...and the squiggle turns into keyframes.

6. Click the check mark in **Figure 7.22** to accept these changes once the process is stopped.

The line changes into one peppered with blue keyframes (**Figure 7.23**).

✔ Tips

■ When you are using this method, only those tracks containing audio have active sliders. Those that contain audio but lie outside the mark-in and mark-out points are grayed out.

■ With the audio track selected, you can also enter the amount in the dB area of the Audio Editor.

Globally adjusting the volume

You may encounter times when you just want to adjust the overall volume of a specific audio clip. Perhaps the crowd clapped too loud, or Granny spoke too quietly. You can adjust the volume this way using one of two methods.

To globally adjust the volume:

1. Open the Audio Editor by pressing F4.

2. *Do one of the following:*

   ▲ Place the mouse pointer over the blue volume line and hold down the Shift key.

   The mouse pointer turns into a horizontal line bracketed by two vertical arrows. Dragging up and down globally adjusts the audio (**Figure 7.24**).

   ▲ Right-click the audio clip and select Adjust audio. In the Adjust Audio box, enter the dB level you require (**Figure 7.25**).

✔ Tips

■ Globally adjusting the volume and adding keyframes will only work if the Audio Editor is open. No Audio Editor, no playtime.

■ Entering a minus (–) in front of the value reduces the volume level.

■ When entering a numerical value, press Tab to apply it.

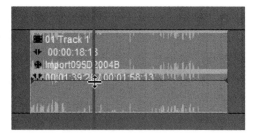

Figure 7.24 Globally adjust the volume of a track using the mouse...

Figure 7.25 ... and with direct numerical entry.

ADJUSTING THE VOLUME ON THE FLY

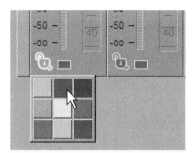

Figure 7.26 Choose a color to lock sliders.

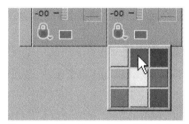

Figure 7.27 Matching colors will be locked.

Locking sliders together

If you have disbanded a stereo track, you might still want to adjust the audio of both tracks an equal amount. If this is the case, you should lock the sliders together.

To lock two sliders:

1. With the Audio Editor open, click once on the lock of the first slider you want to use.

   A three-by-three color matrix is displayed. Gray is unlocked.

2. Click once on any of the other colors—red for example (**Figure 7.26**).

3. Click the lock of the second slider and select the same color as you did for the first (**Figure 7.27**).

   The two sliders are now locked together. To unlock them, for each slider, simply click the lock and select the gray square.

Creating a Fade

Creating a Cross Fade is one of the most common audio adjustments you can make in video editing. It's the audio equivalent of a Dissolve, and it allows the volume to rise gradually so that it does not sound harsh. For example, cutting from a quiet room to a crowd scene creates a large jump in volume if you don't use a Cross Fade.

You can create a Cross Fade in a number of ways, including using the slider bar as detailed earlier. But Liquid Edition has two shortcut methods for achieving this much used audio effect: using the one-click fade and the Cross Fade button.

A one-click fade is quick and easy because it automatically adjusts the volume so that it fades gracefully in and out. If that's all you need, then this is the quickest way to do it.

The Cross Fade is the audio companion to the Dissolve, which creates a gradual visual change from one scene to the other (see Chapter 8 for details). The Cross Fade complements this by doing the same job but with audio.

To use a one-click Cross Fade:

1. Open the Audio Editor by clicking F4.

2. Place the mouse cursor over the volume line so that a pointing finger appears (**Figure 7.28**).

3. Hold down the Ctrl key and the mouse pointer changes into an arrow with a plus sign (+) next to it.

   Near the mark-in point of a clip, the arrow points to the left (**Figure 7.29**). Near the mark-out point of a clip, the arrow points to the right (**Figure 7.30**). This tells you in which direction the Cross Fade will be applied.

Figure 7.28 The pointing finger, only seen when the Audio Editor is open.

Figure 7.29 When you press the Ctrl key, this turns into the one-click fade arrow—here to the mark-in point...

Figure 7.30 ...and here to the mark-out point.

Figure 7.31 Click once in each place to create the one-click fade.

CREATING A FADE

Figure 7.32 The Add Dissolve is also used to add a Cross Fade.

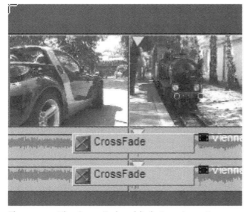

Figure 7.33 The Cross Fade added at center cut.

Cross Fades Not Appearing

There are two reasons a Cross Fade does not appear.

◆ The audio track is not active. (More details on active and deactivated tracks can be found in Chapter 6.)

◆ You don't have enough overlapping material to legally call a Cross Fade. (In this case, see Chapter 8 for details on trimming overlapping clips.)

---

4. Click once where you want the fade to end or begin.

A keyframe is placed at the start of the audio volume line at zero dB (null volume), and a second one is placed where you clicked, thus creating a fade-in.

By clicking the mark-out point, you can create a fade-out with the first keyframe at normal volume levels and the second one at the end of the clip at zero dB (**Figure 7.31**).

✔ Tip

■ You can also use the method described here on a clip with embedded audio.

To add a Cross Fade:

1. Make sure the timeline cursor is over the cut or edit decision point.

2. Click the Add Dissolve/Cross Fade button , and choose your duration and alignment in the dialog box (**Figure 7.32**).

The default alignment is Centered on Cut, but you can also either end or start the Cross Fade at the cut.

3. Click the check mark to insert the Cross Fade into the Timeline (**Figure 7.33**).

✔ Tips

■ Cross Fade does not work with an embedded audio clip.

■ If the audio track is attached to a video track, then a Dissolve is automatically added to it. If you don't want this to happen, toggle the video track off while you apply the Cross Fade by clicking it once.

Using Audio Scrubbing

Once you have adjusted the audio you will want to play it back to preview the changes. But sometimes an audio event, like the single click of a camera, is difficult to isolate when it is being played back at normal speed. To get around this, you can scrub the Timeline with the mouse by moving it backward and forward over the sound event until you have found the exact spot you need to change.

However, audio scrubbing is turned off by default. This is set that way so that the majority of editing tasks can be performed while your machine is enjoying the full computer resources available to it.

Once audio scrubbing is turned on, you will see a performance hit, so I recommend that you only turn it on when you need it and then turn it back off again once the audio job is done.

Audio scrubbing in the Source Viewer

This is useful when you're placing makers or setting mark-in and mark-out points for your media clips. Both video and audio tracks can be scrubbed in the Source Viewer.

To activate audio scrubbing in the Source Viewer:

1. Press the Scroll Lock key on your keyboard to activate audio scrubbing.

   A small A appears over the Audio icon in the Liquid Edition taskbar (**Figure 7.34**).

2. Scrub through the Source Viewer to hear the audio.

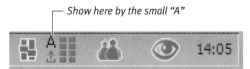

Show here by the small "A"

Figure 7.34 Audio scrubbing activated.

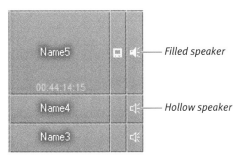

Filled speaker

Hollow speaker

Figure 7.35 The track names showing both examples.

Audio scrubbing the Timeline

This type of scrubbing is a little more complex to activate, but it follows the same basic path—you must press the Scroll Lock key to activate it. However, you then need to make sure the speaker icon on the track you want to hear is hollow, as shown in **Figure 7.35**. Here, the Name 4 and Name 3 tracks display a hollow speaker icon, and audio scrubbing will be heard on these tracks. Name 5 shows a solid speaker icon, and audio scrubbing will not be heard on this track.

To set a Timeline track for audio scrubbing:

◆ Hold down the Shift key and click once on the speaker representing that Timeline track you want to scrub.

The speaker becomes hollow, indicating that audio scrubbing is active for this track.

✔ Tip

■ Only two Timeline tracks can be activated for audio scrubbing at any one time. Activating a third will turn one of the other two off.

Digital or Analog Output

You have two choices of output when you're using audio scrubbing: digital or analog.

These can be toggled on or off by activating audio scrubbing with the Scroll Lock key and then right-clicking the small A that appears next to the Audio Editor in the Liquid Edition taskbar (**Figure 7.36**).

◆ Digital output has one big advantage over analog: its performance is much better.

◆ Analog output has one big advantage over digital: its audio quality is much clearer and easier to work with.

Which one you use depends on how powerful your computer is and how badly you need the quality offered by analog.

Figure 7.36 Switching to digital scrubbing.

Trimming Audio Clips

In Chapter 6, I covered trimming and showed you how to adjust video and image clips. You can apply the same principles to audio clips, meaning that trimming is simply the method you use to get rid of those elements you no longer need, such as a long musical intro, or perhaps even the lyrics from a song.

With clever trimming, you can even create a looping musical track that contains only instrumentals.

The Source Viewer is the natural place to preview and trim an audio clip because it is only a double-click away. But the steps outlined here work equally well in the Clip Viewer.

To trim with the Source Viewer:

1. Double-click an audio clip to load it into the Source Viewer.

2. Turn on audio scrubbing by pressing the Scroll Lock key.

3. Scrub through the clip until you find the point where you want your clip to begin.

4. Press the I key to insert a new mark-in point.

5. Scrub through again until you find a suitable end point.

6. Press the O key to set the mark-out point.

To send to the Timeline:

You can send audio clips directly to the Timeline by *doing one of the following:*

◆ Press the insert arrow (for the keyboard shortcut, press B).

◆ Drag the audio clips from the Source Viewer by holding down the Ctrl key and the left mouse button.

✔ Tip

■ When sending an audio clip to the Timeline, you should be aware of which mode you are in—Overwrite Style or Film Style—and also which tracks are mapped to receive your clip. You can find more details on both of these modes in Chapter 6.

To trim audio clips on the Timeline:

◆ To trim an audio clip directly on the Timeline, you follow the same procedure as when you are trimming a video clip. Simply grab the mark-in or mark-out point of the clip and drag it to its new position. See Chapter 6 for more details.

✔ Tip

■ A clip cannot be dragged further than its own physical length.

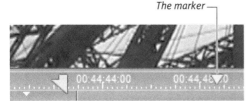

The marker

Figure 7.37 The marker appears as a small gray triangle.

Adding Markers to Audio Clips

You will find that markers are particularly useful in audio editing because the WAV forms—the somewhat complex-looking lines that appear in the Source Viewer when an audio clip is sent there—are not always as useful as you might need them to be. Picking out a specific audio section may be virtually impossible among the mass of lines displayed.

It is quicker and smarter to place a marker at every audio event you deem important. This can be as extreme as a marking the beat of the music, to something as simple as marking the start of the lyrics or the banging of a car door.

To add a marker to an audio clip:

1. Double-click the audio clip to send it to the Source Viewer.

2. Scrub or play the audio clip until you reach the point you want to mark.

3. Press the M key or click the Set Marker button ▼ if you have this button on your interface.

A small gray triangle appears at this point (**Figure 7.37**).

✔ Tips

■ When adding a marker to the beat of a song, you can simply play the clip and press the M key every time you hear the beat change. If you miscalculate the placement of a marker, you can adjust this later by holding down the Alt key and dragging the marker to a better position.

■ For more information on markers and how to name and delete them, see Chapter 6.

Activating and Deactivating Audio

You can temporarily mute audio tracks so that you can hear the other audio tracks on the Timeline or simply to preserve your sanity when you are listening to the same clip over and over.

To mute a Timeline track:

Do one of the following:

- Click once on the speaker icon that belongs to the track you want to mute (**Figure 7.38**).

- Open the Audio Editor and click the speaker icon at the top of the sliders (**Figure 7.39**).

✔ Tip

- You can mute as many tracks as you like and bring them back again by clicking in the speaker column and selecting Audio Playback On (**Figure 7.40**).

Figure 7.38 Click here to mute the volume of this track...

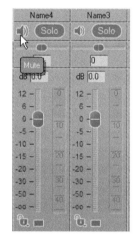

Figure 7.39 ...or here.

Figure 7.40 Activating audio on all tracks.

Deleting an Audio Track from a Video Clip

In some cases, you might want to rid the video of its audio completely. In this case, you have two options: turning the audio off in the clip's properties, or disbanding the audio and deleting just the audio section.

To turn off the audio track:

◆ Right-click the media clip in the Timeline, select Properties, and deselect any audio boxes that are not grayed out (**Figure 7.41**).

✔ Tip

■ Deselecting the audio in this way leaves the original media clip in the Project Browser untouched.

To delete an audio track:

1. Select the clip on the Timeline by clicking it once.

2. Right-click and select Disband Clip(s) from the menu if the clip is not already disbanded.

   If you needed to perform this extra step, you need to reselect the clip again by clicking it once.

3. With the clip selected, hold down the Ctrl key and click once on the video section of the clip so that it turns a lighter shade marking it as deselected (**Figure 7.42**).

4. Press the Delete key on your keyboard and the audio part of this clip is deleted.

✔ Tip

■ Deleting an audio track on the Timeline only affects the clip on the Timeline. The parent clip in the Project Browser retains its audio tracks.

Figure 7.41 Turning off audio in the clip's properties.

Figure 7.42 The audio remains selected but not the video.

Lowering the Monitor Output

The *monitor output* is the level of audio you hear when editing. This is controlled by the Audio tool, which you access by clicking the Audio Tool icon 🎛 in the Liquid Edition taskbar (**Figure 7.43**).

You control the output via the sliders, which you can lock together by clicking the Lock button at the bottom of Audio tool.

It is important to remember that adjusting the volume here does not place keyframes on the Timeline, nor does it alter the final output volume of your project. You simply use it to adjust the playback level of the Timeline while you are editing.

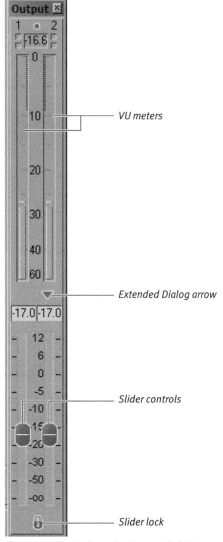

VU meters

Extended Dialog arrow

Slider controls

Slider lock

Figure 7.43 The Audio tool with Extended dialog open.

Exploring Advanced Audio Techniques

So far, you can think of everything covered by this chapter as the basics of audio editing. The next section covers the more advanced concepts such as panning, voice-over, filters, synchronization problems, and last but not least, surround sound.

Although these features are classified as advanced, implementing them is simple and easy to understand.

LOWERING MONITOR OUTPUT

Figure 7.44 Showing the Panning line.

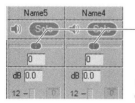

— *Panning controls*

Figure 7.45 The panning controls.

Figure 7.46 An example of the panning keyframes.

Figure 7.47 Panning keyframes are left behind when the clip is moved.

Using Audio Panning

Audio panning is simply the swapping of audio from the left channel to the right. Like volume adjustment, you alter this using keyframes that you add to the Timeline via the Audio Editor.

To use panning:

1. Activate Show Panning by clicking the speaker column for the track you are working with and selecting Show Track output Panning (**Figure 7.44**).

2. Open the Audio Editor by pressing F4 on the keyboard.

3. Slide the horizontal slider under the Solo button to the left or right to control panning (**Figure 7.45**).

   Sliding it in either direction adds a green keyframe to the Timeline signifying that the panning changes at this point (**Figure 7.46**).

✔ Tips

■ Track panning is independent of the actual clips and runs the length of the Timeline, not the length of the clip. If you set a panning keyframe and then move the clip, the keyframes do not follow (**Figure 7.47**).

■ Panning keyframes are undone from the Timeline Undo button (Ctrl+Z), not the audio Undo button.

USING AUDIO PANNING

Left and Right

When panning audio streams, you need to remember that odd-numbered channels are assigned to the left speakers (A1 & A3) by default, and even numbers (A2 & A4) are assigned to the right speakers.

Voice-Over

A voice-over is a standard part of any professional video project. Its inclusion often separates an amateur project from a polished one, but only if it is done correctly. Liquid Edition has the ability to record a voice-over directly to the Timeline using a standard microphone linked to the computer's sound card.

To create a voice-over:

1. Place a mark-in point on the Timeline where you would like the voice-over to begin. You can also place a mark-out point where you would like the voice-over to end. If you do not, the recording continues until you turn it off.

2. Open the Audio Editor by pressing F4.

3. Select which track you want the voice-over applied to by clicking the Audio Recording rectangle at the bottom of the slider. When it goes red, it has been selected (**Figure 7.48**).

4. Click the Microphone button ![icon], and the timeline cursor is placed five seconds before the mark-in point, and then the clip begins playing back.

5. You should begin speaking when the clip reaches the mark-in point.

   If you have defined a mark-out point, the recording stops there. If you haven't, you must stop the recording by clicking the Microphone button once more.

6. Once recording has stopped, a dialog box appears asking you to name the clip and to accept it (**Figure 7.49**).

7. Click the check mark and your recorded voice-over is inserted at the mark-in point (**Figure 7.50**).

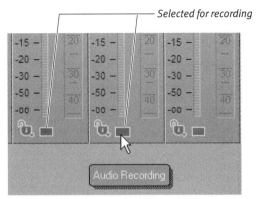

Selected for recording

Figure 7.48 Activating Audio Recording for this track.

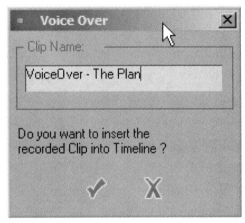

Figure 7.49 Naming the voice-over.

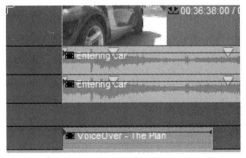

Figure 7.50 The voice-over inserted on the mark-in point.

Figure 7.51 The new Voice-Over rack with your voice-over recordings inside.

✔ Tips

- When the Voice-Over function is used, a new Rack called Voice-Over is created in the Project Browser and all your recordings are sent there (**Figure 7.51**).

- When you first click the Microphone button, the cursor jumps back 5 seconds before playing. This is known as the *preroll time,* and you can alter it by opening the Audio properties box found in the Control Panel.

Creating a Better Voice-Over

But there is a problem with using the voice-over feature in Liquid Edition. By and large, computers are noisy beasts; they whirr in the background with a variety of fans while their hard drives click mysteriously away. In short, this is not an environment for producing a clear-sounding voice-over.

And on top of that, how good a narrator are you? Can you cope with the pressure of reading from a script and getting each word perfect as the video rolls by your slightly anxious face?

The answer, perhaps, is to use a professional microphone, a well-prepared script, and a quiet (computer-free) room to record your voice. You can also use the camera you use for video to capture your voice, probably with better quality than most PC microphones produce, and you can capture it via the Logging Tool by deselecting the video channel (see Chapter 2 for details).

Once you have captured or imported this, you are free to trim it in the Source Viewer, cut it up, or simply use the bits that you now need.

Personally, I find this a better way to work, but if you need to insert a simple voice-over of a few seconds, then the Voice-Over function in Liquid Edition is probably the way to go. Of course if you are looking to create a rough edit for client approval, this direct voice recording may also help you save time and effort.

VOICE-OVER

233

Applying Audio Filters

An *audio filter* is simply a mask that is added to the audio so that it can be artificially altered in various ways. Earlier versions of Liquid Edition featured very few audio filters, but then Pinnacle Systems purchased Steinberg and all that changed.

Version 6 features seven new audio filters and also the ability to use any VST plug-in, which essentially allows you to use one of the many audio plug-ins commercially available for video editing.

You can apply an audio filter in one of three ways: directly to a clip; to an entire audio track; to an entire track but via the Audio Editor.

To add an Audio Clip FX (filter) to a clip:

1. Click once on the Lib tab in the Project Browser to show the filters.

2. Select the Audio Filters Rack in the Realtime Clip FX folder to display the available filters (**Figure 7.52**).

3. Click the filter you want and drag and drop it onto the clip you want to adjust.

   The affected clip displays a large purple line along the top; embedded audio clips also show a small speaker symbol (**Figure 7.53**).

Figure 7.52 The Audio Filters Rack.

Figure 7.53 The small speaker indicates the presence of an audio filter.

VST Plug-Ins

Additional VST plug-ins can be added to Liquid Edition by copying them to the \Plugins\VST folder. You can find this in the Pinnacle directory on your hard drive.

Once the application is restarted, Liquid Edition should automatically detect the extra plug-ins and add them to the Audio Filters Rack.

Figure 7.54 Audio filter added to an entire track.

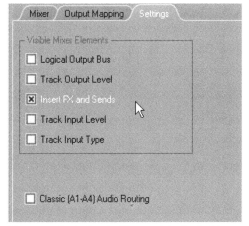

Figure 7.55 Activating the FX area of the Audio Editor.

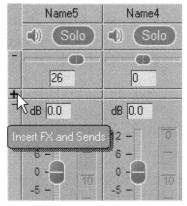

Figure 7.56 Open up the FX area...

To add an Audio Clip FX to a track:

1. Click once on the Lib tab in the Project Browser to show the filters.

2. Select the Audio Filters Rack in the Realtime Clip FX folder to display the available filters.

3. Click the filter you want, and drag and drop it onto the track you want to adjust.

   A purple line is displayed along the track name area (**Figure 7.54**).

To add an audio filter in the Audio Editor interface:

1. Open the Audio Editor by pressing F4.

2. If the Insert FX box is not already displayed in the Audio Editor, click the Settings tab, and click the check box next to Insert FX and Sends (**Figure 7.55**).

3. Return to the Mixer tab area and expand the Insert FX area by clicking the plus sign (+) (**Figure 7.56**).

continues on next page

4. Place the mouse cursor over the Insert FX box until it turns into a downward-facing black arrow; click here, selecting Insert Audio FX from the two choices, and then select the filter you require (**Figure 7.57**).

5. Click once on the small blue square next to the filter to activate the filter without first editing its parameters (**Figure 7.58**).

A purple line appears on the track to which you have applied these filters. Placing a mouse cursor over this line displays the name(s).

✔ Tip

■ You can add as many filters as you like to a single track, but beyond a certain limit (dictated by what is on the Timeline), Liquid Edition needs to render the audio.

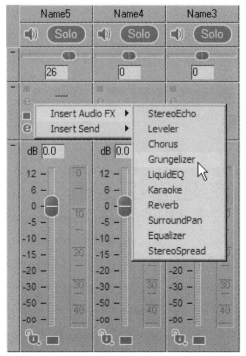

Figure 7.57 ... and choose a filter to insert.

Figure 7.58 Activate the filter by clicking the red square.

APPLYING AUDIO FILTERS

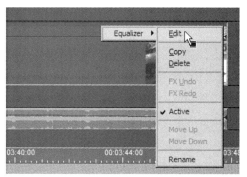

Figure 7.59 Accessing the Edit screen on the Timeline.

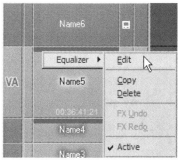

Figure 7.60 For the track-based filter...

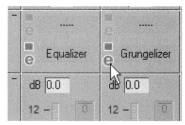

Figure 7.61 ...and in the Audio Editor.

Editing a Filter

Once you have added a filter in any of the ways described earlier, you will want to edit the parameters, which is, after all, the whole point of adding a filter.

To edit a filter:

1. Depending on which method you used to add the filter, open the editor by *doing one of the following:*

   ▲ Right-click the purple line running along the top of the clip, or click the speaker icon and choose Edit from the menu (**Figure 7.59**).

   ▲ Right-click the purple line running along the top of the track name and select Edit (**Figure 7.60**).

   ▲ Click the small "e" next to the filter in the Audio Editor (**Figure 7.61**).

continues on next page

Depending on which type of filter you are using, you see either a standard Liquid Edition interface (**Figure 7.62**) or one of the new VST plug-in interfaces (**Figure 7.63**).

2. First set a mark-in and mark-out point around the audio clip you are working on so that you can edit the parameters on any of these interfaces; then click the Play from Mark-In to Mark-Out button ▮▶▮ to loop the audio.

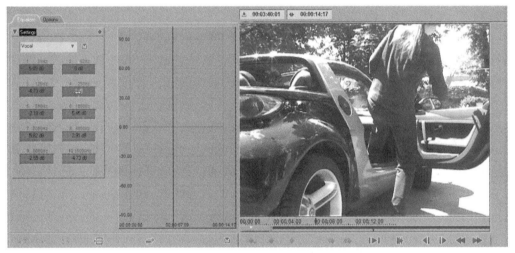

Figure 7.62 The standard Liquid Edition Filter Editor.

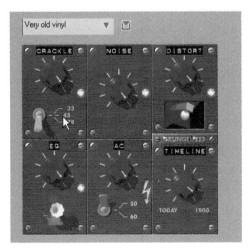

Figure 7.63 The VST Filter Editor.

EDITING A FILTER

Figure 7.64 Dragging the mouse over the values to alter them.

Figure 7.65 Deleting a filter.

Figure 7.66 Moving a filter down in priority.

3. Once the audio starts, you can adjust the setting using the mouse for the VST interfaces and a combination of mouse and direct number entry for the standard Liquid Edition interfaces (**Figure 7.64**).

4. Once you have finished adjusting the filter, click the Running Man button to exit the filter.

✔ Tips

■ Some of these filters do not use keyframes. This means any alterations affect the whole length of the clip.

■ Once you have found a set of parameters that work well, you can save them by clicking the small envelope button and selecting Save VST Bank.

To delete an audio filter:

◆ Right-click and select Delete (**Figure 7.65**).

✔ Tips

■ You can also deactivate a filter from this menu, although if you added the filter via the Audio Editor, you need to click the red square to deactivate it.

■ Stacking effects is possible, but the order in which they affect the clip is from top to bottom. If you are not hearing the effect you think you should, try adjusting the stack order by moving it up or down via the right-click menu (**Figure 7.66**).

Keep It Simple

Be brave and ask yourself these honest questions: Am I a sound engineer? Do I have any practical, real-life experience working with audio? Do I, in fact, have any idea what I am doing with audio? If the answer to any of these questions is no, then you need to use audio editing with extreme caution.

Audio, as I mention at the start of this chapter, is a very important part of the whole video project; try not to ruin this by overusing the filters available just because they are available. Less is often more.

Keeping Audio and Video in Sync

Although my recommendation is to use embedded audio wherever possible, it's a given that you will come across instances where it is far simpler to use disbanded audio. This may be the case when you are adding filters or simply having trouble visualizing how your project is pieced together. Many people find it useful to see the WAV form under the video and then just trim to the sound.

If you do disband your audio, you need to activate the Sync Break feature so that you can be made aware of any video and audio sync problems. See the "To activate Sync Break" task below.

Working with ungrouped files

If you send your media clips to the Timeline ungrouped, generally speaking, these files automatically stick together unless a new media clip causes others to move up the Timeline, thus leaving the audio behind.

If you can't prevent audio sync problems from occurring, then you can at least use Sync Break so you can get a warning that it has happened. Once activated, Sync Break displays a red line along the bottom of any audio files that are out of sync; it also displays how many frames out of alignment the track is (**Figure 7.67**).

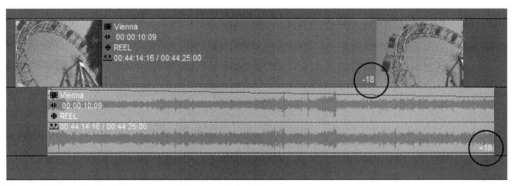

Figure 7.67 Sync Break alerts you to an 18-frame sync problem.

Figure 7.68 Linking two or more items together.

To activate Sync Break:

◆ Right-click the track name and drag the mouse down this menu to the View options. Here you can toggle Sync Break on. You need to toggle this on for all tracks that you want to monitor.

✔ Tip

■ Note that this does not prevent sync problems, but it does alert you to prudent use of the Undo key once you see what is occurring.

Linking objects

If the audio and video were brought in separately—as in the case of a voice-over—then you can line these objects up on the Timeline and then link them together. Once linked, you can trim these objects on the Timeline or in the Trim Editor while always keeping them together.

To link Timeline objects:

1. Use the Ctrl key to select the objects you want to link together.

2. Right-click any of the objects and select Item Link and then Link Items (**Figure 7.68**).

✔ Tip

■ This menu also allows you to unlink the media clips.

Working with 5.1 Surround Sound

The most exciting thing about DVD players is the 5.1 surround sound they offer home users. All of a sudden, we can watch a movie at home and not feel cheated on the sound effects front. It was inevitable that home video editors would want to include this capability in their bag of tricks.

Liquid Edition offers a very simple and intuitive interface for controlling 5.1 sound, but before you start, you must understand some of the basics involved.

The right equipment

To start with, you are going to need a 5.1 sound card and the means to monitor the 5.1 output. This might sound obvious, but it's a detail overlooked by many would-be Spielbergs who are rushing to produce the next Oscar winner.

The sound card specifically needs to be an ASIO 2.0–compliant card, and it needs to have a genuine 5.1 output (usually this is achieved via an optical cable). This output needs to be connected to a 5.1 speaker system via a 5.1 amplifier.

You must check to make sure your system meets all these requirements before you can even think about 5.1 editing.

The right noises

Once you establish that you have the right equipment, you need enough audio to fill up 5.1 speakers. Yes, you can have the normal audio track reverberating from 5 different places in the room, but that kind of destroys the whole concept of "surround sound," that is, being surrounded by sound.

To do this effectively, the sound needs to make sense of the video. If you have two people talking onscreen, make sure their voices come from the center speaker, not the left and right. Using the left and right speakers makes them sound like they are further apart than your eyes are telling you they are.

But if someone off camera to stage left shouts into the shot, put them on that left speaker. If the shout comes from behind the camera, put it on both the rear speakers. Is the shot of a crowded room where speeches are being given? Then have the speeches come from the center speakers and, at a much lower volume, use the other speakers for the crowd noises.

Ambient sound effects such as cars, birds, and cows mooing can all be placed (at a much lower volume) on the speakers out of sight. All come together to create a surround of sound!

.1?

The .1 in the 5.1 surround sound equation stands for the subwoofer, the mysterious big box that sits on the floor producing harmonious amounts of bass as if by magic; allowing your other speakers to be improbably small.

You don't need to deal with this on the Timeline because the bass from all tracks is naturally diverted to the subwoofer by the 5.1 sound system you are using.

Figure 7.69 The ideal track layout for editing 5.1 sound.

Setting up the Timeline and Audio Editor

Obviously you are going to need five audio tracks on the Timeline; the logical way to set them up and name them is displayed in **Figure 7.69**.

This allows you to use the Audio Editor to full effect when it comes to editing the five sound streams.

By default, the Audio Editor does not display the 5.1 panning boxes; you need to add them manually through the Logical Output Bus setting.

To access the Logical Output Bus setting:

1. Open the Audio Editor by clicking F4.

2. Switch to the Setting tab and mark the Logical Output Bus check box (**Figure 7.70**).

3. Switch back to the Mixer tab and see that a small (almost invisible) extra row has been inserted between the dB box and the Panning box.

   Click the small plus sign (+) to expand this (**Figure 7.71**).

continues on next page

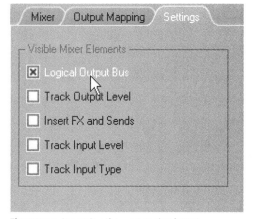

Figure 7.70 Accessing the 5.1 panning boxes.

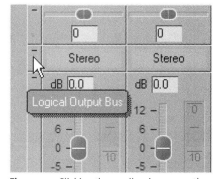

Figure 7.71 Clicking the small + sign opens the interface to display the stereo boxes.

WORKING WITH 5.1 SURROUND SOUND

4. Place the mouse cursor over the word Stereo and click. From the menu, select Surround 5.1 (**Figure 7.72**).

Repeat this for the other four sound channels until the Audio Editor looks like **Figure 7.73**.

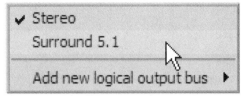

Figure 7.72 Right-click to access the 5.1 option.

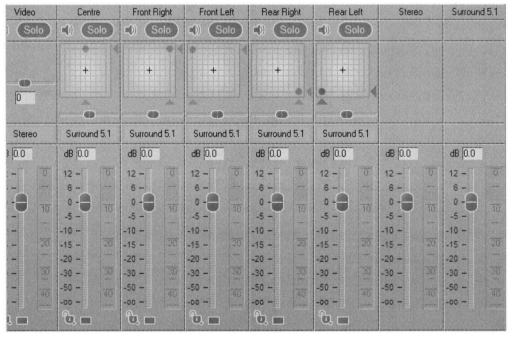

Figure 7.73 The 5.1 panning area, at last displayed.

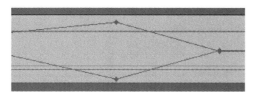

Figure 7.74 An example of surround sound panning. The first keyframes (top and bottom) are with panning set to the rear speaker on the right. The second keyframe is with panning set to the center of the room (all speakers).

Figure 7.75 Activate the panning display from here.

DVD Creation

Once you have successfully created a surround sound mix, you can burn it to DVD to hear how it sounds on a full DVD setup.

For more details on exporting your projects to DVD, see Chapter 12.

Creating surround sound

Once the preparations just discussed are complete, you can actually begin creating your surround sound effects, placing audio clips carefully on those areas you have predefined as routing to various speaker locations.

The fun, of course, comes when you begin panning the surround sound. This can create marvelous effects. For example, imagine a plane that appears from behind the camera and moves off into the distance in front; now imagine that this video clip is matched perfectly with the sound, which also starts behind the audience and follows the plane away.

To pan surround sound

◆ Simply move the dot around the panning box.

As you do this, red and green lines appear on the clip (**Figure 7.74**) with red and green keyframes.

✔ Tips

■ In the diagram, the + symbol in the middle is the listener. Toward the top of the box is the front of the room; toward the bottom of the box is the back of the room.

■ Similar to normal panning, surround sound keyframes are related to the Timeline, not the clip.

■ If you don't see the red and green panning lines, check that the panning display is selected (**Figure 7.75**). The third option—Show Track output LFE—displays the volume line associated with the subwoofer.

Working with Transitions

A transition is a jump from one video clip to the next, or from one scene to another. Typically, this jump changes the location, but it can also indicate time passing or a simple mood change. Often, you accomplish this change with a cut, as described in Chapter 6, but occasionally you need to employ a more subtle approach—something that doesn't visually jar the audience. For example, you need to gradually change the image from a rampant party to the aftermath of the room the next day so that the audience isn't left thinking, "What am I looking at?"

Sometimes you don't need subtlety; the change itself clearly alerts the audience that the scene is about to shift. An example of this type of change might be to signify the start of an advertising break or mark the end of your video production. In either example, you use a transition. Liquid Edition offers you a great selection of subtle and not-sot-subtle transitions for use in your video projects. In this chapter, you learn how to use and abuse these, placing them on the Timeline and editing their parameters to create totally original effects.

Understanding Transitions and the Single-Track Edit

Liquid Edition uses a single-track edit system, which means all the media clips exist on a single track. However, you can have as many tracks as you want, and then you can combine them together to create some spectacular effects.

On the opposite side of the fence is the A/B roll method, which some other NLE programs use. This method needs three lines to create a transition; these lines are often static and can't be customized to your individual needs.

Both single-track edit and A/B roll have advantages and disadvantages, particularly when it comes to the everyday use of transitions, which you look at in the next few pages.

The A/B roll method

The A/B roll method uses the concept of two tracks—Track A at the top, and Track B at the bottom—and in between them, you insert a transition. **Figure 8.1** shows a graphical representation of this. The mark-in point of the clip on Track B is the start of the transition; the mark-out point of the clip on Track A is the end of the transition.

The A/B roll method is easy to understand visually and thus easier to understand on straightforward projects. You simply position the clips to overlap and then place the transition in the middle to fill the overlapping gap. But you may encounter a problem. Suppose you want to add a title above Track A and then add a transition at the beginning of that title so that it fades into the rest of the track smoothly. Well, you can't. Your only option is to alter the transparency levels of the title, but this isn't going to help you if you want a much more advanced type of transition, such as a band wipe or a water ripple.

Figure 8.1 The A/B roll method with overlapping clips.

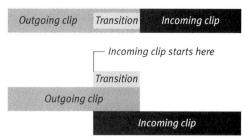

Figure 8.2 The top image shows the single track edit with hidden overlapping clips. Below this is a "side-on" graphical representation of that same image.

Figure 8.3 Two video clips are midway through a Dissolve, while over the top a title is coming to the end of a water drop transition.

The single-track edit system

In contrast, the single-track edit system is a little more complex on the surface. The clips still overlap, but you can't see this overlap like you can in the A/B roll method. Instead, the clips are snuggled in behind each other (**Figure 8.2**). You can still manipulate the clips in the Trim Editor, but how you do this isn't quite as obvious as being able to see the overlapping gap between twp clips as is shown using the A/B roll system.

This makes using the single-track edit system a little more challenging, but not dramatically so. It's not as if you have to be a nuclear physicist to understand the concept, but the process is a little more cerebral than the building-block system used by the A/B roll method.

You'll be happy to know there is an advantage to using this method that should alleviate any potential headaches you feel coming on. Unlike the A/B roll method, the single-track edit system can support transitions on any video clip on any track. This means that if you need a transition—regardless of its complexity (take the example of adding a title or any other clip above your main clips, for instance)—you can do this. It's not a problem, as you can see in **Figure 8.3**.

This clear technical advantage goes a long way toward explaining why many NLE software programs prefer the single-track edit system to the A/B roll method.

TRANSITIONS AND THE SINGLE-TRACK EDIT

Avoiding Transition Problems

Although the single-track edit system is indisputably the more flexible of the two approaches to NLE, you don't get something for nothing.

Because of the sheer power you wield by being able to place a transition on any track you want, you'll find that you have rules to follow. Liquid Edition needs you to follow these if it is to fully understand exactly what you want it to do. These rules are not that complex, and if you take certain precautions, you can avoid the confusion that comes with learning how to use the single-track edit system.

The most important thing to know about the rules is to make sure you have enough available handles (on both clips) and that you know how to adjust a clip if you don't have enough.

Using available handles

A *handle* is the bit of a clip you don't see. It's the bit that a transition needs in order to have a tangible piece of video with which it can work. It's also one of the more challenging aspects of single track editing, particularly for users transferring from the easy A/B roll system. But in fact handles are simple enough once you know exactly what you are looking for.

To visualize the handle of a clip:

1. Place any video clip in the Source Viewer.

2. Insert a mark-in a few seconds after the start and a mark-out point a few seconds from the end on the Source Viewer Timeline (see Chapter 6 for details on this).

   The first handle of the clip is the gap between the start of the media clip and the mark-in point. The other handle is the gap between the mark-out point and the end of the clip (**Figure 8.4**).

3. Send this clip to the Timeline using the insert arrow ![insert arrow icon] twice so that the clip appears as shown in **Figure 8.5**, the invisible areas before and after the mark-in and mark-out points—the handles—are used by the transition.

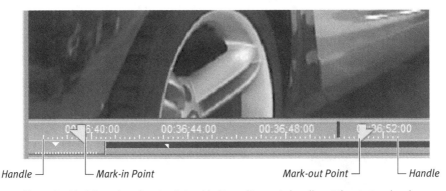

Handle —   └─ Mark-in Point   Mark-out Point ┘   └─ Handle

Figure 8.4 Mark-in and mark-out points added to a clip create handles at the start and end.

However, if you try to use a clip whose mark-in and mark-out points are the same as its clip-in and clip-out points—in other words, its natural length—you'll encounter a problem (**Figure 8.6**).

Repeat the last set of instructions but set the mark-in and mark-out points at the start and end of the clip respectively. This creates a Timeline that appears to be exactly the same as Figure 8.5, but you'll find that attempting to place a transition isn't possible. Instead, if you are dragging and dropping a transition, you see the error message "not enough media available to place transition" (**Figure 8.7**).

Worse still, if you're using the Add Dissolve button , nothing happens and no error message is displayed. This is because a transition needs these overlapping points—a set of handles—to which it can attach itself. Without them, the transition can't work.

Figure 8.5 Two clips on the Timeline waiting for a transition.

Figure 8.6 Liquid Edition uses the clip-in and clip-out points of a media clip that has no mark-in and mark-out points.

Figure 8.7 The error message you see if no handles exist for a transition to latch onto.

AVOIDING TRANSITION PROBLEMS

If you don't have enough handle length

In Chapter 6, I recommended—perhaps a little controversially—that you use embedded audio wherever possible to avoid audio sync issues. To avoid transition problems, I recommend that you alter a setting in Liquid Edition that prevents transitions from being placed if you don't have enough available handle length.

This means that the transition can appear even if it doesn't work correctly, allowing you to continue working without constantly worrying about available handle lengths. I cover trimming these clips so that they work with transitions in the "Trimming Associated Clips" section later in this chapter.

To turn off "Restrict dragged Transitions to available handles":

1. Right-click the Timeline to bring up the Timeline properties dialog box.

2. Switch to the General tab and uncheck the box next to "Restrict dragged Transitions to available handles" (**Figure 8.8**).

3. Click the check mark to accept this change.

✔ Tip

■ Once you make this change, you'll have to manually trim any clips that don't have enough handle space. See the "Trimming Associated Clips" section later in this chapter.

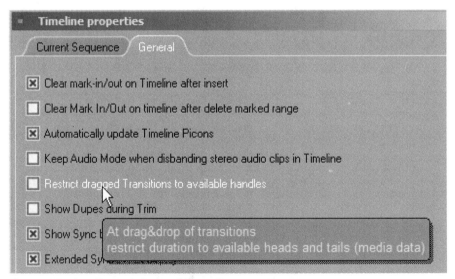

Figure 8.8 Turning off a restrictive transition setting.

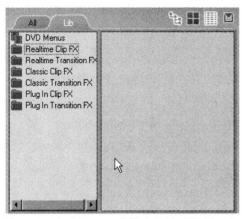

Figure 8.9 The full range of effects in Liquid Edition 6.

Figure 8.10 The Realtime Transition FX folder.

Figure 8.11 The Classic Transition FX folder.

Adding a Transition

Once you understand the basic concept of using transitions on a single-track edit system, you'll find that actually applying them is very easy. You can achieve this by either dragging and dropping or by right-clicking and sending.

To apply a transition to the Timeline:

1. Click the Open Project Browser in Timeline button ![icon] if the Project Browser is not yet open in the Timeline.

   If you are using a dual-screen setup, the Project Browser will already be open in one of you monitors. The Lib tab referred to in this chapter will read Library.

2. Click once on the Lib tab to show the effects Liquid Edition has to offer (**Figure 8.9**).

3. *Do one of the following:*
   - ▲ Open the Realtime Transition FX folder if you intend to add a Realtime transition (**Figure 8.10**).
   - ▲ Open the Classic Transition FX folder if you intend to use a non-Realtime transition (**Figure 8.11**).

   continues on next page

4. Once you've selected the type of transition you want, click once on the Rack to display its contents (**Figure 8.12**).

5. Highlight the actual transition you want by clicking it once.

6. Apply the transition to the Timeline by *doing one of the following:*

▲ Left-click and hold the mouse button over the transition, then drag it into the Timeline. Release the mouse button when the transition is over the point where the two clips meet (**Figure 8.13**).

▲ Place the timeline cursor roughly at the point where the two clips meet, then right-click the transition and select Send To > Timeline (**Figure 8.14**).

✔ Tips

■ If you're dragging a clip to the Timeline and you see the message "not enough media available to place transition," or you send to the Timeline and nothing happens, then refer to the earlier task "To turn off 'Restrict dragged Transitions to available handles.'"

■ Transitions obey the same magnetic rules that I outlined in Chapter 6. By holding down the Shift key, you can toggle the magnets on and off. Press the Alt key to shift the polarity of the magnet from center to mark-out point, to mark-in point, and back to center.

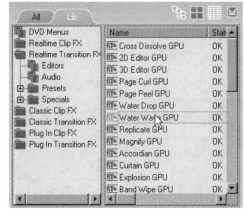

Figure 8.12 A selection of real-time editors.

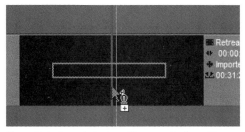

Figure 8.13 Dragging a transition over to the edit point of two clips.

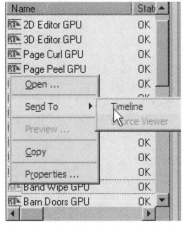

Figure 8.14 Sending the transition to the edit point by right-clicking.

- You can't stack transitions. If you try adding another transition on top of an existing transition, you'll discover that it replaces the original.

- Both the Realtime and Classic transitions offer a choice between Editors and Presets. The Realtime folder also has a Specials subfolder that contains a large collection of Hollywood FX presets. I deal with this folder in the "Adding a Preset Hollywood FX Transition" later in this chapter.

Realtime vs. Classic Transitions

The world of Liquid Edition is divided into two classes: Realtime effects that require no rendering in order to be previewed, and non-Realtime or Classic effects that must be rendered before you can see the results.

Realtime effects are further subdivided into CPU effects, which use the power of your computer's processor to display a Realtime transition; and GPU effects, which use the processor fitted to your graphics card.

The advantage of using Realtime effects is that they clearly increase the speed of your workflow so that you don't have to wait for a render to complete. But Classic effects also have a unique place in Liquid Edition because of the extended options they offer, a few of which are detailed here.

The following is a list of extended parameters that are only available to Classic effects:

- **Pan and Scan:** Realtime effects can only function within the boundaries of the TV standard you're working with. This means all images are cropped to that standard and anything outside the standard area appears black if you try to pan and scan it.

- **Full Screen:** Classic editors can display the effect using the entire PC monitor.

- **Keyframe Interpolation:** This parameter allows you to accelerate the rate at which an effect occurs between two keyframes. Again, this is only available in Classic mode. See "Keyframe Interpolation" later in this chapter for more information.

- **Priority:** Known in Photoshop and various composting programs as *blending*, this feature allows you to choose the transfer mode the transition uses, which allows you to utilize any of the recognized industry standard modes such as Multiply and Color Dodge.

- **More Gradient Wipes:** Although gradient wipes (formally known as the Spice Rack) are available in a real-time format, presets of a more organic variety are available in the Classic version.

Applying the Default Transition

The most common type of transition, and arguably the only transition you ever need, is the Dissolve. This transition gradually changes the scene from one image to the next using a series of subtle onscreen fades over a user-defined length of time (**Figure 8.15**).

Because this is such a commonly used effect, it's the only transition to earn a place as a shortcut button on the Liquid Edition Toolbar (**Figure 8.16**).

To apply the default transition:

1. Once you have two clips on the Timeline, place the timeline cursor roughly where the two clips meet (**Figure 8.17**).

2. Click once on the Add Dissolve/Cross Fade with Options button  to bring up the Add Dissolve dialog box (**Figure 8.18**).

Figure 8.15 Midway through a Dissolve you can see both clips.

Figure 8.16 The Dissolve button has its own interface button.

Figure 8.17 Two clips on the Timeline. The timeline cursor is over the edit point.

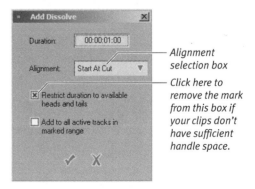

Alignment selection box

Click here to remove the mark from this box if your clips don't have sufficient handle space.

Figure 8.18 The Add Dissolve dialog box.

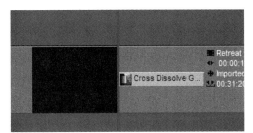

Figure 8.19 A Dissolve added to the start of a cut.

3. Alter the duration by entering numbers directly into this box and decide which alignment you want to use.

See the "Alignment Types" sidebar for more details.

4. Click the check mark to apply the transition (the result is shown in **Figure 8.19**).

✔ Tip

■ If the transition doesn't appear, this means you don't have enough overlap between the two clips. Uncheck the "Restrict duration to available heads and tails" check box to work around this. Then trim the handles of your clips to fit the transition. See the "Trimming Associated Clips" section later in this chapter.

Alignment Types

You have three types of alignment to choose from when applying the default transition: Start at Cut, Centered at Cut, and End at Cut. Which one you use depends entirely on the clip you're applying it to and what is contained inside the handles of that clip.

For example, when you're using the center alignment, the transition uses an equal number of frames from each handle area. In this handle area, you may encounter material not relevant to the clips with which you're working. If this is the case, you need to use the left or right alignment, depending on which clip is giving you problems.

If both clips contain a certain amount of unwanted material, you need to trim one or the other with the Trim Editor.

See the "To trim clips under a transition" task later in this chapter.

APPLYING THE DEFAULT TRANSITION

Changing the Default Transition

If you don't happen to agree with Pinnacle's choice of default transition, you'll be pleased to know that you can change it. But be warned, this is not a simple task and is not for the fainthearted. If you make a mistake, you may lose the ability to have the Dissolve as your default transition.

Changing the default transition is a two-stage operation. First you must create a backup of the Dissolve, and then you can create the link to a new default transition.

To create a backup of the Dissolve:

1. Under the All tab, create a new Rack in your Project Browser called Transitions (**Figure 8.20**).

2. Click the Lib tab to open the FX selection menu.

3. Locate the Cross Dissolve GPU transition in the Realtime Transitions FX/Editors folder and then right-click it, and select copy (**Figure 8.21**).

4. Return to the All tab and select the Transitions Rack that you created in Step 1 by clicking it once.

5. Then right-click the mouse in the right pane of the Project Browser and select Paste (**Figure 8.22**).

   You've now created a fallback position so that you can easily return the default transition to a Cross Dissolve when you want to (**Figure 8.23**).

Figure 8.20 Create a Rack to save your backup into.

Figure 8.21 Find the Cross Dissolve GPU transition and right-click to copy...

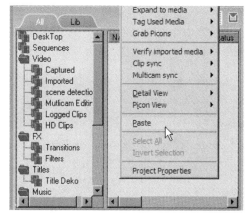

Figure 8.22 ...then paste it into your FX Rack.

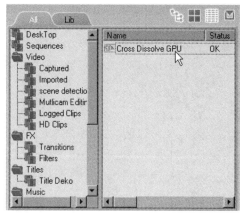

Figure 8.23 The Cross Dissolve transition safely stored in your backup Rack.

CHANGING THE DEFAULT TRANSITION

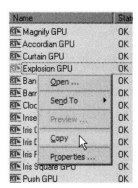

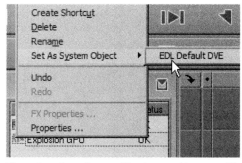

Figure 8.24 Copy the transition you want to use as the new default.

Figure 8.25 Once the transition is pasted into your FX Rack, right-click with the Ctrl key held down to reveal a new option.

To change the default transition:

1. Return to the FX selection menu by clicking the Lib tab again.

2. Choose a transition from any on display here.

   You can use any of the Presets, the Specials, or the Editors. You can even choose a Hollywood Effect, although you might want to avoid using a non-Realtime transition.

3. Once you have made your choice, right-click it and select Copy (**Figure 8.24**).

4. Click the All tab to return to your Transitions Rack.

5. Then right-click the mouse in the right pane of the Project Browser and select Paste.

6. Highlight this transition by clicking it once, and then hold down the Ctrl key and right-click the transition.

   The Set As System Object now appears on the menu.

7. Place the mouse over this item and the EDL Default DVE selection appears (**Figure 8.25**).

8. Click this and the transition you've highlighted is set as the default transition.

✔ Tips

- If you try holding down the Ctrl key while in the FX selection area, the Set As System Object option doesn't appear. The transition must first be copied and pasted into a folder inside the All section of the Project Browser.

- To return your default transition to that of a Cross Dissolve GPU, simply return to the Default Transitions folder you created, and while holding down the Ctrl key, right-click the Cross Dissolve, and select Set As System Object > EDL Default DVE.

CHANGING THE DEFAULT TRANSITION

Trimming Transitions

You trim the overall length of a transition in the Timeline; this is a separate task from trimming the clips you use in the transition.

This process is fairly easy and painless, but trimming the clips underneath the transition is somewhat more complex, as you'll see momentarily.

To trim a transition:

◆ Grab the mark-in or mark-out point of the transition and drag it whichever way you want (**Figure 8.26**).

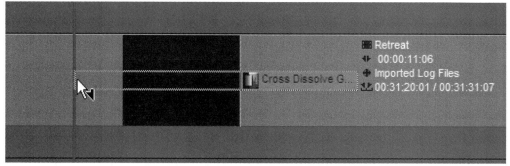

Figure 8.26 You can trim transitions on the Timeline by grabbing the end and dragging it.

Trimming Associated Clips

If you're using the setting I recommended earlier in the "Avoiding Transition Problems" section, you may need to trim your clips. If the transitions contain red areas that indicate that they don't have enough handle to function correctly, you need to trim them (**Figure 8.27**).

I cover trimming clips with the Trim Editor in detail in Chapter 6; refer to that chapter for a more detailed explanation of how the Trim Editor works. However, when you're dealing with a transition, the Trim Editor operates slightly differently.

In order to see the problem clearly, you need to prepare the Timeline before you attempt to trim clips under a transition.

To prepare the Timeline:

1. Send a clip to the Source Viewer and remove any mark-in or mark-out points.

2. Send this clip to an empty sequence twice so that the Timeline looks like **Figure 8.28.**

3. Drag and drop a transition to where the two clips join up.

   The transition appears on the Timeline colored completely red (**Figure 8.29**).

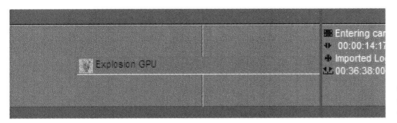

Figure 8.27 A transition with no handle area to work with appears red from end to end.

Figure 8.28 If two clips with no handles are sent to the Timeline...

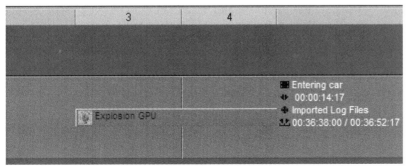

Figure 8.29 ...the transition will be red from end to end. *(See color insert.)*

To trim clips under a transition:

1. Place the timeline cursor so that it falls roughly over the middle of the transition.

2. Open the Trim Editor by pressing F5.

3. Press the P key to select the incoming clip—the right-hand window in the Trim Editor.

4. To remove the red area from the transition, do one of the following until all the red has disappeared.

   ▲ Press the right arrow on the keyboard.

   ▲ Place the mouse cursor over the right-hand window, hold down the left mouse button, and drag to the right (**Figure 8.30**).

   Both of these methods slice the right clip underneath the left clip.

5. Now trim the left clip by pressing the P key again; this sends the black selection bar to the left window. Then press the left arrow key or use the mouse to slide the left clip over the top of the right clip. Stop when the transition has turned from red to gray.

6. Click the Play Preview button ▐▌ in the middle of the Trim interface to see the result. Don't try to scrub with the mouse because doing so alters the trim points in the same way that pressing the left and right arrow keys does.

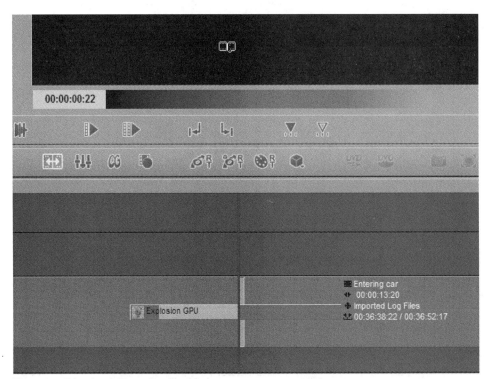

Figure 8.30 Trimming the incoming clip with the mouse.

✔ Tips

- When sliding the right clip underneath the left clip, take careful note of the frame displayed when you've finished pressing the right arrow key; this is the first frame of your transition for the incoming clip. When you trim the left clip, the last frame displayed is the mark-out point.

- If you place the transition at the beginning of the cut or at the end of the cut, you only need to slide one clip under or over the other. When you center the transition, you must slide both clips under or over the other for the transition to work correctly.

- If you delete or remove the transition using the Undo key, the clips remain in their trimmed position and you can add another transition without needing to retrim.

- Slip Trim mode doesn't work for this example because it doesn't have enough material—handles—to work with.

Rendering a Realtime Transition

Although the phrase "rendering a Realtime transition" sounds like a contradiction of terms, you have to remember that what you are seeing with a Realtime transition is a preview of that effect. With the right hardware (MovieBox Pro, or the AGP Pro card from Pinnacle), you can even view these transitions on an external TV. The quality is so good that you might mistakenly think that it already has rendered, but the clue is the slice above the transition (**Figure 8.31**).

If this is yellow, then you are looking at a real-time preview and you need to render this before you can create a DVD or output the Timeline to tape.

continues on next page

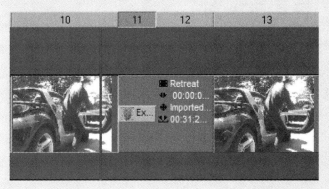

Figure 8.31 A yellow slice above an effect indicates that it is a real-time preview.

Rendering a Realtime Transition *continued*

To render a yellow slice, click the Render symbol in the Liquid Edition taskbar (**Figure 8.32**). Place an X in the include yellow slices check box and all yellow slices on the Timeline begin to render (**Figure 8.33**). Once the render has finished, the yellow slices will turn green.

If the rendering doesn't start, check that you haven't previously clicked the Stopped Rendering button to the left of the include yellow slices check box. If you have it will read "Start Rendering" and the render progress bar next to the render symbol will not move.

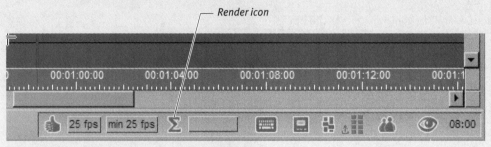

Figure 8.32 The Render icon opens the render box...

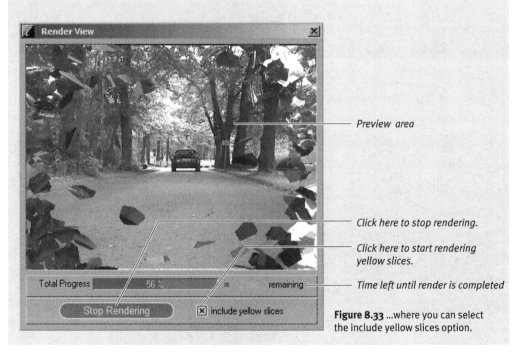

Figure 8.33 ...where you can select the include yellow slices option.

Figure 8.34 Opening the Transition Editor via a right-click.

Editing with Keyframes

As you can see from the earlier examples, actually adding a transition is relatively easy. The fun really starts when you want to alter the basic parameters of that transition to create something unique in your project. This is called editing with keyframes (I explain keyframes in more depth in the "Understanding Keyframes" sidebar).

The Transition Editor is similar in look and operation to the non-VST audio editors I introduced you to in Chapter 7, and you open them in a similar fashion.

To open a Transition Editor:

Do one of the following:

◆ Double-click the transition in the Timeline.

◆ Right-click the transition in the Timeline and select Edit from the menu (**Figure 8.34**).

Either of these methods brings up the editor for that transition. **Figure 8.35** shows the Explosion Transition Editor, which has several interesting adjustable parameters.

✔ Tips

■ Right-clicking a transition allows you to access the full range of editing options allowed for each transition.

■ Clicking on the Maximum Inlay Size button 🔲 on the Liquid Edition toolbar will create a bigger preview screen for you to use when adding transitions.

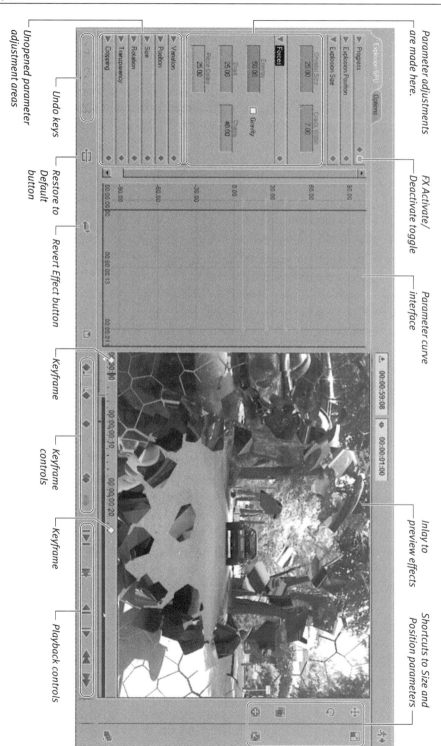

Figure 8.35 The Realtime Explosion Editor.

Parameter adjustments
are made here.

Undo keys

Unopened parameter
adjustment areas

Restore to
Default
button

Revert Effect button

FX Activate/
Deactivate toggle

Parameter curve
interface

Keyframe

Keyframe
controls

Keyframe

Inlay to
preview effects

Shortcuts to Size and
Position parameters

Playback controls

Understanding Keyframes

When you adjust the parameters in the transition editor, a small gray diamond appears on the editor's Source Viewer Timeline (**Figure 8.36**).

These diamond marks are keyframes and are part of the magic behind the NLE system.

A *keyframe* does pretty much what it says on the box—it creates a key point around which a certain action or event occurs.

When you adjust any of the parameters inside the Transition Editor, you create a keyframe. In Figure 8.36, you can see that multiple changes have been made, creating multiple gray diamonds (keyframes) on the Timeline. These control the way in which the transition behaves when it plays back.

Once you've created these keyframes, you can manipulate, move, copy, or delete them at will; this is the true power of a keyframe editing system.

Liquid Edition also uses keyframes to control audio levels. You can find details on this in Chapter 7.

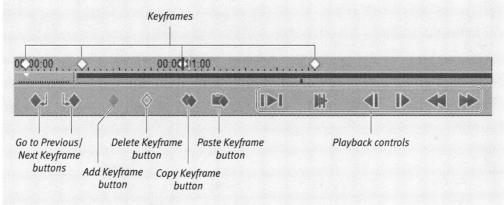

Figure 8.36 The keyframe control bar.

Editing a Transition

To create your own custom-made transition, you need to open the editor and then scrub through the Timeline deciding where and when to alter the various parameters. Experimenting is the only way to find out what each setting can do.

Figure 8.37 Click this triangle to open the parameter settings.

To edit a transition:

1. Open the Transition Editor by *doing one of the following*:

   ▲ Double-click the transition.

   ▲ Right-click and select Edit to open the Edit interface.

Figure 8.38 Use the mouse to alter the parameter...

2. Open the parameter you wish to alter by clicking once on the small triangle to the left of the name (**Figure 8.37**).

3. You can alter this parameter in one of the following ways:

   ▲ Place the mouse cursor over any of the parameter boxes and a double-headed cursor appears (**Figure 8.38**). Hold down the mouse button and drag to the right to increase the value displayed. Drag back to the left to reduce the value displayed.

Figure 8.39 ...enter the numerical value directly...

   ▲ Double-click inside the display area, enter the numerical value required (**Figure 8.39**), and press Enter.

   ▲ Click inside the parameter curve area on the line color that represents the parameter you wish to alter (**Figure 8.40**).

   Parameter lines and boxes always match up with coloring, but the line only appears if the parameter box is open, or if the parameter was previously adjusted.

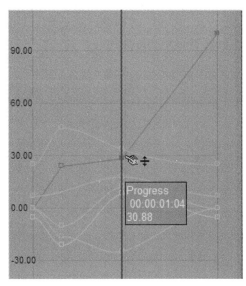

Figure 8.40 ...or use the parameter curve interface to dynamically add and alter keyframes.

✔ Tips

- After altering a parameter, you can play this clip inside the editor to see how your keyframes affect the final image. If it's a Classic transition, you can only scrub through the image. To play a Classic transition, you must first exit the editor and allow the transition to render.

- Undo and redo are fully supported when you're editing keyframes.

Applying a Parameter

If you need to apply any parameter to the whole length of a transition—for example, if you are using Mirror to flip an image—then drag the Keyframe symbol from the parameter's label area into the preview screen of the editor. Those settings in the parameter box then apply to the whole transition (**Figure 8.41**).

continues on next page

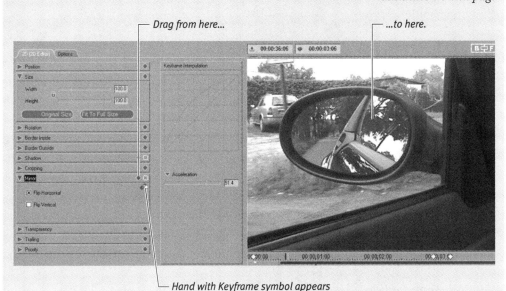

Drag from here...   ...to here.

Hand with Keyframe symbol appears while dragging the keyframe

Figure 8.41 Apply a parameter setting to the whole length of the transition.

EDITING A TRANSITION

269

Applying a Parameter *continued*

If you just want to apply these parameter settings to one specific keyframe that already exists on the Timeline, then drag the Keyframe symbol from the parameters label area onto that keyframe (**Figure 8.42**).

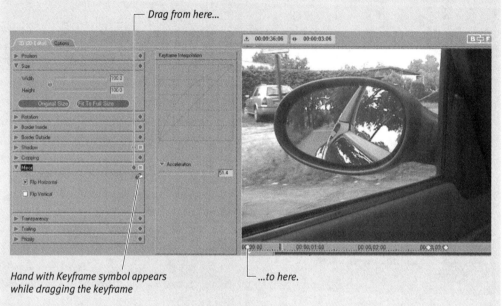

Drag from here...

Hand with Keyframe symbol appears while dragging the keyframe

...to here.

Figure 8.42 Apply a parameter setting to an individual keyframe.

Controlling Keyframes

After the last example, you should now have some understanding of how keyframes can enhance and customize your own transitions. But you must carefully control keyframes if you're to get the best from them.

It's possible to add a keyframe to the Timeline at any time in order to attach an effect to it. This is useful when you're using such advanced techniques as Keyframe Interpolation covered in the section "Working with Classic Transitions" later in this chapter.

You copy and paste keyframes if you need a parameter to stay the same throughout the length of the transition. Moving a keyframe is a quick-and-dirty but useful technique if you have a keyframe that requires just a little tweaking to get it in the ideal position.

In this section, you learn how to manually add and delete a keyframe, and how to copy/paste and move a keyframe inside the editor.

To add a keyframe:

1. With the editor open, scrub through the Timeline until you find the spot where you want to add a keyframe.

2. When the cursor is over this spot, click the Set Keyframe button ◆.

To delete a keyframe:

1. With the editor open, scrub through the Timeline until you are on a keyframe, or use the Go to Next Keyframe buttons ◆ ◆ to find each keyframe.

2. When the cursor is over the keyframe, the Delete Keyframe button ◆ becomes active. Click it and the keyframe vanishes.

To copy and paste a keyframe:

1. Place a keyframe anywhere on the Timeline using the methods detailed in the "To add a keyframe" task.

2. With the cursor over the keyframe, click the Copy Keyframe button ◆.

3. Move the cursor to the new point by scrubbing or playing, then click the Paste Keyframe button ◆ to apply this keyframe.

✔ Tips

■ A copied keyframe is entirely independent of the original and vice versa. Altering one doesn't change the other.

■ The last keyframe on the editor's Timeline cannot be moved.

To move a keyframe:

◆ Hold down the Alt key, then using the mouse, left-click the keyframe and drag it to the new position.

Deactivating a keyframe area

Occasionally you may want to turn off certain parameters in order to see the interaction of the other keyframes on the Timeline more clearly. You accomplish this using the keyframe toggle.

To deactivate a set of keyframes:

◆ Click the Activate square at the end of the row.

It turns from gold to blue and the parameters become grayed out (**Figure 8.43**).

If you scrub through this effect window, the keyframes won't be used.

Activated keyframes (gold color)

Deactivated keyframes (blue color)

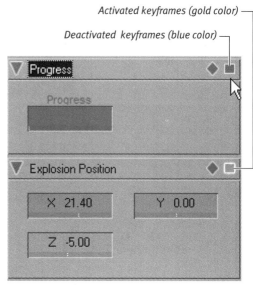

Figure 8.43 Toggle a set of keyframe parameters on or off with this symbol.

Reversing Keyframes

One effect common to both the Classic and RT interfaces is the Revert Direction of Effect button. This button inverts the keyframes you have created, effectively playing the effect backward.

Note: Due to technical restrictions, not all transitions have this button.

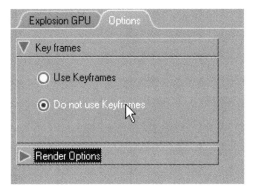

Figure 8.44 Turning off keyframes.

Working Without Keyframes

Although keyframes are a very valuable tool, you may encounter times when you don't want to use them. For example, you might have an exact transparency you want to carry through until the clip jumps into focus on the last frame of the transition.

To disable keyframes:

1. With the editor open, click the Options tab.

2. Open the keyframes area by clicking the small triangle.

3. Click the Do not use Keyframes radio button (**Figure 8.44**).

✔ Tips

■ Turning off keyframes is not generally that useful in a transition because it tends to nullify its effectiveness. Turning off keyframes is more useful when you're dealing with filters. See Chapter 9 for more details on this.

■ When you turn off keyframes, you turn them all off. To deactivate specific keyframes, see "Deactivating a keyframe area" on the previous page.

Working with Classic Transitions

Classic transitions are the old non-Realtime transitions from previous incarnations of Liquid Edition. They need to be rendered (in the background) before you can view them, which should put them at an immediate disadvantage. But because rules restrict the way Realtime transitions work, non-Realtime effects have some additional tricks they can pull from their hypothetical sleeves.

To apply a Classic transition:

◆ Open the Classic Transition FX folder and apply a classic filter (2D Editor in this example) after following the instructions above for adding a Realtime transitions. Double-clicking the transition will open the editor. Here, you immediately see a different interface and a different set of parameters to alter (**Figure 8.45**).

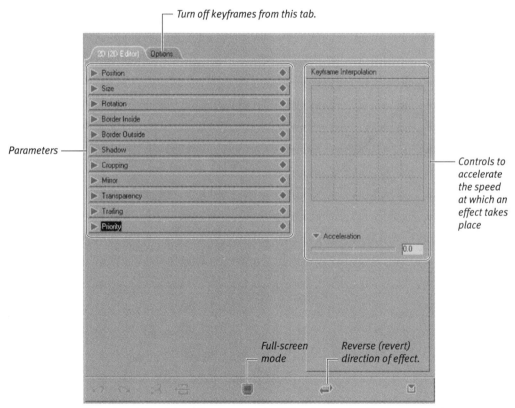

Turn off keyframes from this tab.

Parameters

Controls to accelerate the speed at which an effect takes place

Full-screen mode

Reverse (revert) direction of effect.

Figure 8.45 A Classic transition has several additional parameters the user can control.

Full-Screen Mode

One clear advantage of working with Classic transitions is that you can toggle full-screen mode on by clicking the Full-Screen Mode button . Doing so allows the Classic editor to take over the screen completely (**Figure 8.46**).

You can return the editor to normal size by clicking the Full-Screen Mode button a second time.

Figure 8.46 Full-screen mode. This is essential when you're using Pan and Scan techniques.

Editing the Classic Transition

Classic transitions work with or without keyframes, and so editing them follows the same procedure as editing Realtime transitions.

Keyframe Interpolation

One of the most interesting parameters available to non-Realtime transition users is Keyframe Interpolation. This governs the speed at which the effect happens between any two keyframes.

Note that this is the "speed at which the effect happens," not the "speed of the actual clip." The speed of a media clip can only be altered using the Timewarp non-Realtime filter (see Chapter 9 for details).

You use Keyframe Interpolation simply to alter the pace of an effect. The following example shows a 2D Editor using this parameter to zoom in on the incoming clip—first slowly, then, when it reaches the halfway mark, the zoom increases in speed until it reaches full speed at the end of the clip.

To alter Keyframe Interpolation:

1. Add one of the Classic transitions to the Timeline.

2. Scrub to a keyframe on the Timeline and alter the interpolation in one of the following ways:
   ▲ Drag the acceleration line toward a positive (faster) or negative (slower) amount (**Figure 8.47**).
   ▲ Double-click inside this box and enter a number.
   ▲ Click inside the parameter curve area and drag the keyframe toward the value you require (**Figure 8.48**).

Figure 8.47 Dragging the acceleration setting of the Keyframe Interpolation...

Figure 8.48 ...can also be accomplished using the Parameter Curve Editor.

3. Exit the editor by clicking the Running Man button 🏃 in the top-right corner of the editor.

The editor exits and the transition begins to render in the background.

4. Once it has finished rendering, set a mark-in and mark-out point on the Timeline on either side of the transition (**Figure 8.49**).

5. Then play back the transition by clicking the Play from Mark-In to Mark-Out button ▮▶▮.

Experimentation is the key for this effect because you can customize transitions to look highly original just by using this under-used parameter.

✔ Tips

- Remember that the parameters of the Transition Editor always affect the incoming clip unless the transition is reversed using the Revert button.

- If you add an acceleration of 100 to the first keyframe, the effect happens immediately.

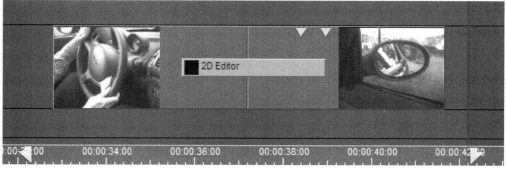

Figure 8.49 Place a mark-in and mark-out point on the Timeline to preview your new transition.

Rendering a Classic Transition

You must render all Classic transitions before you can see them on the PC or through the MovieBox Pro or the AGP Pro card from Pinnacle.

Once you add a Classic transition to the Timeline and you finished editing it, the slice above that transition goes red. Unless you have turned off background rendering, the slice immediately begins to render and gradually changes from red to green. During this render stage, you can still edit the Timeline.

Saving a Customized Transition

Once you have created the most awesome transition the world has ever seen, you will probably be keen on saving it for future use. You can do this with just a few clicks of your mouse.

To save a customized transition:

1. Switch to the All tab in the Project Browser and create a Folder called FX.

2. In the newly created FX folder create a Rack called Transitions (**Figure 8.50**).

3. Return to the transition in the Timeline and right-click it, then select Copy from the menu (**Figure 8.51**).

4. Right-click inside the right pane of the Project Browser and select Paste from the menu, and the transition is copied into this Rack for use later in your project (**Figure 8.52**).

✔ Tips

- The transition appears in the Rack with its default name. To change this to something you will recognize in the future, right-click the effect and select Rename from the menu.

- You can also use saved transitions as the default transition. You can find instructions for altering the default transition in the "Changing the Default Transition" section earlier in this chapter.

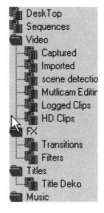

Figure 8.50 Creating a place to save your customized FX.

Figure 8.51 Right-click and select Copy...

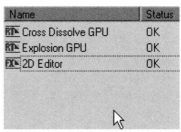

Figure 8.52 ...then paste it into your FX Rack.

Using the Transitions

To help you visualize what the Transition Editor can do and how cool keyframes are, the following sections show you how the basic concepts in the chapter actually work with a Realtime transition and a Classic transition.

RT 2D transition

The 2D and 3D transitions and their cousins, the 2D/3D filters, are probably the most used effects in NLE. Their effectiveness and lack of subtely is open to question and at the mercy of what happens to be in vogue at any one time, but there is no denying that they are great fun to play with.

The video clips used in the following example can be downloaded from www.peachpit.com/liquid6vqp but you can also use your own clips to complete this task.

First you need to create sufficient handles on these clips to prepare them to be inserted, then you can begin working with the editor.

To prepare the clips:

1. Send the first clip (Entering car; if you have downloaded the sample clips) to the Source Viewer, and place a mark-out point just after the door slams shut, about two seconds before the end (**Figure 8.53**). This creates a handle at the end of this clip one second in duration.

2. Send the clip to the Timeline using the Insert Source into Master button .

continues on next page

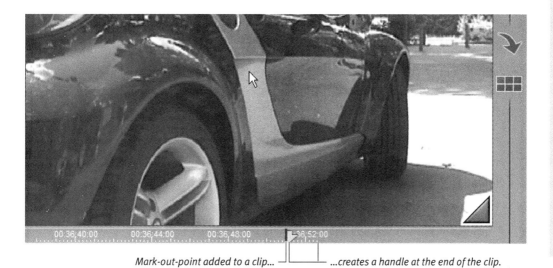

Mark-out-point added to a clip... ...creates a handle at the end of the clip.

Figure 8.53 Creating a handle by inserting a mark-out point in the Source Viewer.

USING THE TRANSITIONS

3. Send the second clip (Retreat) to the Source Viewer and add a mark-in point a few seconds from the start of the clip (**Figure 8.54**). This creates a handle at the start of this clip a few seconds in duration.

4. Send this clip to the Timeline so that it adjoins the first clip (**Figure 8.55**).

✔ Tip

■ Figure 8.55 shows the clips with embedded audio. See Chapter 6 for details on this.

Mark-in-point added to a clip...

...creates a handle at the start of the clip.

Figure 8.54 Creating a handle by adding a mark-in point in the Source Viewer.

Figure 8.55 Both clips on the Timeline. They overlap each other using the handles created in steps 1, 2, and 3 but these handles can't be seen on a single-track edit system.

To add the 2D transition:

1. Select the Lib tab from the Project Browser.

2. Open the Realtime Transitions FX folder by clicking on it once. Locate the Editors rack and click on this so the Editors are displayed in the right pane of the Project Browser.

3. Drag and drop the 2D Editor GPU to the point where the two clips meet.

To edit the transition:

1. Open the 2D Editor GPU by double-clicking the actual transition that should now be sitting on the line between the two clips (**Figure 8.56**).

   The 2D Transition Editor comes with a built-in preset that brings in the incoming clip with a zoom and a rotation effect. Although you like the zoom effect, suppose you decide you don't want the rotation.

continues on next page

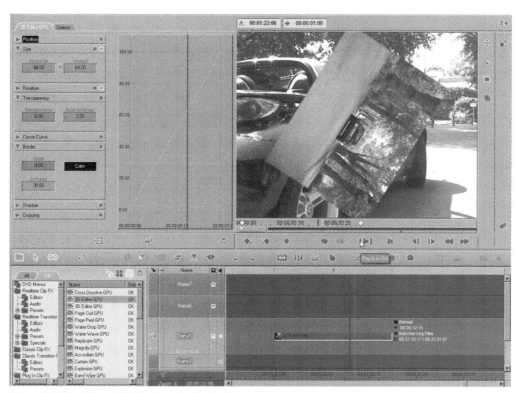

Figure 8.56 The default effect for the 2D editor GPU.

2. Turn rotation off by clicking the Activate button in the Rotation text area (**Figure 8.57**).

Now the clip plays just the zoom effect. But what you really want is for the clip to stop at about 50 percent of its actual size around a third of the way through the transition.

3. To do this, scrub the Timeline until the cursor is about a third of the way through the transition.

4. Then type the numerical value "50" into the horizontal size box (**Figure 8.58**).

5. Press the Tab key.

Once you do, this value is applied to both the horizontal and vertical boxes (because they are locked together with the padlock in the middle) and then a keyframe is created that holds this value.

Now the clip zooms in much faster, but you decide that want it to hold the zoom at 50 percent of its total size and stay that way until the transition is two thirds of the way through.

6. Using the Next Keyframe button, you advance the timeline cursor until it reaches the keyframe you created in steps 4 and 5. This should be the second keyframe on the edit window Timeline. The first is the start keyframe at the very beginning. The third is the end keyframe at the very end.

7. Click the Copy Keyframe button .

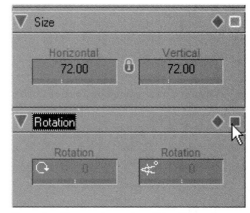

Figure 8.57 You toggle rotation off by clicking the Activate/Deactivate toggle.

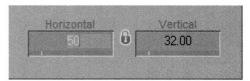

Figure 8.58 Directly entering a numerical value.

8. Move the timeline cursor to about two thirds of the way through the transition, and click the Paste Keyframe  button to create a copy of the keyframe at this point (**Figure 8.59**).

This now creates a transition that zooms in quickly to 50 percent of its total size, stays like that for a second, and then zooms to 100 percent of its total size when it reaches the original keyframe at the end of the Timeline.

In this example, I've set it up so the first zoom finishes with the sound of the door closing to make it feel more dramatic. Combining effects with the natural audio on a video clip is always more effective.

This transition still seems a little flat and you decide you want to add a border to make it look a little livelier.

Figure 8.59 Adding another keyframe via copy and paste.

To add a border:

1. Using the Next Keyframe button, move the timeline cursor until it reaches the last frame in the transition.

2. Open the Border Parameter settings and create a yellow border with a width of 6 and an edge softness of 100 (**Figure 8.60**).

3. Because you want this yellow border to be present throughout the entire transition, drag the Keyframe symbol from the Border Text area into the preview window so that these values are applied throughout the transition (**Figure 8.61**).

   You're almost happy, but you decide you really want this to be a little more subtle at the beginning. You can create this effect by adding a fade to the incoming clip as it zooms toward its first keyframe.

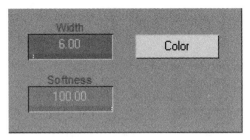

Figure 8.60 Adjusting the border color and parameters.

Drag the keyframe symbol from here...

The cursor shows a hand when dragging the keyframe.

...to here.

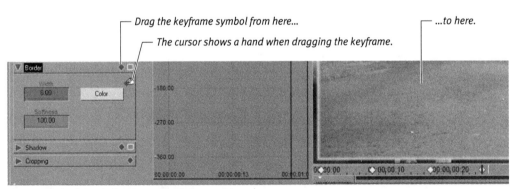

Figure 8.61 Applying the border to the whole transition.

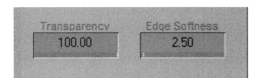

Figure 8.62 Setting the transparency to 100 makes it see-through.

To add a fade using the transparency setting:

1. Using the Previous Keyframe button, move the cursor to the first keyframe on the Timeline.

2. Open the Transparency parameter settings and set the Transparency to 100.

   This makes the clip almost entirely see-through (**Figure 8.62**).

3. Move the cursor to the second keyframe and enter the numerical value "0" into the Transparency Parameter box.

   The incoming clip gradually becomes more solid during the first zoom, and then it is 100-percent solid for the rest of the transition (**Figure 8.63**).

If you play back the transition now, it looks promising, although you're probably going to have to do a little more tweaking to make it look a whole lot better. Perhaps you can do so by using the position parameters to make the incoming clip float around the screen before it zooms to 100 percent. Or perhaps you can add a shadow to accentuate the border. As I've said before, you must experiment with Liquid Edition if you ever want to get the best from it.

Figure 8.63 The finished result. Each picture here represents the keyframes 1 to 4 from left to right.

Classic 2D transition

The tasks in this section show the same two clips used in the "RT 2D transition" section: Entering car and Retreat. But with the Classic 2D, you also have the option of using Keyframe Interpolation to alter the rate at which your keyframes occur.

First you need to create sufficient handles on your clips to prepare them for insertion. Then you can begin working with the editor. You prepare these the same way I described in the "To prepare the clips" task in the "RT 2D transition" section. If you have not read this, do so now and then return here once you've prepared your clips.

To apply the Classic 2D Editor :

1. After you place the two prepared clips on the Timeline, select the Lib tab from the Project Browser.

2. Open the Classic Transitions FX folder and then click once on the Editors Rack to display the list of editors in the right pane.

3. Drag and drop the 2D Editor to the point where the two clips meet.

To open the 2D editor:

◆ Open the 2D editor by double-clicking the actual transition that should now be sitting on the line between the two clips (**Figure 8.64**).

Unlike its RT cousin, the 2D Classic Transition Editor has no preset effect built in, so you must build your transitions from scratch.

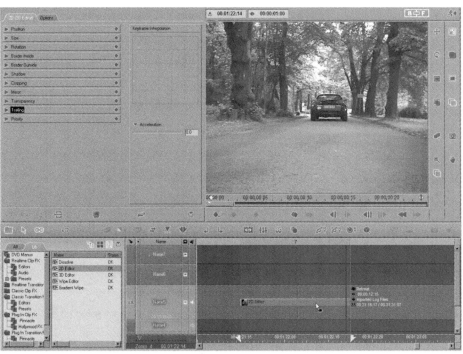

Figure 8.64 The 2D Classic Editor—a non-Realtime transition.

Figure 8.65 Dragging the sliders.

To create a 2D transition

1. Using the mouse, move the cursor to the first frame of the Timeline and open the Size Parameter box. Alter the size in one of the following ways:

   ▲ Enter the numerical value in one of the boxes and press the Tab key to apply it.

   ▲ Drag the sliders to the size you require (**Figure 8.65**).

   ▲ Use the One Click Size button found to the right of the preview window (**Figure 8.66**). To use this One Click Size button, select it, then with the mouse cursor inside the preview area, click and hold the left mouse button while pushing the mouse forward to expand the image and pulling it back to reduce the image (**Figure 8.67**).

continues on next page

One Click Position button —
One Click Size button —

Figure 8.66 The one click adjust buttons provide a helpful shortcut.

USING THE TRANSITIONS

2. To make the Retreat clip zoom from nothing, drag the mouse back until the size is 0.

Now the clip plays the zoom effect from start to finish. But what you really want is the clip to stop at about 50 percent of its actual size at around a third of the way through the transition.

3. To do this, scrub the Timeline until the cursor is at about a third of the way through the transition, and then type a numerical value of "50" into the width size box.

4. Press the Tab key and this value is applied to both the width and height boxes because they are locked together using the padlock in the middle.

Now the clip looks like the first stages of the example you created in the RT section of this chapter. You can go on to finish building your effect so that it resembles the RT version in every detail, but before you do that, you decide you want to alter the speed at which the zooms occurs between the first and second keyframe. This is done using the middle graph area labeled "Keyframe Interpolation."

The cursor becomes a Resize cursor as you drag the image forward or backward.

Figure 8.67 The One Click Size button in action.

Figure 8.68 Adjusting the Keyframe Interpolation to 50.

To use Keyframe Interpolation:

1. *Do one of the following:*

   ▲ Return the cursor to the first keyframe and drag the acceleration line in the Keyframe Interpolation over until the number box reads 50 (**Figure 8.68**).

   ▲ Double-click inside this box and enter the number "50" with the keyboard.

   Adding this interpolation causes the zoom to rush in much more dramatically, which causes it to stutter slightly as it reaches the next keyframe.

2. To soften this stutter, add a second Keyframe Interpolation to the next keyframe and reduce the acceleration to −10.

   This cushions the slowdown of the interpolation so that it doesn't seem so abrupt when it returns to normal speed.

3. Because this is a Classic effect, you must exit the editor and wait for it to finish rendering before you can see the final results.

USING THE TRANSITIONS

To view the transition after rendering:

1. Once it has finished rendering, set a mark-in and mark-out point on the Timeline on either side of the transition.

2. Then play back the transition by clicking the Play from Mark-In to Mark-Out button ▮▶▮.

The result should be an incoming clip that zooms quickly into view until it reaches the first keyframe. At this point, it slows down, then gradually speeds up until it reaches the default speed at the last keyframe.

If you wish, you can now continue to build this effect using the instruction found in the "RT 2D transition" section of this chapter.

✔ Tips

■ Remember that the parameters of the Transition Editor always affect the incoming clip unless the transition is reversed using the Revert button.

■ If you add an acceleration of 100 to the first keyframe, the effect happens immediately.

■ The One Click Size button used in step 1 of the "To create a 2D transition" task is available in both Realtime and Classic effects. Using this as a shortcut can contribute greatly to a smooth workflow.

■ Experimentation is the key for this effect because you can customize many simple transitions to look highly original just by using this underused parameter.

Pan and Scan

Panning and scanning oversized clips is another action only a Classic effect can perform. Although it is possible to do this in a transition, the effect can be limited; this type of FX is usually used with the 2D Classic filter. For more details on this, see Chapter 9.

Gradient Wipe

The gradient wipe transitions are something a little special in Liquid Edition and they deserve a special mention. Previously known as the Spice Rack, they're a collection of organic transitions you can use in special effects and introduction sequences.

Version 6 offers both Realtime and Classic versions. Although the Realtime version (**Figure 8.69**) has the practicality of nonrendering on its side, the Classic version (**Figure 8.70**) has a much better range of presets.

Once more, experimentation is the key to realizing the full potential of this range of truly unique transitions.

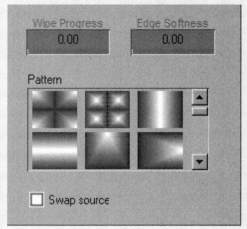

Figure 8.69 The limited range of Realtime gradient wipes.

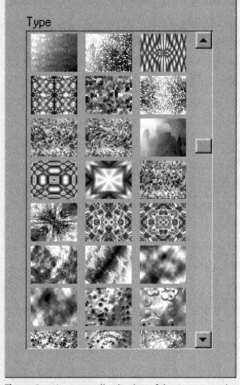

Figure 8.70 Just a small selection of the more organic range of non-Realtime gradient wipes.

Introducing Hollywood FX

Hollywood Effects (HFX) is a popular plug-in integrated into Liquid Edition for both filters (see Chapter 9) and transitions. The plug-in offers a specific type of transition that is of the less subtle and more dramatic variety. Using these transitions, you will always be alerting the audience to a scene change because using HFX is like holding up a flashing neon sign that says, "yep, the scene is changing and I want you to know about it."

You'll probably see HFX used mainly in wedding videos; in fact, a number of templates are included with the plug-in for just this purpose (**Figure 8.71**). You might also see a great many other HFX transitions in various hokey holiday videos (**Figure 8.72**).

Most of these transitions are real-time, meaning they display a preview version under a yellow slice, which must be rendered before you can export to DVD or tape. But some are slightly more complex and require rendering. In such cases, they're marked with a small red ball in the bottom-left corner of the effects thumbnail (**Figure 8.73**).

Some HFX transitions render with a big Pinnacle "P" watermark across the screen. To unlock these extra effects, you need to buy a serial number from Pinnacle. You can accomplish this online via their Web site, www.pinnaclesys.com.

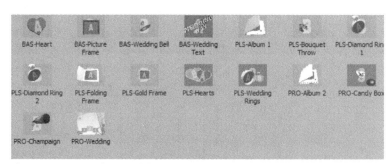

Figure 8.71 A range of HFX wedding templates...

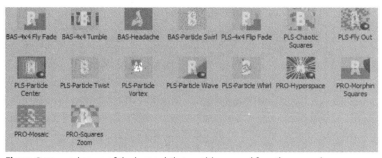

Figure 8.72 ...and some of the less subtle transitions used for other occasions.

— Red ball

Figure 8.73 The red ball marks a non-Realtime effect.

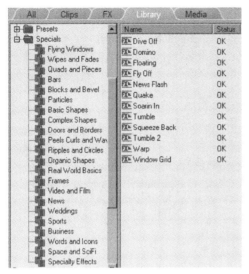

Figure 8.74 HFX presets in the Specials folder.

Adding a Preset Hollywood FX Transition

You add HFX preset transitions the same way as normal transitions; you just need to drag them from a different folder. The rules of handles and overlapping clips still apply, as does your ability to add an HFX transition to any video clip on any track, including titles and graphics.

To add a preset Hollywood FX transition:

1. With two clips on the Timeline, click the Lib tab in the Project Browser and open the Realtime Transition FX Folder.

   Contained within this folder is the Specials subfolder, which holds the various preset Hollywood FX transitions (**Figure 8.74**). If you want to view this folder in its entirety, press Shift+F3 to switch over to Storyboard view.

2. Click through each of these Racks until you find the transition you're looking for. Drag it over to the Timeline and drop it where the two clips meet.

   HFX Presets are real-time, so once you drop it onto the Timeline, you can immediately scrub or play it back to view the effect at work.

✔ Tips

- Switching to Picon View can make it easier to see what each of the preset transitions do to your clips.

- HFX transitions don't stack on top of each other. Dragging a preset transition on top of another erases the one underneath.

Editing a Hollywood FX Transition

Once the HFX transition has been applied, you can edit many, many different parameters. In fact, HFX is a somewhat complex program to work with outside of the presets; and it really needs a separate book to fully explain the vast potential this it has to offer.

To open the Hollywood FX Editor:

◆ Double-click the HFX transition in the Timeline and the HFX Editor loads, taking over the desktop (**Figure 8.75**).

✔ Tip

■ The editor of HFX has a frightening number of parameters to alter, and is, by and large, one of the more complex editors within the Liquid Edition editing suite. Some documentation comes with the program, but I recommend that you do some further reading on this subject.

Keyframable parameters — Edit View buttons

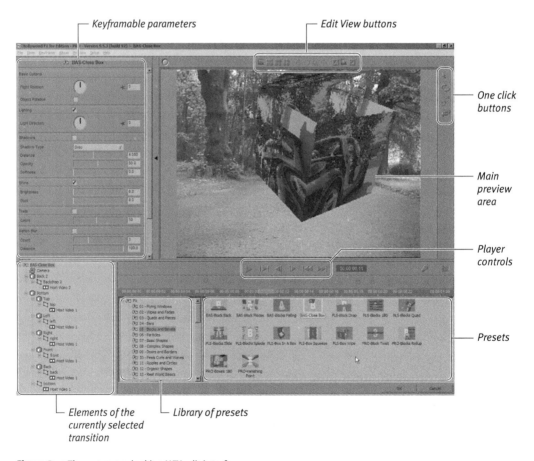

One click buttons

Main preview area

Player controls

Presets

Elements of the currently selected transition — Library of presets

Figure 8.75 The very scary-looking HFX edit interface.

To select a preset:

1. Open the editor.

2. Select any of the presets by simply selecting the category from the left of the album and double-clicking on the preset you want.

✔ Tips

■ Adjust the preset you choose in any way you like, but always save your altered version under a different name; otherwise, you'll overwrite the original.

■ At the bottom of the menu selection is a range of real-world objects and preset movements that allow you to build your own FX from scratch.

■ Many fan sites exist for HFX. You might find Mike Shaw's (www.mikeshaw.co.uk) of particular interest. He has been running this popular HFX Web site for many years. His site offers CD tutorials and a range of downloadable HFX presets, assuming, of course, that you've already worked your way through all those that came with version 6 of Liquid Edition.

EDITING A HOLLYWOOD FX TRANSITION

WORKING WITH FILTERS

Filters—or Clip FX as they are referred to in Liquid Edition—are similar to transitions; they're keyframable effects you use to visually alter the properties of a media clip. But whereas a transition only works on the overlapping point between two separate clips, you can apply filters to the whole clip, allowing for some interesting creative options.

Liquid Edition offers a great selection of filters for various tasks—from adjusting the size and scale all the way through to visually altering the clip beyond recognition— and just like with transitions, Liquid Edition also offers a whole pile of Hollywood FX (HFX) filters to really add some spice to your video productions.

Learning to apply and edit a filter is relatively easy and draws on those skills you learned with transitions. Adjusting parameters and adding keyframes involves the same procedure, and the only real difference between the two (filters and transitions) is the greater complexity you can achieve using filters.

In this chapter, you learn how to apply a filter, alter the basic parameters, and adjust keyframes. You also look into the complexity of HFX and delve into the most used filter of them all, the Timewarp—Liquid Edition's method of creating slow-motion speed effects. Once you have mastered these concepts, you can create some really original effects.

Using Filters— The Basic Concept

As we discussed in Chapter 8, the world of Liquid Edition is divided into two classes: Realtime (RT) effects, which you don't need to render in order to preview; and non-Realtime or Classic effects, which you must render before you can see the results.

Realtime and Classic filters offer you a choice of editors and presets, and both options have a Presets folder. The Realtime folder contains a large collection of edited 2D variations both in CPU and GPU format (**Figure 9.1**), whereas the Classic presets offer some interesting color correction and Picture in Picture (PiP) effects (**Figure 9.2**).

The Classic filters also have access to some extended parameters including the following:

◆ **Full Screen:** Realtime effects can only function within the boundaries of the TV standard with which you're working. This means all images are cropped to that standard, and anything outside that area appears black if you try to pan and scan it. However, Classic effects can work in full-screen mode, allowing you to move the image around using a technique called Pan and Scan (**Figure 9.3**). See "Using Classic Filters" later in this chapter for details.

◆ **Keyframe Interpolation:** This allows you to accelerate the rate at which an effect occurs between two keyframes. Again, this is only available in Classic mode. See "Keyframe Interpolation" later in this chapter.

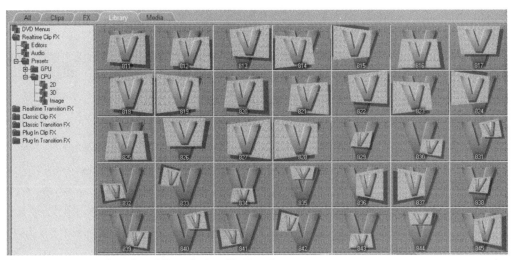

Figure 9.1 A selection of CPU-based filters displayed in Picon form.

✔ Tip

- I deal with the Color Correction and Chromakey filters in Chapters 11 and 14, respectively. Their complexity and specialized application demanded a separate discussion.

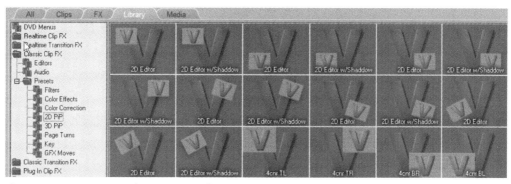

Figure 9.2 Various preset PiP (Picture in Picture) filters used by the Classic presets.

Figure 9.3 An oversized image displayed in a Classic filter using the Full Screen function.

CPU and GPU Effects

Realtime effects are subdivided into CPU and GPU effects. Here's the difference:

♦ CPU filters use the power of your computer's processor to display a real-time preview.

♦ GPU filters use the processor fitted to your graphics card to display a real-time preview.

Eventually, you'll probably want to use GPU effects to exploit the power of your graphics card's on-board processor and free up some valuable processing time for your computer's CPU. But if your graphics card isn't a particularly fast or modern one, you may have to consider using the CPU filters. Otherwise, your Realtime effects display with so many dropped frames that they become unwatchable.

Some of the filters—2D, 3D, and Cross Dissolve—have both CPU and GPU for you to choose from in order to help you overcome this problem (**Figure 9.4**).

Name ▼
RT⇤ 2D Editor CPU
RT⇤ 2D Editor GPU
RT⇤ 3D Editor CPU
RT⇤ 3D Editor GPU

Figure 9.4 The 2D and 3D Editors come in both CPU and GPU flavors.

Stacking Filters

Unlike with transitions, you can stack filters one on top of the other on a single clip (**Figure 9.5**).

Liquid Edition doesn't have an official limit on how many filters you can stack together, but RT filters consume an ever-incresing amount of CPU or GPU power in order to play back in real-time. At some point, you may find that your computer can no longer display the clip in anything approaching a watchable format; then you have to go ahead and render.

Be careful when you mix CPU and GPU filters together because some combinations don't mix. If you're experiencing problems with two types of RT filters, you may find you need to use another combination to achieve the effect you're looking for.

Figure 9.5 Four filters stacked to create a rotation (2D filter), a Lens Flare (upper-right), a Water Ripple, and a Page Curl.

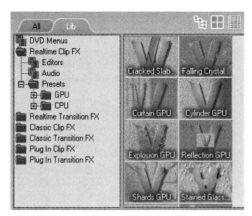

Figure 9.6 The effects tree displayed in the Project Browser.

Adding a Filter

Once you understand the basic concept of using filters, actually applying them is easy and can be achieved by drag and drop.

✔ Tip

■ Some filters have no value until you open the editor and adjust some of the parameters, and therefore, they show no immediate change to the clip. See "Taking Filters Further" later in this chapter for more information on this.

To apply a filter:

1. Place a clip on the Timeline and if the Project Browser isn't yet open in the Timeline, click the Open Project Browser in Timeline button 🖼.

2. Click once on the Lib tab to show the effects Liquid Edition has to offer (**Figure 9.6**).

   Dual-screen users will probably have the Project Browser open on the second monitor; in this case the tab will be marked Library.

3. *Do one of the following:*
   ▲ Open the Realtime Clip FX folder if you intend to add Realtime filters.
   ▲ Open the Classic Clip FX folder if you intend to use non-Realtime filters.

4. Once you have selected the type of filter you want, click a Rack to display its contents.

   continues on next page

Premiere Translation

Many of the filters used in Premiere are found in Liquid Edition; many even have the same names. However Liquid Edition refers to filters as Clip FXs—that is, FXs that you apply to clips.

Other than that minor difference, the Clip FXs of Liquid Edition behave in a similar fashion to the filters in Premiere.

5. Highlight the actual filter you want by clicking it, and apply the filter to the Timeline by *doing one of the following:*

▲ Drag the filter into the Timeline and release the mouse button when the filter is over the clip (**Figure 9.7**)

▲ Right-click the filter and select Copy (**Figure 9.8**). Then right-click the clip and select Paste > Clip FX from the menu (**Figure 9.9**).

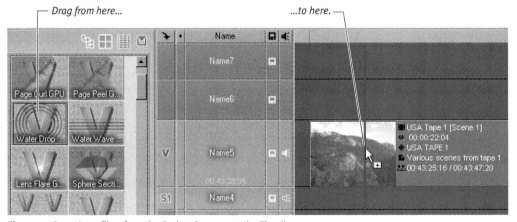

Figure 9.7 Dragging a filter from the Project Browser to the Timeline.

Figure 9.8 Applying a filter using the copy and...

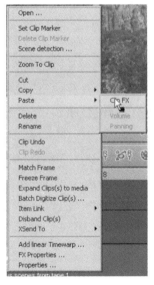

Figure 9.9 ...paste method.

ADDING A FILTER

Figure 9.10 Deleting a filter using Clip Undo.

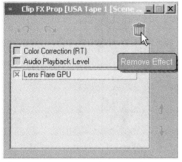

Figure 9.11 Deleting a filter via the Clip FX Properties dialog.

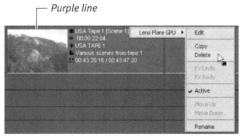

— Purple line

Figure 9.12 Deleting a filter via a right-click on the purple FX line.

6. To remove this filter, *do one of the following:*

▲ Right-click the clip in the Timeline and select Clip Undo from the menu (**Figure 9.10**).

▲ Right-click the clip in the Timeline and select FX Properties from the menu. Then highlight the filter you want to delete and click the Trash can (**Figure 9.11**).

▲ Right-click the purple line running along the top of the clip and select Delete from the menu (**Figure 9.12**).

✔ Tip

■ If you are dragging a filter to the Timeline and you see the message "No Filter Target," then you don't have the mouse cursor over a valid media clip.

Clip Undo

The Undo function for filters—like the Undo function for audio keyframes—is a separate entity from the Undo command you normally use.

If you add a filter to a clip on the Timeline and then use Ctrl+Z or the Timeline Undo key, then an Undo occurs on the Timeline, but the filter remains firmly on the clip. In this case, I advise you to click the Redo key to redo whatever it is that you've accidentally undone.

This becomes slightly more complex when you're dealing with filters you've added to tracks and to clips in the Project Browser. To keep this from frying your brain early on in the chapter, I've listed the removal method in the last step for each of the three application techniques.

ADDING A FILTER

303

Applying a Filter in the Project Browser

You can also add a filter directly to the clip in the Project Browser. This allows you to always have the corrected clip ready and waiting in the Project Browser whenever you need to use it.

Of course, to gain full advantage of this technique, you need to edit this filter too. For details on this, see "Taking Filters Further" later in this chapter.

To apply a filter to a clip in the Project Browser:

1. Select the filter you need by following the instructions in the "Adding a Filter" section earlier in this chapter.

2. Right-click the filter and select Copy.

3. Click the All tab to take you back to your media clips, and open the Rack where the clip you are interested in is stored.

4. Right-click anywhere in the right pane and select Paste from the menu (**Figure 9.13**).

5. Click anywhere inside the right pane to deselect all clips (this must be done or the next step will not work), then click the filter and drag and drop it over the clip (**Figure 9.14**).

6. To remove this filter, right-click the clip inside the Project Browser and select FX Properties from the menu. Then highlight the filter and click the Trash can (**Figure 9.15**).

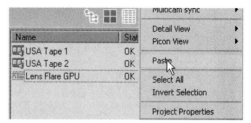

Figure 9.13 Pasting a filter into a Rack in the Project Browser.

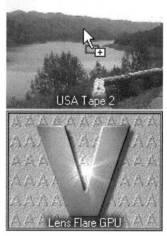

Figure 9.14 Applying the filter to a clip in the Project Browser.

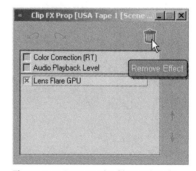

Figure 9.15 Remove the filter using the Clip FX properties and the Trash can.

Figure 9.16 The correct cursor for successfully dragging a filter to a clip in the Project Browser.

Figure 9.17 This cursor indicates that it isn't central enough in the clip for you to successfully apply the filter.

✔ Tips

- The cursor must have a small, white box with a plus sign (+) inside it before you can drop the filter (**Figure 9.16**). If the cursor looks like it does in **Figure 9.17**, then you have not dragged it exactly into the middle of the clip.

- Make sure no other clip in the Rack is selected before you select the filter and try to drag it; otherwise the filter only moves around the Rack and isn't applied to the clip.

Adding a Filter to a Timeline Track

You may want to add a filter to an entire Track—the Autocolor Corrector, for example—in order to make a change to all the clips on a particular Track in your project Timeline. This is a global change and you need to use it with care, but it can prove helpful if you have a lot of images on the same Track, and they all need to be cropped in a similar fashion.

Drag from here... ...to here.

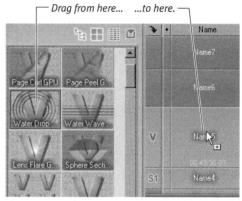

Figure 9.18 Adding a filter to a Timeline Track.

To add a filter to a Timeline Track:

1. Select the filter you need by following the instructions in the "To apply a filter" task earlier in this chapter.

2. Highlight the actual filter you want by clicking it, and apply it to the Timeline by dragging it into the Track name and releasing the mouse button (**Figure 9.18**).

   A purple line appears indicating that the filter is successfully applied (**Figure 9.19**).

3. To remove this filter, right-click the purple line running along the top of the Timeline Track and select Delete from the menu (**Figure 9.20**).

Figure 9.19 The purple line indicates a filter present on this Track.

✔ Tip

■ Once again, to take full advantage of this technique, you need to edit this filter before it has any dramatic effect on your Timeline.

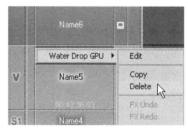

Figure 9.20 Deleting the filter via a right-click menu.

Figure 9.21 The Toolbar buttons for the RT filters: 2D, 3D, and Base Color Corrector.

Figure 9.22 Apply the filter with a single click...

Working with the Default RT Filters

The most common type of filters are the 2D/3D filters and the Base Color Corrector. Because they are such commonly used effects, each one has a shortcut button on Liquid Edition's Toolbar (**Figure 9.21**).

To apply one of the default filters from the toolbar:

1. Select a clip in the Timeline by clicking on it once.

2. Click once on any of the default filters—but not the Effects Editor menu button, which I deal with in the "Applying the Default Classic Filters" section—to apply the filter (**Figure 9.22**).

   Once you've applied the filter, the editor for that filter automatically opens (**Figure 9.23**).

✔ Tip

■ If you exit a filter without making any changes, the filter will be removed from the clip.

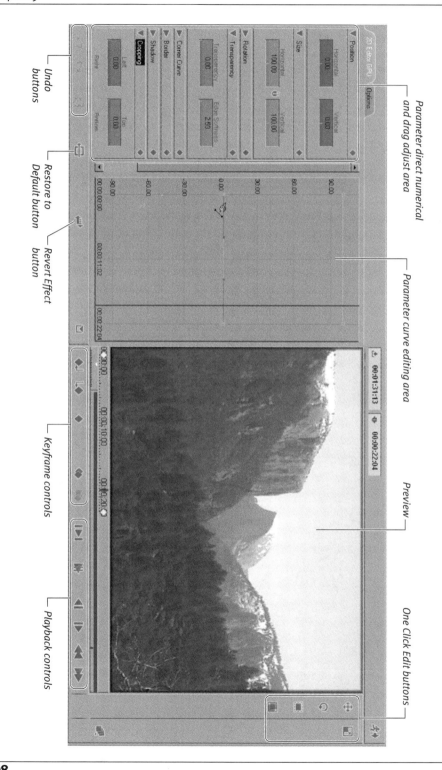

Figure 9.23 ...and the editor automatically opens.

Undo buttons

Restore to Default button

Revert Effect button

Keyframe controls

Playback controls

Parameter direct numerical and drag adjust area

Parameter curve editing area

Preview

One Click Edit buttons

Rendering a Realtime Filter

Realtime filters provide a preview of the effect without having to render it. To do so, they use a complex set of codecs, which allow you to see the effect right away. With the right hardware (the MovieBox Pro or the AGP Pro card from Pinnacle) you can even view these filters on an external TV. The quality is so good that you're forgiven for thinking it has already been rendered.

The clue is the slice above the clips that have filters applied to them (**Figure 9.24**). If this is yellow, then you're looking at a real-time preview and you need to render this before you can create a DVD or output the Timeline to tape.

To render a yellow slice, simply click the Render icon Σ in the Liquid Edition taskbar (**Figure 9.25**). Then, check the include yellow slices check box. When you do, all yellow slices on the Timeline begin to render (**Figure 9.26**). If the rendering doesn't start, make sure you haven't previously stopped it by clicking the Stop/Start Rendering button to the left of the include yellow slices check box.

Note: A red slice indicates the presence of a non-Realtime filter. A green slice indicates a clip has been rendered. A gray slice indicates a clip that does not require rendering.

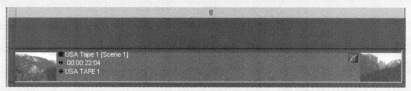

Figure 9.24 A yellow slice above a clip indicates the presence of an RT filter.

Figure 9.25 The Liquid Edition taskbar containing the Render icon. (PAL, top. NTSC, bottom.)

Figure 9.26
The Render View.

Applying the Default Classic Filters

Classic filters also have a shortcut root key—the Effect Editor Menu button 🔲— from which you can access the most commonly used non-Realtime filers. These filters are compressed into one menu button that displays its contents when you click the Effects Editor Menu button (**Figure 9.27**).

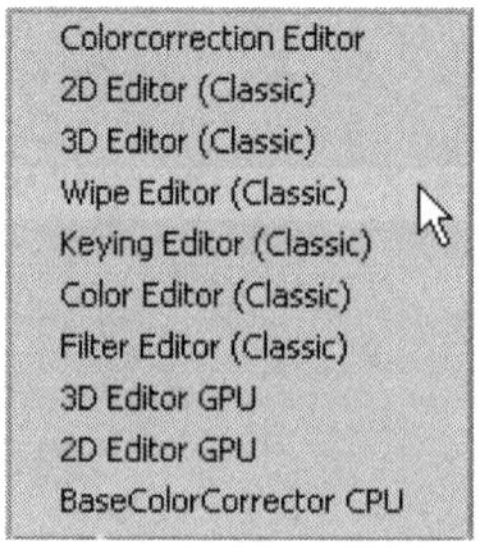

There are ten filters you can access from this button. The bottom three are the Realtime filters that you can access through their own buttons on the interface. They're included here only to allow you to use the workflow with which you feel most comfortable.

✔ Tip

■ You can also access the Audio Editor (see Chapter 7) and the title creation program, Title Deko (see Chapter 10), from this button.

To apply the 2D or 3D filter from the toolbar:

1. Select a clip on the Timeline by clicking it once.

2. Click the Effects Editor button and select either the 2D Editor (Classic) or 3D Editor (Classic).

   The filter applies to the clip you selected and the edit window opens automatically.

   Once you exit the editor, the clip begins to render. See the "Rendering a Classic Filter" sidebar for details.

Figure 9.27 The list of editors available via the Effects Editor Menu button.

Colorcorrection Editor
2D Editor (Classic)
3D Editor (Classic)
Wipe Editor (Classic)
Keying Editor (Classic)
Color Editor (Classic)
Filter Editor (Classic)
3D Editor GPU
2D Editor GPU
BaseColorCorrector CPU

APPLYING THE DEFAULT CLASSIC FILTERS

Rendering a Classic Filter

You must render all Classic filters before you can see them on the PC or through the MovieBox Pro or AGP Pro card from Pinnacle.

Once you've added a Classic filter to the Timeline and you've finished editing it, the slice above that filter goes red. Unless you have turned off background rendering, the slice immediately begins to render. The slice gradually changes from red to green, although some users may see the change occur only when rendering has finished. This is due to a technical limitation some machines have when working with Liquid Edition. During this render stage, you can still edit the Timeline.

If you want to disable background rendering, click the Render icon (**Figure 9.28**) in the Liquid Edition taskbar to open the Render View. Then click once on the Stop Rendering button (**Figure 9.29**). To restart the rendering, open the Render View again and click the Start Rendering button.

Figure 9.28 The Render icon and progress bar.

Click here to stop rendering.

Figure 9.29 You can also use the Render View to pause background rendering.

APPLYING THE DEFAULT CLASSIC FILTERS

Editing a Filter

As you can see from the previous tasks, actually adding a filter is relatively easy. The creative fun starts when you want to alter the wide range of parameters that come with each filter, hopefully with the aim of creating something unique. This is called *editing with keyframes*. Keyframes are explained in more depth in the "Keyframes" sidebar.

The Filter Editor is similar in look and operation to the Transition Editor you looked at in Chapter 8. In fact, many of filters have similar names and similar parameters.

To create your own custom-made filter, you need to open the editor and then scrub through the Source Viewer Timeline deciding where and when to alter the various parameters.

To understand filters, you need to experiment with them; because of their many complex parameters, it's impossible to show everything in the pages of a book. You need to see every living variation on the screen; otherwise you'll never know what sort of highly original effects you can create just by tweaking one underused parameter.

To open the Filter Editor:

With a filter present on a clip, *do one of the following*:

◆ Double-click the Filter icon if it is visible (**Figure 9.30**).

◆ Double-click the purple line running across the top of a clip and select a filter from the menu that appears (**Figure 9.31**).

◆ Right-click the purple line running across the top of a clip and select Edit from the menu that appears (**Figure 9.32**).

Any of these methods brings up the Filter Editor (**Figure 9.33**).

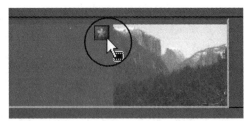

Figure 9.30 Open a filter by clicking the Filter icon or...

Figure 9.31 ...double-click the purple line at the top of the clip...

Figure 9.32 ...or right-click the purple line and select Edit.

✔ Tips

■ If you open an editor for the first time and then close it again without making any adjustments, you cause it to be removed from the clip.

■ Right-clicking a filter by accessing the FX Properties allows you to access the full range of editing options allowed for each filter, including Copy and Delete.

EDITING A FILTER

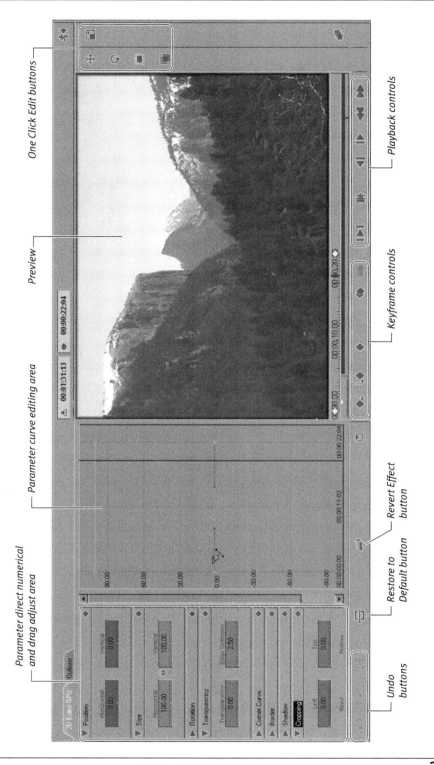

One Click Edit buttons

Preview

Playback controls

Keyframe controls

Parameter curve editing area

Parameter direct numerical
and drag adjust area

Revert Effect
button

Restore to
Default button

Undo
buttons

Figure 9.33 The RT Filter Editor interface.

Keyframes

When you adjust the parameters in the Filter Editor, a small gray diamond appears on the editor's Timeline (**Figure 9.34**). These diamond marks are *keyframes* and they are part of the magic behind the NLE system.

A keyframe does pretty much what it says on the box: It creates a key point around which a certain action or event occurs.

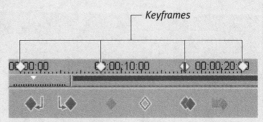

Figure 9.34 Keyframes on the Timeline of the Filter Editor.

When you adjust any of the parameters inside the Filter Editor, you create a keyframe. If you look at Figure 9-34 again, you can see that multiple changes have been made creating multiple gray diamonds—keyframes—on the editor's Timeline. These control the way in which the filters behave when they're played back.

Once you create these keyframes, you can manipulate, move, copy, or delete them at will; this is the true power of a keyframe editing system.

Keyframes are also used in Liquid Edition to control audio levels and transitions. You can find details on this in Chapters 7 and 8.

Click here to open the parameter.

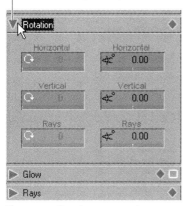

Figure 9.35 Opening a parameter area.

Figure 9.36 Work with the double-headed arrow...

Figure 9.37 ...or enter the number directly.

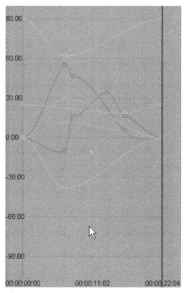

Figure 9.38 You can add and manipulate keyframes inside the parameter curve area.

To edit a filter:

1. Open the Filters Editor using one of the methods detailed in the "To open the Filter Editor" task earlier in this chapter.

2. Open the parameter you wish to alter by clicking once on the small triangle to the left of the name (**Figure 9.35**).

3. If this is an RT filter, you see various colored boxes and you can alter the parameters in the following ways:

   ▲ Place the mouse cursor over any of the parameter boxes and wait for a double-headed cursor to appear (**Figure 9.36**). Hold down the mouse button and drag to the right to increase the value displayed. Drag back to the left to reduce the value displayed.

   ▲ Double-click inside the display area and enter the numerical value you need; then press Enter (**Figure 9.37**).

   ▲ Click inside the parameter curve area on the line color that represents the parameter you wish to alter. Parameter lines and boxes always match up with coloring, but the line only appears if the parameter box is open, or if the parameter was previously adjusted (**Figure 9.38**).

continues on next page

If you are using a Classic filter, you can adjust the parameters using sliders or by entering numbers directly into the boxes at the end of the slider controls (**Figure 9.39**).

✔ Tips

- RT filters can be played inside the editor to see how your keyframes have affected the final image. If it's a Classic filter, you can only scrub through the image. To play a Classic filter, you must first exit the editor and allow the filter to render.

- To return the Classic slider to the default value, click the small button that appears on the right side of the slider once a parameter has been altered (**Figure 9.40**).

- You can increase the size of any editor window by clicking the Maximum Inlay Size button 🔲 on the Liquid Edition toolbar.

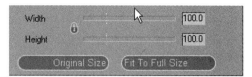

Figure 9.39 Classic editors used simpler sliders.

Figure 9.40 To reset a slider, click the small button next to the numbers.

Applying a Parameter

If you need to apply any parameter to the whole length of a filter—for example, using Mirror to flip an image—then drag the Keyframe symbol from the parameters label area into the preview screen of the editor. Those settings in the parameter box then apply to the whole filter (**Figure 9.41**).

continues on next page

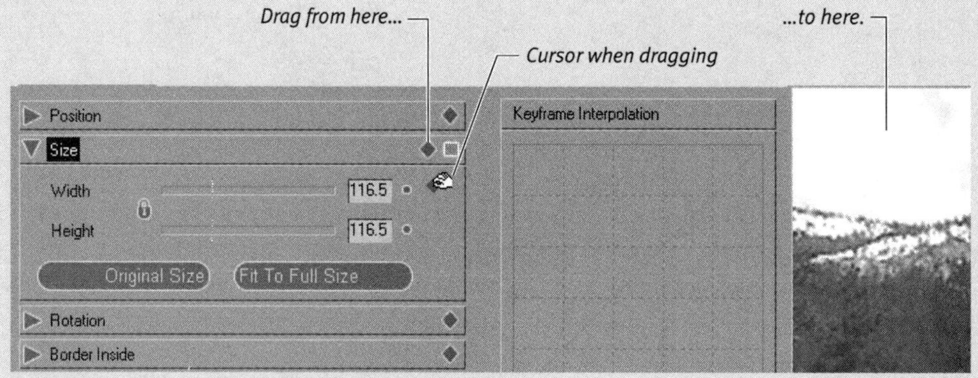

Figure 9.41 Applying a keyframe across the duration of a clip.

EDITING A FILTER

Applying a Parameter *continued*

If you just want to apply these parameter settings to one specific keyframe that already exists on the Timeline, then drag the Keyframe symbol from the parameters label area onto that keyframe (**Figure 9.42**).

Drag from here...

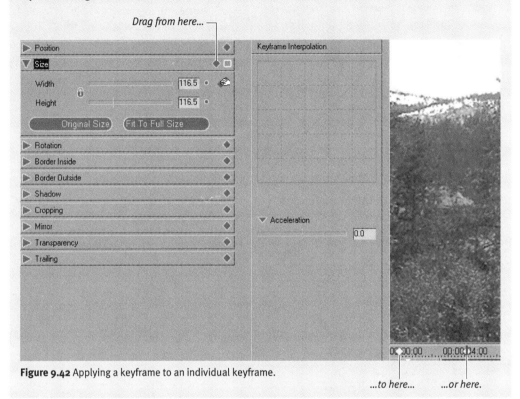

Figure 9.42 Applying a keyframe to an individual keyframe.

...to here...   *...or here.*

Controlling Keyframes

At this stage in the chapter you should now understand how keyframes can enhance and customize your own filters. But you must carefully control keyframes if you're to get the best from them.

In this section, you learn how to manually add and delete a keyframe and how to copy/paste and move a keyframe inside the Filter Editor.

To add a keyframe:

1. With the editor open, scrub through the Timeline until you find the spot where you want to add a keyframe.

2. When the cursor is over this spot, click the Set Keyframe button ◆ .

To delete a keyframe:

1. With the editor open, scrub through the Timeline until you are on a keyframe, or use the Go to Next Keyframe buttons ◆ ◆ to find each keyframe.

2. When the cursor is over the keyframe, the Delete Keyframe button ◇ becomes active. Click it and the keyframe vanishes.

To copy and paste a keyframe:

1. Place a keyframe anywhere on the Timeline using the methods detailed above.

2. With the cursor over the keyframe, click the copy Keyframe button ◆ .

3. Move the cursor to the new point by scrubbing or playing, then click the Paste Keyframe button ◆ to apply this keyframe.

✔ Tip

■ The keyframes copied in the manner described above are entirely independent of their original keyframes and vice versa. Altering one doesn't change the other.

To move a keyframe:

◆ Hold down the Alt key, then, using the mouse, left-click the keyframe and drag it to the new position. Note: the last keyframe cannot be moved.

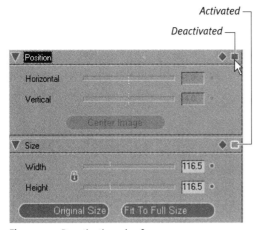

Activated

Deactivated

Figure 9.43 Deactivating a keyframe range.

Deactivating a keyframe area

Occasionally you may want to turn off certain parameters to see the interaction of the other keyframes on the Timeline more clearly. You can accomplish this using the Keyframe toggle.

To deactivate a set of keyframes:

◆ Click the Activate square at the end of the row.

It turns from gold to blue and the parameters become grayed out (**Figure 9.43**).

If you scrub through this effect window, these keyframes won't be used.

Reversing Keyframes

One button common to both the RT and Classic interfaces is the Revert Direction of Effect button ![icon], which inverts the keyframes you've created, effectively playing the filter backward.

Due to technical restrictions, not all filters have this button.

CONTROLLING KEYFRAMES

Working Without Keyframes

Although keyframes are a very valuable tool, you may encounter times when you don't want to use them. For example, you might want to zoom in on clip and keep that level of zoom from the first frame to the last.

✔ Tip

■ Some filters, such as the Basic Color Corrector, have keyframes turned off by default and you need to activate them before you can use them.

To deactivate/activate keyframes:

1. With the editor open, click the Options tab.

2. Open the keyframes area by clicking the small triangle.

3. Click the "Do not use Keyframes" or "Use Keyframes" radio button, depending on what you want to do (**Figure 9.44**).

✔ Tips

■ In a filter, turning off keyframes is useful for creating global effects, such as correcting a poorly framed camera shot or for color correction. Don't forget that you can stack filters, which allows you to use the same filter with or without keyframes as the need arises.

■ Turning off keyframes in this way is global. To deactivate specific keyframes, see "Deactivating a keyframe area" earlier in this chapter.

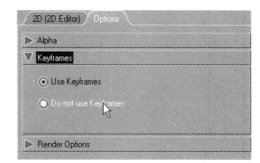

Figure 9.44 Turning off all keyframes.

Working with Classic Filters

As with Classic transitions, Classic filters are the old non-Realtime filter from previous incarnations of Liquid Edition. You need to render them—in the background—before you can view them, which should put them at an immediate disadvantage. But because you can find several very interesting non-Realtime filters within the Classic collection, they are still used by editors everywhere (**Figure 9.45**).

Check here for new parameters in the Classic filters.

Keyframe Interpolation is unique to the Classic FX range.

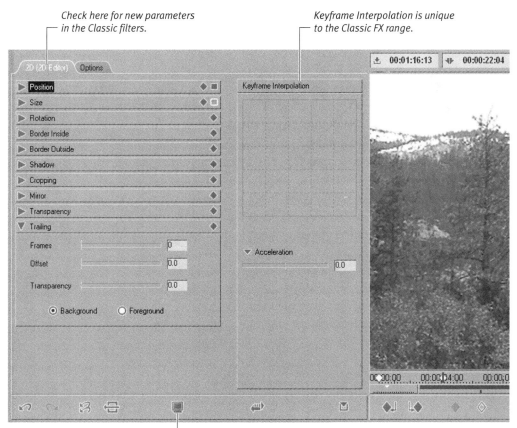

Figure 9.45 A Classic Filter Editor.

Full-screen mode

Full-screen mode

One clear advantage of using a Classic filter is the full-screen mode. You can toggle this on by clicking the Full-Screen Mode button ▦, which allows the Classic Editor to completely take over the screen (**Figure 9.46**).You can return to normal size by clicking the Full-Screen Mode button a second time.

Figure 9.46 Full-screen mode showing the hidden areas of an oversized image.

Editing the Classic Filters

Classic filters work with or without keyframes, and so you can edit following the same procedure you did when you edited Realtime filters. However, there are a number of additional parameters for you to adjust. You need to look at each filter in turn to see to which extra parameters you can gain access.

Keyframe Interpolation

One of the most interesting parameters available using Classic filters is Keyframe Interpolation. This governs the speed at which the effect happens between any two keyframes.

Remember; this is the "speed at which the effect happens" and not the "speed of the actual clip." You can only alter the speed of a media clip using the Timewarp non-Realtime filter, which I discuss later in this chapter.

You use Keyframe Interpolation simply to alter the pace of an effect. The following example shows a 2D Editor using this parameter to zoom in on the incoming clip. This happens slowly at first, then when it reaches the halfway mark, the zoom increases in speed until it reaches full speed at the end of the clip.

To alter Keyframe Interpolation:

1. Add one of the Classic filters to a clip on the Timeline.

2. Scrub to a keyframe on the Timeline and alter the interpolation in one of the following ways:

   ▲ Drag the acceleration line toward a positive (faster) or negative (slower) amount.

   ▲ Double-click inside this box and enter a number.

   ▲ Click inside the parameter curve area and drag the keyframe toward the value you require.

3. Exit the editor by clicking the Running Man button 🏃 in the top-right corner of the editor.

   The editor exits and the filter begins to render in the background.

4. Once it has finished rendering, set a mark-in and mark-out point on the Timeline on either side of the filter.

5. Then play back the filter by clicking the Play from Mark-In to Mark-Out button.

✔ Tip

■ If you add a Keyframe Interpolation of 100 to the first keyframe, the effect happens immediately.

Saving a Customized Filter

Once you have altered just the right the combination of parameters to create your dream filter, you probably want to save it for future use. You can do this with just a few clicks of your mouse.

To save a customized filter:

1. Switch to the All tab in the Project Browser and create a Folder called FX.

2. In the newly created FX folder, create a Rack called Filters (**Figure 9.47**).

3. Right-click the purple line that runs the length of the clip in the Timeline, and then select Copy from the menu (**Figure 9.48**).

4. Right-click inside the right pane of the Project Browser and select Paste from the menu. The filter is copied into this Rack complete with your parameters safely stored so that you can use it again in the future with just a drag and a drop (**Figure 9.49**).

✔ Tip

■ The filter appears in the Rack with its default name. To change this, right-click the effect and select Rename from the menu.

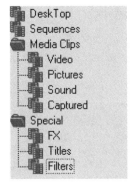

Figure 9.47
Creating a new FX Rack.

Figure 9.48 Copying the effect with your unique parameter settings.

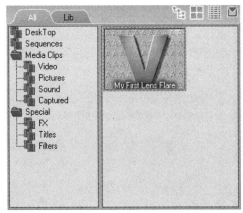

Figure 9.49 Pasted and renamed in the newly created FX Rack.

Figure 9.50 The clip as filmed...

Figure 9.51 ... and the corrected version using a 2D filter.

Working with RT Filters

It is sometimes difficult to visualize what the Filter Editor can really do. To help you overcome this, I have created two examples that show the basic concepts detailed in this chapter. The video clips used in the following sections can be downloaded at www.peachpit.com/liquid6vqp but you can use your own clips to work through these tasks.

Using the 2D RT Editor

It used to be that a cameraperson could get fired for bringing back a shot that was poorly framed, but now no one needs to panic because the 2D filter is there to crop away our mistakes.

In this example, you'll probably agree that the shot of the Ferris wheel would look better if you reduced the metal base in the lower-left corner a little (**Figure 9.50**).

To do this, you need to zoom in on the image using the 2D RT filter and then move the image to the right until it looks like **Figure 9.51**.

To use the 2D RT Editor:

1. With the clip on the Timeline, add the 2D filter by clicking the 2D Filter button.

   The filter is applied to the clip and the editor opens.

2. Scrub through the clip until you find the right spot.

   For my example, this is right at the end of the clip. I zoom in just as the metal outcrop appears.

   continues on next page

3. Click the One Click Size button ▦ and, with the cursor over the preview screen, push the mouse forward to zoom in (**Figure 9.52**).

On my copy, the size looks okay, but now I want to reposition the clip to bring the carriage back toward the center.

4. To do this, click the One Click Position button ✥, and with the cursor inside the preview area, drag the clip into the correct position (**Figure 9.53**).

✔ Tips

- To correct an entire clip keyframing can be turned off.

- Using the 2D editor to zoom in on a shoot is often used to correct an interview shot where the subject isn't correctly framed or something is distracting in the background. You can also use it to zoom in during a dramatic moment in the interview.

Figure 9.52 The cursor for the One Click Size tool.

Figure 9.53 The cursor for the One Click Position tool.

Figure 9.54 An example Picture in Picture. I created this using three clips stacked on top of each other and two preset PiP filters.

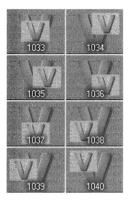

Figure 9.55 A selection of PiPs in the RT CPU Presets folder.

Figure 9.56 Setting up a PiP by stacking two clips on top of each other.

Creating a Picture in Picture effect

You can also use the 2D or 3D Editor to create a PiP—a Picture in Picture effect—where one video clip sits inside a small window playing over top of another (**Figure 9.54**).

A PiP is probably one of the easiest effects to create and is among the most used. There are even several presets in the GPU and CPU Presets folder for you to use as starters (**Figure 9.55**).

To create a PiP:

1. Place two clips on the Timeline, one on top of the other (**Figure 9.56**).

2. Select a preset PiP by clicking on the Lib tab (Library for dual-screen users), then opening the GPU Presets folder. Click on the 2D rack and scroll down to effect number 1033. The PiP effects start at this number.

continues on next page

3. Drag effect 1049 onto the topmost clip to add a PiP to the top-left corner of the screen (**Figure 9.57**).

Right away a PiP forms. It's a little too big.

4. You can fix this size problem quickly enough by opening the editor and using the One Click Size and Position tools to resize it (**Figure 9.58**).

✔ Tip

■ If you want the PiP to remain the same size and in the same position as I did in this example, turn the keyframes off so the filter works with only one set of parameters. You can see that I did this here by the lack of gray diamonds on the Source Viewer Timeline.

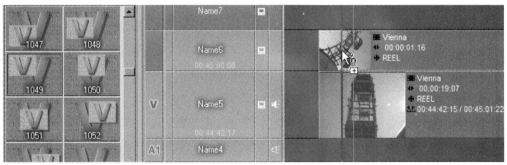

Figure 9.57 Drag and drop the preset PiP to apply it.

Figure 9.58 Adjusting the size of the PiP using the One Click Size tool.

Figure 9.59 Default application of a Lens Flare.

Figure 9.60 A Lens Flare with just a few parameters adjusted.

Working with the Lens Flare effect

The Lens Flare is a nice RT filter that you can use to subtly enhance a shot. In this example, you're going to create a glint in the mirror of the car as it drives along just to give the shot a sunnier, warmer feel.

To use the Lens Flare:

1. Open the Lib tab (Library for dual-screen users).

2. Select the Realtime Clip FX Rack and then the Editors Rack.

3. Drag and drop the Lens Flare onto the clip to get an instant result.

But you can see that you need to readjust the flare's placement (**Figure 9.59**).

To readjust Flare placement:

◆ Open the editor to use the One Click Position tool to move the Lens Flare to a more effective position.

By playing with the Intensity and Glow settings, you can work toward a really unique effect (**Figure 9.60**).

✔ Tips

■ The Lens Flare has an additional One Click button called Intensity; you use this to build more light into the flare.

■ Don't forget that you can save effects once you've created them to use in future projects.

Using Classic Filters

Panning and scanning oversized clips is one thing a Classic effect can do that an RT effect cannot. This is a useful trick when you're trying to create a dramatic video using a still image such as a panoramic landscape.

For this example, I am using an imported graphic that is much larger than the 720 by 480 NTSC pixel image or the 720 by 540 PAL pixel image that would normally fit inside the Master Viewer. This means that you won't be able to use a Realtime filter because anything outside of this area appears black if you try to move it (**Figure 9.61**).

However, by using a Classic filter, you can use the unseen areas. In this case, you create a vertical pan of the Yosemite falls. (The photograph used in this section can be downloaded at www.peachpit.com/liquid6vqp.)

Figure 9.61 The area outside of the TV standard is not visible when you're using a Realtime filter.

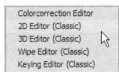

Colorcorrection Editor
2D Editor (Classic)
3D Editor (Classic)
Wipe Editor (Classic)
Keying Editor (Classic)

Figure 9.62 Applying a 2D Classic Editor using the Effects Editor button.

To pan and scan a clip:

1. After you place the oversized image on the Timeline, select it by clicking on it once and then add the 2D Classic filter by clicking the Effects Editor button and selecting 2D Editor (Classic) (**Figure 9.62**).

2. The editor opens automatically; click once on the media clip to select the image if it isn't shown in the inlay.

3. Now open the editor to full screen by clicking the Full Screen Mode button (**Figure 9.63**).

continues on next page

— One Click Position cursor

Figure 9.63 The Classic filter allows you to work with oversized images.

4. From here, use the One Click Position tool to move the image around.

   Each time you move the clip, you create a keyframe. If you move the clip twice at the same keyframe position, you overwrite the last value.

   In this example, you want to pan from the top of the photo to the bottom.

5. To do this, move the Timeline cursor to the first keyframe, and then using the One Click Position tool, reposition the image so that the top shows.

6. Also maneuver the waterfall so that it appears on the second third of the screen, thus obeying all good film school rules (**Figure 9.64**).

7. Now scrub to the last keyframe and maneuver the clip toward the person at the bottom of the picture to complete this part of the example (**Figure 9.65**).

8. Select the One Click Size tool and zoom in on the image until the person fills the screen.

   You need to add a keyframe a couple of seconds before you do this with the size set to 100; otherwise the zoom begins at the start of the clip.

9. Finally, add a transparency of 100 to the last keyframe so that the clip fades to black, and insert an extra keyframe a few seconds before the last with a transparency of 0 (**Figure 9.66**).

   Done. After rendering, the clip plays back pretty much as planned. All it needs now is some music or a voice-over to make it complete (**Figure 9.67**).

Figure 9.64 The image is repositioned using the "Rule of Thirds"...

USING CLASSIC FILTERS

Figure 9.65 ...then moved to the bottom of the picture at the last keyframe.

Keyframe to begin zoom

Keyframe to begin transparency

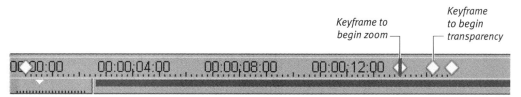

Figure 9.66 The Timeline displaying the final amount of keyframes.

Figure 9.67 The final effect. Start at the top of the waterfall, move slowly down, finish at the person at the bottom, zoom in on her, and fade to black.

Understanding Timewarp

Timewarp is one the most commonly used filters in Liquid Edition, but it's rarely recognized as actually being a filter. But that's what it functions as; slowing down a clip or speeding it up is a way of filtering it in order to alter its appearance.

I touched on Timewarp briefly in Chapter 6, when I used it during a four-point edit. In that case, Liquid Edition added Timewarp automatically, but in this chapter, you're going to learn how to manually add Linear and Dynamic Timewarps to your clips in order to alter the speed at which they play back.

Both versions of Timewarp are Classic filters even though the Dynamic Timewarp is relatively new. This means you need to render Timewarp filters before you can view the results.

Understanding Dynamic and Linear Timewarps

The words *Dynamic Timewarp* and *Linear Timewarp* tend to cause some confusion among first-time Liquid Edition users, as does the word *Timewarp* all on its own.

Timewarp is simply a way to alter—or warp—the way time plays back on your media clip. The two variations are also easy to understand. A Dynamic Timewarp alters the clip using keyframes, and a Linear Timewarp alters the clip without using keyframes. It really is that simple.

However, although the definitions are simple enough, the actual use of these is somewhat more complex.

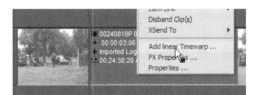

Figure 9.68 Adding a Linear Timewarp using the right-click menu.

Adding a Linear Timewarp Filter

Linear Timewarp is the simpler of the two speed-change filters, and it is also the one you used during the four-point edit technique we looked at in Chapter 6. Unlike Dynamic Timewarp, this filter has no keyframable abilities, but it still has many uses for everyday editing.

✔ Tip

■ New to version 6 is the ability to add a Timewarp to an audio clip. Media clips with audio automatically adjust any attached audio, but only down to a minimum of 50 percent and up to a maximum of 200 percent.

To add a Linear Timewarp filter:

1. Right-click the clip on the Timeline and select Add linear Timewarp from the menu (**Figure 9.68**).

   This automatically opens the Add Timewarp dialog (**Figure 9.69**).

continues on next page

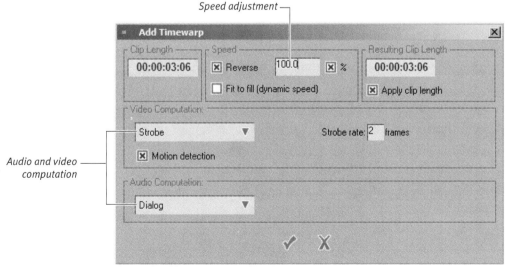

Figure 9.69 The Add Timewarp dialog.

ADDING A LINEAR TIMEWARP FILTER

335

2. To speed your clip up, alter the number in the Speed box so that it is greater than 100; to slow it down, enter a number less than 100.

3. To reverse the direction of the clip, click the Reverse check box and then alter the speed if you want.

4. Select the Video Computation method (see the sidebar "Which Computation Method Should You Use?" for details).

5. If you're applying a Timewarp to an audio track, select the Audio Computation most suitable for the clip you've selected.

6. Once you are happy with the settings, click the check mark at the bottom of the dialog to apply these changes.

✔ **Tips**

■ When increasing the speed of a clip, Liquid Edition subtracts frames from a clip, making it physically smaller on the Timeline. When decreasing the speed, Liquid Edition adds frames to a clip, making the clip physically larger on the Timeline. Therefore, you need to make sure you know which Timeline mode you are working in, Film Style or Overwrite Style. You can find details of these Timeline modes and the effects they have in Chapter 6.

■ You can undo a Dynamic Timewarp using the Timeline Undo key or the Ctrl+Z shortcut.

■ In the Speed section, you can click the check box next to the percent sign (%) to change the settings so that the speed shows as a decimal value rather than a percentage.

The Fit to Fill Check Box

You'll find the Fit to fill (dynamic speed) check box just under the Reverse box in the Speed section of the Add Timewarp dialog. Checking this is exceptionally useful when you want to fill areas of your video that, for one reason or another, you no longer want to move on the Timeline—a clip that matches a voice-over, for example.

In this case, you can add a clip to the Timeline and then select the Fit to fill (dynamic speed) check box. When you do so, this clip automatically increases the speed the required amount to exactly fill the gap to the next clip on the Timeline.

This is effectively the same as the four-point edit technique, but you can use it on clips you have dragged onto the Timeline.

Clips with Fit to fill selected don't overwrite other clips on the Timeline.

ADDING A LINEAR TIMEWARP FILTER

Which Computation Method Should You Use?

You can use seven different computation methods in both Linear and Dynamic Timewarps.

The default is Cut Fields, but for DV editing, many find that Mix Fields is the better choice because it tends to play back more smoothly, although the focus may be a little soft. If the sharpness of the picture is an issue—on a close-up, for example—then Cut Fields provides a clean image, but the speed increase/decrease isn't as smooth. In all cases, I recommend that you leave Motion Detection selected if the clip contains a lot of action.

You obviously have to experiment with each different clip to find out which setting suits it best. If you don't like either Cut Fields or Mix Fields, try Cut Frames or Mix Frames, but be aware that both of these filters are really aimed at film users as opposed to DV users, so results may vary.

You use the other computation methods for special effects, and these directly affect the visual finish of the clip.

Strobe cuts frames out to create a strobe light effect. You can select the flicker rate of this strobe by altering the Strobe rate.

When you use Trailing, you can get the effect of a ghost image following the moving object—the swing of a golf club, for example. With a bit of imagination, you can use this setting so your clip looks like the viewpoint of a recently concussed man. You can select the severity of the trails by altering the Trail Length.

You can use the final computational method, Progressive, to convert interlaced clips to non-interlaced clips. Normally you use a speed setting of 100 percent.

ADDING A LINEAR TIMEWARP FILTER

Editing a Linear Timewarp

You can edit a Linear Timewarp to tweak any of the settings you find in the Add Timewarp dialog, but make sure you're editing the filter and not asking Liquid Edition to add another Linear Filter on top of the one that already exists. Timewarp doesn't stack particularly well, which leads to strange results and possibly some green flashes on the screen—something you will be keen to avoid.

To edit a Linear Timewarp:

◆ To edit a clip, you must right-click directly on the small purple and black speckled line that runs along the bottom of the clip, and select Edit linear TimeWarp from the menu (**Figure 6.70**).

✔ Tips

■ You can also delete the Timewarp using the menu shown in Figure 6.70.

■ Some GPU filters don't mix well with Linear Timewarp. If you get results that don't fit the filter you have applied, use a CPU alternative.

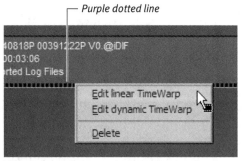

Purple dotted line

Figure 9.70 Click the purple dotted line to edit a Linear Timewarp, not add another one.

Adding a Dynamic Timewarp

Dynamic Timewarp, the more complex cousin of Linear Timewarp, was introduced in Liquid Edition version 5.5. Dynamic Timewarp is fully keyframable and you can use it to add a very professional look to your project by selecting at which point a clip should increase or decrease its speed.

However, using it is much more complex than using Linear Timewarp. As a result, you need to spend a great deal more time learning how it works.

✔ Tip

- Dynamic Timewarp doesn't support audio. Once the filter is applied, audio only plays when the clip is running at normal speed.

To add a Dynamic Timewarp filter:

1. Click the Lib tab (or Library if you are a dual-screen user) in the Project Browser, open the Classic Clip FX folder, and drag the Timewarp Editor filter to the clip on the Timeline.

2. Right-click the black and purple spotted line that runs along the bottom of the clip and select Edit dynamic TimeWarp.

   This brings up the complex-looking Dynamic Timewarp Editor (**Figure 9.71**).

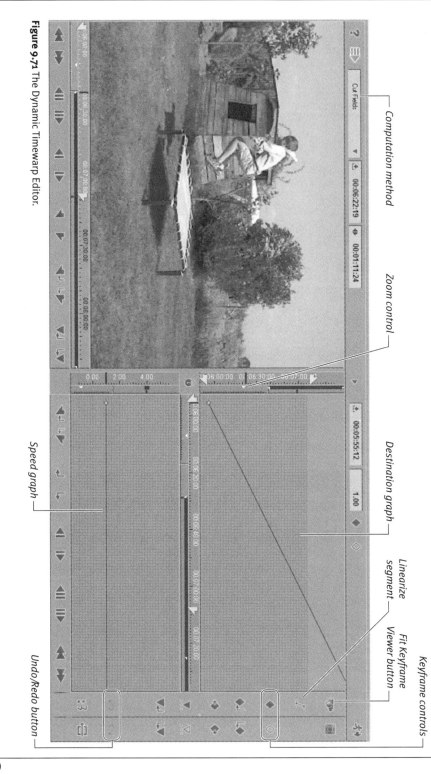

Figure 9-71 The Dynamic Timewarp Editor.

Computation method

Zoom control

Destination graph

Linearize segment

Fit Keyframe

Viewer button

Keyframe controls

Speed graph

Undo/Redo button

✔ Tips

■ There is nothing different here about working with Timewarp keyframes; the only variation is that by slowing down or speeding up a clip, you are adding frames to or subtracting frames from the overall length of the clip rather than visually altering the clip.

■ The two graphs on the right display motion (top) and speed (bottom). Most of the time you work with the bottom screen, but don't ignore the top one, because experimenting here uncovers more secrets.

■ Click the extended dialog arrow to make the Dynamic Timewarp Editor full screen (**Figure 9.72**).

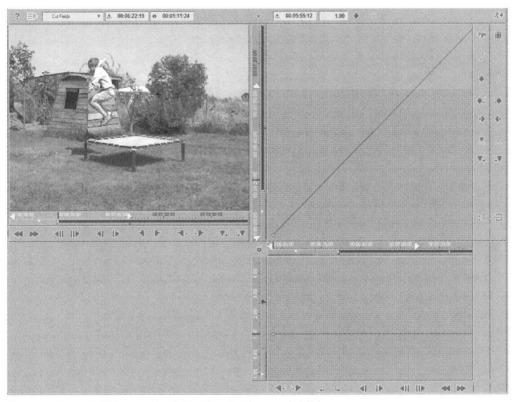

Figure 9.72 Dynamic Editor opened to full height using the extended dialog arrow.

Editing a Dynamic Timewarp

Trying to explain the Dynamic Timewarp on the flat medium of paper is a little tricky. It's difficult to get excited about a screen-shot of a slow-motion sequence. To try and make this as clear as possible, I'll first explain the basics of how to add and edit keyframes, and then I'll offer you a real-world example of what you can try to do with your own clips.

To edit a Dynamic Timewarp:

1. Before you begin editing, use the Go to Mark In button to place a keyframe at the start of the clip by clicking the Set Keyframe button (**Figure 9.73**).

   This creates a golden diamond in both of the graphs. This is your keyframe. When it is selected, it is gold; when it is deselected it is white.

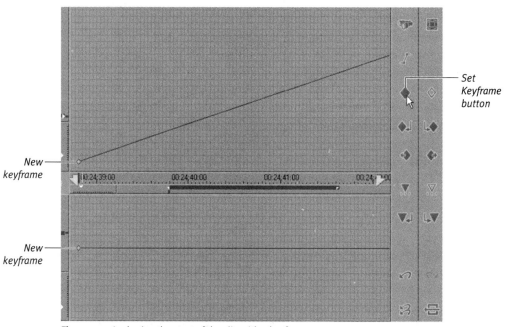

New keyframe

New keyframe

Set Keyframe button

Figure 9.73 Anchoring the start of the clip with a keyframe.

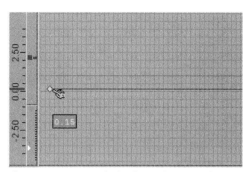

Figure 9.74 Dragging the keyframe down to reduce speed (0.15 or 15 percent of normal speed).

Figure 9.75 Entering the speed value directly.

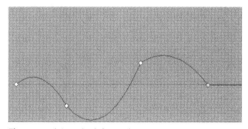

Figure 9.76 A typical dynamic curve.

2. To alter the speed of a specific keyframe do one of the following:

▲ In the bottom graph, drag the golden keyframe up to speed it up or down to slow it down (**Figure 9.74**).

▲ Enter a speed value in the speed box at the top of the interface (**Figure 9.75**).

Adding more than one keyframe creates a series of parameter curves between the keyframes that exist to smooth out the change between the two points (**Figure 9.76**).

3. Once you've finished altering your keyframes, exit the interface by clicking the running man 🏃 and allow the filter to render.

✔ Tips

■ The Dynamic Timewarp Editor doesn't automatically insert a keyframe at the beginning or end of your clip, but it does place a mark-in and mark-out point that indicates the length of the clip.

■ To show the mark-in and mark-out points of your clip on the Timeline, click once on the Fit Keyframe Viewers button 🔲.

Adding a Linear Keyframe

In the task above, "To edit a Dynamic Timewarp," you created a speed change (perhaps several) using the bottom graph. The parameter curve this creates may cause a problem if the curve dips down too low, causing the video to slow more than you intend. Worse still, if the curve dips below the green line at the bottom of the graph, the clip begins going backward, which is almost definitely not what you want.

To solve this, you need to instruct the Dynamic Timewarp Editor to create a linear link between the keyframes, which then ignores this curve and creates a straight speed change.

To add a linear keyframe:

1. *Do one of the following:*

   ▲ Place the mouse cursor slightly to the left or the right of the keyframe in question so that a small plus sign (+) appears next to the hand icon. Then drag a straight line up or down; the straight line indicates this is a linear keyframe (**Figure 9.77**).

   ▲ A slightly easier method is to highlight the keyframe that occurs *before* the keyframe you want to linearize, and then click the Linear Adjustment button to automatically create a Linear Timewarp between these two keyframes (**Figure 9.78**).

2. Once you have finished altering the parameters, exit the editor by clicking the running man in the top-right corner of the interface. The filter has to render before you can see the result.

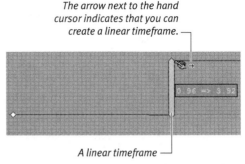

The arrow next to the hand cursor indicates that you can create a linear timeframe.

A linear timeframe

Figure 9.77 Creating a linear speed change using the mouse.

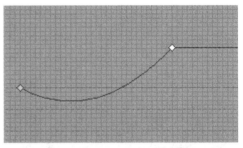

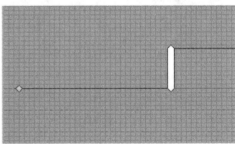

Figure 9.78 Before and after. On the top, the speed change created a curve. On the bottom, the Linear Adjustment button turned it into a linear timeframe.

Using the Dynamic Timewarp

So much for the theory. As you can see from the descriptions, Dynamic Timewarp is a lot more brain intensive than its cousin, the relatively cuddly and friendly Linear Timewarp. And of course it doesn't help when the Dynamic version also utilizes linear terminology.

To try and get you comfortable with this theory with as little pain as possible, you can download a clip from the book's Web site (www.peachpit.com/liquid6vqp) called Boy Jumping, import it into Liquid Edition, and use it to follow along in this next section.

In the tasks that follow, a sequence is created that shows a boy jumping at normal speed until his hat flips off in the wind. At this point I want to slow down to 25% until the hat hits the floor, then speed back up to normal speed. This creates the classic "slow-suspend" effect during an event, something that is often seen in TV commercials. It's all made possible by using keyframes to control the speed and—more importantly—the interpolation of that speed between the keyframes.

To create a slowdown/speed-up effect:

1. Add the Dynamic Timewarp as described in the "To add a Dynamic Timewarp filter" task earlier in this chapter.

2. Open the editor by right-clicking the bottom purple spotted line and selecting Edit dynamic TimeWarp.

3. Once the editor is open, click the Fit Keyframe Viewers button [▼] to see both the mark-in and mark-out points of your clip inside the graph and to highlight the opening keyframe.

To anchor the speed:

◆ Navigate to the start of the clip, click the Go to Mark-In button [◀·], and then add a keyframe by clicking the Set Keyframe button [◆] (**Figure 9.79**).

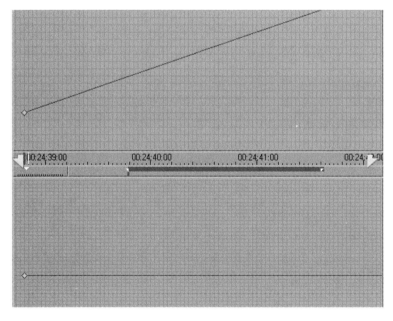

Figure 9.79
Creating a start point using Set Keyframe.

To add a speed change:

1. Scrub to the point just before you want the speed to change; in this example, just before the boy's cap lifts off his head.

   Now that you have found the correct position on the Timeline, you want to slow down to a quarter of normal speed.

2. To adjust the speed, double-click the Speed value box, enter a value, and either click the Set Keyframe button or press Enter on the keyboard to apply this change.

3. As you can see in **Figure 9.80**, in this example version, you should enter 0.25, the decimal equivalent of 25 percent or 1/4.

   In the lower graph, notice that the blue line passes over the red line before it dips down toward the keyframe that was last added (**Figure 9.81**). This means the clip increases speed before it decreases.

   This isn't what you want. You want it to play at normal speed and then dip down immediately to slow motion. To achieve this, you need to add a linear segment between the two keyframes.

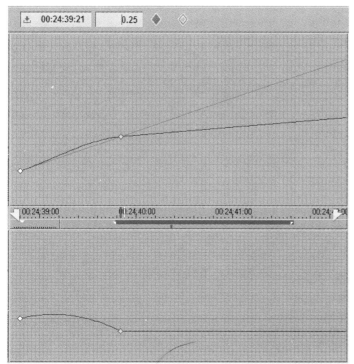

Figure 9.80 Slowing the speed down to 25 percent of normal by creating a new keyframe using direct number entry.

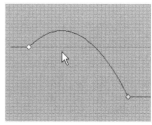

Figure 9.81 The result is a parabolic climb in speed before the reduction occurs…

To add a linear segment:

1. Select the keyframe before the one that holds the speed change (in this case the opening keyframe), and then press the Linear Segment button (**Figure 9.82**).

   Now the clip does exactly what you want. It plays at normal speed—indicated by the blue line in the bottom graph following the red line—then it dips suddenly down to 25 percent of normal speed.

   At this point, you should exit the editor to check the results before moving on.

2. To exit the editor, click the running man button in the top right of the interface.

   After you render it, the clip plays fine except it now ends too early. This is another difficult area to understand, but put simply, when the Dynamic Timewarp slows something down, it adds frames to the clip to create something from nothing. But unlike the Linear Timewarp, Dynamic Timewarp doesn't alter the overall length of the original clip.

To correct a shortened clip:

◆ Trim the clip on the Timeline, dragging the handle outward until the Master Viewer displays the correct last frame for this media clip (**Figure 9.83**). Allow the clip to render again.

   Okay, that worked fine. If you are using the downloaded example, the boy's cap flips off and the clip ends where we want it to. But the boy now moves in slow motion until the end of the clip. What we want to see is the clip return again to normal speed once the cap hits the floor.

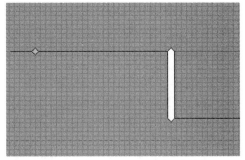

Figure 9.82 ... but it's turned into a Linear Time adjustment by using the Linearize Segment tool.

Figure 9.83 Adjusting the length of a clip to compensate for the additional frames.

Green line

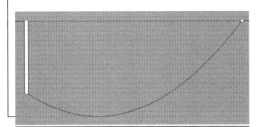

Figure 9.84 The green line indicates zero speed or stop. If the line hits this, the clip pauses. If the line goes beneath this, it moves into reverse.

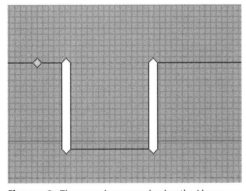

Figure 9.85 The curve is removed using the Linear Segment button.

To return the speed to normal:

1. Open the editor as described earlier in this chapter and click the Fit Keyframe Viewers button to realign the graph. If you are using the downloaded example, scrub through until you reach the point where the cap touches the ground. Enter "1" in the speed box and press Enter.

Now you have another problem. The bottom graph in the last parabolic curve—between the slowdown keyframe and the normal speed keyframe—touches the green line, indicating a speed of zero—a freeze-frame, in other words (**Figure 9.84**).

This isn't what you want. You need the clip to return to normal speed when the cap lands, for this example.

2. Remove the parameter curve between the two keyframes by selecting the keyframe to the left of the one you added last and click the Linear Segment button (**Figure 9.85**).

Okay! Now if you exit the editor and allow it to render in this example, the cap falls in slow motion, but the boy jumps after it at normal speed.

continues on next page

USING THE DYNAMIC TIMEWARP

One Step at a Time

Try not to get too advanced too quickly when moving through the exercise. Make a small adjustment, then exit the editor to see what you've created. Add keyframes one at a time to see the collaborative effect. Dynamic Timewarp is best learned in small steps; if you go too far to fast, you may just end up confused.

To build the slowdown/speed-up effect exercise, I added one keyframe at a time, starting from the left and moving to the right. I had a clear idea of what I wanted before I even opened the editor, and I rendered each keyframe to make sure I got exactly what I wanted.

If you follow this approach, you'll get excellent results from the Dynamic Timewarp and your video production will stand out from the crowd.

However, because you've effectively increased the speed—you adjusted the clip from .25 to 1.0—the opposite problem to the one you experienced when you decreased the speed occurs. The clip now shows a few more frames at the end than you want. This is because when speeding up a clip, Liquid Edition subtracts frames—in this case, the frames it added during the slow motion—but again, Dynamic Timewarp doesn't alter the physical length of the clip.

3. To solve this problem, trim the clip again, this time taking the mark-out point down the Timeline until the Master Viewer displays the correct frame for this clip's mark-out point.

   When trimming a clip down the Timeline, you may notice that it doesn't need to be rendered. This is as good an example as any of how intelligent the Liquid Edition render engine can be.

✔ Tips

■ Audio is not supported by the Dynamic Timewarp filter. However, if the speed returns to 1.0 at any point during the clip, audio returns. Outside of that, audio is lost.

■ If you want to take the Dynamic Timewarp example further, try adding a keyframe to speed the boy up as he jumps after his cap. Remember to take it a step at a time and always allow to render after each change.

■ Insert a marker at the end of the clip before you add the Dynamic Timewarp filter. That way you can always locate the end point during the Timewarp edit process.

USING THE DYNAMIC TIMEWARP

Introducing Hollywood FX Filters

Hollywood Effects (HFX) is a popular plug-in integrated into Liquid Edition for both transitions (see Chapter 8) and filters. This plug-in offers a specific range of filters that are never going to be described as subtle. Using these filters is like holding a flashing neon sign that says, "yep, this is an impressive filter and I'm proud of it." If that's what you want, then with HFX filters, that's exactly what you're going to get.

Most HFX filters are real-time, meaning they display a preview version under a yellow slice, which must be rendered before you can export to DVD or tape. But some filters are slightly more complex and require rendering first. In these cases, they are marked with a small red ball in the bottom-left corner of the effects thumbnail.

There is also a range of filters that render with the word Pro displayed across them. To unlock these filters, you need to buy a Pro serial number from Pinnacle. You can do this online via their Web site www.pinnaclesys.com.

Adding a Hollywood FX Filter

You add a Hollywood FX filter the same way you add a normal filter; you just need to drag it from a different folder. HFX filters obey the same rules as normal filters and you can add them to any video clip on any Track, including titles and graphics.

✔ Tip

■ You can also stack HFX filters with normal filters, although their visual complexity may mean this isn't exceptionally practical or visually digestible.

To add a Hollywood FX filter:

1. Click the Lib tab in the Project Browser and open the Realtime Clip FX folder.

   Inside the Editor Rack, right at the bottom, is the HFX Filter Editor (**Figure 9.86**).

2. To apply this filer, drag and drop it to the required clip. Once it's applied, a yellow slice appears above the clip indicating the effect is real-time.

   By default, HFX displays the Fly-Away filter when it is first applied to a clip.

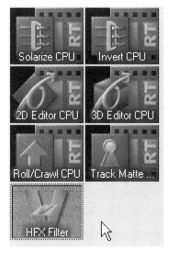

Figure 9.86 The HFX filter is located at the bottom of the RT Clip FX Editors Rack.

Editing a Hollywood FX Filter

Unlike the HFX transitions, no preset Hollywood FX filters are stored in the Project Browser Racks; however, a large number are inside the HFX interface. Once you've applied the HFX Filter, you can access any of these presets by opening the HFX Editor.

To open the Hollywood FX editor:

Do one of the following:

- Double-click the purple line running along the top of the clip or click the filter symbol if it's visible.

- Right-click the clip and select FX Properties from the menu, then double-click the HFX Filter from the Clip FX Properties box.

  Once it's loaded, the HFX Editor loads, taking over the desktop (**Figure 9.87**).

Keyframable parameters   *Edit Views toggle buttons*

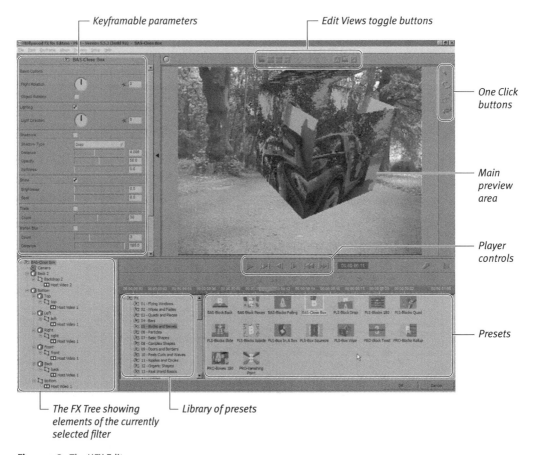

One Click buttons

Main preview area

Player controls

Presets

The FX Tree showing elements of the currently selected filter   *Library of presets*

Figure 9.87 The HFX Editor.

✔ Tip

- HFX has many fan sites; of particular interest is Mike Shaw's site (www.mikeshaw.co.uk). Mike has been running his popular HFX Web site for many years. On this site, he offers CD tutorials and a range of downloadable HFX presets, assuming, of course, you've already worked your way through all those that came with version 6 of Liquid Edition. One such tutorial expands greatly on the wedding book example shown briefly at the end of this chapter and another shows you how to create a "Beam me up, Scotty" effect. All good stuff.

INTRODUCING HOLLYWOOD FX FILTERS

Working with Hollywood FX Filters

Although I recommend buying an HFX book to get the best of out of this plug-in, in this section, I provide a very basic introduction to using HFX in a real-world scenario.

In this example, I want to show you how to reproduce a film effect similar to that seen in the *Harry Potter* films.

Creating a Harry Potter–type photo

One of the things I like about the universe Harry Potter lives in are the magical photographs. In these, people and things actually move around and wave at the camera. Using HFX, you can simulate this without too much difficulty.

To create a moving photograph:

1. Place a clip on the Timeline, preferably one with a close-up of a person.

2. Open the Realtime Clip FX folder and look for the HFX Filter Editor at the bottom of the Rack.

3. Drag this over to the clip, then right-click the purple line and select Edit to open the editor.

4. Once inside the editor, select the Frames Rack (number 14), and choose from one of the frames offered by double-clicking it. Scrub though the HFX Timeline to make sure you like the look of it (**Figure 9.88**).

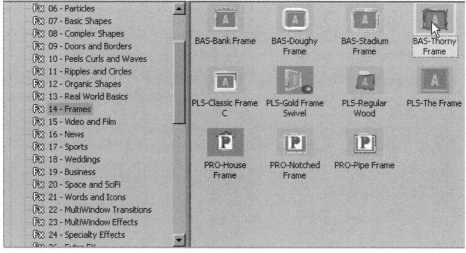

Figure 9.88 Selecting a frame from the presets.

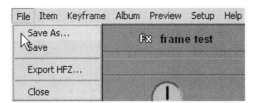

Figure 9.89 Saving a copy of the preset.

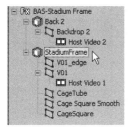

Figure 9.90 Movement for the BAS-Stadium frame is controlled from this highlighted branch.

5. Now save a copy of this filter by clicking File and then selecting Save As from the menu (**Figure 9.89**).

All of the frames have motion, but that's not what you want. You need to immobilize the frame so that your clip plays in it, thus simulating a Harry Potter experience.

6. To freeze the motion, you need to alter the keyframes that are hidden under the Presets album. Click the Show/Hide Album button ▨ to reveal the Frame Editor.

By default, this is empty even though frames exist on this clip.

7. To reveal the frames, first highlight the FX group that controls movement; this is found in the FX tree panel.

In this example, you are using the BAS-Stadium frame, and its movement is controlled on the Stadium Frame branch (**Figure 9.90**).

8. Confirm that you have the right branch by scrubbing the Timeline.

If it is the correct one, the X, Y, and Z settings move as the frame moves.

continues on next page

9. Now that you have the correct branch, click once in any of the numerical boxes to reveal the keyframes (**Figure 9.91**).

10. Delete all the keyframes except the start and the end ones using the Go to Next Keyframe and Delete Keyframe buttons.

11. Return to the first frame and alter the X, Y, and Z settings until you have the frame on the screen where you want it.

You can also use the One Click buttons on the side of the HFX interface to adjust the image.

— Click once in any of these boxes...

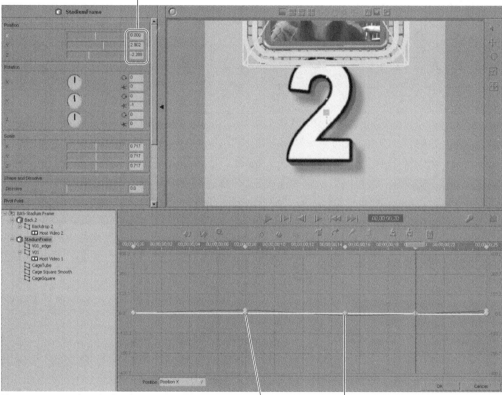

Figure 9.91 Revealing the keyframes.

...to reveal these keyframes.

Figure 9.92 A moving portrait—aka Harry Potter style.

12. When you are happy with the placement, click the Copy Current Keyframe button, move to the last keyframe, and click Paste Keyframe.

13. Exit the editor and the clip displays inside a frame.

14. If you want to get rid of the black behind this clip, create a color clip and place it underneath the filtered clip (**Figure 9.92**).

✔ Tips

- Animated backgrounds look particularly cool when you use them as a backdrop for this type of effect.

- Add a 2D filter to improve the framing of the original clip if you need to.

WORKING WITH HOLLYWOOD FX FILTERS

Doing More with Hollywood FX

Hollywood FX is capable of a lot more than you have seen in this chapter. But the version that comes with Liquid Edition has some restrictions that limit its use. For example, it isn't possible to edit FX and add objects so that you can place your own images on transitions and filters unless you upgrade to one of the more powerful versions of HFX.

For an example of the Hollywood FX's capabilities, take a look at **Figure 9.93**. This shows the Wedding Album effect edited so that it includes a graphic on the front cover. This effect isn't possible with the standard HFX that comes with Liquid Edition.

You can find full details on where you can buy these upgrades on the Pinnacle Web site at www.pinnaclesys.com. Unfortunately, I can't give you any more details here because specifications are likely to change after this book goes to press.

Figure 9.93 A more advanced version of HFX allows the use of graphic mapping.

Using Title Deko

It's easy to overlook the significance good titles can bring to your video productions, but like most elements of video editing, a title works best as an enhancement rather than as a glaring object on the screen. Therefore, before you can move on to being creative, you need to understand at least the basic fundamentals of title creation.

In Liquid Edition 6, you can make titles using any image creation program, but generally speaking, most are created using Title Deko, which has been supplied with a number of different NLE packages in a variety of formats over the years. It's a relatively easy program to use, and although it's beginning to look a little dated, it still packs a significant punch.

In this chapter, you learn how to create a basic title, adjust it using the templates available, and finally, add movement and backgrounds to enhance the title's visual appeal.

Introducing Title Deko

Title Deko is essentially a text editor that creates bitmaps of your text so that you can manipulate them on the Liquid Edition Timeline. If this all sounds a little complicated, don't worry; the majority of this happens in the background. All you need to do is type out the text and decide which design to use. Once you've completed this, Title Deko creates the bitmap for you and Liquid Edition automatically imports it.

Title Deko is a separate application, but it's integrated in such a way that you never really see the join or feel removed from your actual video project. For most editors, using Title Deko is a quick and resourceful way to create titles without having to break the creative flow.

Advantages of Title Deko Pro

Title Deko Pro is an upgrade Pinnacle has made available as a separate purchase or as part of their Productivity Pack. It has many enhanced features, including curved text and textured fonts. In addition, you can type text in any direction and spell-check your title (**Figure 10.1**).

 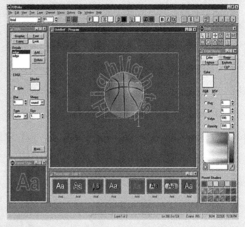

Figure 10.1 Title Deko Pro with support for various advanced text features.

Once it's installed on your computer, Title Deko Pro replaces the earlier version and responds when you activate the Title function in Liquid Edition. To get further upgrade information, click the Upgrade to TitleDeko Pro button found on the left side of the Title Deko program (**Figure 10.2**).

Figure 10.2
Upgrade to Pro via
the Title Deko interface.

Opening Title Deko

Opening Title Deko (or Pro if it is installed) is a simple matter of clicking the Toolbar button or using the keyboard shortcut. Once you open Title Deko, it takes over your monitor with a full-sized interface (**Figures 10.3a** and **3b**).

To open Title Deko:

Do one of the following:

◆ Press F2 on the keyboard.

◆ Click the Character Generator button on the Liquid Edition Toolbar.

✔ Tip

■ By default, the background of the Title Deko editor displays whatever is underneath the timeline cursor. If this happens to be a blank space in the Timeline, the background is black; if not, video from the Timeline is displayed as a single frame (**Figure 10.4**).

Text cursor   *Presets*

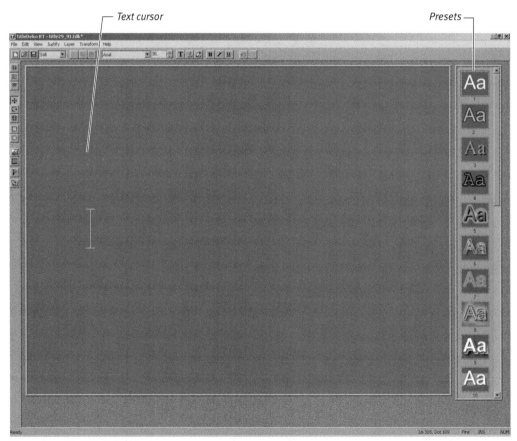

Figure 10.3a The Title Deko interface.

Figure 10.3b The Title Deko interface (buttons detail).

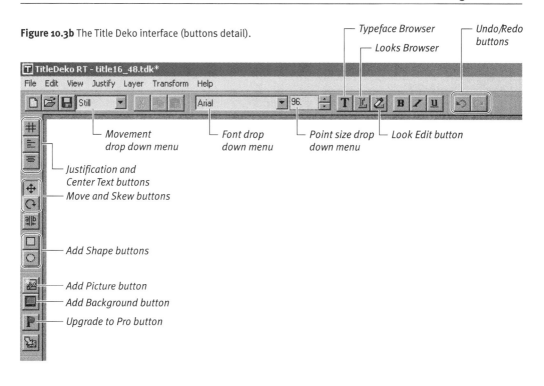

Typeface Browser

Looks Browser

Undo/Redo buttons

Movement drop down menu

Font drop down menu

Point size drop down menu

Look Edit button

Justification and Center Text buttons

Move and Skew buttons

Add Shape buttons

Add Picture button

Add Background button

Upgrade to Pro button

Figure 10.4 When video is present on the Timeline, you see a single frame in Title Deko.

Creating a Basic Title

Once Title Deko opens on your screen, the text cursor is ready. To create a title, just type and the text appears on your screen (**Figure 10.5**). If you make a mistake, navigate using the left and right arrows to delete or retype the word.

When you get to the end of a line, the text wraps around to the next line; if you press Enter, you create a carriage return. If you drop below the window, you'll need to scroll up using the standard Windows scroll bar.

✔ Tips

■ You can also use a wheel mouse to scroll through the text window.

■ Undo/Redo via the Ctrl+Z shortcut is supported, as are the search and replace functions found in most text editors. You can access most of these edit features from the Edit menu (**Figure 10.6**).

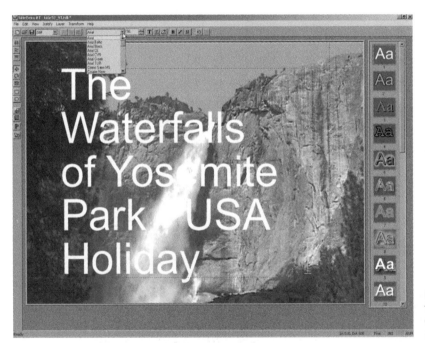

Figure 10.5 Basic text entry using the default font and point size.

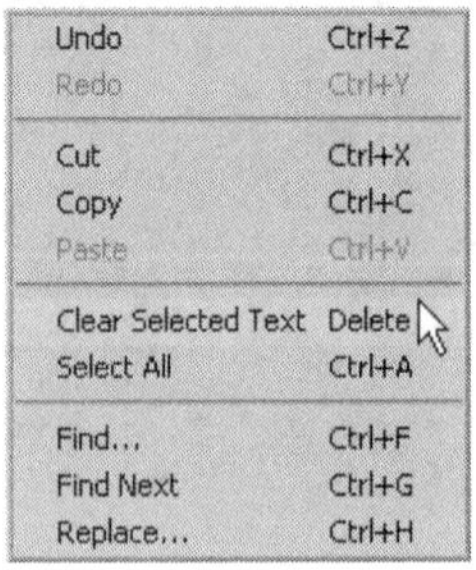

Figure 10.6 The Edit drop-down menu.

Changing the Typing Direction

If you need to type from right to left or top to bottom, click the Layer menu and select the style you want from the four choices at the bottom of this menu (**Figure 10.7**).

This feature is only available on a newly created title *before* you type anything. Once you start typing, you're committed to using the selected style, and the direction change options are grayed out.

Figure 10.7 Altering the direction in which text is entered.

The Alpha Channel

When you create a simple title with what appears to be a black background, you are in fact creating a title with an alpha channel.

An *alpha channel* is a part of an image that allows anything behind—or in Liquid Edition's case, underneath—to show through. This effectively means that you can use titles with alpha channels on top of video clips without totally obscuring the clip (**Figure 10.8**).

However, if you add a picture or colored background to the title inside of the Title Deko interface, the alpha channel isn't visible (**Figure 10.9**).

Figure 10.8 A title showing the clip below using its alpha channel.

Figure 10.9 The same title with a colored background loses its alpha channel.

Altering the Text Properties of a Title

Once you have created a basic title, you'll want to customize it. In this section, you'll learn how to alter the font and point size, and also how to enhance the title using shadows, colored backgrounds, and background images.

Changing the font and point size

The text defaults to Arial 96 points whenever you open the application. This is a rather large point size, and it's easy for your titles to start looking messy once you've entered only a little bit of text. At this stage, you'll want to adjust the point size of the text and think about altering the font you are using.

To change the font:

1. Highlight your text by dragging a lasso around it with the mouse (**Figure 10.10**).

2. Select the font you want by doing one of the following:

   ▲ Click the drop-down font menu and choose from the list (**Figure 10.11**).

   ▲ Click the Browse Typefaces button **T**, or press Ctrl+T and make your selection by double-clicking any of the available fonts (**Figure 10.12**).

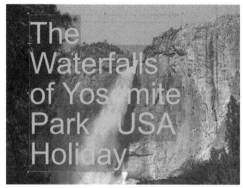

Figure 10.10 Dragging the lasso around the text selects it. You must do this to apply any changes to text or objects in Title Deko.

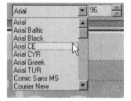

Figure 10.11 The drop-down font menu.

Figure 10.12 The Typeface browser allows you a better look at the fonts that are available.

Figure 10.13 Bits of your text *not* highlighted retain their previous font.

Figure 10.14 Adjusting the point size using the up and down arrows...

Figure 10.15 ...or by directly entering the numerical value...

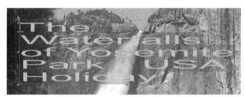

Figure 10.16 ...or by dynamically dragging the text to a new size using the selection box.

✔ Tip

■ Text that isn't highlighted doesn't change. Make sure you highlight all of your text; otherwise missing letters remain in the old font style (**Figure 10.13**).

To change the point size:

1. Highlight your text by dragging a lasso around it with the mouse (Figure 10.10).

2. Then do one of the following:

   ▲ Click the up and down arrows next to the point size (**Figure 10.14**).

   ▲ Double-click inside the point size box and directly enter the size you want (**Figure 10.15**).

   ▲ Click one of the adjustment handles around your text and drag it to the size required (**Figure 10.16**).

Aligning text

Once you have the right point size and font style, you can move the text by surrounding either all of it or just one word (or even one letter) and dragging it to wherever you want to place it.

However, to align the text with a bit more accuracy, you should use the alignment tools. You can find these arranged down the left side of the interface.

To align the text:

1. Highlight your text by dragging a lasso around it with the mouse (Figure 10.10).

2. Click one of the three alignment buttons (Top, Center, Bottom) and make your choice (**Figure 10.17**).

✔ Tip

■ You can also access these options from the Justify menu and the keyboard shortcuts listed in it (**Figure 10.18**).

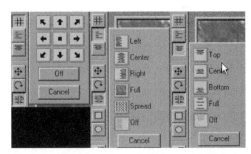

Figure 10.17 The three types of alignments in Title Deko.

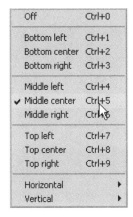

Figure 10.18 Adjusting alignments via the Justify drop-down menu.

ALTERING THE TEXT PROPERTIES OF A TITLE

Safe Areas

When you're working with alignment, be aware of the safe area markers, which are displayed as dotted red lines inside the Title Deko interface (**Figure 10.19**).

These lines indicate where a title is likely to be viewable on the majority of TV sets; I'd advise you to play it safe and always keep your titles within the confines of these lines.

Figure 10.19 The safe area for a title is inside these dotted red lines.

Enhancing the Text

Once the point size is under control and you have decided which font to use, you can refine things a little further by enhancing the text in various ways. Although you really need the Pro version of Title Deko to create some truly startling changes, the standard version can still add shadows, create colored backgrounds, and even insert a picture into the frame.

To add a shadow:

1. Highlight your text by dragging a lasso around it with the mouse (Figure 10.10).

2. Click the Edit Current Look button, or press Ctrl+P and select the Shadow tab in the Look edit dialog (**Figure 10.20**).

3. Choose a solid or gradient color for your shadow, and then click the colored tiles to pick the actual color (**Figure 10.21**).

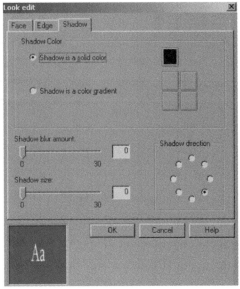

Figure 10.20 The Shadow tab in the Look edit dialog.

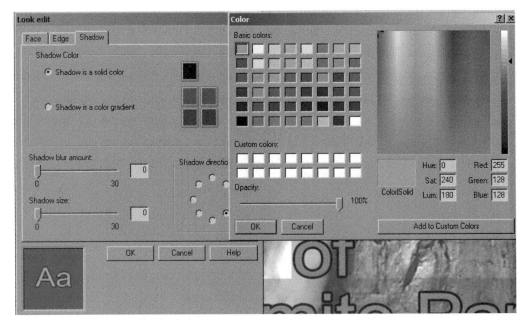

Figure 10.21 Adjusting the color of a shadow.

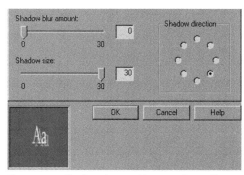

Figure 10.22 Shadow size must be more than 1 if you want to see a shadow at all.

Figure 10.23 A title with shadow and blur added.

4. To activate the shadow, give it a direction and a size.

You can find the controls for both of these at the bottom of this interface along with the shadow blur slider. As you adjust these three controls, a real-time preview of your shadow is created (**Figure 10.22**).

✔ Tips

■ If your shadow has a size of zero, no shadow displays. Occasionally Title Deko picks up the last shadow setting in a new title. If you don't need it, just return to the Edit look dialog and reduce the shadow to zero.

■ If your shadow is black, you can't see it against the standard black background Title Deko uses to represent the alpha channel.

■ When you use it constructively with bright colors, the Shadow Blur can produce a very nice looking title (**Figure 10.23**).

ENHANCING THE TEXT

Look Edit—Further Functions

You can also use the Look edit dialog to add a colored edge to the letters and to offset the face with a blur effect.

All you need is a little imagination to create some really unique titles using a combination of settings on the dialog's three tabs: Face, Edge, and Shadow (**Figure 10.24**).

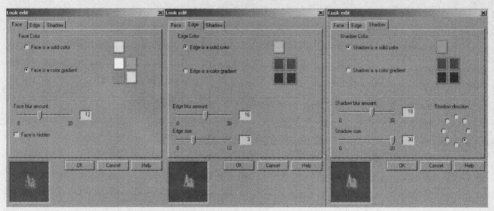

Figure 10.24 The three tabs of the Look edit dialog.

I generated **Figure 10.25** using such settings.

Figure 10.25 A title generated after adjusting a setting in each of the three tabs.

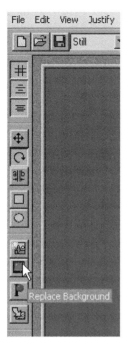

Figure 10.26 The Set Background button.

To add a colored background:

1. Click the Set Background button once (**Figure 10.26**).

2. From the Set Background dialog, select whether the color will be a solid or gradient and then choose the actual color by clicking the colored tile(s) (**Figure 10.27**).

3. Click OK to close this dialog; the background color is created as a result.

✔ Tips

■ You can add a colored background before or after you add text to the title image.

■ To return the alpha channel so that you can see through the title again, select the Background is transparent option (**Figure 10.28**).

Figure 10.27 Choosing a color for the background.

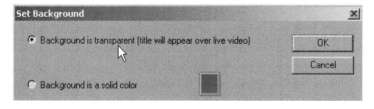

Figure 10.28 Returning the title's alpha channel and removing the colored background.

To add a picture background:

1. Click the Insert Picture button once (**Figure 10.29**).

2. From the Open dialog, browse to the image you want, and click once to select that picture (**Figure 10.30**).

3. Click Open to close this dialog, and the picture is inserted into the title.

4. To expand the picture to full-screen size, select Make Full Screen in the Layer menu (**Figure 10.31**).

Figure 10.29 The Insert Picture button...

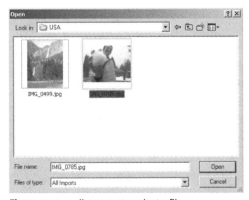

Figure 10.30 ...allows you to select a file.

Figure 10.31 The Make Full Screen option in the Layer menu.

ENHANCING THE TEXT

✔ Tips

- If the picture obscures the text, click the Layer menu and select Send to Back from the choices available, or press Alt+hyphen on the keyboard (**Figure 10.32**).

- You can incorporate small images, such as company logos, into the title using the Insert Picture button (**Figure 10.33**).

Figure 10.32 This shows the before and after of sending an image to the back so that you can see the text.

Figure 10.33 In addition to adding an image, you can also include a logo.

Image Dimensions

When you import a picture, it automatically adjusts to the TV standard with which you are currently working. If the Y or X axis of this picture doesn't match the same ratio as the TV standard, the picture stretches and becomes distorted.

To avoid this, either change the picture inside a photo manipulation program or drag it back to the right dimensions in Title Deko.

Using the Preset Templates

If you don't want to spend time creating your own enhanced text, make sure you become familiar with Title Deko's presets. Title Deko comes with a full list of presets that you can either use as they are or adapt to fit your own needs.

The presets are displayed down the right side of the Title Deko interface. When you first scroll through them, many don't display right away; this is because their font type and enhancement must first load into the Windows memory cache. Once this completes, you can scroll down to see which one you need.

To apply a Title Deko preset:

1. Highlight your text by dragging a lasso around it with the mouse (Figure 10.10).

2. Click the Browse Looks button or press Ctrl+L and select from the choices on display (**Figure 10.34**).

3. Apply the change by double-clicking the Font style or by single-clicking the style and clicking OK.

✔ Tip

■ You can edit the Title Deko presets in the same way as I described in "Changing the font and point size" section earlier in this chapter.

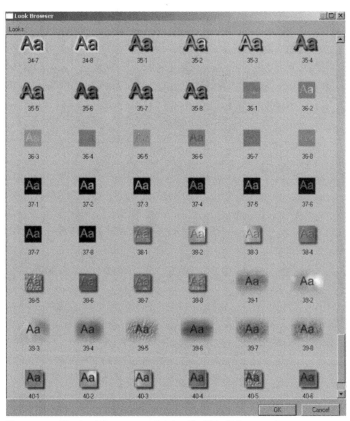

Figure 10.34 The Look Browser containing the Title Deko presets.

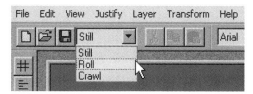

Figure 10.35 Adding a basic animation to the title via the Movement menu.

Making a Title Move

Title Deko can also animate a title in one of two directions: the title can roll up the screen, or crawl across it. These features can be a bit limiting, and you might find that a well-placed Realtime filter is more practical (see Chapter 9 for more on filters). But if you want to quickly add movement to a title, the Title Deko interface offers a quick and tidy method of doing so.

To add movement to a title:

1. Highlight your text by dragging a lasso around it with the mouse (Figure 10.10).

2. Select Roll or Crawl from the Movement drop-down menu (**Figure 10.35**).

✔ Tips

■ You can't see movement in Title Deko. You must exit the editor and add the title to the Timeline before you can see it move.

■ In the Project Browser, titles with movements appear as either Picons with a white star in the corner or, in detail view, with a small arrow Picon next to the text.

Saving a Title and Adding It to the Timeline

Once you've created a title, you can save it in a couple of ways—either by creating a stand-alone title that you might want to import into future projects, or by saving the title and importing it directly into the Project Browser.

The default way to save your title is to send it to the Project Browser where it can be stored for future use. Once in the Project Browser, you can also use it in other sequences, not just the one on which you're working.

Once you've created your title and saved it to the Project Browser, you can add it to the Timeline. This process is exactly the same as placing a video, music, or image file into your project.

To save a title:

Do one of the following:

◆ Press F12 or Ctrl+E or select File and then Save as new to Liquid to automatically add this title to the Project Browser, but to keep the Title Deko interface open.

◆ Press F11 to automatically add this title to the Project Browser and to close the Title Deko interface.

✔ Tip

■ To return to the Liquid Edition interface without saving the title you've created, select Exit from the File menu or click the window's X in the top right of the interface.

To place a title on the Timeline:

Do one of the following:

◆ Drag and drop the title to where you need it to be (**Figure 10.36**).

◆ Send the title to the Source Viewer; then use the insert arrow to send it to the current location of the timeline cursor.

◆ Right-click the Title and select Send To > Timeline to send the title to the current location of the Timeline cursor (**Figure 10.37**).

✔ Tip

■ You can dynamically resize a title on the Timeline by clicking the mark-in or mark-out point to reveal the red handle. Grab this with the mouse to adjust the size (**Figure 10.38**).

Drag from here...   *...to here*

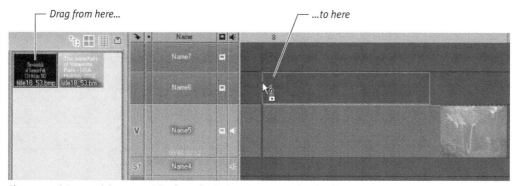

Figure 10.36 Drag and drop your titles from the Project Browser to the Timeline...

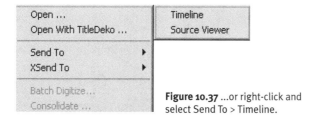

Figure 10.37 ...or right-click and select Send To > Timeline.

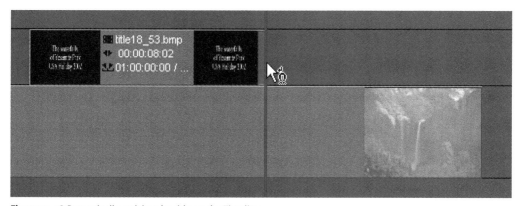

Figure 10.38 Dynamically resizing the title on the Timeline.

The Default Duration of a Title

Chapter 3 looked at importing an image file and predefining its default duration using the Liquid Edition Control Panel. This function also applies to titles, so the default duration you list for your images is used when you add a title to the Timeline.

Changing this setting is global and applies to all images you add to the Timeline after you make the change.

Editing the Title Again

Once a title is in the Project Browser or on the Timeline, you can reedited it quite simply using Title Deko. However, be careful—editing the title in the Project Browser doesn't affect any instance of the title that already exists on the Timeline. Similarly, editing a title on the Timeline doesn't affect its parent in the Project Browser.

To edit a title:

◆ Right-click the title either on the Timeline or in the Project Browser and select Open With TitleDeko from the menu (**Figure 10.39**).

Figure 10.39 You can use the right-click menu to reedit a title in the Project Browser.

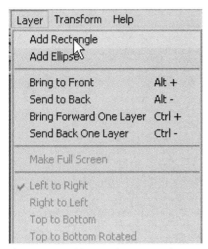

Figure 10.40 Adding an object using the Layer menu.

Figure 10.41 A standard title enhanced by adding a rectangle and adjusting the rectangle using the Look edit dialog.

Advanced Title Deko Techniques

Once you have mastered the basics of creating and saving your own customized titles, you can move on to add some greater enhancements to your text. You can achieve this by adding objects to the image; doing so isn't complicated and can create impressive results.

Two different objects can be added to a title: Rectangle and Ellipse. They can be any color, and you can resize and overlap them to create a whole range of different shapes.

To add an object:

◆ Within the Title Deko interface, open the Layer menu and choose Add Rectangle or Add Ellipse (**Figure 10.40**).

✔ Tips

■ To move an object, simply select it and move it with the mouse.

■ To resize an object, drag any of the handles out in the direction you want to expand it.

■ To delete an object, press the Delete key with the object selected.

To change the object color:

◆ Click the Edit Current Look button or press Ctrl+ P. You must make sure the object is highlighted for the changes to affect it. Once the object is highlighted, you can adjust the color using the Look edit interface (**Figure 10.41**).

ADVANCED TITLE DEKO TECHNIQUES

Using Filters to Animate Titles

When you use a combination of filters and transitions on titles, it's possible to give Title Deko a whole new lease on life. For instance, by adding the 2D filters, you can create—in real time—a title with real movement. You can command it to move about the screen rather than simply rolling up the screen or crawling across its bottom.

With transitions, you can use Dissolve, Band Wipe, and Water Drop to add some unique features to your titles. The only tool you really need here is your imagination (**Figure 10.42**).

Figure 10.42 A title with one or more filters from the Realtime Clip FX folder applied.

COLOR CORRECTION

Color correction is a way to correct camera exposure so that it conforms to how we want it to look. It's a complex process that's almost an art in itself—you'll need to practice and cultivate patience if you're to create stunning movies from badly shot video.

In this chapter, you learn how to use the four different types of color correction filters that come with Liquid Edition: the Base Color Corrector, the Auto Color Corrector, the Color Editor (Classic), and the ColorCorrection Editor (sometimes referred to as the Secondary or CX Color Editor). I also show you the basics of correcting some pretty commonplace color problems, such as white balance, and also how to create special effects using only color.

Please note that a number of illustrations in this chapter are duplicated in the color insert section of this book.

Introducing the Color Correctors

There are four color correction filters that are suitable for different kinds of jobs. Two of them are Realtime filters (denoted by the RT stamp after their name), and the other two need to be rendered before you can see their results. No one filter does everything you want it to, so to get the best possible color correction for your project, you need to use each different filter at some stage.

- **Base Color Correction CPU:** A Realtime filter you can use to quickly correct problem areas, such as brightness and contrast and also for adding basic color casting.

- **Auto Color Correct CPU:** Use this to automatically correct certain instances of poor lighting or bad white balance.

- **Color Editor (Classic):** This is essentially the same as the Base Color Corrector but it isn't a Realtime filter, although it does have additional functions.

- **ColorCorrection Editor:** Use this to make major alterations to color. It comes with a set of powerful tools and you can also use it for special effects; however, it is not a Realtime effect and will need to be rendered.

Each of these filters has an invaluable and unique place in Liquid Edition. You need to experiment with them all if you want to get the best from them.

✔ Tips

- All the color correctors follow the same rules as all other filters, and you can apply them to a Timeline clip, a Timeline Track, or a clip in the Project Browser. They are also stackable.

- None of the color correctors have keyframes turned on by default, and the Auto Color Corrector doesn't support them at all. Generally speaking, you should carry out color correction uniformly over the entire clip, unless, of course, you're trying to achieve a special effect using a momentary color shift.

Color Calibration

To successfully use any of the color correctors, you need to be sure that what you are looking at on your PC monitor is an accurate depiction of true colors. With video editing, the easiest way to do this is to compare your monitor's output to the signal from a good quality TV so that you can see how close the match is. If there is a discrepancy between the two, you need to find a way to calibrate your monitor, but don't forget to allow your monitor to warm up first.

If you have no TV output, then you're going to need to perform a lot of trial and error before you find the right calibration settings because things can look different on an RGB or LCD monitor—particularly on inexpensive models. Tools for calibrating monitors are widely available via the Internet, and most graphics cards include some kind of rudimentary setup instructions in the driver (**Figure 11.1**).

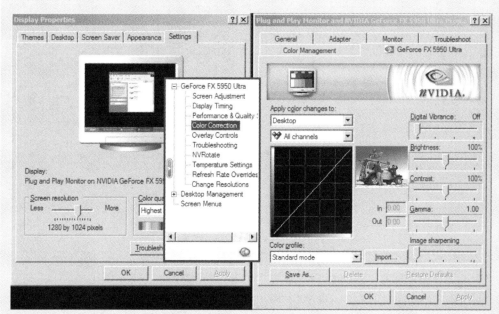

Figure 11.1 An example of the NVIDIA color calibration tool found in the Windows Display Properties.

Applying and Adjusting the Base Color Corrector (RT)

The Base Color Corrector allows you to alter the color parameters of a clip and then see the results without having to render. It has a simple enough interface, and although it has certain limitations, you can use it both for basic color corrections and for creating effects, such as adding a blue shift to the scene to create the illusion of night (**Figure 11.2**).

To apply the Base Color Corrector:

Do one of the following:

◆ Click the Lib tab and open the Realtime Clip FX folder. From the Editors Rack drag and drop the Base Color Corrector to the clip or to the Timeline Track (**Figure 11.3**).

Figure 11.2 Night effect created by increasing blue and gamma. The original clip is on the bottom. (See color insert.)

You'll find RT color correctors in this folder.

— Drag from here...

...to here —

...or here.

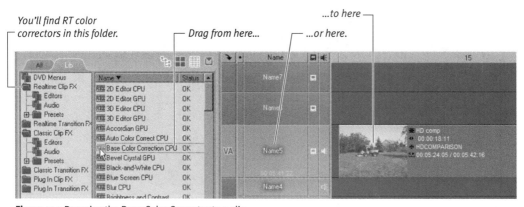

Figure 11.3 Dragging the Base Color Corrector to a clip.

BASE COLOR CORRECTOR (RT)

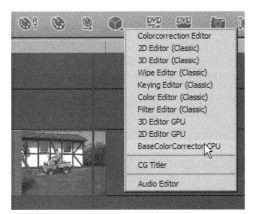

Figure 11.4 The Effects Editor menu.

Figure 11.5 The shortcut button on the toolbar.

◆ With the clip selected, click once on the Effects Editor Menu on the Toolbar, and select BaseColorCorrector CPU from the list (**Figure 11.4**).

◆ With the clip selected, click once on the Open BaseColorCorrector CPU shortcut button ▨ on the Toolbar (**Figure 11.5**).

✔ Tip

■ Inside the Base Color Corrector, you can use a number of quick and easy one-click tools including Hue, Saturation, Brightness, and Contrast. These alone should be enough to enhance most video clips. If you need more, or you want to add a keyframable special effect, you can delve into the 3D color space channels and edit one of the RGB colors. As with any aspect of Liquid Edition, experimentation is the only way to learn.

To adjust the Base Color Corrector:

1. If the editor for the Base Color Corrector is not already open right-click the purple line that runs along the top of the clip and choose Edit (**Figure 11.6**).

2. Once the editor is open, adjust the parameters the same way you do for any other filter.

   For a full explanation of filter editing and using Keyframe tools, see Chapter 9.

✔ Tips

- To turn on keyframes, open the Options tab and select Use Keyframes from the Keyframe options.

- You can revert any of the settings you make in this editor back to the default by clicking the Restore to Default button .

- If you close the editor without making any alterations, the filter will be removed from the clip.

You can adjust parameters from here and here.

You can turn on keyframes from here.

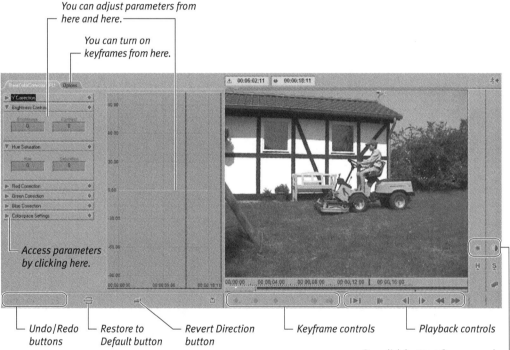

Access parameters by clicking here.

Undo/Redo buttons — Restore to Default button — Revert Direction button — Keyframe controls — Playback controls

One-click buttons for commonly used color corrections

Figure 11.6 The editor for the Base Color Corrector.

Working with the Color Editor (Classic)

The Color Editor (Classic) isn't a Realtime filter, and as a result, you need to render before you can see the results. However, this filter does have several options that aren't available in the Base Color Corrector, such as Transparency settings and the Keyframe Interpolation setting, which allows you to alter the speed at which effects occur between keyframes. There is also the ever-present full screen mode. For more details on how to use the extra features you'll find only on classic filters, see the relevant section in Chapter 9.

To apply the Color Editor (Classic):

Do one of the following:

◆ Click the Lib tab and open the Classic Clip FX folder. From the Editors Rack, drag and drop the Color Editor to the clip or Timeline Track (**Figure 11.7**).

continues on next page

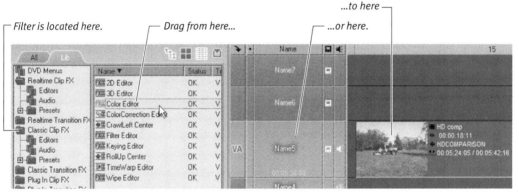

Figure 11.7 Dragging the Color Editor (Classic) to a clip.

◆ With the clip selected, click once on the Effects Editor menu on the Toolbar, and select Color Editor (Classic) from the list (**Figure 11.8**).

◆ With the clip selected, click once on the Open Classic Color Editor shortcut button 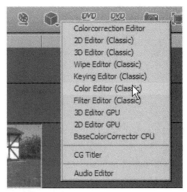 on the Toolbar (**Figure 11.9**).

✔ Tip

■ If you don't have the Open Classic Color Editor on your toolbar, you need to add it by customizing your interface. You can find further information on this in Chapter 1.

Figure 11.8 The Effects Editor menu.

Figure 11.9 The shortcut button on the Toolbar.

To adjust the Color Editor (Classic):

1. If the editor for the Color Editor is not already open, right-click the purple line running along the top of the clip and select Edit to open the editor (**Figure 11.10**).

2. Once you've opened the editor, adjust the parameters the same way you do for any other filter.

   See Chapter 9 for more details on this.

✔ Tips

- You can revert to default any of the settings you make in this editor by clicking the Restore to Default button ⬚ .

- If you close the editor without making any alterations, the filter will be removed from the clip.

―Additional parameters

┌ This parameter is only available with classic effects.

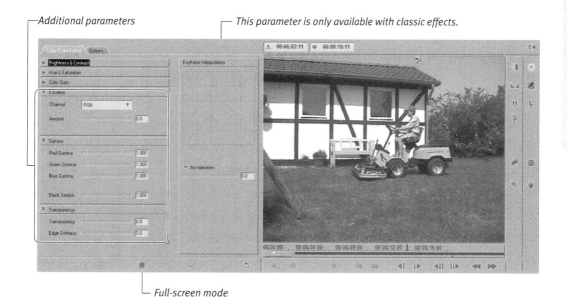

└ Full-screen mode

Figure 11.10 The Color Editor (Classic).

Exploring the Auto Color Corrector

Pinnacle designed this unique Realtime filter to add a quick fix to any video clips that suffer from common faults such as low-level lighting or an incorrect white balance. It works pretty much like magic; you just apply it and all your problems melt away (**Figure 11.11**).

Of course it doesn't always work, but if it doesn't, you can try tweaking the setting or you can fall back on the ColorCorrection Editor.

To apply the Auto Color Corrector (RT):

1. Click the Lib tab and open the Realtime Clip FX folder.

2. From the Editors Rack, drag and drop the Auto Color Corrector to the clip or Timeline Track (**Figure 11.12**).

Figure 11.11 This clip isn't perfect after using the Auto Color corrector, but at least you can now view it. (See color insert.)

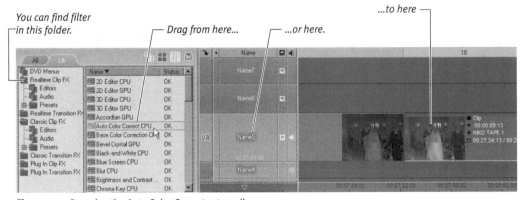

Figure 11.12 Dragging the Auto Color Corrector to a clip.

EXPLORING THE AUTO COLOR CORRECTOR

To adjust the Auto Color Corrector:

1. Right-click the purple line running along the top of the clip to open the editor (**Figure 11.13**).

2. Once you've openedthe editor, adjust the parameters—such as they are—the same way you do for any other filter. See Chapter 9 for more details on this.

✔ Tips

■ The color picker option allows you to select which color the Auto Color Corrector uses as its reference. To use this, open the color picker tool, then drag the picker onto the best source of white in the picture.

■ You can revert any settings you make in this editor back to default by clicking the Restore to Default button ⊟.

Reference color button opens the color picker.

Drag and drop the color picker onto the nearest source of white.

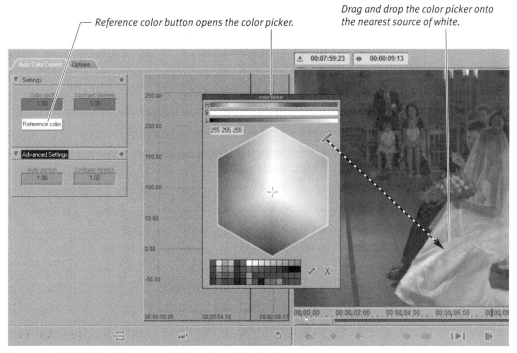

Figure 11.13 The Effects Editor menu with the color picker tool open.

Applying the ColorCorrection Editor

This is such a functional tool that it has a variety of names, includ-ing CX Color Correction and, Secondary Color Correction. In the manual and the program, however, it is referred to as the ColorCorrection Editor.

This editor has a variety of different tools you can use to correct color and create some pretty amazing special effects. You'll discover an amazing amount of cool stuff you can do with this tool, but use it like you do most powerful functions—with restraint. More is sometimes too much!

In this section, you learn how to apply and open the editor and how to use one-click tools to solve some of the more common color and lighting problems. At the end of this section, I demonstrate how to apply a special effect using the ColorCorrection Editor.

To apply the ColorCorrection Editor:

Do one of the following:

◆ Click the Lib tab and open the Classic Clip FX folder. From the Editors Rack drag and drop the ColorCorrection Editor to the clip or Timeline Track (**Figure 11.14**).

You can find this filter in this folder. — *Drag from here...* — *...to here* — *...or here.*

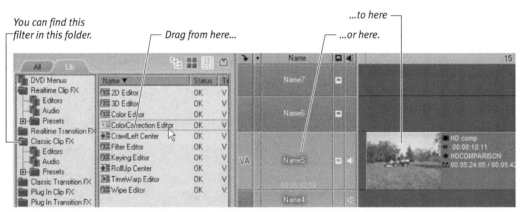

Figure 11.14 Dragging the ColorCorrection Editor to a clip.

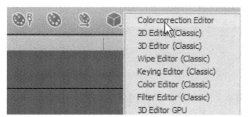

Figure 11.15 The Effects Editor menu.

Figure 11.16 The shortcut button on the toolbar.

◆ With the clip selected, click once on the Effects Editor menu button on the Toolbar and select Colorcorrection Editor from the list (**Figure 11.15**).

◆ With the clip selected, click once on the Open Colorcorrection Editor shortcut button ▦ on the Toolbar (**Figure 11.16**).

✔ Tip

■ If you don't have the Open ColorCorrection Editor shortcut on your Toolbar, you need to add it by customizing your interface. You can find further information on this in Chapter 1.

To adjust the ColorCorrection Editor:

1. Right-click the purple line running along the top of the clip and select Edit to open the Editor (**Figure 11.17**, on the following page).

2. Once you've opened the editor, adjust the parameters the same way you do for any other filter.

   However, if you click the small extended dialog arrow, you expose a wealth of options.

✔ Tip

■ You can revert any of the settings you make in this editor back to their default by clicking the Restore to Default button ▦ .

APPLYING THE COLORCORRECTION EDITOR

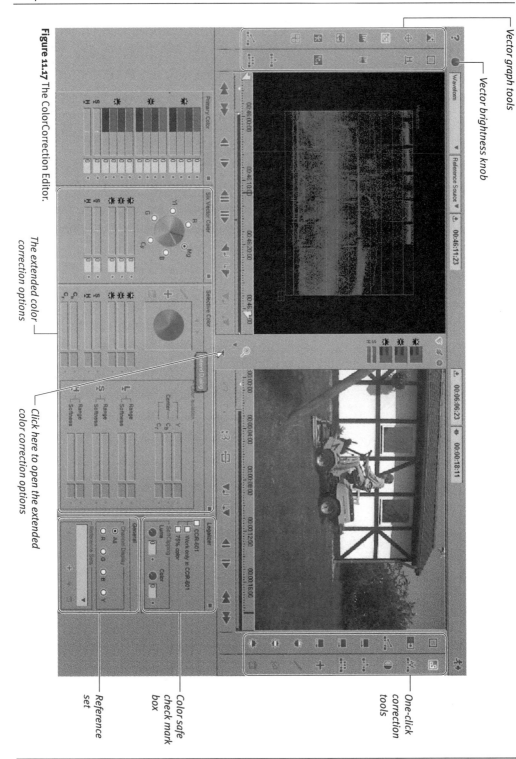

Vector graph tools

Vector brightness knob

One-click correction tools

Color safe check mark box

Reference set

Click here to open the extended color correction options

The extended color correction options

Figure 11.17 The ColorCorrection Editor.

Legalizing Color

Also known as broadcast legal, color legalizing refers to a range of colors accepted as a standard by the broadcast community. To help you stay within the boundaries recognized by the broadcast legal system, the ColorCorrection Editor has a set of options that limit the amount of gain and luminance you can add to your color corrections.

To activate this, put a check mark in the box next to CCIR-601 in the Legalizer section of the interface (**Figure 11.18**).

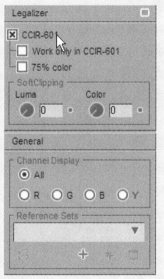

Figure 11.18 The color legalizer.

Matching Color

Color matching is the process of taking two video clips and correcting the color so that shades of white and black appear matched in each clip. For example, a scene filmed with two cameras that cuts from person to person must contain the same color tones or it will jar the viewer as the colors shift in each different viewpoint. This process might involve correcting the white balance on a clip that resulted from using two different cameras or accounting for filters used incorrectly on the same camera from shot to shot.

To help you perform color matching, you have a veritable army of tools at your disposal. These include a vector scope and a selection of vector color tools that allow you to edit every color element in a clip. How good your results turn out depends greatly on how much you know about color editing. To be honest, unless you're well versed in the technique, you should approach it with caution and never let your mouse wander too far from the Undo key.

The one-click tools

If you find yourself daunted by the vector scope and find no clues in the color selection area, you still don't need to give up. Pinnacle has incorporated a number of tools into the ColorCorrection Editor that are designed to automatically help out with the most common color and lighting problems (**Figure 11.19**).

To make it even easier, most of these tools allow you to use a reference clip against which to match the color correction.

The reference clip

A reference clip must be another clip on the Timeline. Once you select it, you can use the colors it contains to adjust the colors in your target clip. For example, you can take this to extremes by matching the sky from a tropical photograph with the sky from your overcast shot to try creating an instantly improved skyline.

To set a reference clip:

1. With the ColorCorrection Editor open, close the extended dialog area so that you can see the Timeline.

2. Right-click the clip on the Timeline that you want to use as a reference and select Set As Reference Clip (**Figure 11.20**).

✔ Tip

■ Clips in the Project Browser cannot be used as a reference.

Figure 11.19 The one-click tools.

Figure 11.20 Setting a clip as your reference point.

Split-Screen Effect

If you set a reference clip, it is also possible to split the right screen of the ColorCorrection Editor so it contains both the reference and the original clip.

To split the screen, first click once on the Set split size button (**Figure 11.21**). Then click the left side of the right window and drag the cursor to the right (**Figure 11.22**).

Figure 11.21 The Set split size button.

Figure 11.22 An example of a split screen.

Using the 3-Point Color Balance Tool

Once you select the reference clip, you can adjust the colors of your original clip using the 3-Point Color Balance tool. This tool requires white, black, and gray references points that you set using the reference clip as the baseline.

To use the 3-Point Color Balance tool:

1. Place your reference clip in the left window and your target clip in the right.

2. Click the 3-Point Color Balance button [icon]. This button is located in the one-click tools on the far right of the ColorCorrection interface.

   Three points linked by two lines appear on both screens. These are colored white, gray, and black.

3. Adjust the squares in the reference clip so that the black one is on the darkest area of the screen, the white is on the lightest area, and the gray one is somewhere in between.

4. Now repeat this for your target clip, dragging each square to the right area.

5. Once you are happy, right-click the mouse *inside* the right window to apply the effect.

   If you forget to do this, the effect isn't applied (**Figure 11.23**).

✔ Tip

■ Use the Zoom tool in the middle of the two windows to get a pixel-sized view of where to place your color balance squares (**Figure 11.24**).

Figure 11.23 A before and after example of correcting a severe white balance problem. (See color insert.)

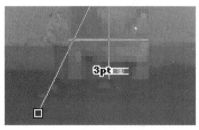

Figure 11.24 Use the zoom tool for accuracy. (See color insert.)

1-*Point Gray*
— *Balance cursor*

1-*Point Gray*
Balance tool —

Figure 11.25 Using the 1-Point Gray Balance tool. (See color insert.)

Examining the Gray Balance Tools

The Gray Balance tools are your main weapons against white balance problems. When you're making adjustments, it's probably best to start with the 1-Point Gray Balance tool and progress to the 2-Point and then the 3-Point tools if you aren't getting the results you're looking for. Remember to return the clip to its original state before you move from tool to tool by clicking the Restore to Default button ; otherwise you'll make alterations on top of alterations.

The 1-Point Gray Balance tool

Using this tool is the simplest and quickest way to alter a clip, but the results may not always be perfect on the first click. You should try clicking several times before you give up and move on to the next tool.

To use the 1-Point Gray Balance tool:

1. With the ColorCorrection Editor open and your target clip in the right window, click once on the 1-Point Gray Balance tool which is located on the far right of the ColorCorrection interface in the one-click tools.

2. Move the cursor over to the target area.

    A crosshair with a sun and a grayscale under it appears.

3. Find an area that's as near to gray as you can and click it (**Figure 11.25**).

    The target adjusts using the information it finds under the cursor.

✔ Tip

■ This method is quick and dirty. If you don't like the results, click somewhere else.

1-Point Color Balance

This is a basic color correction tool that simply matches one color in the reference shot to a frame displayed in the right-hand window. Its effectiveness is limited and for corrections of this nature you would be best to use either the 1-Point Gray Balance tool or the 3-Point Color Balance tool, as both tend to give better results.

The 2-Point Gray Balance tool

Using this tool is a slightly more complex process than using the 1-Point Gray Balance tool. It gives you two points with which to correct the target. For it to work correctly, you need a target clip that has both an area of light gray and an area of dark gray.

To use the 2-Point Gray Balance tool:

1. With the ColorCorrection Editor open and your target clip in the right window, click once on the 2-Point Gray Balance tool.

2. Move the cursor over to the target area. A "2pt" appears under the crosshair where the sun was in the 1-Point tool.

3. Find an area that's as near to light gray as you can, then click and drag the mouse to an area of dark gray (**Figure 11.26**).

4. Release the mouse and the color balance is applied using information it finds under both cursor positions.

✔ Tip

■ This method is a little more refined, but you may still need to select some more sample areas before the clip looks right.

Drag from here...

...to here.

2-Point Gray Balance tool

Figure 11.26 Using the 2-Point Gray Balance tool. (See color insert.)

The 3-Point Gray Balance tool

The 3-Point Gray Balance tool requires the same reference points that the 3-Point Color Balance tool required, but it doesn't need a reference clip. Instead it uses the target clip as its own reference in an attempt to adjust the levels of white, gray, and black.

To use the 3-Point Gray Balance tool:

1. With the target clip in the right window, click the 3-Point Gray Balance button.

Three points linked by two lines appear on both screens. These are colored white, gray, and black.

2. Adjust the squares in the reference clip so that the black one is in the darkest area of the screen, the white one is in the lightest area, and the gray one is somewhere in between.

3. Once you're happy, right-click the mouse *inside* the right window to apply the effect.

If you forget to do this, the effect isn't applied.

✔ Tip

■ Use the Zoom tool in the middle of the two windows to get a pixel-sized view of where to place your color balance squares.

EXAMINING THE GRAY BALANCE TOOLS

Using the Vector Scope

This area of the ColorCorrection Editor is only for professional color editors who really know what they are doing, and perhaps for anyone with Photoshop experience because the way you use the histogram is fairly similar.

To open the vector scope:

◆ Click once on the Vector button on the left side of the ColorCorrection Editor interface (**Figure 11.27**).

✔ Tip

■ You can display vector scopes in five other formats; the most popular are the Waveform (**Figure 11.28**) and the Histogram (**Figure 11.29**). These two are most commonly used by color editors to adjust and finely tweak their color selections. With the Histogram, you can even adjust the color by dragging the cursor over one of the three RGB graph areas.

Figure 11.27 The vector scope and control buttons.

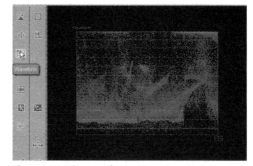

Figure 11.28 The waveform—Top = 100; Bottom = 0.

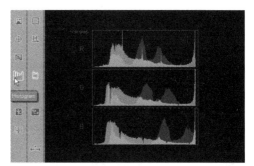

Figure 11.29 The Histogram.

Further Reading

Vector editing is a specialist's subject; so I don't deal with it within this book, but for further advice on this subject, read through Chapter 8 of the Pinnacle Liquid Edition Reference Manual.

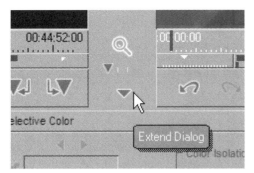

Figure 11.30 The extended dialog arrow.

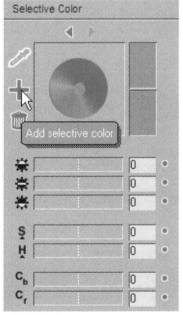

Figure 11.31 Add a color to the Selective Color wheel.

Adjusting Colors Selectively

You can also use the ColorCorrection Editor to selectively enhance or remove individual colors from the clip. This technique has been widely used in films and TV to show a black and white object in a colored world, or vice versa. The actual process of doing this in Liquid Edition is simple enough; however it is painstakingly slow to achieve, and you only get good results if you are prepared to put in the work.

The other neat trick you often see on TV is an object, such as a car, changing color. You can do this in Liquid Edition using the ColorCorrection Editor. But you do need to select your subject carefully; this trick only really works on objects that have the same uniform color and exist on a background that doesn't repeat that color.

To explain color removal, it's easier for me to show you an example where one color is retained and all the others are reduced to black and white. After you've seen this, you can use this experience to remove single colors.

To remove all colors from a clip except one:

1. Open the ColorCorrection Editor and select a clip so that it appears in the right window.

2. Click the extended dialog arrow to open up the interface (**Figure 11.30**).

3. To select a color, click once on the plus sign (+) next to the Selective Color wheel (**Figure 11.31**).

   The wheel opens two color windows to its right and highlights the ink dropper tool to its left.

continues on next page

4. Place the cursor over the right window and over the color you want to keep.

5. Hold down the left mouse key and drag out a square across the color you want to keep yellow in this example.

   This color is added to the Selective Color wheel as a small circle. Try not to let any other colors infect this sample (**Figure 11.32**).

6. Click anywhere outside the wheel, but inside the square that contains the wheel (**Figure 11.33**).

   You can now adjust all colors other than the one you just selected using the sliders underneath the Selective Color wheel.

Figure 11.32 Selecting the color in the clip with the Zoom tool active. (See color insert.)

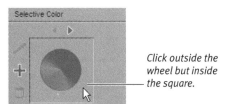

Click outside the wheel but inside the square.

Figure 11.33 Select all colors except the one you have just picked in step 3. (See color insert.)

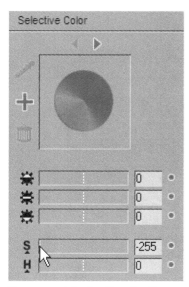

Figure 11.34 Adjusting the saturation level of all colors except the one you picked in step 3

7. To remove all the other colors, slide the saturation slider all the way over to the left so the box reads –255 (**Figure 11.34**).

The entire picture is now black and white except for the color you selected (**Figure 11.35**).

✔ Tips

- To restore saturation to 0, click the small button to the right of the figures.

- A single JPEG of this video clip (color correction example 1) is available for download at www.peachpit.com/liquid6vqp.

Figure 11.35 Before and after saturation is adjusted to all colors except the one you picked in step 3. The picture still needs some fine-tuning, but for a single adjustment, it looks good. (See color insert.)

To change one color from a clip:

1. Open the ColorCorrection Editor and select the target clip in the right window.

2. Click the extended dialog arrow to open up the interface.

3. Click once on the color you want to change in the Six Vector Color area (**Figure 11.36**).

4. To alter the color, drag the Hue slider to the left or right (**Figure 11.37**).

   This cycles your selected color through a range of alternatives.

In this example, the color I selected was red and I adjusted the Hue to 221. With these settings, I created some purple tomatoes and some blue carrots. Note that the blanket and the parsley remain relatively untouched by this filter, but the breadboard (which contains an element of red in its grain) has changed slightly (**Figure 11.38**).

✔ Tip

■ A single JPEG of this video clip (color correction example 2) is available for download at www.peachpit.com/liquid6vqp.

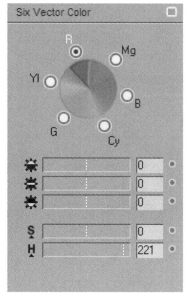

Figure 11.36 Selecting the color you want to adjust using the Six Vector Color wheel. (See color insert.)

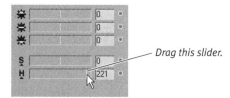

Drag this slider.

Figure 11.37 Altering the Hue changes the color.

Figure 11.38 Before and after shots demonstrating color removal. (See color insert.)

ADJUSTING COLORS SELECTIVELY

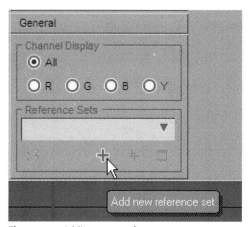

Figure 11.39 Adding a new reference set.

Saving a Reference Set

If you have a certain setting, a simple effect, or a color correction that you know you'll needed in the future, then you can save this as a reference set for later use. You can then load the reference set back in with just a click on a drop-down menu.

To save a reference set:

1. Click once on the Add new reference set button (**Figure 11.39**).

2. Enter the name of your reference set and click the check mark (**Figure 11.40**).

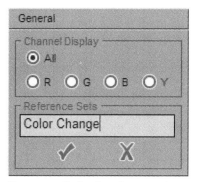

Figure 11.40 Saving the reference set.

Further Reading for Color Correction

As you can see, color correction is complex and not for the fainthearted. Certainly, it's an interesting and sometimes exciting tool, but it's also a dangerous one. You can easily create more of a mess than a masterpiece if you don't know what you are doing or if you don't use it with restraint and care.

To find out more about color correction try the following books, DVDs, and online tutorials.

◆ *Real World Color Management* by Bruce Fraser (Peachpit Press)

◆ *Color Correction for Digital Video*, by Steve Hullfish and Jaime Fowler (CMP Books)

◆ Adita – Liquid Edition Color Correction training DVD (www.adita.com)

◆ PBN (Pinnacle Broadcast Network) – A range of online tutorials. www.pinnaclesys.com/PBN/

DVD Authoring

Without a doubt, DVD is now the medium of choice for the buying public. Go to any major video store and you'll find VHS breathing those final breaths of a format on the wane; meanwhile, you'll see that DVDs are confidently ascending to claim the home movie throne. With this in mind, DVD authoring should be your target when you're constructing a project, and if you want to use 5.1 sound, then DVD is your only format choice.

Liquid Edition makes life easy for would-be DVD authors by allowing the whole process to take place on the Timeline. In fact, you never leave the Liquid Edition interface, which means you can still fine-tune edits to the project while you create a DVD menu. The benefits of this are liberating, to say the least, for producers and editors with challenging schedules.

In this chapter, you first learn the basics of DVD authoring; you produce a standard DVD with a menu before you move on to more advanced topics such as customizing a menu template, creating animated backgrounds and buttons, and using nested menus.

Authoring DVDs with Liquid Edition 6

You can make DVD authoring in Liquid Edition as complex as you want. Creating a standard menu should create no real problems, but animated menus, variable bit rate, and nested menus can confuse the beginner and professional user alike.

I cover creating a DVD with a one-page menu in the first half of this chapter, and spend the second half with more complex topics. By the end of this chapter, you should completely understand how to create some impressive-looking DVD menus with fully animated backgrounds and buttons too, if you so desire.

✔ Tip

■ The DVD Editor doesn't open unless a DVD menu is on the Timeline.

SVCD and VCD

SVCD (super video CD) and VCD (video CD) are formats you use to burn video to ordinary CDs. Although this might sound intriguing—if only because CD media is cheaper than DVD—be aware of the catch in the quality department. Because SVCD and VCD have a smaller physical storage area, video must be compressed at a much lower rate, which produces poorer quality videos. The quality of SVCD isn't that bad when you view it on a computer, but when you see it on a DVD player, it isn't comparable to DVD quality.

Although I'm primarily interested in DVD authoring in this chapter, you can use all of the techniques you find here to make an SVCD or VCD. The only real difference is the burn settings you use in the final stage.

The Mini DV setting is a variation on the burn settings theme that allows you to burn your DVD to an 8cm DVD or to a CD-R/RW. When you do so, you'll find that quality is high, but the amount of space you have is restricted to 750 MB.

Preparing the Timeline

DVD authoring is all about preparation. This is the sort of preparation you need to think about even before you place your first clip on the Timeline. Only so much material fits on a single-sided DVD, so you can forget the luxury of three-hour VHS tapes; in the world of DVD; you need to justify every scene you place on the Timeline.

Dual-layer DVDs are on the way, but most of you will use single-sided DVDs with this version of the software, so you need to be aware of how quickly the space is gobbled up.

How much material you can fit on a DVD depends on two things: the amount of motion in your clips—higher motion creates a higher data rate, which needs more storage area—and the actual data rate you use to burn the DVD—the higher the rate, the less room you have. Sacrificing quality for quantity might seem like a workable option, but be careful, lower data rates produce *pixelization*—visible when there is fast movement on the screen. This makes your production look anything but professional.

On the other hand, a static interview doesn't benefit from a high data rate; by giving it one, you're simply wasting space you could use for something else. With these facts in mind, you need to limit the Timeline to the maximum you can fit on a DVD at an acceptable data rate.

Using Sequences

In Chapter 6, you saw how to build a Timeline in stages by creating a Sequence for each scene. Once you reach the DVD stage of your project, it is time to bring these Sequences together into one Timeline.

Remember, the real advantage of creating DVDs on the Timeline is that you can change or edit a scene when you realize that it will become a DVD chapter button. For instance, by adding a fade to the background noise or the music at this point, you help ensure that the chapter point doesn't jar the audience with a suddenly enhanced audio level if they directly select that button. All of these edit options are open to you now, or they will be when you begin to edit your DVD menu. You don't have this kind of control if you have to export this project to a third party application.

To create a Timeline from Sequences:

1. Start a new Sequence and call it DVD compilation of *project name* or something similar.

2. Open the Sequences Rack by clicking it once to show all the Sequences you've created in this project (**Figure 12.1**).

3. Drag and drop each Sequence onto the Timeline in order until you have a complete project displayed (**Figure 12.2**).

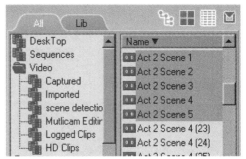

Figure 12.1 Every Sequence you create is stored in the Sequences Rack.

Figure 12.2 Dragging sequences directly to the Timeline creates your movie from individual scenes.

USING SEQUENCES

✔ Tips

- Make sure you place the first Sequence at about the 15-second mark of the Timeline. This gives you the room you need to insert the DVD menu. If you want to insert a preplay message, you need to leave more room. If you want a really long animated menu, you'll have to calculate for that too (**Figure 12.3**).

- The alternative to using Sequences is to place the whole Timeline inside a container. For more information on using containers, see Chapter 14.

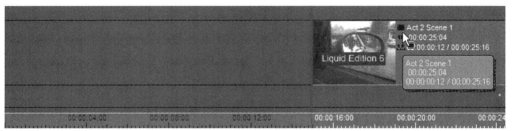

Figure 12.3 When you're constructing a Timeline for DVD export, leave around 15 seconds at the beginning for the menu.

Creating a FirstPlay Message

At the start of most commercial DVDs, a FirstPlay message plays just once—when you first insert the DVD into the player, just before the DVD menu displays. This can be the standard anti-piracy message, or it can be a company logo, or simply a sound and color bar test.

To add your own FirstPlay item to a DVD project, insert the video or image, preferably with a music track, just before the DVD menu (**Figure 12.4**).

This then burns to the DVD as a FirstPlay item that displays before your menu appears.

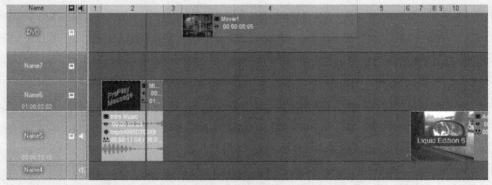

Figure 12.4 Adding a FirstPlay message to the start of your DVD.

Using Markers

Before you start the DVD authoring process, take a moment to make one more time-saving preparation. In Chapter 6, you learned how to place markers on a clip or on the Timeline so key events are more visible. You can use the same technique to scrub through the Timeline, find each potential chapter point, place a marker on it, and then rename the marker to reflect what it represents. Once inside the DVD Editor, you can use these markers to navigate the Timeline much more quickly.

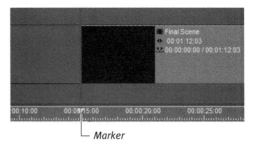

Figure 12.5 Placing a marker on the Timeline.

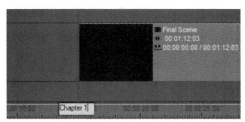

Figure 12.6 Naming a marker. Here I have typed in "Chapter 1."

To place and name markers:

1. Scrub through the Timeline until you find a suitable point.

2. Press the M key to place your marker (**Figure 12.5**).

3. Double-click the marker to open the name dialog (**Figure 12.6**).

4. Give it a logical name and press Enter.

5. Move on to the next maker.

✔ Tip

■ If you want a single page menu, then don't place any more than six markers on any one Timeline.

Converting 16:9 Footage

Liquid Edition DVD menus don't support the 16:9 wide-screen format. As a result, you have to either accept that your TV changes from 4:3 to 16:9 each time you transfer from the menu to the footage, or you need to convert the footage.

You can make this conversion by first fusing the Timeline (you can find details on fusing in Chapter 14) and then placing the fused clip on a new 4:3 timeline. Then you need to add a 2D filter to the fused clip to reduce the size to around 70 to 80 percent depending on your footage. Remember, to use this trick, you must use the classic filters because the RT filters show anything outside the normal TV standard as black.

See Chapter 9 for more filter details.

Building Your DVD Menu

Your first DVD should be a simple one that establishes two things: how the process works, and if any technical problems may stop you from actually burning a DVD.

Technical problems usually occur if you're using a DVD burner that Liquid Edition doesn't recognize. In this case, you need to download an update from the Pinnacle Web site (www.Pinnaclesys.com). Pinnacle releases these patches on a regular basis, and you'll find full instructions on how to install them on the download site.

✔ Tip

- If you do experience a technical problem, it's better that you experience it with a simple DVD project that hasn't taken too much time to build. Experiencing it after you spend several hours building the most awesome menu the world has ever seen is tragic, to say the least.

No Menu DVDs

You can also burn a DVD without a menu if you want to create a promotional demo DVD. In this case, you can ignore the DVD wizard completely and read the "Understanding the Export Dialog Box" section later in this chapter.

DVDs burnt without a menu are produced with a giant blue play button at the start. You can avoid seeing this and create an autoplay DVD by clicking the Autoplay check box in the Options tab of the Export dialog and specify a delay time of 0 (zero) and whether or not you want the DVD to loop (**Figure 12.7**).

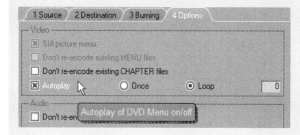

Figure 12.7
Creating an Autoplay DVD with no menu.

Using the DVD Wizard

Building a simple DVD menu is—like just about everything in Liquid Edition—very easy to accomplish. The built-in DVD wizard holds your hand through the first important stages; it just leaves you to decide which burn option you want to make at the end. This wizard has its own help files built in, and if you get anything wrong, you can always use the Undo command.

Figure 12.8 Opening the DVD wizard.

To open the DVD wizard:

1. Prepare the Timeline as I laid out in the "Preparing the Timeline" section earlier in this chapter.

2. Click once on the DVD Menu wizard button 🖳 (**Figure 12.8**).

   This opens the wizard at step 1, which is choosing a DVD menu.

Choosing a Menu

Once the DVD wizard's interface opens, you can choose from any of the menus available. These menus are all editable, so don't worry too much about choosing one that doesn't quite match your project. Later in this chapter, you learn how to change everything inside the preset menu (**Figure 12.9**).

Preset Template menus   *Insertion arrow*

Text instructions
for placing a menu

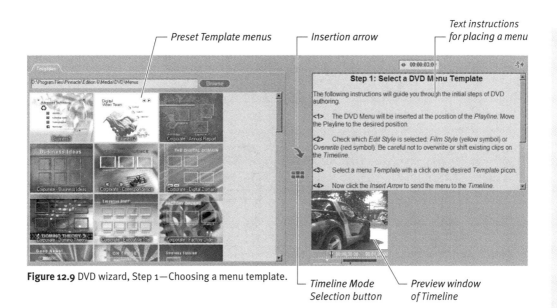

Figure 12.9 DVD wizard, Step 1—Choosing a menu template.

Timeline Mode
Selection button

Preview window
of Timeline

To choose a menu:

1. Make sure the timeline cursor is at the point where you want to place the menu (**Figure 12.10**).

2. Place the DVD menu on the Timeline by *doing one of the following:*

   ▲ Double-click the menu you want.

   ▲ Click once on the menu and then click the Insert Arrow button 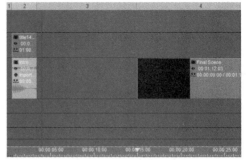.

   Once you've placed the DVD menu, a track called DVD is created on the Timeline and this menu is inserted into it (**Figure 12.11**).

✔ Tip

■ The default menu size is a few seconds, but you can drag it out to any size you want by clicking the handle on the right and dragging it up the Timeline (**Figure 12.12**).

Figure 12.10 Place the menu just after the preplay message (if you have one on the Timeline) but before the first Sequence or clip.

New DVD track created

DVD menu placed into it

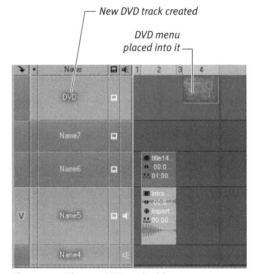

Figure 12.11 The new DVD track with menu.

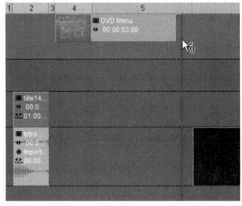

Figure 12.12 Drag out the menu to make it last longer.

Adding Links

You use links to create a logical relationship between a scene on the Timeline and a button on the DVD menu. Once you choose your menu, you are presented with the AutoLink screen (**Figure 12.13**).

By default, this screen contains a list of every edit decision point on the Timeline. If you have a lot of these, which is highly likely, this list will be large, and quite possibly, unmanageable. You can highlight each link on the list to see each point on the Timeline, but setting links in this manner is a painstaking affair.

Filtering links

In order to see which links you really need, the DVD editor can filter the links to various criteria so you're looking at fewer of them. This should help you see beyond the fog of "everything," but it still might not help you enough to create the links without spending some time doing so.

However, if you prepared the Timeline as I describe in the "Using Markers" section earlier in this chapter, then you already have named markers on your Timeline at all the relevant points; you can now use these.

To filter out unwanted links:

◆ Deselect the Clip Ins option to display just the named makers (**Figure 12.14**).

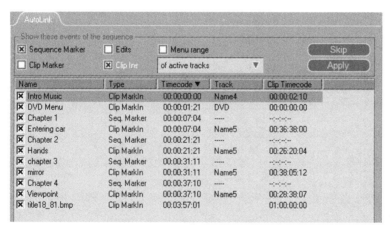

Figure 12.13 The AutoLink screen showing all edit decision points on your Timeline.

Click here to filter links.

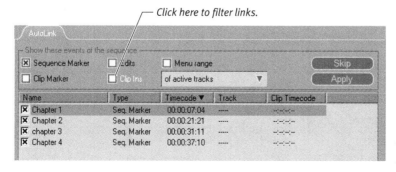

Figure 12.14 Deselecting the Clip Ins option shows just your markers.

Selecting links

Now that you can see the forest for the trees, you can decide if you really want all of the chapter points. You can see which chapter point contains what material by scrubbing through the Timeline and watching the playback on the tiny preview window. This window also has its own scrub bar for previewing and displays all relevant markers.

To select/deselect a chapter point:

◆ Remove or place an X in the box next to the chapters you want to subtract or add to your DVD menu (**Figure 12.15**).

Applying the links

Once you've made your decision on which links you want to add and which you don't, applying them is a simple matter of clicking the Apply button (**Figure 12.16**). If you want to proceed without applying any chapter points at this stage, just click the Skip button.

The wizard exits after you click either button; you can then preview your menu.

✔ Tip

■ Don't worry too much if you aren't sure about the number of buttons you have selected or their relative positions. You can change all this later in the process.

Name	Type
☒ Chapter 1	Seq. Marker
☐ Chapter 2	Seq. Marker
☒ Chapter 3	Seq. Marker
☒ Chapter 4	Seq. Marker

Figure 12.15 Deselecting a link removes it from the DVD menu.

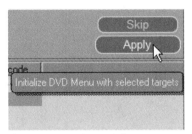

Figure 12.16 Hit the Apply button to include these links in your menu.

Changing a Thumbnail

When you set a link, it takes the first frame it finds and displays it as the thumbnail inside the button. If your clip starts with a fade to black or a frame you don't like, you can change it from within the DVD Editor.

To change the thumbnail, first open the DVD Editor. Then select the Master View tab and the button you want to change. Next, scrub through the clip until you find a better frame, and then click the Set picon button (**Figure 12.17**).

The thumbnail now updates to the frame under the timeline cursor (**Figure 12.18**).

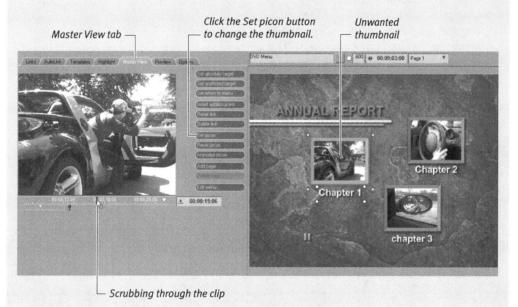

Figure 12.17 Using the Master View tab to change the thumbnail of a button.

Figure 12.18
The updated thumbnail.

Previewing Your Menu

You can preview what you've created by clicking the Preview button ⬛ anytime time during your DVD menu's construction. Once it finds the menu, the preview function plays it in an endless loop until you click the Preview button again (**Figure 12.19**).

✔ Tips

■ While you are previewing your menu, double-click any of the buttons to see if they play the correct clips. The keypad on the left of the display simulates the DVD remote control's Play and Pause buttons as well as the four direction buttons for selecting which button to activate.

■ If you scrub the Timeline outside of the DVD Editor, the menu buttons aren't visible.

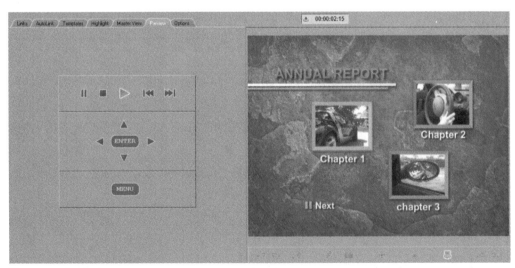

Figure 12.19 Previewing your menu.

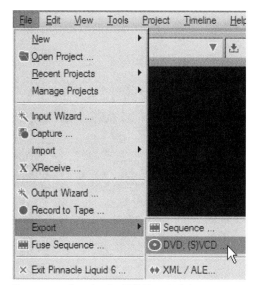

Figure 12.20 Opening the DVD Export dialog.

Understanding the Export Dialog

The Export dialog is one of the more complex areas of Liquid Edition because the DVD burn engine is a very versatile program with many variables you can alter for every DVD you burn. Fortunately, you can use a number of presets to avoid getting too deep into the technical ramifications of this.

Once your menu is complete, you need to exit the DVD editing screen by clicking the running man and then entering the Export dialog. Here you find all the settings you need to burn your project, and its menu, to a DVD.

To open the Export dialog:

◆ Click File and select Export > DVD.(S)VCD (**Figure 12.20**).

All four tabs of the DVD export dialog open, which are shown on the next page (**Figure 12.21**).

Figure 12.21 The DVD Export dialog showing all four tabs open.

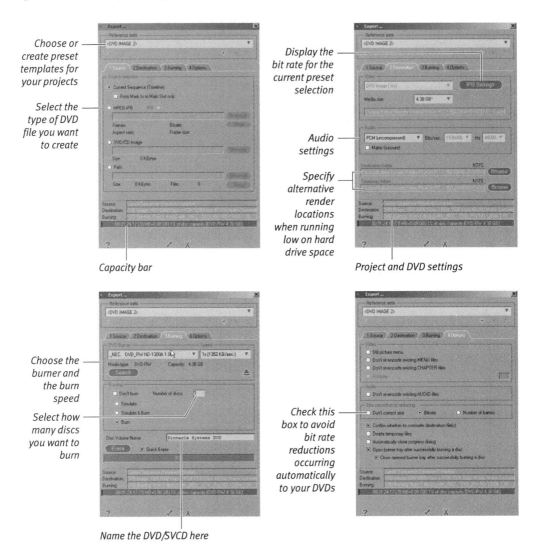

Choose or create preset templates for your projects

Select the type of DVD file you want to create

Capacity bar

Display the bit rate for the current preset selection

Audio settings

Specify alternative render locations when running low on hard drive space

Project and DVD settings

Choose the burner and the burn speed

Select how many discs you want to burn

Check this box to avoid bit rate reductions occurring automatically to your DVDs

Name the DVD/SVCD here

The Capacity Bar

The most important area on the entire interface is the bar that runs along the bottom of the Export dialog; it indicates how much room your project takes up on a single DVD (**Figure 12.22**). You can see this line no matter what tab you are in.

Source:	Current Sequence (Timeline) Complete
Destination:	DVD Image: VBR 8000 Kbps + PCM 1536 Kbps 48 kHz Matrix Surround
Burning:	No burning

00:59:46:22 [3317 MB=3.24 GB] 73% of disc capacity [DVD-RW 4.38 GB]

Figure 12.22 The capacity bar lets you know when your Timeline is too big for the DVD.

As the line approaches the right side of the box, it indicates that the DVD is nearing its maximum capacity. If the line flashes at you in red, this indicates that your project is too big. You either have to reduce its size or tweak the data rates you're using to burn the DVD so that it all fits on.

By default, the data rate is reduced automatically to fit your project on the DVD. If Liquid Edition detects a large project, then the data rate reduces until the project fits. However, a reduction in data rate means a reduction in overall quality, and this might not be what you want.

To turn off the automatic data reduction, check the Don't correct size option on the Options tab of the Export dialog. When you do so, the data rate reverts back to normal (**Figure 12.23**).

Once you've disabled this feature, you can see the true size of your project at the data rate you've selected. But as the warning says, disabling this feature may also cause your DVD to fail if the Timeline exceeds the DVD's limit.

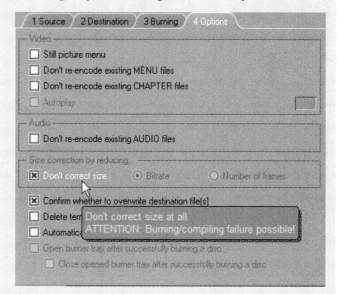

Figure 12.23 Turning off the auto size reduction feature in the Options tab.

The Source Tab

By default, the dialog box opens with the Source tab. Here you can select a preset for burning your DVD or you can create your own reference set. For more information see the "Reference Sets" sidebar, but if you think of a reference set as being a preset for various DVD qualities, you aren't too far off.

To select a preset reference set:

◆ Click the downward-pointing arrow and select from the choices available (**Figure 12.24**).

Once you make your choice, the IPB Settings box pops up to alert you to what that preset contains (**Figure 12.25**).

✔ Tip

■ Using any of the last four presets in the list that appears in Figure 12.24 (PROGRAM STREAM 2, PROGRAM STREAM 1, ELEMENTARY STREAM, or IMPRESSION DVD) will not burn a DVD but will create an MPEG file on your hard drive. See the "Alternatives to Creating DVDs..." section at the end of this chapter for more details.

Figure 12.24 Accessing the bit rate reference sets.

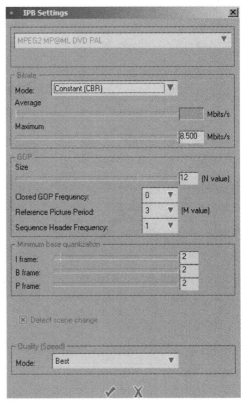

Figure 12.25 The IPB settings associated with the reference set you have selected.

THE SOURCE TAB

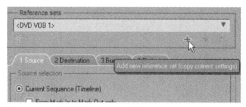

Figure 12.26 Adding a new reference set.

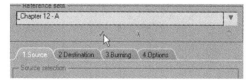

Figure 12.27 Naming your new reference set.

To create your own reference set:

1. Click once on the Add new reference set button (**Figure 12.26**).

   This copies the currently selected reference set but allows you to give it a new name.

2. Enter the name of your reference set and click the check mark (**Figure 12.27**).

✔ Tip

■ To delete a reference set, click the Trash can.

Reference Sets

Pinnacle provides reference sets so that you can burn DVDs at a variety of different data rates. But what does this mean in real terms?

Someone could write a book on DVD data rates; however, it would be a rather large book and one that wouldn't be terribly interesting. In a nutshell, DVD rates break down into two groups: variable bit rate (VBR) and constant bit rate (CBR). VBR is then subdivided into two further groups: Statistical VBR and Storage VBR. These attempt to use a lower data rate for static scenes and a higher data rate for scenes that contain rapid movement. Both of these settings save you some space on your DVD, but using them may be at the expense of image quality in some scenes.

It's worth noting that the capacity bar can't always measure VBR discs with any true accuracy. Thus, you should be cautious when using VBR with a long Timeline that could fill the DVD to the threshold of its capacity. Such a DVD is sometimes known as a coffee coaster. Therefore, I don't recommend that you use VBR settings if your DVD is nearly full. If you do, you could easily end up with another coffee coaster.

CBR does what it says; it keeps the bit rate set to a constant no matter what's going on in the scene. The default setting is 8.5 Mbits/s, but most users find that 6 Mbits/s produces a good quality DVD and doesn't eat up as much DVD space.

Experimentation is the key here. Try burning a selection of scenes to DVD+RW and then look at the results using your DVD player.

THE SOURCE TAB

Selecting the Source

The middle of the Source tab is where you can choose what burns to the DVD. By default, the current Sequence is selected—in other words, the Timeline. You can further specify From Mark In to Mark Out only (**Figure 12.28**).

Here are your other three choices:

◆ **MPEG-IPB:** This option allows you to select a file on your hard drive that conforms to the MPEG IPB standard.

◆ **DVD/CD-Image:** This option is looking specifically for an ISO or IMG file created by another program, but one that is suitable for DVD burning.

◆ **Path:** This isn't actually used for DVD burning; instead, it allows you to specify a directory you want to back up, your media files, for instance. Once selected, these files are burnt to DVD.

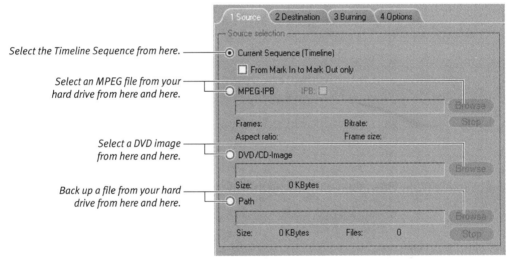

Figure 12.28 Selecting exactly what you want to export to DVD.

Working with the Destination Tab

You use the Destination tab to fine-tune your IPB settings, select the format the audio tracks use, and adjust your render folders. These settings are altered when you choose a reference set, so you can skip this tab, but if you need to tweak the bit rate setting to squeeze the project onto one DVD, this is the place to visit (**Figure 12.29**).

✔ Tip

- When creating a file with, for example, the Program Stream preset, you can choose the file's final destination using the Destination Folder browse button.

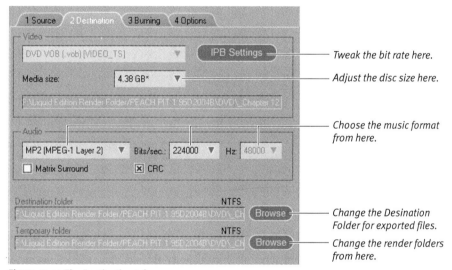

Tweak the bit rate here.

Adjust the disc size here.

Choose the music format from here.

Change the Desination Folder for exported files.

Change the render folders from here.

Figure 12.29 The Destination tab.

Fine-tuning IPB settings

You can preset these using reference sets or adjust them to your own individual requirements. You need to experiment to find the right settings for your DVD, but generally speaking, a setting lower than 3 Mbps for the Maximum and Average bit rates doesn't produce good quality results.

To adjust the bit rate:

1. Click once on the IPB Settings button to bring up the IPB Setting box (**Figure 12.30**).

2. Drag any of these bars to increase or decrease the bit rate. You can also directly enter the numbers into the value boxes. (You also alter the GOP size here, but it's best not to alter it unless you really know what you are doing.)

✔ Tip

■ If you are using a dual-layer DVD, you can adjust the potential size of the media by clicking the drop-down menu and selecting 7.95 GB (**Figure 12.31**).

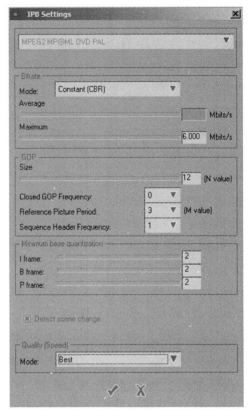

Figure 12.30 The IPB settings displaying a CBR reference set but with the bit rate reduced to 6Mbps.

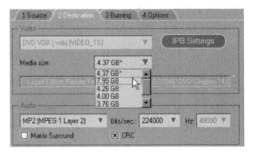

Figure 12.31 The media size options.

Selecting sound format

If you are using 5.1 sound, this selection area is where you instruct the burn engine to create the surround sound tracks the DVD player recognizes. Here are your other options:

- **PCM uncompressed:** This is the default sound selection the majority of DVD players recognize.

- **MP2 (MPEG-1 Layer 2):** This is a space-saving audio codec you can use if your DVD is approaching maximum capacity. However, this may not be 100-percent compatible with all DVD players.

- **Dolby Digital Stereo:** This setting formats your audio into Dolby stereo to give it an added boost.

- **Dolby Digital 5.1:** This setting is the one you need if you have created a surround sound Timeline. Using this setting will encode those audio tracks so they are recognized by a surround sound decoder with each sound channel being sent to the correct speaker.

Adjusting your render files

To render a DVD, you need an eye-watering amount of hard drive space. The default location is the Render folder Liquid Edition uses to render Realtime and non-Realtime effects. However, if you're running short of space, you can change this by clicking the Temporary folder Browse button (see Figure 12.29) and steering the Windows browser to a new location.

Make sure this new location is an NTFS partition; otherwise you'll be bitten by the 4 GB limitation of the FAT32 file system.

WORKING WITH THE DESTINATION TAB

Using the Burning Tab

The actual process of transferring your project to DVD happens on this tab (**Figure 12.32**). This interface is fairly straightforward, but here are some tips for using this tab:

◆ If your DVD player doesn't show up in the DVD Burner box, click Search and Liquid Edition scans for it.

◆ If your DVDs fail to burn correctly, try lowering the speed if you can.

◆ Don't forget to rename the disc volume; otherwise, whenever you put this DVD into a computer, it appears in Windows Explorer with the default Disc Volume Name—Pinnacle Systems DVD.

◆ Use a DVD+RW or -RW for your first copy to make sure the DVD burns correctly and that it contains no errors when you play it back. You can use rewritable DVDs many times, so they can prove to be an economical saving when you're dealing with the not entirely risk-free world of DVD burning.

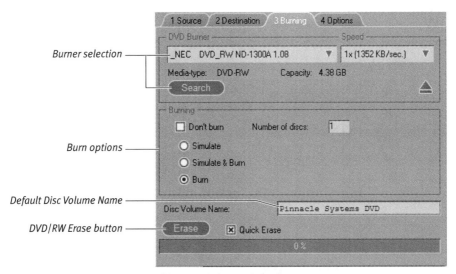

Figure 12.32 The Burning tab.

USING THE BURNING TAB

To start the burn process:

◆ Once you're happy with all the settings, start the burn process by clicking the check mark at the bottom of the Export dialog box (**Figure 12.33**).

Once you click here, the DVD Render engine begins its long job of getting everything rendered before it burns to DVD.

✔ Tips

■ If you haven't rendered the Timeline and yellow or red slices are present, you receive an error message telling you that the process can't continue because of missing media. In this case, the missing media are the render files. To correct this, simply exit the error message and then open up the Render box to make sure the Include yellow slices box is selected. Don't forget, the DVD menu generates a yellow slice all by itself.

■ If you are creating a file with the Program Stream preset, for example, the burn options will be grayed out. In this case, clicking the check mark will create an MPEG file. See the section "Alternatives to creating DVDs…" later in this chapter for more details.

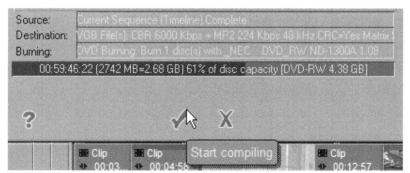

Figure 12.33 Click the check mark to begin the burn process.

Exploring the Options Tab

Don't overlook the Options tab because it contains a couple of useful settings, including the dreaded Don't correct size check box (**Figure 12.34**).

✔ Tip

■ If you're doing an overnight render and burn of your DVD, don't forget to check the "Close opened burner tray…" option so that your DVD burner doesn't spend the rest of the night open and collecting dust.

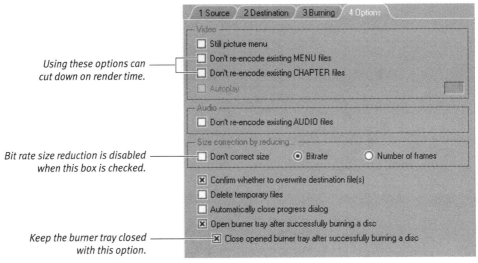

Using these options can cut down on render time.

Bit rate size reduction is disabled when this box is checked.

Keep the burner tray closed with this option.

Figure 12.34 The Options tab.

Automatic Bit Rate Reduction and How to Remove It

The "Don't correct size" option is a bit of a control freak. I recommend that you get into the habit of opening the Options tab right away and marking this box to deactivate it. If you don't, Liquid Edition takes control of your bit rates depending on whether your project is too big. You may not want this because you may find that altering audio from PCM to MP2 is enough to bring your DVD down to the required size. Remember, if this option is active (unmarked), altering the IPB settings does you no good because the Size Correction control freak just corrects it right back to where it thinks it should be.

Using the Template Editor

If you use the DVD wizard to add a menu to your Timeline, you probably want to alter the text on the background and around the buttons. You may also want to replace the buttons themselves and the background. All of this is possible using the Template Editor.

If you experimented with Title Deko in Chapter 10, you'll recognize that the Template Editor works in a similar fashion but with a slightly different, perhaps cleaner interface. The basics of highlighting text to change its font or point size are the same, and the way you use color and shadow follows a similar principle.

✔ Tips

■ Although you accomplish most menu editing in this interface, including changing buttons and backgrounds, animation takes place outside this interface. I deal with this later in this chapter in the "Adding Animation on a DVD Menu" section.

■ To use the Template Editor you must have a DVD menu on the Timeline.

Manually Adding a Menu to the Timeline

Although this chapter covers modifying a preset, you can create your own from scratch by using the Blank DVD menu. To add a blank menu, first switch to the Lib tab in the Project Browser and click once on the DVD Rack. Then drag and drop the menu into the Timeline (**Figure 12.35**).

After you have added a blank menu, you can use the tasks described throughout the rest of this chapter to build your DVD menu.

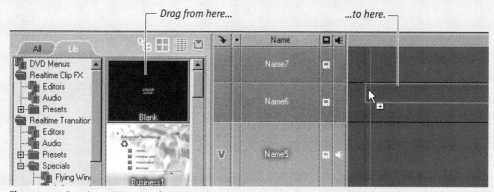

Figure 12.35 Creating a DVD menu from scratch.

To open the Template Editor:

1. With the DVD menu on the Timeline, open the DVD Editor by double-clicking on the actual menu or by clicking on the DVD Editor button .

2. Click the Pencil button or press the Z key on the keyboard (**Figure 12.36**).

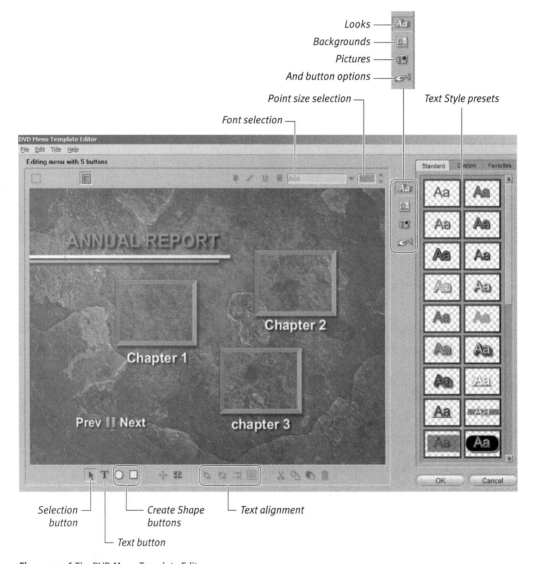

Figure 12.36 The DVD Menu Template Editor.

Figure 12.37 Looks button is activated.

Figure 12.38 Highlight the text.

Figure 12.39 Enter your own text.

Editing a DVD Menu

Once the interface is open, you can change pretty much every element of the menu to one degree or another. You can accomplish this using preset fonts and letter styles or by creating your own in Photoshop and then importing the file.

By default, the Looks menu button is active when you open the interface. This allows you to change the style, font, and point size of the background and button text.

To edit the menu text:

1. Make sure the Looks button is activated (**Figure 12.37**).

2. Highlight the text by dragging the cursor across it (**Figure 12.38**).

3. Press Delete to remove the text and then enter your own via the keyboard (**Figure 12.39**).

To alter the style:

1. Select the text again by dragging the cursor across it.

2. *Do one of the following:*

   ▲ From the preset text styles running down the right side of the interface, single-click the style you want (**Figure 12.40**).

   ▲ From the drop-down font menu, select which font style you want (**Figure 12.41**).

3. Adjust the point size in both cases by either entering the size you want into the font size box or by clicking the up and down arrows (**Figure 12.42**).

Figure 12.40 Applying a new style to the text.

Figure 12.41 Changing the font via the drop-down menu.

Figure 12.42 Alter the point size here.

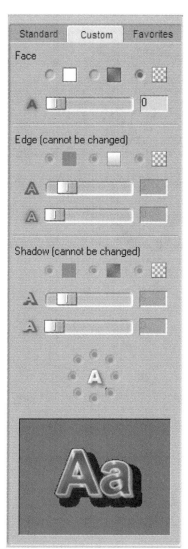

Figure 12.43 You can adjust shadows and face styles in the Custom tab.

✔ Tips

- To adjust the style further, open the Custom tab and adjust any of its settings (**Figure 12.43**). These alterations only affect the text you highlight.

- Hold the cursor over the styles to see all the color variations that are available (**Figure 12.44**).

Figure 12.44 Color variations exist for each style.

Saving a style

Once you've created the most awesome font and colored shadow style known to humankind, you'll probably want to save it. You do this by simply adding it to the favorites area.

To save the current look:

1. Highlight the text, then click the Favorites tab.

2. Click the suitcase icon.

   The highlighted text is added to your collection, ready for you to use next time (**Figure 12.45**).

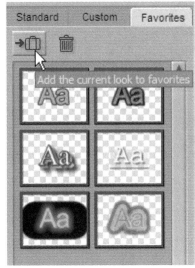

Figure 12.45 Saving a favorite text style.

EDITING A DVD MENU

Editing a Button

You follow the same process to change the button text that you did to edit the menu text, but sometimes this is a bit painful. The first step is to highlight the text, and because the text is often part of a button, it can be difficult to access.

The only advice I can offer is to double-click inside the text area of the button. Once at least a single letter becomes highlighted and once you have the text cursor inside the text area of the button, you can simply delete the old text and enter your own. The procedure for changing the text properties follows the same rules as those you used to change the menu text I dealt with in the "To edit the menu text" and "To alter the style" tasks earlier in this chapter.

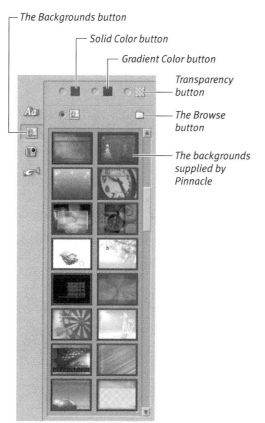

The Backgrounds button

Solid Color button

Gradient Color button

Transparency button

The Browse button

The backgrounds supplied by Pinnacle

Figure 12.46 With the Backgrounds button active, you can see the large selection of high-quality backgrounds that Pinnacle supplies.

Changing the Background

Liquid Edition supplies you with a stunning range of backgrounds to use in your DVD menus. I'm sure you'll find at least one here to suit the project you are working on, but if you don't want to use a preset, you can always import your own graphics files.

To change the background:

1. Click once on the Backgrounds button (**Figure 12.46**).

2. *Do one of the following:*

   ▲ Drag and drop any of the preset styles that run down the right side of the interface into the main interface.

   ▲ Click the Solid Color button and select a single color.

   ▲ Click the Gradient button and select a gradient-colored background.

   ▲ Click the Transparency button to select a transparent background.

   ▲ Click the Browse button to use one of your own backgrounds, then drag and drop it to the main interface.

The Picture Button

The third button in the column just underneath the background is the Picture button 🔟. This normally displays any pictures inside your Media folder, but you can use it to browse to any location on your hard drive.

If you want to keep the Liquid Edition Backgrounds safe in the backgrounds area, then this is a better place to import your pictures or graphics.

Changing and Adding Buttons

As with backgrounds, the number of buttons Liquid Edition supplies for its users is excellent. And again, if you really want to, you can import your own buttons as PSD files directly from Photoshop. Most templates come with a nominal amount of buttons per template, but you can easily add another button to the menu using drag and drop.

Buttons are preset graphic files with two states: highlighted (when selected) and non-highlighted (when not selected). If this means nothing to you, then stick with the preset buttons and modify those within the DVD Menu Template Editor.

To alter a button's style:

1. Make sure the Buttons option is selected.

2. Highlight the button you want to change by clicking it once (**Figure 12.47**).

3. Select a different button from the preset area that runs down the right side of the interface by clicking it once.

To change the size of a button:

◆ With the button selected, grab any one of the corner handles and drag it out to the required size (**Figure 12.48**).

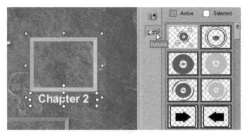

Figure 12.47 Select the button and click the Button option to open up the preset styles.

Figure 12.48 Dragging out a button to adjust its size.

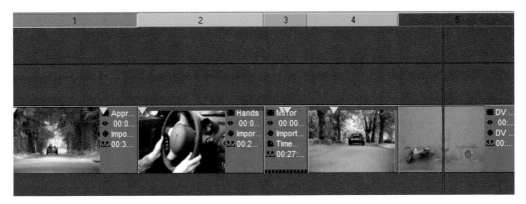

Figure 8.27 A transition with no handle area to work with appears red from end to end.

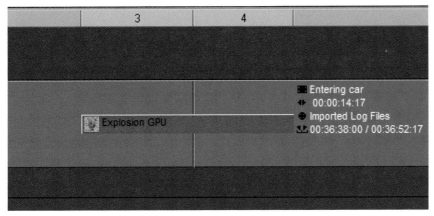

Figure 8.29 If two clips with no handles are sent to the Timeline the transition will be red from end to end.

Figure 11.2 Night effect created by increasing blue and gamma. The original clip is on the right.

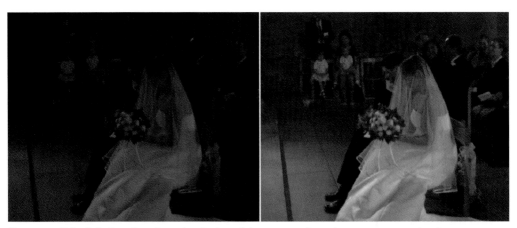

Figure 11.11 This clip isn't perfect after using the Auto Color corrector, but at least you can now view it.

Figure 11.23 A before and after example of correcting a severe white balance problem.

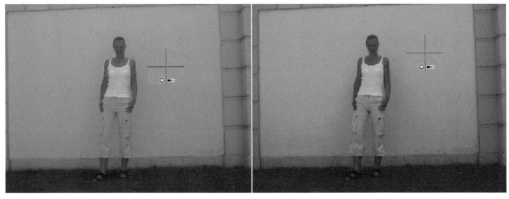

Using the 1-Point Gray Balance tool—before and after.

Figure 11.26 Using the 2-Point Gray Balance tool.

Figure 11.32 Selecting a color in the clip with the Zoom tool active.

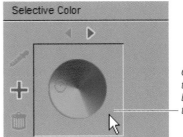

Click outside the circle but inside the square

Figure 11.33 Select all colors except the one you have just picked in step 3.

Figure 11.35 Before and after saturation is adjusted to all colors except the one you picked in step 3. The picture still needs some fine-tuning, but for a single adjustment, it looks good.

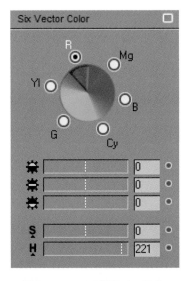

Figure 11.36
Selecting the color you want to adjust using the Six Vector Color wheel.

Figure 11.38 Before and after shots demonstrating color removal.

To change the active and selected colors:

◆ Click the Active or Selected color square, then change the color in the color picker (**Figure 12.49**).

✔ Tip

■ The default active color is yellow. When you select another color, consider your choice carefully in case the active color is no longer obvious when the button is displayed as "selected" on the TV.

To add another button:

◆ Make sure the Button option is selected and then drag your button from the right side of the interface to the menu.

✔ Tips

■ When you add additional buttons to the interface, always check for collisions using the Collision Detection button. You can find details on this in the "Collision Detection" sidebar.

■ If you add Next and Previous buttons to a DVD menu that currently only has one page, they don't show up until you add a second page to your menu. See the "Adding a New Page" section later in this chapter.

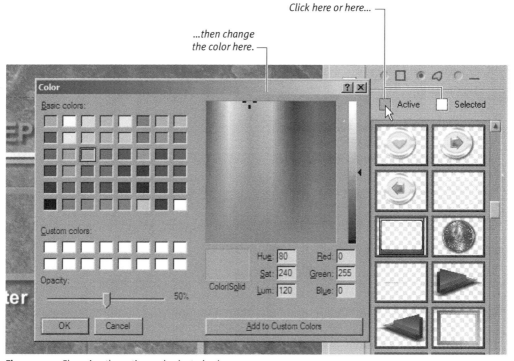

Click here or here...

...then change the color here.

Figure 12.49 Changing the active and selected colors.

CHANGING AND ADDING BUTTONS

Creating a Text Button

You can also use text to create a button. You're probably familiar with this format from seeing commercial DVDs. For example, you choose the language of the DVD by clicking the actual language name.

To create a text button, first highlight the text you want to turn into a button. Then click the drop-down menu in the Button area and select Normal button from the list (**Figure 12.50**).

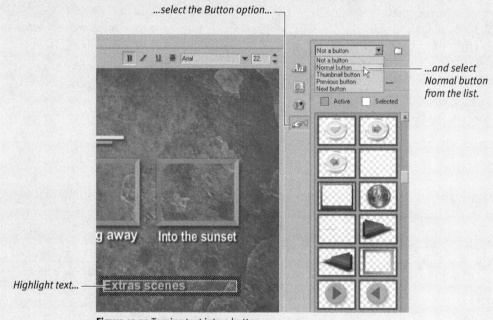

...*select the Button option...*

...*and select Normal button from the list.*

Highlight text...

Figure 12.50 Turning text into a button.

CHANGING AND ADDING BUTTONS

Collision Detection

When you're adding buttons, it's important to make sure the pixels don't overlap; otherwise the DVD you burn may not work. Overlapping buttons are a common problem caused either by the user placing them badly, or by the highlighted state of the button spreading further than expected.

If a collision occurs in the DVD edit menu, Liquid Edition automatically detects this and the Collision Detection button begins to flash. Click once on this button and the area of collision shows in red (**Figure 12.51**).

The button flashes when there is a problem.

The collision is marked here in red.

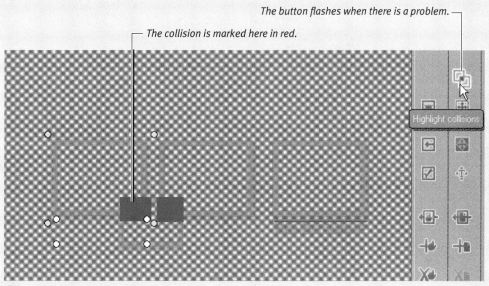

Figure 12.51 The collision detection interface.

Adding a New Page

If you have more than six buttons on a single DVD page, it begins to look a little cramped. At this point, it's best to add another page to spread the buttons out a bit. Once you've added a second page, you can see the Previous and Next buttons on your DVD menu.

✔ Tips

■ If you start with a blank template and you haven't yet added these Previous and Next buttons, don't forget to add them. Otherwise you won't be able to access the second page either in preview mode or on the final DVD.

■ If you add a second page to a DVD, you can't use animated buttons. However, if you use nested menus (multiple DVD menus all linked to each other), you can still have a multipage menu system with animation. See the "Creating Nested Menus" section later in this chapter.

To add a new page:

1. Open the DVD Editor and switch to the Links tab if it isn't already open.

2. Click once on the New Page button to add a new page.

Once the new page is added, the page indicator in the top right of the DVD interface changes to 2 and the buttons all appear empty, waiting for you to provide new links for them (**Figure 12.52**).

✔ Tips

■ To switch between the pages, use the page selector or click once on the Next/Previous button.

■ To delete a page, select it with the page selector, and then click the Delete page button.

Navigate to new pages using the drop-down menu.

Click here to add a new page.

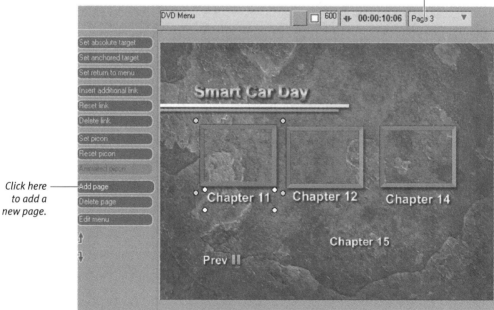

Figure 12.52 Adding a new page.

Adding a New Page

Navigation View

To conform with all DVD programs, Liquid Edition must know where to place the cursor on the menu when the up, down, left, or right key on the DVD remote control is pressed. This is automatically included when you build a DVD menu, but you can also change this.

To view the actions of the remote cursor, first press the Navigation View button to display the paths between the buttons. Then click any button, and move the mouse to the top, bottom, left, or right of the button to display an up, down, left, or right arrow. The trails you see indicate where the DVD cursor goes when you press a button on the remote control (**Figure 12.53**).

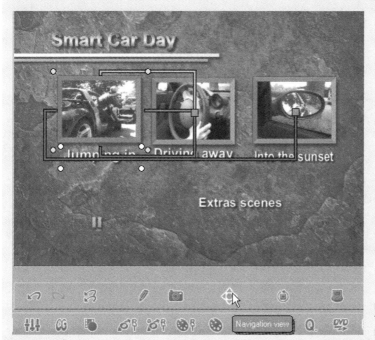

Figure 12.53
The remote pad
Navigation view.

To alter the direction, place the mouse over the button, click and hold the mouse button, and move the mouse around until the direction you want appears. Then drag the colored line to the button you want to associate with this remote control action.

Adding Animation on a DVD Menu

One of the coolest things you can do with a DVD menu is add animation to the buttons and the backgrounds. This is probably the killer feature for DVD menus, one that elevates them and gives your productions an immediate WOW factor. In Liquid Edition 6.0, adding animation is also easy to accomplish and a lot of fun to play around with.

To create an animated background, you first must have a suitable clip in the Project Browser. Before you start adding this clip to the background, carefully consider which clip will work best. You can also create a color animation in any Photoshop-type program.

✔ Tip

■ To complete the next taks, you should already have a DVD menu on the Timeline and a basic understanding of how the DVD Editor can be accessed and operated. If you don't, please read this chapter from the beginning.

To add an animated background:

1. First prepare a clip in the Source Viewer by adding a mark-in point where you want the animation to begin.

   Don't worry about the mark-out point; it's automatically set as the overall length of the DVD menu.

2. Once you've prepared your clip, enter the DVD menu by clicking the DVD Editor button on the Toolbar.

3. Make sure the Links tab is displayed, then drag the clip up into the background area of the menu (**Figure 12.54**).

   As a result, a separate track called DVD-B is created and the background of the menu changes to a checkerboard pattern to indicate that it is now transparent (**Figure 12.55**).

4. Click the DVD preview button to see your background motion in action.

   The preview function always displays the first DVD menu in a loop. To preview a nested menu, click the link that leads to that menu.

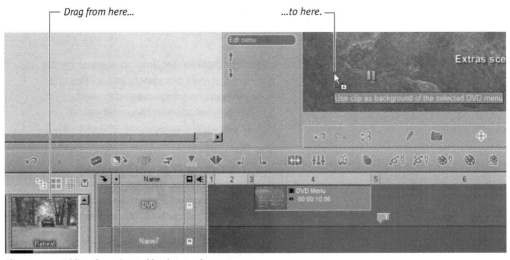

Figure 12.54 Adding the animated background.

✔ Tips

- You can add a filter to the track on DVD-B. See the instructions found in the "Saving a Customized Filter" section in Chapter 9.

- If the DVD menu isn't quite long enough to show what you want on the animated background, drag it out to the required length instead of trimming the clip. This is another advantage of DVD authoring on the Timeline.

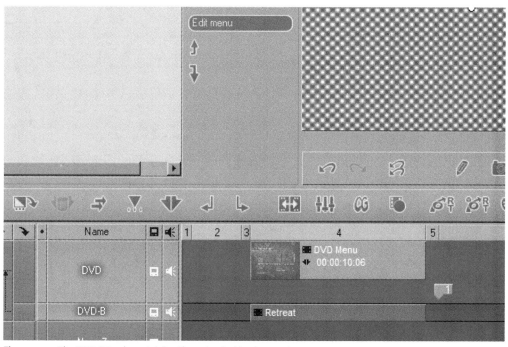

Figure 12.55 The DVD-B track containing the animated background.

Animating Buttons

An animated button looks even cooler than the animated background because you can actually show a small preview of the scene related to that button. When you're using this effect, Liquid Edition automatically adds a 2D filter to this clip, which resizes it to the size of the button and repositions it to the button's location. You can do this yourself, but doing so takes much longer than the simple drag-and-drop method I describe here.

To add an animated button:

1. First prepare a clip in the Source Viewer by adding a mark-in point where you want the animation to begin. Don't worry about the mark-out point; it is set automatically to the overall length of the DVD menu.

2. Once you've prepared the clip, enter the DVD menu by clicking the DVD Editor button on the Toolbar [icon].

3. Make sure the Links tab displays, then drag the clip up into the button (**Figure 12.56**).

   At this stage, a separate track is created called DVD-*number*, where *number* is the button you select. The background of the button changes to a checkerboard pattern to indicate that it is now transparent (**Figure 12.57**).

4. Click the DVD preview button to see your button in action.

   The preview function always displays the first DVD menu in a loop. To preview a nested menu, click the link that leads to that menu.

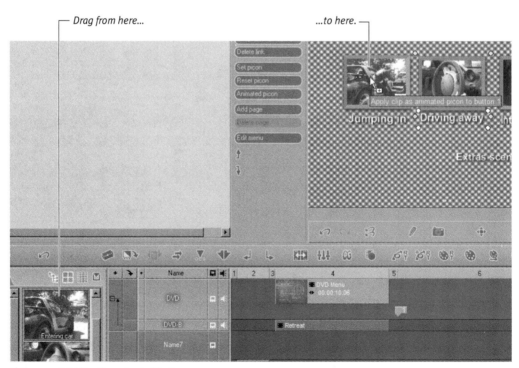

Figure 12.56 Adding the animated button.

✔ Tips

- The animations—background and buttons—must be the same length; otherwise, black shows on some areas when the menu plays back.

- You can add a filter to the clip on the DVD-*number* track as described in the "Saving a Customized Filter" section in Chapter 9.

- Warning: Animated buttons (and backgrounds) can also look corny and overstated when not used with care and restraint.

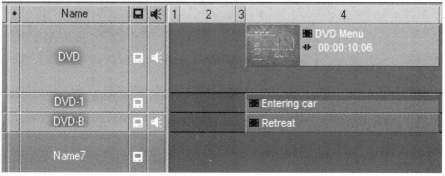

Figure 12.57 The DVD-1 track created by animating button number 1.

Adding Music to the Menu

You can add music to a DVD menu by simply dragging an audio clip down onto the Timeline below the DVD menu. This audio clip should be the same length as the DVD menu and any animated clips, but make sure you pay attention to how well the audio loops. At the end of the menu playback (10 or 20 seconds), the play starts again, so you may want to add Cross Fades at the start and end of the audio clip so that it doesn't begin or finish too abruptly, thus spoiling the overall animation of the menu.

If your DVD background contains audio, you need to mute it by clicking once on the DVD-B speaker icon (**Figure 12.58**).

Deactivate the DVD-B speaker by clicking here.

Activate the audio speaker by clicking here.

Figure 12.58 Adding music to the menu.

ANIMATING BUTTONS

Creating Nested Menus

A nested menu is simply a menu that leads to another menu. You've seen this often on commercial DVDs; a menu leads from the main film to the bonus area where you normally find cut scenes, trailers, and perhaps interviews with the cast.

Creating a nested menu inside Liquid Edition is just a matter of adding another menu to the Timeline and then creating some extra links. However, the trick is to place the nested menu at the end of the Timeline, beyond the point where your project finishes.

To insert a new menu:

1. Click once on the Lib tab; then open up the DVD Menu Rack.

2. Drag a preset or blank menu to a point after your movie finishes (**Figure 12.59**).

3. Open this menu in the DVD wizard, and link it to the buttons for the main film using the techniques I described in the "Adding Links" section earlier in this chapter.

✔ Tip

■ You can also add animated buttons and an animated background to this menu. If you saved the type style from the first menu, this is a good time to use it.

— Drag from here...   ...to here. —

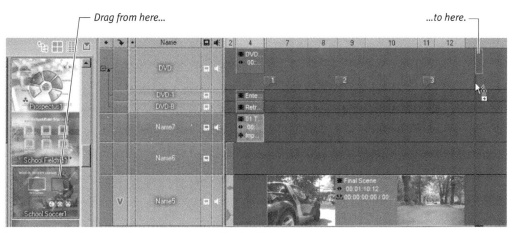

Figure 12.59 Adding a second menu after the Timeline has finished.

Excluding a Nested Menu from Playback

If you create a menu at the end of the Timeline, you need to make sure that the DVD doesn't play this menu when it reaches the end of the film. To do this, you need to insert a jump marker at the end of the last clip and before the new menu.

To add a jump marker:

1. Open the DVD editor and make sure you are displaying the first DVD menu in the Timeline and that the first button is selected.

2. Move the cursor to the mark-out point of the last clip.

3. Click the Set Return to Menu button. A small jump marker is added to the Timeline (**Figure 12.60**).

Click here to add the jump marker.

Figure 12.60 Adding a jump marker back to the first menu.

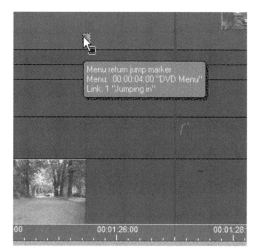

Figure 12.61 Displaying the details of a jump marker by hovering the cursor over it.

✔ Tips

■ If you place the cursor over the jump maker, it displays its jump point location (**Figure 12.61**).

■ To move a jump marker, simply drag and drop it.

Linking to a Nested Menu

Now that you have the new menu in place and the jump marker to stop the playline from seeing it, you have to create a link to it; otherwise you won't be able to use it.

Remember that a single-page DVD menu doesn't allow you to see the Next and Previous buttons, so you won't be able to use any of those presets. In fact, the easiest way to create your own button to link to a nested menu is to create a Text button. You can do this by following the instructions in the "Changing and Adding Buttons" section earlier in this chapter. Once you've created a Text button, return to these instructions.

To create a link to the nested menu:

1. Scrub down the Timeline until you reach the start of your second DVD menu.

2. To add a link, do one of the following:

   ▲ Click the Set Absolute Target button.

   ▲ Drag and drop the button onto the Timeline at the point where the second menu starts (**Figure 12.62**).

   A link is now created between this menu and the first one.

✔ Tip

■ Using this method, you can have as many nested menus as you like, although you must be aware that each one eats up a bit of valuable space on your DVD.

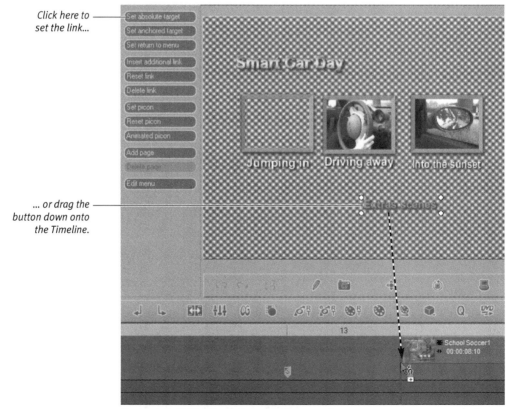

Click here to set the link...

... or drag the button down onto the Timeline.

Figure 12.62 Linking the first menu to the second.

Alternatives to Creating DVDs on the Timeline

Maybe you don't want to burn inside Liquid Edition for whatever reason—perhaps you want to create MPEG files from your AVI clips. In this case, you don't create a menu; you simply export the Timeline as is to your application in a format it can handle. Generally speaking, this means it needs to be an MPEG stream of some sort, but you need to check your program's handbook to see which setting you should use.

To export your Timeline:

1. Click on File > Export > DVD/SVCD.

2. Select Program Stream 1 or 2, or the Elementary stream.

   The IPB settings appear. If you're going to use the Impression DVD maker, use the Impression preset.

3. Check the IPB settings to make sure they are correct and/or suitable for your application; then click the check mark.

4. In the Destination tab, click the Browse button next to the Destination Folder box and browse to your target location.

5. Switch to the Burning tab—note that the DVD burner is now grayed out—and click the check mark to begin the process.

6. Once the export finishes, you can import this into the application of your choice.

✔ Tip

■ The files at www.peachpit.com/liquid6vqp that can be used in this book were created using the Program Stream 2 preset to convert a single clip on the Timeline into an MPEG clip that is $1/10$th the size of the original AVI.

Understanding Links

Links come in three different flavors:

◆ **Absolute link:** A point relative to the clip but not to the Timeline

◆ **Anchored link:** A point relative to the Timeline but not to the clip

◆ **Jump link:** A link that always returns the viewer to a specific menu

You can find more information on links in the Pinnacle Liquid Edition Reference manual.

EXPORTING THE TIMELINE

13

DVD may be the first export choice for many home and semiprofessional users, but you'll find plenty of other ways to get your project out of Liquid Edition and into the real world. In fact, Liquid Edition is capable of exporting your project to a number of different formats, including Internet-based distributions such as Windows Media Player, or to a file that can be incorporated into an application that can create Flash presentations. With Liquid Edition, you really can "create once and publish many times."

In this chapter, you learn how to use all of these methods to output your project to the tape and file destination media of your choice, which allows you to incorporate your projects into Web sites and even applications such as Microsoft PowerPoint.

Using the Output Wizard

Version 6 introduces the Output wizard as a way to simplify the process of getting your work out of the computer, especially for first-time users. There aren't that many steps to using the wizard, but it does demonstrate how the export workflow works, which can, at least, be illuminating. If you are new to NLE or Liquid Edition, it is best if you start by exploring the export functions of this program by using the wizards first.

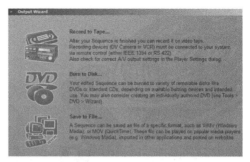

Figure 13.1 The Output wizard is new to version 6.

To use the Output wizard:

◆ Click File > Output Wizard to display the choices available (**Figure 13.1**).

Each of these choices is clearly explained by the text beside the button. Click any of the buttons to launch the appropriate application (**Figure 13.2**).

✔ Tips

■ Fuse Sequence is not an option in the Output wizard; you must access it directly from the File menu. See the "Fusing a Sequence" section later in this chapter for more information on this.

■ For complete details on the Burn to Disk option, see Chapter 12.

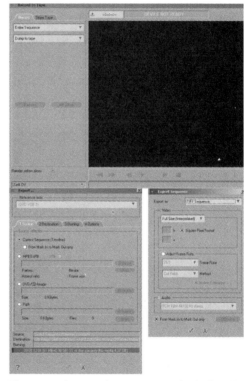

Figure 13.2 The Record To Tape, Export (to disc), and Export Sequence (to file) interfaces.

USING THE OUTPUT WIZARD

Figure 13.3 Check whether the include yellow slices box is marked and that rendering has finished.

Click here to open the output options.

Figure 13.4 The analog outputs options available when you're using the MovieBox.

Analog Outputs and Inputs

CVBS (Composite video baseband signal.): Uses the round yellow output plug for video.

Y/C (Brightness [luma, Y] and color [chroma, C]. Also called S-video): Uses the 5-pin connector for video.

Recording to Tape

You can export the Timeline or a section of it to create an archive of your finished project to digital or analog tape, such as DV or BetacamSP, or to supply your viewer with a VHS copy of the finished movie. However, unless you're using BetacamSP or an RS422 interface between the analog (VHS) deck and your computer, you have no control over the deck and need to export simply by playing back the Timeline with the analog outputs selected.

When exporting to DV, you have full control over the recording deck.

✔ Tip

- Consider exporting the Timeline to a DV device and then playing the DV device into the VHS recorder to avoid sound synchronization problems that can beset analog output.

To record to an analog tape:

1. Make sure the Timeline has finished rendering by clicking the Render icon Σ and checking to see if include yellow slices has been selected (**Figure 13.3**).

2. Click the Monitor icon in the Liquid Edition Timeline and select your analog output (**Figure 13.4**).

   Note: Analog outputs are only displayed if you have a recognized analog output device connected, such as the MovieBox Pro, or if you are using the AGP Pro card from Pinnacle.

3. Click the Record button on the deck and then click Play on the Liquid Edition Timeline.

✔ Tip

- During analog output, make sure background devices aren't operating and avoid using the computer for any other activities until the export is complete.

463

To record to a DV tape:

1. Make sure the Timeline has finished rendering by clicking the render icon and checking to see if include yellow slices has been selected (**Figure 13.5**).

2. Connect your DV device to the Firewire cable Liquid Edition uses, then make sure it's in Player mode and that you've inserted a non–copy-protected tape.

3. Click the Monitor icon in the Liquid Edition Timeline and select Liquid: IEEE 1394 to activate the FireWire output (**Figure 13.6**).

4. Click File > Record to tape or use the Output wizard to open the Record To Tape interface (**Figure 13.7**).

Figure 13.5 Check whether the include yellow slices box is marked and that rendering has finished.

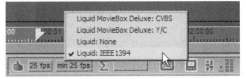

Figure 13.6 Selecting the FireWire output. This should occur automatically once your DV device is connected, but always check before you attempt a DV export.

Current position of tape

DV device status

Export options

Activate Record button

Render yellow slices check box

DV Device Selection menu

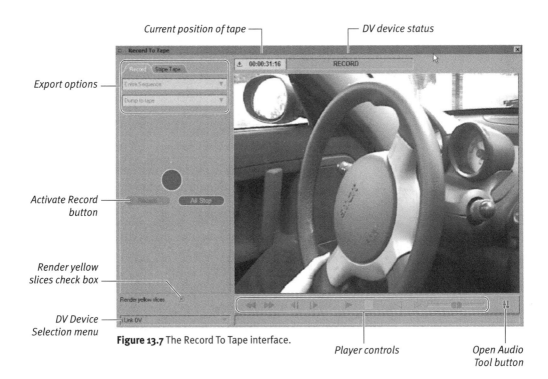

Figure 13.7 The Record To Tape interface.

Player controls

Open Audio Tool button

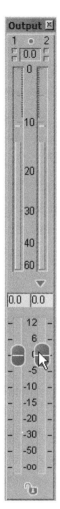

Figure 13.8 The Audio tool.

5. Select Entire Sequence or Mark In to Mark Out from the top drop-down menu.

6. Review the tape you're planning to use by using the player controls and find the place you want your recording to begin.

7. Click the Record button to send the Timeline to the DV tape. Click Stop to end this at any time.

✔ Tips

■ Although the Record To Tape interface has a Render yellow slices option, it's always best to render the Timeline first to avoid potential output problems.

■ You can also monitor and alter the output volume by clicking the Open Audio Tool button 🔢 and adjusting the volume with the slider controls (**Figure 13.8**).

■ By default, the Shuttle control is absent from the Record To Tape interface (**Figure 13.9**), but you can add it by customizing the interface. See Chapter 1 for more on this.

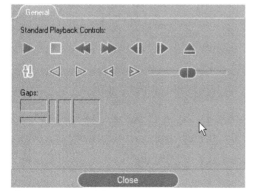

Figure 13.9 Some of the controls you can add to the Record To Tape interface.

Fusing a Sequence

The Fuse function is used to literally fuse together all the clips on the Timeline to create a single AVI file on your hard drive. You can also automatically import the fused clip back into the Project Browser so that you can use the clip in future productions or with other techniques such as XSend to Flash (see the "Using XSend" section later in this chapter).

To fuse a Sequence:

1. Click File > Fuse Sequence to open the interface (**Figure 13.10**).

2. Browse to a directory of your choice and then click OK.

   The Timeline is now rendered into a single AVI at the location you specify. Once it is finished rendering, it imports this into the Rack you last used, unless you deselected that option.

✔ Tips

- If you're exporting a particularly large Timeline, make sure that the destination drive has plenty of room. Allow 4 GB for every 10 minutes on the Timeline.

- Due to a file size restriction placed on the AVI format by Microsoft, an AVI can't be longer than 4 GB. The Fuse method gets around this limitation by using an Open DML format that is immune to this restriction and can create an AVI of any length on an NTFS partition.

- The Fuse method is also useful when you compile a standard introduction sequence that you want to use at the start of each of your videos. Rather than dumping this to a DV tape or DVD and then capturing or importing it, you can quickly create a single clip that you can store in the Rack of your choice.

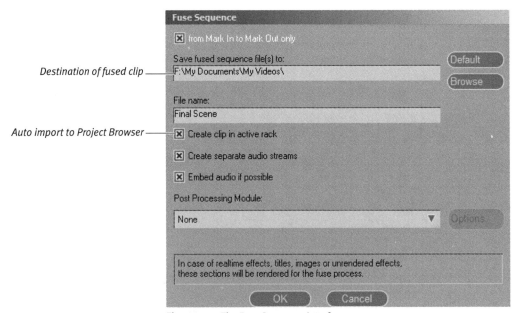

Destination of fused clip

Auto import to Project Browser

Figure 13.10 The Fuse Sequence interface.

Exporting a Sequence to a Specific File Format

The Internet is the perfect place to distribute your video productions, or at least to expose them to a wider audience. In this case, distribution is simply a matter of deciding which format you want to use and what sort of quality levels you require. Remember, large-scale formats such as AVI create large files that aren't always suitable for downloading. The QuickTime format can create a more compact version of the same Timeline, but the users must have this application installed on their computer.

Trial and error reveals which format is best for which production, and which one offers the best download time versus the optimal quality setting.

To export a Sequence to a specific file format:

1. Click File > Export and then select Sequence to open the Export Sequence interface (**Figure 13.11**).

2. Select the frame size you want and then click the Options button.

continues on next page

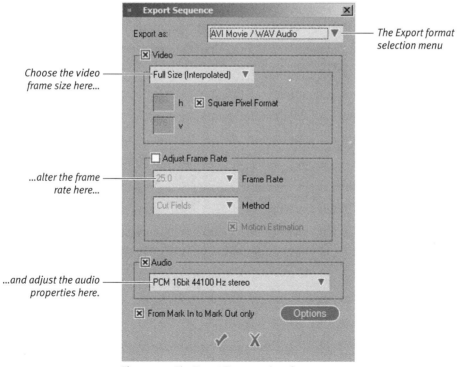

Choose the video frame size here...

...alter the frame rate here...

...and adjust the audio properties here.

The Export format selection menu

Figure 13.11 The Export Sequence interface.

EXPORTING TO A SPECIFIC FILE FORMAT

3. From the AVI Options dialog, select the codec you want to use from the drop-down list (**Figure 13.12**).

4. When you click the check mark at the bottom of the AVI Options dialog in Figure 13.12, you're prompted for a target location for that file. Make your selection and click Save.

✔ Tips

- Most Internet videos are reduced to a smaller file size by using the "Quarter Size" option. This lowers the frame size and decreases quality, but it also creates a smaller file size that is easier to download.

- You need to install some codecs on your computer before they show up on the list in the Options dialog.

- By changing the frame rate of a video from 25 to 15, you reduce the overall size of the exported file but you'll find the video playback jerky.

- For better compression without quality loss, consider using the DVD Export function and the Program Stream 1 preset. Details on this can be found in the "Alternatives to Creating DVDs…" section at the end of Chapter 12.

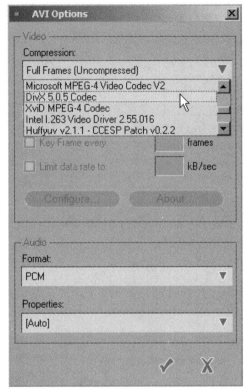

Figure 13.12 In the AVI Options dialog, select which codec you want to use.

Miscellaneous Export Methods

Three other options are available to you in the Export menu: XML/ALE, EDL, and OMF. Strictly speaking, these aren't export options because they don't export the Timeline as such; instead, they export various properties associated with that Timeline or Project. Their use is fairly specific and most users never need to go anywhere with them. Further information regarding their use and abuse can be found in Chapter 7 of the Pinnacle Liquid Edition Reference manual.

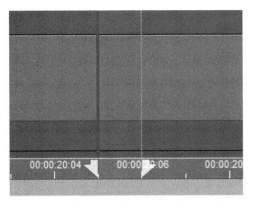

Figure 13.13 Defining a mark-in and mark-out point that is one frame long.

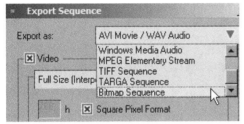

Figure 13.14 The picture format options are at the bottom of the drop-down list.

Using the Snapshot Function

A very quick way to export a single frame bitmap is to use the Snapshot button. This simply creates a bitmap out of whatever frame is currently in the Master Viewer and then places it in the current Rack. While this appears to be an easier method than the contorted method described above, it should be noted that this will only create a bitmap inside the current Media folder. If you want to export it to a program like Photoshop, then you are going to have to spend time hunting it down. Not impossible, but not exactly a timesaving method either. You'll probably find that the contorted method produces usable snapshots of your video into a directory you can easily find in the future.

Exporting a Single Frame

The real beauty of film is that it captures a whole range of events in motion; this is something only an experienced cameraperson can do with a normal photograph. But with video, you have the option of isolating one specific frame from a whole range and using that to create a photograph, either to include in your video project, or to place on the cover of the DVD case.

To export a single frame:

1. Scrub through the Timeline until you find the frame you want to export.

2. Press the I key and then the O key on the keyboard without moving the timeline cursor to place the mark-in and mark-out points one frame apart (**Figure 13.13**).

3. Click File > Export and then select Sequence to open the Export Sequence interface.

4. Select from the image formats at the bottom of the list (Bitmap, TARGA, and TIFF) as shown in **Figure 13.14**, and then select the frame size and decide whether or not to use the interpolated or the interlaced option.

5. Click the check mark and browse the folder to which you want to export this file.

   Once you click the Save button, a single frame suitable for use inside applications like Paint Shop Pro is exported.

Using XSend

One of Liquid Edition's most powerful features is its ability to export a clip from the Timeline or Project Browser to another application outside of Liquid Edition. This clip can then be edited in a compositing program such as Commotion or After Effects or, in the case of audio, you can clean it using any number of audio programs.

You accomplish this using the XSend command, which literally sends to *X*, where *X* is the application of your choice.

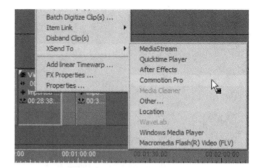

Figure 13.15 Right-click a clip, access the XSend To option, and select the target program.

To use XSend:

◆ Right-click any clip in the Timeline or in the Project Browser and select XSend and any application from the available list (**Figure 13.15**).

Liquid Edition then exports the clip and loads it into the application you selected (**Figure 13.16**).

Figure 13.16 The selected clip opened inside Commotion ready for some serious compositing work.

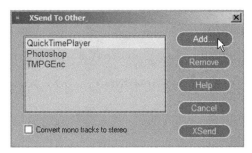

Figure 13.17 You can add any suitable application to the XSend list.

✔ Tips

- If the application you want to use isn't listed, click Other. Then add the application by clicking the Add button and browsing to the .exe file of the application you have in mind (**Figure 13.17**).

- To XSend the whole Timeline, you need to fuse the clip and then XSend that to the application from the Project Browser. See the "Fusing a Sequence" section earlier in this chapter.

- As an alternative to fusing the entire Timeline, you can build a container and XSend that. For details on containers, see Chapter 14.

XSend to Flash

Pinnacle offer the Flash file creation plug-in as a free download to all registered users of Liquid Edition. This plug-in allows you to create a file that's compatible with Flash authoring programs. Once installed, the Flash plug-in shows up automatically in the list of XSend choices.

Its worth noting that you still need a Flash authoring program to do anything meaningful with this file; this is because the file itself isn't something that you can play immediately inside a Flash application. However, because Flash is one of the most widely distributed formats on the Internet, buying such a program is probably a wise decision.

ADVANCED TECHNIQUES

The title of this chapter is somewhat of a contradiction in terms because pretty much everything in Liquid Edition is advanced, but it's so easy to use, it appears simple. The effects team that worked on *Star Wars: The Empire Strikes Back* created a scene that involved the largest number of models to appear simultaneously in one place. It was the first film to achieve something like this (copied endlessly now with CGI), and at the time it was impressive, but one of the team members later made this comment: "It looked good, but it didn't look nearly as good or as complex as the effort needed to accomplish it." Liquid Edition reverses this concept so that your project looks complex, but you don't need to apply that much effort to get the sort of polish usually reserved for professional productions.

The techniques you learn in this chapter are primarily about workflow and special effects—the former being an area that every editor wants to smooth out, the latter being something that most users want to dabble in, but an area that is perhaps only really applicable to the professional user.

This chapter appears at the end of the book because most of the techniques I describe here require you to understand at least the basics of how Liquid Edition works. For example, because compositing uses the various chroma keying filters, they follow the rules you learned about in Chapter 9. Similarly, you'll better understand how to create and consolidate Subclips to save space if you've already read about media management in Chapter 4. In short, this chapter deals with the icing on the cake and techniques that polish your production to the highest level.

Creating the Sequence

I've touched on Sequences in various chapters throughout this book, but here I'd like to hammer home what a Sequence is and how you can use it to effectively improve your workflow. Simply put, a *Sequence* is the end result of placing clips, titles, images, and filters on the Timeline. During the life of a project, you can, and should, create as many Sequences as you want. Here are some examples of sequences:

◆ Act 1, Scene 1; Act 1, Scene 2; Car chase—Scene 1.

   or

◆ The wedding of Jim & Joan— Registrar

◆ The wedding of Jim & Joan— Church service

◆ The wedding of Jim & Joan— Reception dinner

◆ The wedding of Jim & Joan— The speeches

With this last example, perhaps you can see more clearly how each part of the overall project—the wedding—can be split into separate parts or even subsections of parts. The use of sequences in this way allows you to concentrate on one specific area of the project at a time, editing that until it's perfect. In this section, you'll learn how to create a new Sequence, switch between Sequences, and combine Sequences together onto a single Timeline.

Figure 14.1 Click the New Sequence button to open the New Sequence dialog.

To create a new Sequence:

1. On the main interface, click once on the New Sequence button [image] in the top-right corner of the interface (**Figure 14.1**).

2. When the New Sequence dialog appears, enter a unique Sequence name in the top box (**Figure 14.2**) and select the settings appropriate to the media clips you're using.

3. Click the check mark to accept these settings.

Give your Sequence a unique name.

Always select a preset that is compatible with the majority of the clips with which you are working.

Check to make sure DV(AVI) or DIF(AVI) is selected here when you're working with DV material.

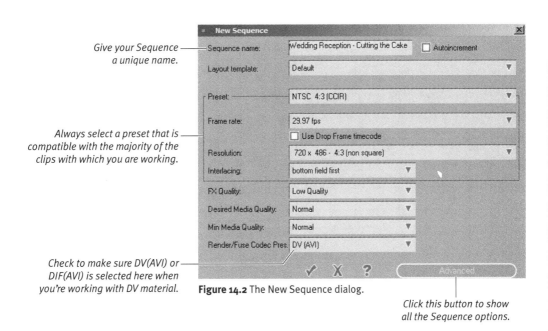

Figure 14.2 The New Sequence dialog.

Click this button to show all the Sequence options.

CREATING THE SEQUENCE

✔ Tips

- To view the New Sequence dialog as it appears in Figure 14.2 click the Advanced button and the rest of the options will appear.

- Check the Render/Fuse Codec Preset (at the bottom of the Advanced menu). This should read either DV (AVI) or DIF(AVI) when you are working with normal DV material. If you use any other codec setting, you may experience problems when you try to apply certain filters and effects such as Timewarp.

- You can rename a Sequence by opening the Sequences Rack, right-clicking it, and then selecting Rename from the pop-up menu.

- Always pick a preset compatible with the format in which the scene was filmed. Although Liquid Edition can support multiple formats in a Timeline, picking a preset closest to the majority of your clips can save unnecessary rendering time every time you place a clip on the Timeline.

Finding Your Sequence after a Software Crash

If your computer crashes while you're editing, Liquid Edition opens with an empty Timeline the next time you launch the application. This protects against corrupted projects or Sequences that might stop the application from opening when you restart it.

However, because Autosave backs up your work 30 times a second, the Sequence and its undo history aren't lost; they're just hidden from view.

To find your Sequence, click the drop-down menu to display a list of all the Sequences in the current project and pick the last sequence you were working on—this is usually the one at the top of the list.

Figure 14.3 The drop-down list reveals all the Sequences stored in the current project.

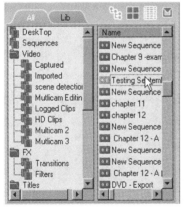

Figure 14.4 You can also find them stored in the Sequences Rack in the Project Browser.

Using and Combining Sequences

Once you've created a new Sequence, you can switch between it and any other Sequences you have made very simply. Remember: NLE is nondestructive, so you can use your media clips in as many different Sequences as you like.

Once the project is finished, you can quickly and easily combine all these separate Sequences into the final assembly Sequence using just the power of drag and drop.

To switch between Sequences:

Do one of the following:

◆ Left-click the drop-down Sequence menu in the top-right corner of the interface and select the Sequence you want (**Figure 14.3**).

◆ Open the Sequence Rack by left-clicking it, then double-click the name of the Sequence you want (**Figure 14.4**).

✔ Tip

■ You can also copy and paste Sequences inside the Project Browser to create a backup of a particular Sequence. The copy always retains the original state and isn't affected by any alterations you make to the original Sequence.

USING AND COMBINING SEQUENCES

To combine Sequences onto one Timeline:

1. Create a new Sequence by clicking once on the New Sequence button  in the top-right corner of the interface.

2. When the New Sequence dialog appears, enter a unique Sequence name in the top box and select the setting appropriate to the media clips you are using.

3. Drag the Sequence you want from the Sequence Rack to an empty Timeline.

   The Sequence appears on the Timeline as the Sequence name without displaying the various cuts the original had, although these are included inside the actual Sequence clip (**Figure 14.5**). Note: Markers will still be displayed.

4. Repeat step 3 until all the Sequences you want are assembled in the Timeline.

✔ Tips

■ Scrub through each sequence to make sure you have the right one. Sequences can't be viewed in the Source Viewer.

■ Switch back to the original Sequence to make last-minute changes.

Figure 14.5 Dragging a Sequence to the Timeline is the same as dragging a clip.

Understanding Multicam Editing

In Chapter 2, you looked briefly at Multicam capture and editing; if you haven't familiarized yourself with this section, it's probably best if you do so now.

But you don't have to capture clips using the Multicam capture technique. Instead, you can sync together any clips in the Project Browser using the clip in, timecode, or a marker on each clip. Then you can instruct Liquid Edition to treat these separate clips as a Multicam set.

✔ Tip

- To fully utilize the Multicam tool, you need to add the Multicam Gang button and the Multicam Display button to the Source Viewer control bar (**Figure 14.6**). For information on adding buttons to the interface, see Chapter 1.

Figure 14.6 The Multicam Display and Multicam Gang buttons added to the Source Viewer toolbar.

To sync clips together:

1. Select the clips you want to sync by holding down the Ctrl key and clicking each until they're all highlighted. Then right-click any of these clips and select Multicam sync from the menu (**Figure 14.7**).

2. In the Multicam sync interface, select which sync method you want to use. See the "Sync By?" sidebar for details (**Figure 14.8**).

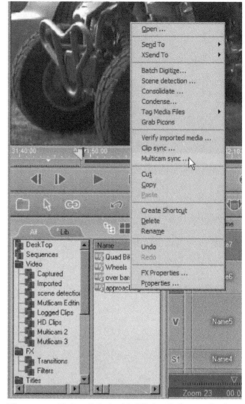

Figure 14.7 Right-click the highlighted clips and select the Multicam sync option from the menu...

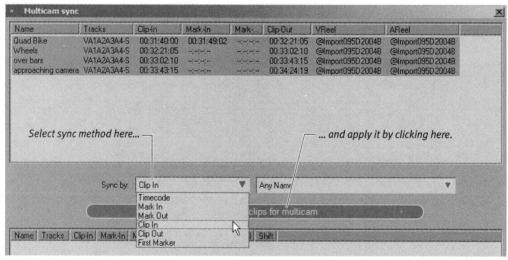

Figure 14.8 ...to display the Multicam sync interface.

3. Once you've selected your sync method, click the large "Sync selected clips for multicam" button (**Figure 14.9**).

The clips should now appear in the bottom window.

4. Click the check mark at the bottom of the interface and the clips sync together.

A clip called *xxxx* sync (where *xxxx* is the name of the first clip in your selection) is created in the Rack in which you're working (**Figure 14.10**).

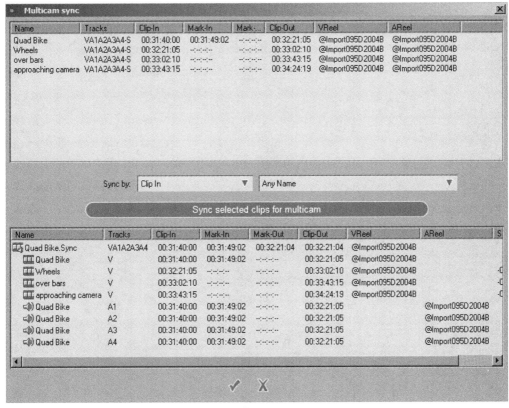

Figure 14.9 The applied clips appear in the bottom window.

Figure 14.10 Multicam sync creates a new clip in the Rack—QuadBike.Sync in this case.

✔ Tips

- You can sync together up to 16 video clips using this technique.

- When clips are synced together, the overall length of the *xxxx* sync clip is only as long as the shortest clip in your selection. This means that if you have a 5-second clip in your selection, all clips are shortened to 5 seconds in the *xxxx* sync clip. Consider adding Timewarp to shorter sections and then fusing the clip to create the new media.

Sync By?

There are six different ways to sync a clip to use with the Multicam tool.

Timecode: Use this for clips that you capture from different tapes but that have identical timecodes—for example, a concert where several different cameras are filming at the same time. In this case, it's better to capture these tapes using the Multicam capture technique, but if that isn't possible, syncing the tapes using this setting simulates that.

Mark In/Mark Out: It's best to use this setting when you're working with Subclips that have a mark-in or mark-out point that the user has defined.

Clip In/Clip Out: It's best to use this setting with Master clips you capture using batch capture or Subclips you've condensed.

First Marker: If you have several clips of the same event—again, a concert is the best example—but they have different timecodes/clip-in points and it isn't practical to alter the mark-in points, then you can add a marker to each clip at a specific event (the audience clapping, a conductor tapping the podium, and so on). Multicam sync can then use this marker to sync all the clips together.

To use the Multicam tool:

1. Double-click the clip created by either the multicamera capture technique or the sync-clip technique (**Figure 14.11**).

2. Select how many cameras you need by right-clicking the Source Viewer and choosing from the top three in the list (**Figure 14.12**).

Each square in the matrix represents a camera, numbered from 1 to 16. A golden square represents the current active camera.

3. Move the timeline cursor along the Source Viewer until you find a spot where you want to change to a different camera.

continues on next page

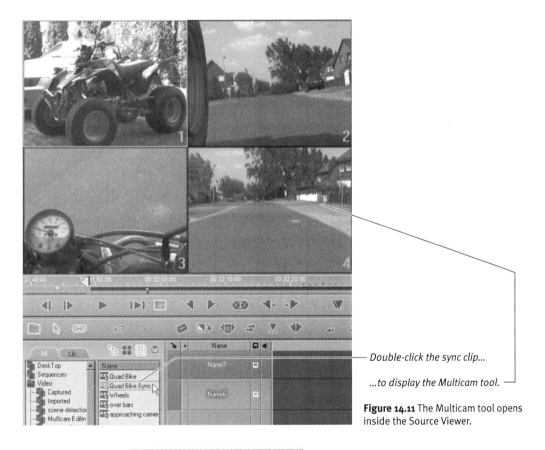

Double-click the sync clip...

...to display the Multicam tool.

Figure 14.11 The Multicam tool opens inside the Source Viewer.

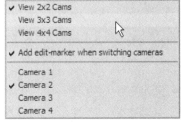

Figure 14.12 The camera matrix selection menu.

4. Click that camera square once and a small gold marker appears with the camera number inside it (**Figure 14.13**). Repeat this until you have selected all the camera positions for the entire clip.

5. Position the timeline cursor at a spot where you want to insert the clip and then click the Insert arrow 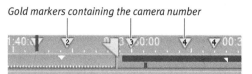 to send your edit decisions directly to the Timeline (**Figure 14.14**).

Gold markers containing the camera number

Figure 14.13 The Source Viewer Timeline displaying the camera selections.

✔ Tips

■ Only one audio track is supported when you're using Multicam, and this is always taken from the first clip in your selection, or from the clip you capture using the Camera 1 setting.

■ If you want to return to the normal Source Viewer at any time, double-click another clip in the Project Browser or click the Multicam display button to toggle the Multicam feature on or off.

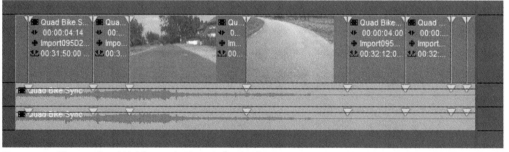

Figure 14.14 The completed Multicam selection on the Timeline.

Configuring the Multicam Display

You can configure the Multicam matrix to display 16, 9, or 4 different clips at any one time. If the number of clips you have doesn't entirely match one of these three matrix settings, then the spare cameras are deactivated and shown only as black squares. Their presence doesn't affect the tool's operation.

Note: You can also turn off the Add Edit Marker function, but this nullifies the functionality of the Multicam display.

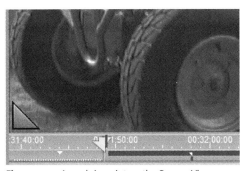

Figure 14.15 A mark-in point on the Source Viewer Timeline.

Using Subclips

When you're working with long clips, it is possible to create a series of proxy or Subclips from the master clips you have stored in your Project Browser. Subclips are proxy representations of media clips that allow you to split very large media clips into bite-sized, manageable lumps.

You can create Subclips in two ways: either by using scene detection, or by manually defining each one in the Source Viewer. Scene Detection is a time-saving tool, but sometimes it pays to do it yourself, particularly if you have just one small segment of a large media clip that you want to use.

To create a Subclip:

1. Place the media clip into the Source Viewer by double-clicking it and then using the mouse or the arrow keys to look for the best place for your subclip to start.

2. Once you've found the ideal start to your subclip, press the I key on the keyboard or click the Mark-In Point button. You can see that a small Mark-In Point icon has now been added to the Timeline of the Clip Viewer (**Figure 14.15**).

continues on next page

3. Select a point where you would like your subclip to finish by pressing the O key or by clicking the Mark-Out Point button .

A small Mark-Out Point icon is added to the Timeline of the Clip Viewer (**Figure 14.16**).

4. To create the Subclip from these new mark-in and mark-out points, press the U key on the keyboard or click the Make Subclip button 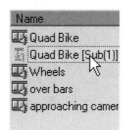.

A clip called *xxxx* (Sub(#))—where *xxxx* is the name of the original clip and # is the number of Subclips created from this master clip—appears in the Rack (**Figure 14.17**).

✔ Tips

■ You can also add the Make a Subclip button to your Source Viewer controls. See Chapter 1 for details on how to add buttons to the Source Viewer.

■ Use the Zoom tool to reduce the view if you can't see both the mark-in and mark-out points on the Timeline display.

Figure 14.16 A mark-out point added to the Source Viewer Timeline.

Figure 14.17
The Subclip is created in the current Rack.

USING SUBCLIPS

Using Scene Detection to Create Subclips

If you don't want to make the Subclips yourself, you can get Liquid Edition to do it by opening the clip in the Clip Viewer and using the Scene Detection tool. This is the automatic and much faster way to create individual Subclips from a long master clip.

To use Scene Detection:

1. Open a clip in the Clip Viewer. The quickest way to do this is to switch to Storyboard mode by pressing Shift+F3.

   This isn't necessary if you have a dual-screen setup. However, on single screens, it's the easiest way to open a clip in the Clip Viewer without adjusting any settings in Liquid Edition.

2. Click the extended dialog arrow ▼ in the top-right corner of the Clip Viewer to display the three tabs: Video, Audio, and Scenes (**Figure 14.18**).

continues on next page

Click here to open and view the three extra control tabs.

Figure 14.18 The Clip Viewer with the extended dialog displayed.

3. Click the Scenes tab (**Figure 14.19**) to bring up the Scene Detection options.

4. Select either the "based on video content" or "based on metadata" radio button.

   See the "Video Content and Metadata Explained" sidebar for an explanation of what these do. Don't worry about the Create clips options just yet. You usually only select these once the scene detection is completed.

5. Click Start to begin the process.

   The Clip Viewer runs through the scene using a low-quality picture to speed up the process. As each scene is detected, a small green marker appears on the Clip Viewer's Timeline marking the start of a scene (**Figure 14.20**).

6. Create either a master clip or a Subclip from these markers by clicking the radio button next to either option and clicking the Create clips button. This creates your clips in the Rack where the original clip is stored.

Figure 14.19 The Scenes tab.

Figure 14.20 After the detection process, green markers set out each scene change.

Using Scene Detection to Create Subclips

✔ Tips

- Clips created as master clips only have the amount of handle length you define in the Scene Detection options. Clips created as Subclips have a handle length that is effectively the same length as the original clip.

- When you are scanning using video content, you may adjust the sensitivity of the detection program using the Interframe Sensitivity slider. You'll need to experiment to find the perfect setting for each of your tapes.

- After scene detection, you can review the results by jumping through each scene marker using the C and V keys on your keyboard. Delete any unnecessary scene markers by clicking the Delete Marker button ▓. The Delete Marker button isn't a default button for the Clip Viewer; therefore you must customize the Clip Viewer and add the Delete Marker button to the interface. See Chapter 1 for more details on adding buttons to the Clip Viewer. You can also clear all scene markers using the Clear all scene markers button.

Video Content and Metadata Explained

Scene detection uses two types of data to create scenes—Video Content and Metadata. Their functions are explained below.

Video Content: The Scene Detection program runs through your clip specifically looking for changes in light level, such as the change from an indoor scene to an outdoor scene. This also occurs at a pixel level, which allows the program to detect changes in screen content—a second person entering the scene, for example.

Metadata: The Scene Detection program looks for the beginning or end of a recording. Each time you click the Pause button on the camera or turn the camera off, a flag is sent to the data on the film to signal this event. This is known as *Metadata*.

So, which one should you use? This depends on the film you've created. If you've used the DV tape over several weeks or months, then obviously the scenes are very much dependent on the camera being turned on and off. In this case, you should use Metadata.

However, if the camera is running continuously for the whole length of the tape—filming a stage play or a concert, for example—then you probably get better results using Video Content.

Using Consolidate

Once you have created Subclips, you can copy them to another hard drive using the information created in the Subclips' mark-in and mark-out properties. This is useful when you need to save hard drive space or when you're looking to consolidate your media before you export a project. The processes of digitizing and importing into a project can create reams of unwanted footage that takes up valuable hard drive space. Liquid Edition uses the Consolidate Media Management function to try and reclaim some of this valuable space.

✔ Tip

■ Consolidate only works with logged clips, not imported clips.

To use Consolidate:

1. Once you have finished editing your Timeline, go to the Sequence Rack and right-click the name of the Sequence you want to consolidate.

2. When the Consolidate box appears, check the box marked Create new MASTER clip(s) in new Rack, then give the Rack a new name (**Figure 14.21**).

3. Click the check mark and the process begins.

   If you have many files or the original file is large, this process may take some time.

4. Once this process finishes, the new master clips appear in the Rack you specified in step 2.

✔ Tip

■ Because these clips are independent of the original media, you can now delete those original clips. Remember to do it from within the Project Browser and not from inside windows. Then test your Timeline Sequence to see if it still works.

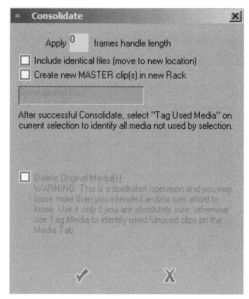

Figure 14.21 The Consolidate dialog.

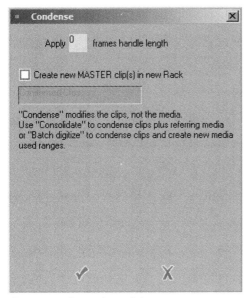

Figure 14.22 The Condense dialog.

Using Condense

Condense is a similar feature to Consolidate, and it uses Subclips simply to create a better, more logical workflow. The major problem with Subclips is that the clips' mark-in and mark-out points remain the same as the original media. This can be distracting if you are using the Source Viewer to fine-tune these points or if you are dragging the clip out in the Timeline. This is because it's possible to skip past the Subclip's mark-out point and find yourself miles down the original clip.

To solve this, Condense allows you to place a block on each Subclip, effectively creating a mini-clip. However, the media actually never changes and can be returned to the original Subclip status at any time; this is something that isn't possible when you're using Consolidate.

To use Condense:

1. Right-click those clips in the Project Browser you want to condense and select Condense from the menu.

2. Apply a handle length if you think you need one, and click the Create new MASTER clip(s) in new Rack option if you want these clips to be created in a new Rack (**Figure 14.22**).

3. Click the check mark to begin the process.

✔ Tip

■ To return the clip to its original state, right-click inside the Rack where the Condensed clip is, and select Expand to media.

Using Containers

You use containers to group certain elements in a Timeline so that you can move them around or send them to external applications using XSend. The container is, in reality, a proxy marker for the clips and effects that you place inside the container. The effects don't change, nor do the relative locations, unless you move them. You can also step into a container to fine-tune the edit at any point.

✔ Tips

■ The Build container of active tracks button ▣ isn't on the default Liquid Edition interface. You need to add it from the customize Edit tab that you access by right-clicking on the Liquid Edition toolbar and selecting Customize from the menu that appears. For more details on adding buttons, see Chapter 1.

■ The Build container of active tracks button is always grayed out unless you've defined a mark-in and mark-out point on the Timeline.

To build a container:

1. Place the timeline cursor at the start of the area where you want to build a container, and press I on the keyboard to create a mark-in point.

2. Place the Timeline cursor at the end of the area where you want to build a container and press the O key on the keyboard to create a mark-out point.

   The Build container of active tracks button now becomes active (**Figure 14.23**).

3. Build the container by *doing one of the following:*

   ▲ Click the Build container of active tracks button.

   ▲ Right-click anywhere on the Timeline button area and select Edit > Build container of active tracks (**Figure 14.24**).

   The resulting container displays on the Timeline as one clip (**Figure 14.25**).

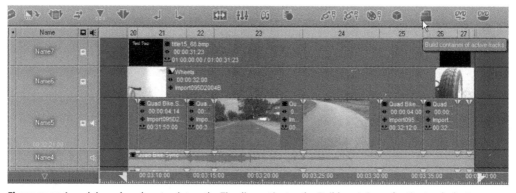

Figure 14.23 A mark-in and mark-out point on the Timeline activates the Build container of active tracks button.

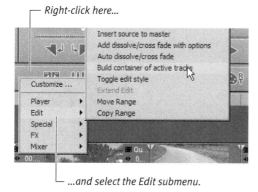

Right-click here...

...and select the Edit submenu.

Figure 14.24 You can also access the build container function without adding the button to the Toolbar.

✔ Tips

- Make sure all the tracks between the mark-in and mark-out points are active before you attempt to build a container, because only active tracks are included.

- Containers can be useful if you want to apply a filter across a set number of clips or even the entire Timeline. An example involves making a container from the whole Timeline and then adding the ColorCorrection Editor to legalize each clip, image, and title to broadcast standards. See Chapter 11 for details on the ColorCorrection Editor.

Figure 14.25 A container as it appears on the Timeline.

To edit a container:

1. Right-click the container and select
   Container > Step Into Container
   (**Figure 14.26**).

2. Once you've stepped into a container,
   you need to exit back to the Timeline by
   clicking the Main Sequence Level tab
   that appears only when you are working
   inside a container (**Figure 14.27**).

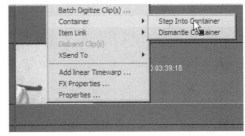

Figure 14.26 Opening a container for further editing...

— *Main Sequence Level tab*

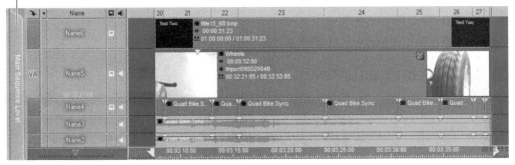

Figure 14.27 ...displays the contents in a sub-Timeline.

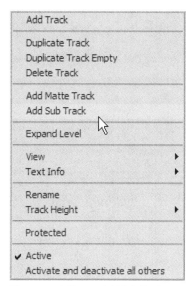

Figure 14.28 Choose Add Sub Track from this menu...

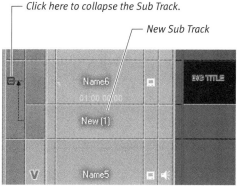

Figure 14.29 ...creates a Sub Track under the selected track.

Working with Sub Tracks

You can use Sub Tracks to conserve your work area and hide tracks that you really don't need to see all the time.

For instance, it's fairly common to add a motion background to a title in NLE. The motion background itself has probably been created in a third-party application and imported into Liquid Edition. Once you place the motion background on the Timeline, you don't really need to see it anymore. In fact it's taking up valuable real estate, which is always an issue for editors who work mainly in special effects.

By using Sub Tracks, you can easily get around this problem by collapsing the Sub Track after you have added the motion background. It can then be opened again at any time if you need to perform any fine-tuning.

To add a Sub Track:

◆ Right-click in the track name area and select Add Sub Track from the menu (**Figure 14.28**).

The Sub Track is created directly under that track, appearing in the name area as a branch (**Figure 14.29**).

✔ Tips

■ To collapse a Sub Track, click the minus sign (–) on the far left of the track name.

■ You can also create a Sub Track within another Sub Track by using the same procedure as you did to create the first Sub Track. You might use this method as an alternative to building a container.

■ The video monitor for a Sub Track isn't always switched on by default when it's created. Watch for this because without the small monitor icon that appears in the Sub Track, no video is visible. Of course, the same rule applies to the speaker icon that again may not appear when you create a Sub Track.

Matte Track

To understand Matte Track, you must first understand what a matte actually is. Imagine a matte as a stencil, the sort a painter might place on the wall, spray paint over, and then peel off to reveal the shape of the stencil in the paint.

In NLE, the Matte Track is the stencil. It allows video through the shape of the matte, but in this case, you can actually move the matte using the 2D Editor and create a stencil that moves across the path of the video clip. Perhaps the most famous example of this is the opening scene of every James Bond film where the barrel of the gun tracks across the screen until it finds 007. Everything else on the screen is black, except the stencil of the gun barrel, which is effectively a still image with a transparent circle in the middle.

To create a Matte Track:

◆ Right-click in the track name area and select Add Matte Track from the menu (**Figure 14.30**).

The Matte Track is created directly under the track you right-clicked on, appearing in the name area as a branch track (**Figure 14.31**). The track is always colored green to differentiate it from a Sub Track.

✔ Tips

■ To collapse a Matte Track, click the minus sign (–) to the far left of the track name.

■ To delete a Matte Track, right-click it and select Delete.

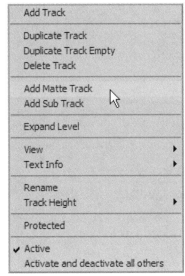

Figure 14.30 Choosing Add Matte Track from this menu...

A created Matte Track with green track

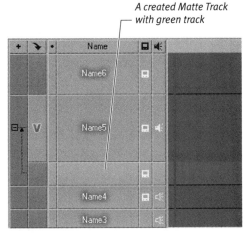

Figure 14.31 ...creates a Matte Track under the selected track.

Matte Track in Action

To see how quick and easy, yet highly impressive Matte Track is, do the following to re-create James Bond's entrance scene.

1. Open Title Deko (see Chapter 10) and create a title with just a circle in the center (**Figure 14.32**).

   This is your matte or stencil.

2. Place a clip on the Timeline and then create a Matte Track under that clip.

3. Place the title you created in step 1 onto the Matte Track and expand it to the length of the clip above (**Figure 14.33**).

4. Place a 2D GPU filter on the title and add movement to the circle, taking it from left to right (**Figure 14.34**).

5. Add James Bond music and perhaps tweak the 2D filter's blurring parameters to give the matte a softer edge, and you're done! It really is that easy.

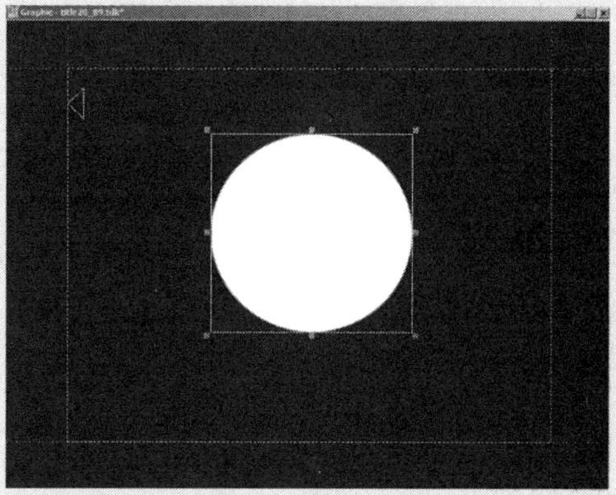

This is only a basic version of what can be done. Mattes that have been created in Photoshop will look

Figure 14.32 Simply add a circle to a blank Title Deko screen to create a matte.

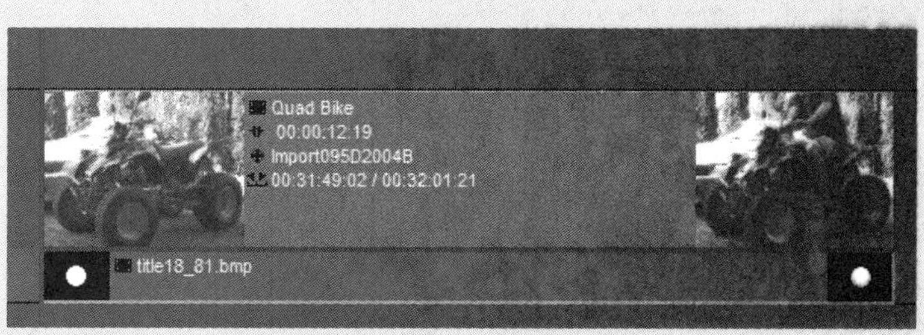

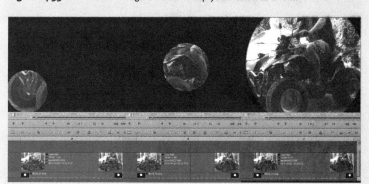

Figure 14.33 The matte must go below the clip you want it to affect.

Figure 14.34 After adding a 2D filter to create some motion to the matte.

better than this simple one. But as you can see, with only a few mouse clicks, you have an effect that works in real time and is very simple to set up.

Mattes can also be bought online from companies such as Digital Juice, which also supplies a range of copyright-free motion backgrounds and themed mattes. See www.holdan.co.uk for details.

Using Chroma Keying

There are a number of different names for chroma keying including the more familiar blue- or green-screen compositing.

You often see this on national TV when the weather appears on a screen behind the weather person. In fact, the presenter is pointing to a blank green or blue screen and is looking at an image on a monitor in front of him or her.

Blue-screen compositing is used extensively in movies to put objects and people into a shot. This is what allows Superman to fly and Spider-Man to spin webs around the city without either of them having to dangle from a helicopter.

To create a chroma-based video clip, you need some fairly special equipment; just having a blue or green background isn't really enough to produce truly professional results. First, you must have the correct lighting to remove shadows and to allow the background to be a uniform shade of blue or green. If you don't do this correctly, the composite suffers from strange areas on the screen that appear to glimmer slightly as the light moves inside the shot. A modern audience will spot these and when they do, your effect falls flat.

However, once you successfully shoot the clip and Liquid Edition captures it, the process of removing the green or blue color background is simply a matter of applying a filter and adjusting the parameters for maximum effect.

The following task-based description refers to any of the chroma keying filters, including the Blue Screen, Green Screen, Chroma Key CPU, and Chromakeyer YUV effects.

To apply one of the chroma key filters:

◆ Place the clip on the Timeline; then drag and drop the chroma key of your choice onto the clip (**Figure14.35**).

✔ Tip

■ To work correctly, the clip with the chroma key filter must be the uppermost clip on the Timeline tracks.

Drag any one of the chroma key filters from here...

...to the clip.

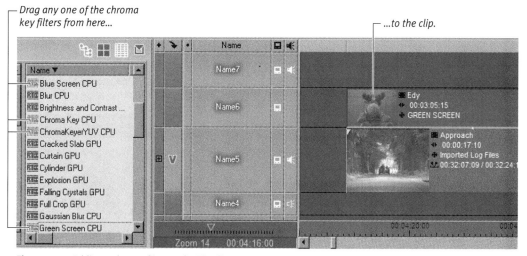

Figure 14.35 Adding a chroma filter to the Timeline.

To use the Blue or Green Screen filters:

◆ Double-click the purple bar that runs the length of the clip to display the Green or Blue Screen Editor (**Figure 14.36**).

Adjusting the threshold produces the most noticeable difference when you're fine-tuning your chroma effect, but don't ignore the other settings as you adjust this clip (**Figure 14.37**).

✔ Tip

■ Don't forget that you're working with video, and as a result, you need to change the parameters for this effect throughout the length of the clip. For more details on adjusting parameters and working with keyframes, see Chapter 9.

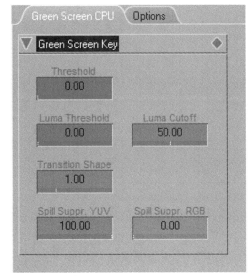

Figure 14.36 The Green Screen Key parameter interface. This is a Realtime filter.

Figure 14.37 Before and after adjusting the Green Screen parameters.

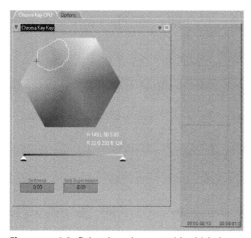

Figure 14.38 Defining the color area with which the filter should work.

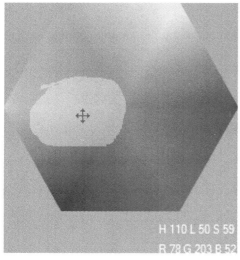

Figure 14.39 Hold the Ctrl key to move the selection area.

To use the chroma key filter:

1. Double-click the purple bar that runs the length of the clip.

2. Draw a circle around the color chart, tracing the color of your background (green in this example) (**Figure 14.38**).

✔ Tips

■ Hold down the Ctrl key and left-click in the drawn area to move it around (**Figure 14.39**).

■ Hold down the Alt key and draw inside the area to subtract areas from your original drawing.

■ Hold down the Shift key to add to the areas of your original drawing.

USING CHROMA KEYING

To use the Chromakeyer YUV filter:

1. Double-click the purple bar that runs the length of the clip).

2. Use the color picker to drag the color band around the circle to achieve the result you are looking for (**Figure 14.40**).

✔ Tip

■ The disc parameter expands the selection area of the color picker.

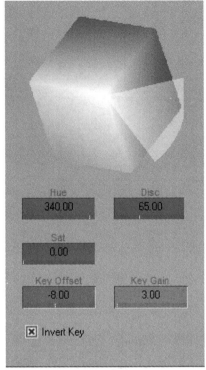

Figure 14.40 You need to rotate the color area of the YUV filter to select the correct color.

Chroma Keying on the Cheap

Although I said that you need professional equipment to produce professional results, you can still experiment with chroma keying without having access to a large budget. To create the examples shown in this chapter, I printed off several sheets of green paper. I stuck these to the wall and tried not to leave gaps or create any ripples in the paper. Then, I just added a bright light source or two to eliminate shadows and voilà—Edy the Elk is now a movie star (**Figure 14.41**).

The top row of Figure 14.41 shows Edy inserted into the clip's Viewpoint, Mirror, and Approach. If you compare these screenshots with ones throughout this book, you'll see how convincing a simple green-screen effect can be. The bottom row shows Edy in front of the big Ferris wheel, and if you look carefully enough, you'll also see that he is sitting on one of the cars in the center right of the middle screenshot. In the last screen shot in this montage, I used the blue sky background behind the big Ferris wheel as the chroma keying color so that you can see the Approach clip through it.

Chroma keying is a very versatile tool, but it's only as good as your imagination and the consistency of your chroma background. Take a look through your clips and see where you might add chroma keying to create unusual and interesting effects from videos that contain uniform amounts of color.

Don't forget that you can combine a 2D filter with a chroma filter to rotate and resize the inserted object so it fits the scene better. For example, it's not hard to shrink someone to make them appear smaller than they are and then place them in a room full of what appears to be giant furniture.

An Edy JPEG is one of the sample files available at www.peachpit.com/liquid6vqp. You can also download a green and blue JPEG to help create your own chroma key studio.

Figure 14.41 Edy the Elk and the Smart Roadster show how easy it is to create a green screen set at home and from suitable clips.

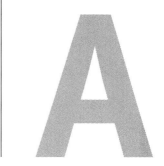

TROUBLESHOOTING

I've designed this appendix to help you understand how you can best set up your computer so it provides optimal performance for NLE work. If you're having trouble with Liquid Edition, I suggest that you read through this appendix and try out the three basic NLE tests before you start altering any significant part of your computer's setup. This appendix does assume that you know the basic functions of Liquid Edition. If you're unsure of how something should work, refer to the specific chapter where it is covered first to make sure what you are seeing is actually a problem.

Ultimately, the best help you can find is via Pinnacle's own support area on its Web site (www.pinnaclesys.com) and on the community-run forums where many problems are solved by ordinary users (http://webboard.pinnaclesys.com). This latter site is a veritable gold mine of information frequented by both longtime expert users of the program and Pinnacle's own technical support team.

Old Computers, New Tricks

In a previous job, I built NLE systems for a U.K.-based company. During that time, I was often presented with a computer—presumably passed down from Noah—into which the user wanted to incorporate an NLE system. Usually, this computer refugee from the stock room was chosen because "It has SCSII hard drives," but the drives themselves would usually turn out to be too small, nearing the end of their useful life, or both. Unsurprisingly, the computer would fail the three basic NLE tests:

◆ Playback

◆ Capture

◆ Output

Here's why they failed:

An NLE program demands the utmost from the computer's resources. Just having a fast SCSII, a SATA, or an EIDE hard drive is a tiny part of the story. For example, having lots of memory (RAM) is seen as a good thing, but is it good quality and fast? A fast processor is wonderful, but is the motherboard going to do it justice or be compatible with NLE? A cutting-edge graphics card is great, but are the drivers going to cause problems?

The answer to all these questions is often that no one really knows until someone tries it out. Computers aren't cars; they aren't assembled from exactly the same parts and the interaction between all the components is not always a definable and known subject. Computer technology is a dark, mysterious subject, fraught with personal tragedy and costly mistakes.

How to test your system:

Complete the thee basic NLE tests in this appendix, but don't panic if your computer fails at any stage; you can do several things to fix this. It is best to get these problems sorted out now, rather than when you're in the middle of a project that has a deadline creeping steadily closer.

Shortly after the launch of Liquid Edition, a demo version of Liquid Edition will be available via a download link from the Peachpit Web site (www.peachpit.com/liquid6vqp). If you have doubts about your computer's capabilities, then use this demo first to make sure it works on your system. The demo is an unrestricted version that allows you to play around with all the features mentioned in this book for 20 days.

The Three Basic Suitability Tests

If you're having problems with Liquid Edition or you want to test your computer to see if it's suitable for running Liquid Edition, then follow these three basic tests. The result of each one should be positive, but if it isn't, refer to the section noted at the end of each of the three basic test stages for possible solutions. Don't give up right away; you'll seldom find a system that works with NLE without a little bit of tweaking here and there.

Test 1: Playback

The first test determines whether your computer can play back the sample project correctly. Playback under yellow slices (indicating Realtime previews are being displayed) will place a greater strain on your system than green slices (indicating that rendering has completed), but you need to know now what your computer is capable of.

If you have started a new project, switch back to the old project by clicking on File > Recent Projects and then selecting C:\program files\projects\start6_NTSC (or PAL). Once you have finished testing, switch back to your project using the same method.

To determine whether your computer can play back:

1. Launch Liquid Edition. A Timeline displays that contains a demo project of a racing track with titles, music, and effects. The sequence lasts less than a minute.

2. Play back this demo first without rendering yellow slices.

   Watch the display carefully to see if it plays out smoothly or if there is any jerkiness. Also, watch the speed indicator in the Liquid Edition taskbar to see if it falls into the red.

3. Open the render box by clicking the Render icon in the bottom-right corner of the interface.

4. Check the include yellow slices check box.

5. Once all slices have changed to green, play the demo sequence back again.

   If you are unsure of how to do this, refer to this book's index and look up "render."

   Once again, watch the display carefully to see if it plays out smoothly and watch the speed indicator to see if it falls into the red.

✔ Tips

■ If you see problems with the display, such as black inlays or a stuttering playback, see the "Playback Problems" sidebar.

■ If the playback is good, the displays aren't black, and you can hear the audio, then you have passed Stage 1. Give a big cheer and move on to Stage 2.

Inlay Problems

If the display is black or partly green, this is referred to as an *inlay error* and is often the result of a driver problem in your system. These problems are caused by either a graphics driver problem—the data not getting through correctly—or a bandwidth problem caused by poor performance from the chipset drivers. As a rule of thumb, always update all your drivers to the latest version. However, if your system is working fine, then leave it as is. If it ain't broke...

However, if your system is broken and not displaying the playback correctly, you should try the following:

- You can download new graphics drivers from the graphics card manufacturer just as you can download the chipset drivers from the motherboard manufacturer. Don't overlook the importance of updating your chipset driver. If it's old and performs poorly, this may stop the correct display on an inlay; in fact, it can be the root cause of many NLE problems.

- Make sure your system has a graphics card suitable for NLE work. For Liquid Edition, it needs to be a suitably fast (and modern) AGP card with at least 64 MB of RAM on board. Cheaper graphics cards probably don't have a fast-enough GPU *or* on-board RAM to cope with NLE work. Check out the Pinnacle forum for advice on which card to buy.

- Check to make sure the AGP aperture in your system's BIOS is set to 64 MB. You can find details of how to do this in your system's manual.

- Reinstall DirectX 9. This is available as a download from Microsoft support pages. The download and installation takes a few minutes and can often solve many problems.

- If you're still having problems, see the "Optimizing for NLE" section later in this appendix.

Playback Problems

If you see a stuttering frame when you're playing back yellow slices, it's probably because your system doesn't have a fast-enough CPU to cope with showing effects in preview quality. You can get an idea of how bad the playback is by monitoring the speed playback readout in the Liquid Edition taskbar (**Figure A.1**).

Figure A.1 The speed indicator shows red and a frame count lower than 25 fps for PAL and lower than 29 fps for NTSC when the playback is below Realtime.

◆ Speed up playback under yellow slices by making sure no unnecessary programs are running in the background that are stealing resources from Liquid Edition.

◆ Alter the quality setting in the FX Editors area of the Control Panel (**Figure A.2**).

◆ If you still have problems, see the "Optimization Tips" section later in this appendix.

Click the FX Editors icon in the Control Panel...

...and adjust this setting to speed up yellow slices.

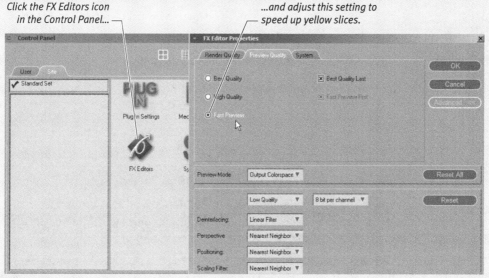

Figure A.2 Altering the FX settings may help speed up playback of Realtime effects.

Test 2: Capture

The second test determines whether your computer can correctly communicate with a FireWire device. This is imperative if you're ever to capture anything into Liquid Edition.

✔ Tip

- Some users who have experienced problems using the Logging tool have found a third-party application, such as scenalyzer from www.scenalyzer.com, can be used instead. The scenalyzer program even has a specific setting for Liquid Edition and a downloadable demo.

To determine whether your computer can capture:

1. Connect your camera *directly* to your FireWire device (don't go through any other kind of connection point).

2. Open the Logging tool by clicking the Logging Tool icon or by pressing F6 on the keyboard.

3. Once the Logging tool opens, begin capturing a tape as described in Chapter 2.

   Always make sure the camera is actually in Playback mode and that some footage is on the film you're using.

4. Open the small LCD panel to monitor the video and audio on the tape. If you fail to check this, you may see a false negative result.

DV Device Problems

Older DV devices have a variety of different communication problems that cause them to fail to connect to the DV device in question. Newer cameras usually only fail if the FireWire card (or on-board socket in the case of a laptop) isn't correctly configured.

You can conduct a quick double-check to see if FireWire is a problem with your computer or just with Liquid Edition. To do so, load up Windows Movie Maker—a program included with XP by default. This tool has a basic capture window that you can use to ascertain if Windows XP sees the DV device.

If XP, Movie Maker, or Liquid Edition can't see the DV device, you probably have a problem with the FireWire card conflicting with another part of your PC. You can often overcome this by downloading the latest drivers; however, you should also watch for on-board FireWire ports (which are included on many deluxe motherboards) that conflict with an extra FireWire port that was installed later. In this case, you need to disable the motherboard variant or remove the PCI version.

You can often solve DV Device problems by visiting the Pinnacle forum and asking if anyone else is having problems with your particular model. If you still have problems, see the "Optimization Tips" section later in this appendix.

5. Capture at least 15 minutes of footage before you end this test. Make sure the hard drive you select has enough free space and is formatted with NTFS.

6. Assuming the captured clip is in the Rack, double-click it to send it to the Source Viewer.

7. Click Play and watch your clip play in the left monitor.

✔ Tips

- If your clip doesn't appear in the left monitor or if the control buttons are grayed out, refer to the "DV Device Problems" sidebar.

- If you have control over your DV device and a clear overlay both during the capture and playback of the captured file, then give another cheer, you have just passed Stage 2.

Test 3: Output

Assuming you've passed the last two tests, you now need to test the output potential of your NLE system. After all, there's little point in creating a video project if no one ever gets to see it.

To determine whether your computer can burn a DVD/SVCD:

1. Return to the sample project by clicking the Sequence menu in the top-right corner, and then select NTSC or PAL from the list.

2. Open the Render box by clicking the Render icon in the bottom-right corner of the interface; then click the include yellow slices check box.

3. Once rendering is complete, access the DVD export menu by clicking File > Export, and then select DVD/SVCD.

4. Keep the defaults settings for burning your DVD/SVCD (Liquid Edition auto-detects your burner's capabilities) and then click the check mark to proceed with the burn.

✔ Tip

- If the burn engine fails to start or gives an error message and doesn't create a DVD/SVCD, refer to the "DVD Problems" sidebar.

To determine whether your computer can output to tape:

1. Make sure your camera is correctly connected and that you've inserted a blank tape.

   If the camera didn't pass the Stage 2 test, you probably won't be able to complete this test either.

2. Click File/Record to Tape.

   This brings up the Record To Tape interface. Make sure Dump to tape and entire sequence are selected.

3. Click Play to determine whether there is a connection between the camera and Liquid Edition and also to check if the tape really is blank. The overlay should display nothing if it is, but you should also view the tape through the camera's LCD screen or viewfinder. Remember: erased is erased.

4. Activate Record to Tape by clicking once on the record button. More details on how to use this interface can be found in Chapter 13.

5. Play back the recorded tape to see if it has successfully transferred the Timeline to the tape.

continues on next page

✔ Tips

- If the tape is fine and you encountered no obvious problems, give a final cheer. Your system has passed all three tests and is suitable for NLE and Liquid Edition.

- If the controls are grayed out and/or the Device is not Ready sign is flashing, go to the "DV Device Problems" sidebar earlier in this appendix.

- If you bought your DV camera in Europe, the camera may not be DV-In enabled. This is a feature the camera makers introduced to benefit from an import tax loophole. You can enable some of these cameras by using a widget that updates the camera's firmware, but doing so voids your warranty.

DVD Problems

Not being able to find the burner is by far the most common error when you're working with DVD authoring. This problem often occurs because the DVD burner is new and Liquid Edition isn't familiar with the firmware.

The Pinnacle programmers are constantly working on new patches that include the latest burners and the process of providing updates is very quick; however, it's likely that by the time a burner is on the market, a patch is on Pinnacle's Web site.

If your burner is very old, then it's highly unlikely a patch will be released for it. In this case, your only alternative is to upgrade.

A number of problems cause error messages during the compile or burn process; check the following if you are having problems.

- Are all slices on the Timeline rendered? Missing render files aren't detected until you begin to compile the DVD.

- Check the DVD menu (if you have one). Do any of the buttons collide? See Chapter 12 for details.

- Try using a different type of media. Some DVD discs may not be suitable for the burner you're using.

- If you're still having problems, see the "Optimizing for NLE" section later in this appendix.

Figuring Out What's Wrong

If you're reading this section, it's because the quick fix techniques listed in the "The Three Basic Suitability Tests" section haven't solved your problems. In this section, I hope to help you out, but please bear in mind this rather brutal truth about PCs in general:

Sometimes there may not be a solution to your problem.

The problem with PCs is simply that not all hardware is created equal; not all the hardware that costs megabucks is guaranteed to be the best; and sadly, not all PCs are destined to ever become NLE workstations.

This all might sound a little on the bleak side, but it's worth bearing this important rule in mind before you start endlessly trying to reconfigure your system. Otherwise you could end up stuck in a circle where you wind up reformatting the drive to reinstall the OS; in order to reconstruct perhaps a little sanity back into your relentlessly PC-persecuted life.

Try to remember that drivers for graphics cards and sound cards can be and often are bugged; hard drives can go wrong just after you buy them; and PC motherboards are updated so often that compatibility lists are often pretty meaningless.

Pretty scary, huh? But if you know about this in advance, then you're prepared (at least mentally) for the road ahead.

Optimizing for NLE

Optimizing a PC is the Holy Grail for NLE workstation owners. They spend hour upon hour adjusting and tweaking the machine so that it runs silky smooth and problem free. The trick, of course, is to spend more time editing. If you follow the basic optimizations tips I describe in the next couple of sections, doing so should be possible.

The optimization of a PC is split into two sections: optimizing Windows XP and optimizing the hardware. Both are complementary, and you'll have more success delving into both rather than just the one. However, a word of warning: always make sure you set a Restore point using the built-in function you find in XP. This, at least, allows you to reset any changes that have screwed up your system beyond usability.

Optimizing Windows XP

Of all the culprits in your PC, of all the suspects for making your NLE experience a painful one, it is unlikely that Windows is it. Really, I am not a Microsoft fan, but I do recognize that finally, after all these years, Windows XP is the operating system they got right. However, as good as this OS is, you can still do some basic things to try to optimize it, or in laymen's terms, get the darn thing to do the job it was designed to do.

Setting the swap file location

The old school of thought with PC optimization was to set your swap file to 2.5 times the amount of physical RAM. However, now that RAM is so cheap and 1 GB is commonplace place, this rule no longer applies. In general, a swap file larger than 640 MB is unnecessary, and it eats up precious hard drive space.

Where the swap file should go is also a matter of heated discussion among the geeky part of the computer community. Some reason that placing the swap file on a second hard drive improves performance, while others say it just needs to be on a separate partition. My advice is to keep it on the C drive unless you see some really serious performance problems.

Windows Updates

Generally speaking you should apply all Windows security updates when they are available. However, it's a good idea to take a look at the Pinnacle Web forum to make sure this will not cause Liquid Edition any problems. For this reason I recommend turning off Automatic Updates and applying updates manually.

However, turning off the auto-update function does mean that you have to remember to check the Microsoft update page on a regular basis to keep your computer secure.

Service Pack 2

If you have SP2 installed, two warning messages from the Windows firewall may appear the first time you start Pinnacle Liquid 6. In this case, you need to click Unblock to add the Render Manager and Desktop applications to the list of allowed applications. These two applications are required by Liquid Edition to function correctly. Once they're added, you should no longer see this prompt.

Access the swap file by entering the System Properties for your computer, clicking the Performance section's Settings button, clicking the Advanced tab on the resulting Performance Options dialog, and then clicking the Change button (**Figure A.3**).

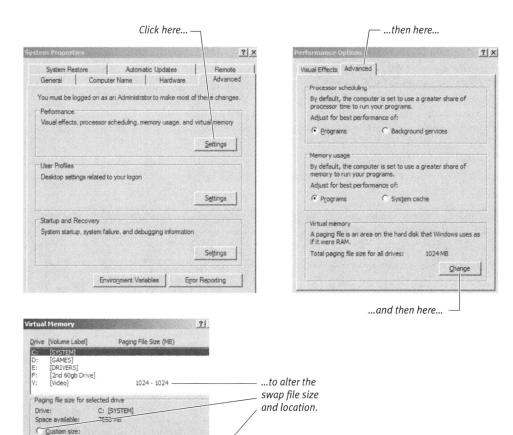

Figure A.3 Setting the Windows XP swap file.

Reducing the XP eye candy

XP has been compared to a toy interface, with too many unwanted features such as fading menus and brightly colored windows buttons. Although this is a subjective comment, it's true to say that the default XP interface uses a lot of resources that could be better used elsewhere.

To reduce the interface overhead, access the System Properties for your computer, click the Advanced tab, then the Performance section's Settings button, and select Adjust for best performance from the resulting Performance Options dialog (**Figure A.4**).

✔ Tip

■ Many Internet sites offer further advice on how to turn off unwanted services—the parts of XP that operate in the background. Performing a Google search for "XP services disable" reveals plenty of help. One such site is www.pcpitstop.com which has an online diagnostic program to help identify areas of your computer that are underperforming. But always make sure you are turning off something you really don't need.

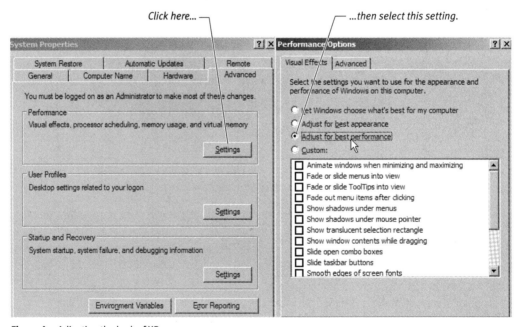

Figure A.4 Adjusting the look of XP.

OPTIMIZING WINDOWS XP

Optimizing Hardware

Hardware optimization is largely about setting up your computer correctly in the first place. To use this section, you need to understand at least the basics of the components that lie beneath your computer's (quite possibly beige-colored) case. If you don't have this knowledge and you also have a deep-rooted fear of all things electrical, you should skip this section and head to "Getting Further Help."

For those of you still reading, here is a breakdown of how your computer should be set up.

Hard drive configuration

If you're using IDE drives (as opposed to SATA) you should have a minimum of two separate hard drives in your system. Note that this means two *separate* drives, not a single drive with two partitions.

A drive with two partitions is still only one drive. It still only has one set of drive heads to read data with and is unlikely to cope with the high data streams that are transferred during a normal editing session.

You should connect these two drives on the primary channel of the motherboard. If you have a separate RAID IDE port, then by all means, use that, but don't, under any circumstances, have either your system drive or your capture drive on the same cable as your CD player or DVD/CD burner. If you do, you slow down the data rate of the hard drive and impair its performance—this is sometimes called *negotiating down*.

✔ Tip

- Avoid filling your hard drive all the way up. Once it gets above 85 percent of its total capacity, you begin to see performance problems.

Memory—RAM

Memory is the central transfer hub for everything. Without good, reliable, fast RAM, the PC suffers problems.

First, you need to make sure you're using the correct slots. Again, your computer system's handbook tells you which slots you should populate first and which amounts you can use. Always consult the handbook before buying more RAM because you want to make sure there is no upper limit to the amount of RAM your system can use. Second, you should buy the fastest RAM your system supports and no faster.

Defrag and Other Disc Maintenance

A hard drive is one of the few moving parts of your PC, and as such, a target for wear and tear. To reduce this, you should defragment your drives on a regular basis. This allows the drive heads to locate the data they are looking for without traveling all over the hard drive to find it, thus cutting down on wear.

XP has a very workable defragmentation program, but others are available that do the job faster and give you more options.

OPTIMIZING HARDWARE

517

Power supply

The power supply is the much-ignored component of your PC, and ironically, one of the most important. Certain processors, particularly AMD, require very specific voltage across specific pins. They are tolerant of minor variations, but a cheap unbranded power supply often fails to deliver (on a constant basis) the correct amps the processor needs when working flat out. As most NLE tasks ask the processor to work flat out, it doesn't take a brain surgeon to figure out what happens when the power supply is erratic.

If you're running large hard drives, a DVD burner, and a fast CPU, you probably want a power supply that delivers in excess of 450 watts. But check to make sure it can deliver the required voltage to the required pins. If in doubt, check the AMD and Intel Web sites, which carry a list of recommended Power Supply Units (PSUs).

When you go to buy a power supply, you might want to give some thought as to how loud it will be. A giant turbine in your computer may become a point of fractious discussion with other members of your household.

Getting Further Help

The Pinnacle Webboard (http://webboard.pinnaclesys.com) is a vast pool of knowledge. Anyone who owns a Pinnacle product of any description should always check here to see if anyone else is experiencing the problems they are having. Often they are, and as a result, you see advice here from other users and Pinnacle technical support people.

But to get the best help from this board, you need to provide correct information. It's a bit like asking an oracle a question; to get the right answer, you must first have the right question. An ideal post to the Pinnacle forum would state the problem clearly (in steps 1 to 10 if necessary) and list the hardware *and* the driver versions you're using.

Once the message is posted, you need to check back regularly to see if anyone has replied. Usually, you receive replies fairly quickly from people who either have this problem and know the solution, or have this problem and can tell you what they've already tried, which in itself is a great timesaver. Pinnacle employees also post to this forum, but bear in mind that they may be anywhere in the world, and as a result, there can be a large time lag getting their responses back to you.

Getting professional help

In each country, there is a network of Pinnacle partners who are very well experienced and can offer either help and advice or (for a fee) take a look at your system. They may be able to save you a great deal of time and money by simply suggesting either an upgrade or confirming that your system will never function correctly as an NLE workstation.

You can find Pinnacle partners via the main Pinnacle Web site from which you can choose which country to search for a dealer near you.

INDEX

INDEX

INDEX

G

H

I

INDEX

INDEX

INDEX

INDEX

X-Y-Z

W

INDEX